Perspectives on Human Capital Development

Ashraf Mishrif
Editor

Perspectives on Human Capital Development

Effects of the COVID-19 Pandemic on Health and Education

palgrave
macmillan

Editor
Ashraf Mishrif
Humanities Research Centre
Sultan Qaboos University
Muscat, Oman

ISBN 978-981-97-5245-4 ISBN 978-981-97-5246-1 (eBook)
https://doi.org/10.1007/978-981-97-5246-1

This Palgrave Macmillan imprint is published by the registered company Springer Nature Singapore Pte Ltd.
The registered company address is: 152 Beach Road, #21-01/04 Gateway East, Singapore 189721, Singapore

To my father, family and
the memory of my beloved mother

Acknowledgments

This book is the outcome of the papers presented at the international conference on the impact of COVID-19 on the economy and society that took place at Sultan Qaboos University on October 10–12, 2022. Under the patronage of the Minister of Commerce, Industry and Investment Promotion, participation of senior officials from the World Trade Organization (WTO), United Nations Conference on Trade and Development (UNCTAD), and Oman Chamber of Commerce and Industry, this conference attracted over 100 scholars and researchers from 16 countries, with extensive participation from the government, the private sector, and the academic community.

The author and editor of this book would like to express his gratitude of Sultan Qaboos University for its generous financial and logistical support to organize this conference. I am also grateful to Oman Chamber of Commerce and Industry for their participation and continuous support to the OCCI Research Chair for Economic Studies. My thanks and appreciation go to all the authors who devoted their time and efforts to write their papers. My thanks also go to my research assistant Maryam Essa Al Maqbali for her excellent support during the preparation of this book. Without their tireless efforts this book would not have been produced and come out in the market.

Special thanks to Vishal Daryanomal, editor of Palgrave Macmillan, and his colleagues for their outstanding support during the publication of this book. My thanks also go to the three anonymous reviewers who provided rigorous comments and feedback that helped us to improve the quality of the manuscript.

The publication of this book comes at a critical junction in the global economy. So, I hope that our analysis will assist policymakers, academics, students, and other stakeholders to understand and respond appropriately to the economic effects of the pandemic for a better future.

Contents

Notes on Contributors

Said Elhussein Abdelli is assistant professor in social sciences at Sultan Qaboos University, and before that at Carthage University in Tunisia. He holds a doctorate in sociology from the University of Tunisia, and a university qualification in research and supervision. He specializes in studying social change in the Arab world in the context of his precise specialty, political and cultural sociology. He authored several books, including Magic in Tunisia: for Money, Power, and Sex (2017) and Social Change in the Arab and Islamic World: Backwardness (2021). He has more than 20 research papers published in peer-reviewed scientific journals and 15 international conferences, in addition to chapters in books. He is a member of the Arab Council for Social Sciences.

Fadi Abdelfattah is an associate professor and department head at the Modern College of Business and Science in Muscat, Sultanate of Oman. He is a recognized academic leader with publications in indexed international journals and roles on editorial and advisory boards. Dr. Abdelfattah has secured multiple research grants, supervised postgraduate students, and was an examiner. His research interests are consumer behavior, Leadership, Entrepreneurship Innovation, Technology Adoption, and healthcare management. He has taught diverse undergraduate and graduate courses and led various committees and initiatives. Notably, Dr. Abdelfattah and his team have developed several successful undergraduate and graduate programs, attracting over 350 students.

Iyad Abusahloub M.B.A., Ph.D., is a seasoned academic and expert in business management, human resources management, and tourism management. Currently a lecturer at Universite IBN KHALDOUN UIK in Tunisia, he holds a Ph.D. in management from ESECT—Tunisia and another in tourism management from Anadolu University in Turkey. Dr. Abusahloub has showcased his expertise through numerous published articles and active participation in conferences. Proficient in English, Turkish, and French, he is dedicated to advancing knowledge in the fields of business and tourism management.

Rashid Aftab has a Ph.D. in Public Policy and Governance from Utrecht University. He is currently the Director of Faculty of Public Policy at Riphah International University, Islamabad, Pakistan. Dr. Aftab possesses rich experience of about 25 years in various public and private sectors. He has been participating in the Planning, Coordination, and Monitoring/ Evaluation of various Socio-economic, Human Resources Development, SME, and Telecom projects with the Ministry of Science & Technology; Ministry of Environment, Local Government & Rural Development; Ministry of Industries & Production; and Telecom sector. The primary areas of his focus are Teaching, Research, Institutional Development and Linkages, Strategic Planning, Programming Analysis, Government/ International Liaison, Human Resource Management, Public Relations, Strategic Alliances, and Project Management.

Omar Al-Farsi is an assistant science teacher at Oman College of Health Sciences. He finished his Ph.D. at Sultan Qaboos University in Epidemiology and Public Health in 2016. He has been working in the Ministry of Health since 2004 and director of Information and statistics department from 2016 to 2022. He has numerous publications in peer-reviewed medical journals. He has been providing oral presentations in various national and international conferences. He was the focal point with the WHO in the Sustainable Development Goals 2030 and National Health Workforce Accounts. He developed lots of national documents such as The National Strategy of Population Policy, Fifth Years plan for the health sector (2021–2025) and Oman vision 2040 for the health field. He is an active in social work and a member in the board of Oman Autism Society.

Yahya Al-Farsi is a Professor of Epidemiology and Public Health at Sultan Qaboos University (SQU), Oman. He served in several leading academic positions among which the Assistant Dean for Training &

Community Service, and Acting Dean of College of Medicine & Health Sciences, Chairman of SQU Hospital, and Member of SQU University Council. He is the Chairman of Oman Autism Society, and Oman Public Health Society. Regionally, he has served as a Public Health Consultant at the Gulf Health Council, Riyadh, Saudi Arabia, where he contributed towards the establishment of the Health Research Unit and the Gulf CDC Center. Internationally, he is an Adjunct Professor at Boston University, USA, and Honorary Clinical Lecturer at Imperial College London, UK. He has numerous publications in peer-reviewed scientific journals and has supervised several master's and PhD dissertations.

Abrar AL Alawi an esteemed lecturer at the University of Nizwa's Department of Business Management, holds a Master's in entrepreneurship. Specializing in Entrepreneurship Innovation and leadership, her research endeavors focus on exploring innovative strategies in business development and organizational leadership. Ms. Al Alawi has excelled in securing various research grants, enabling her to delve into essential topics such as e-entrepreneurial intention and the design of effective teaching and learning frameworks. Her dedication to advancing knowledge in these areas highlights her commitment to enhancing entrepreneurial education and fostering a culture of innovation within academic circles.

Raniya Al-Kiyumi is a professional and dedicated individual with 23 years of experience, accomplished acting dean and lecturer roles at Oman Health Information Management Institute and College of Health Sciences, respectively. Served as the Head of the Health information management department in a regional hospital under the Ministry of Health. Al Kiyumi is a qualified Health Information Management professional with Ph.D. from Queensland University of Technology, Australia. Dr Raniya's research explores the status of Health Information Management in Oman. She is an associate member of The International Federation of Health Information Management Associations (IFHIMA) and a global member of The American Health Information Management Association (AHIMA). Research interests: Health information management and education, legal and ethical aspects of health information, electronic health records, clinical classification, workforce development.

Najla Yahya Al Mashaikhya has over six years of administrative experience in higher education institutions, specializing in management, coordination, and quality service. Initially starting as an administrative specialist at A'Sharqiyah University, she now holds the senior quality assurance administrator position at the Global College of Engineering and Technology. With a B.Sc. in Statistics from Sultan Qaboos University and an M.B.A. from A'Sharqiyah University, her research focuses on leadership styles, innovative employee behavior, e-learning, and student engagement. Al-Mashaikhya has obtained various research grants investigating digital readiness, e-entrepreneurial intention, teaching, and learning frameworks.

Salim Al-Salmi has been witnessing the development of the health informatics and information management in Oman for the last 32 years. He worked as the director of the health information management department at the Royal Hospital, Dean of Oman Health Information Management Institute. Currently he is the associate dean for health information management program in Oman College of Health Sciences. He is also the health information management adviser for the Ministry of Health, Oman. He holds a degree in Health Information Management from the USA, master's in health informatics from UK, PG certificate in medical education from UK and Ph.D. in health informatics and information management from UK. He is a registered health information technician by AHIMA. He is interested in electronic health record, electronic clinical documentation and coding standards, and information privacy policy and practice.

NABEEL ALOBAIDI is a specialist in International Law and expert on combating extremism and international terrorism. He served as an international arbitrator and reviewer of journals including Babir International Center for Humanities and Social Sciences, Turkey, Arab Democratic Center for Political and Legal Sciences, Germany, Arab Society for Forensic Sciences, Naif Arab University for Security Sciences, Saudi Arabia, Arab Council for Social Sciences, Qatar, Journal of Constitutional Law and Political, Nile Journal for Humanitarian Studies, Egypt, Garmian University Journal, Iraq, Faculty of Law and Political Science, Algeria. He has fifteen legal books published in Arabic, English, and French, forty-three research papers, and attended more than thirty international conferences.

Salah Al Awaidy is a medical doctor and holds a Masters in Epidemiology with current post is senior consultant epidemiologist and Communicable Disease Surveillance and Control Adviser to the office of the Undersecretary of Health Affairs at the Ministry of Health, Oman. He currently advises on eradication, elimination, and control of communicable diseases of public health importance, in addition to the EPI, vaccine supply chain system and International Health Regulations. At national arena, in the MOH, Oman, he played a pivotal role in reducing the national under five mortality and morbidity, preparedness, management and control of infectious diseases like SARS, avian influenza, pH1N1 and in establishing national communicable diseases, AEFI and Rotavirus surveillance, as well as in the eradication of Polio, Measles, Rubella, CRS and leprosy in Oman.

Afra Al Balushi is a senior specialist in the Pulmonary Unit at Department of Medicine, Royal Hospital, Muscat, Oman.

Amal Al Balushi is Senior Specialist, at the Department of Medicine, acute medicine unit, Royal Hospital, Oman. My scope of work involves inpatient care, referrals, procedures, teaching medical students, interns, and residents. During my working years I was a member of several committees: VTE steering committee and the focal point for the department of medicine, internship committee, morbidity and mortality review audit committee, and Associate faculty in Oman medical specialty board. I was an active member of the Covid team and one of the front-liners.

Jawaher Al Balushi is an experienced assistant lecturer with a demonstrated history of working in the higher education industry. Skilled in Entrepreneurship Education, she is a strong education professional with an M.Sc. focused on International Business from Coventry University. She is a Ph.D. student and researcher in entrepreneurship and entrepreneurial inclination. She is an entrepreneurship coach and trainer certified TOT by a recognized international organization. Not only that, but she has published many book chapters and papers in very important and recognized reviews.

Sabah Al Balushi holds a Ph.D. in education, with a concentration in quality management in higher education. She is an Expert at the Deputy Vice-Chancellor for Academic Affairs and Community Service at Sultan Qaboos University (SQU), Oman. Prior to that, she was Deputy Director for Professional Development and Research in the Centre for Preparatory Studies (CPS), SQU. She was also Head of the Quality Management Unit in the CPS for four years. Her areas of interest include higher education in the Arab Gulf, quality management, and blended learning.

Shabnam Chhetri is a medical officer in the Infectious Diseases Unit at Department of Medicine, the Royal Hospital, Muscat, Oman.

Ayman El-Saleh earned his Ph.D. in Wireless Communications from UKM in 2012. Currently, he serves as an Associate Professor at A'Sharqiyah University, Oman. El-Saleh is a Senior IEEE Member and has served on the Executive Committee of the IEEE Malaysia ComSoc/VTS Joint Chapter. He has reviewed various ISI-indexed journals and authored approximately 60 journal and conference articles, focusing on cognitive radio networks, heterogeneous LTE/LTE-Advanced cellular networks, and applications of artificial intelligence and evolutionary algorithms in wireless communications.

Thamra Al Ghafri is a senior consultant in public health and currently the director general of health services in Muscat, Oman. She is supervising all primary and secondary health services in Muscat under Oman ministry of health. She is the chairman of the administrative board for Almasara hospital (the only psychiatric hospital in Oman). She is interested in health promotion and disease prevention through structured behavior change initiatives. She has several publications and enjoys working in interventional research health projects.

Hisham Ghunaimi has started his career in the banking sector in Oman, worked in various multinational commercial and diplomatic organizations in finance, accounting, and HR sections. He worked as a faculty member for different higher education institutions where he taught financial and management courses and now in A 'Sharqiyah University in the college of business administration as an accounting and finance lecturer. He is certified from the International Academy of Financial Management as Master Financial Controller and Chartered Cost Controller. Furthermore, he is also a recognized quality management internal auditor and certified as organizational Manager from the Leadership and Learning Organization Centre.

Mudabera Gulzar is an emerging researcher in the field of psychiatric nursing, behavioral sciences, and psychology. Mudabera's academic journey is marked by a multidisciplinary approach to understanding behavioral aspects of humans including mental health and psycho-social wellbeing. She earned her M.Sc. and B.Sc. degrees from the prestigious Sher-i-Kashmir Institute of Medical Sciences, SKIMS, Soura, Srinagar, Jammu and Kashmir. She is committed to advancing knowledge through publications that showcase a profound comprehension of the intersection between psychiatric nursing, psychology, human behavior, and socio-economic development.

Saira Hafeez is a policy researcher with a master's degree in public policy. She is currently building her career in policy research and analysis through a Ph.D. in Political Science at Colorado State University, United States of America. Her noteworthy contributions to esteemed academic journals, her policy briefs with the Institute of Strategic Studies Islamabad, and her conference papers and newspaper articles ratify her scholarly expertise. Her primary area of focus is policy research, analysis, and communication to empower change, embrace hope, and uplift vulnerable communities in the face of contemporary development challenges.

Ahmed Al Harthi is a fifth-year medical student at Sultan Qaboos University in Oman. He has several publications in medical research and is passionate about scientific inquiry, particularly in behavioral medicine. He actively participates in extracurricular activities and is committed to volunteer work aimed at improving public health.

Jibran Hussain is a distinguished official of the Ministry of Overseas Pakistanis & Human Resource Development with a multifaceted career spanning academia and public services. His tenure as an Adjunct Professor of Economics and Finance for Policymakers at various esteemed institutions in Pakistan and his membership in the Science Committee at the International Institute of Knowledge Management, Sri Lanka substantiate his academic prowess. Dr. Hussain's recognition in domains like energy economics, financial economics, and quantitative methods is founded on rigorous research showcased through his prolific contributions to reputable academic journals. His commitment to continuous growth is evident in his pursuit of advanced knowledge through specialized courses in data science, actuarial modeling in social security, and innovation in governance, among other specialized fields.

N. Ramdas Iyer is the Director of National Science Centre of India, New Delhi and is a science communicator with an experience of over thirty-three years. During these years, he has served with the Birla Industrial and Technological Museum in Kolkata, National Science Centre in Delhi and Raman Science Centre in Nagpur. Having Master's degree in Applied Electronics, his area of interest is development of new exhibition/galleries, museum management, public relations and creating public understanding of science. He has curated over 20 galleries in the past 25 years and over 12 travelling exhibitions.

Faryal Khamis is a Senior Consultant in Infectious Diseases and Head of Internal Medicine Subspecialities and Deputy of Directorate of Internal Medicine at the Royal Hospital in Muscat, Oman, where she Chairs both the Antimicrobial Stewardship Committee and the Infection Prevention and Control Committee. Prior to this She was working as a consultant in Infectious Diseases at the Sultan Qaboos University Hospital. She is a member of several National Committees and task forces in the Ministry of Health, Oman. She completed her medical school training with honors at the Sultan Qaboos University in Oman in 1993. Following her completion of a residency program in Internal Medicine at the University of Minnesota, Minneapolis, MN, USA in 1999, she completed two fellowships programs both in Infectious Diseases and in Medical Microbiology at Duke University Medical Center, Durham, North Carolina. She has authored several publications in scientific journals and has received several research awards including the National Research Award in 2021. She is editor in a few scientific journals such as Oman Medical Journal. Her main research interests include respiratory viral infections, infections in immunocompromised patients, including those with HIV, antimicrobial Stewardship and SARS-CoV-2.

Mohammed Athar Khan holds a Ph.D. in language assessment and has been teaching ESL for over 20 years. He is the Head of the Sustainable Development Unit, Centre for Preparatory Studies, Sultan Qaboos University, Muscat, Oman. His research interests include quality management, language assessment, and critical thinking.

Sameer Ahmad Khan is a dedicated research scholar affiliated with the Department of Management Studies at Jamia Millia Islamia in New Delhi, India. His primary focus lies in exploring the intricacies of Organizational Citizenship Behavior within the realm of higher education. Passionate about contributing to the enhancement of the academic environment, he delves into the dynamics of organizational behavior in educational settings. Beyond his research pursuits, he actively engages with the broader discourse on public policy in higher education. A prolific writer, he regularly contributes insightful articles to various national newspapers. His expertise and interest in this domain reflect a commitment to fostering positive changes and advancements in the field of higher education through both scholarly research and public discourse.

Mohd Hussain Kunroo is currently serving as an Assistant Professor in the Department of Economics & Business Environment, Indian Institute of Management Sirmaur, India. Prior to that he was affiliated with Central University of Rajasthan, Institute of Economic Growth New Delhi, The NorthCap University Gurgaon, Indian Institute of Foreign Trade New Delhi, and Amity University Noida. He earned his Hons. Economics from Aligarh Muslim University, master's in economics from University of Hyderabad, and Doctor of Philosophy in Economics from Jamia Millia Islamia, New Delhi. Dr. Kunroo has been a recipient of the prestigious Sir Ratan Tata Trust Fellowship hosted by the Institute of Economic Growth, New Delhi. The fellowship is awarded from the Sir Ratan Tata Trust Fund for Young Social Scientists. He has worked extensively in the field of International Trade and International Finance, with a special focus on the Euro Currency Union. His research works have been published in peer-reviewed journals of major publishing houses such as Springer, Taylor & Francis, Sage, Routledge, Economic and Political Weekly, and Wiley Blackwell.

Abdulraman Al Mirza is a resident in Emergency department, Oman Medical Specialty board, Sultanate of Oman.

Ashraf Mishrif is the founding director and research chair of Oman Chamber of Commerce and Industry Research Chair for Economic Studies, Sultan Qaboos University, Oman. Prior to that he was Associate Professor at King's College London and taught at various universities including Qatar University, Ahmed bin Mohammed Military College Qatar, Anglia Ruskin University Cambridge, and the University of Greenwich, London, UK. He is an expert in economic development and the political economy of the Middle East, with a special focus on the Gulf region. He is Fellow of International Society for Development and Sustainability (Japan) and the Book Series Editor of Palgrave Macmillan Political Economy of the Middle East. He authored and edited more than 80 books, book chapters and peer-reviewed papers, including two volumes on economic diversification and nationalization of the labour market in the GCC.

AbdulHakim Mohamed a senior IEEE member, holds a Ph.D. in computer science from the University of Liverpool (UK). Currently serving as an Associate Professor and eLearning Director at A'Sharqiyah University, Oman, he brings extensive experience from esteemed UK higher education institutions. With a background as a Lead Systems Analyst and Senior Software Engineer, Dr. Hakim's research focuses on intelligent agents, User Experience Design, and health informatics. He actively coordinates multiple programs and serves as an external examiner. Dr. Hakim has played pivotal roles in developing and submitting various programs at A'Sharqiyah University, including B.Sc. in Cybersecurity, Bachelor of Technology in Internet and Information Technology, Ph.D. in Management, M.B.A., B.Sc. in Data Science and Business Analytics, and Bachelor of Business in Logistics and Supply Chain Management programs. His expertise lies in delivering substantial returns on technology investments, implementing cost-effective technologies, and enhancing revenue streams through cutting-edge technology services.

Furqan Qamar presently a Professor of Management at Jamia Millia Islamia's Centre for Management Studies in New Delhi, boasts an impressive career marked by significant leadership roles in academia and policy. Formerly the Secretary General of the Association of Indian Universities (AIU), he contributed to shaping the landscape of higher education globally. With notable stints as Vice Chancellor at the University of Rajasthan and the Central University of Himachal Pradesh, along with serving as an Advisor (Education) in the Planning Commission of India, Dr. Qamar brings extensive experience in educational planning, administration, and financing. His research focus encompasses public policy in higher education, reflected in numerous reputable publications. Renowned for his academic eminence, leadership, and global exposure, Dr. Qamar's expertise extends to educational planning, administration, financing, public policy, and research methodologies, demonstrating a commitment to advancing best practices in higher education.

Ramzi Sallem is an Assistant Professor in Management at A' Sharqiyah university. He is also a coach and expert in the field of entrepreneurship for more than 15 years that gave him significant experience in the development of entrepreneurial potential among the youths. His experience has been the major inspiration for his academic research. He has always been interested in studying the complexity of entrepreneurial phenomenon given the cultural differences between the different regions, namely those that belong to the same nation. He is conducting continual research on how to change the inherited culture by designing different entrepreneurship training programs that aim to enhance entrepreneurial skills among the students of HE, especially in Arab countries.

Muna Al Shaaibi is a statistical specialist at Ministry of Education since 2010, Sultanate of Oman. She obtained her Ph.D. at Sultan Qaboos University in statistics with distinction. She was the first student in the department to create an integrated package in the R program. She was a member of the Royal Hospital's study team during the COVID-19 period. She has participated in many conferences internally and externally and produced several publications. Further, she peer-reviewed papers for PLOS-ONE journal. Assistant Professor at the College of Economics and Political Science. Member of the Royal Statistical Society in Britain.

Mubarak Al Shukeili is a PhD. student in the Department of Statistics, College of Science, Sultan Qaboos University, Muscat, Oman.

Hamed Al Sinawi is a senior consultant old age Psychiatrist and the head of department of behavioral medicine, Sultan Qaboos University. He is the founder and Chairman Oman's Alzheimer's Society and a member of the national bioethics committee. He completed his training in the UK and specializes in Geriatric Psychiatry and became a fellow of the Royal college of Psychiatrist in the UK in 2011. His special interest is in cognitive impartment, mood disorder, and medical education. He is involved in teaching medical students, psychiatry residents, and other health care professionals and has few publications and book chapters in areas related to mental health.

Bharat Bhusan Srivastava is working as Education Officer at senior level in National Science Centre, Govt. of India, Pragati Maidan, New Delhi, India. Having a Master's degree in applied physics; Education; & Science Communication, he has an interest in writing articles in science journals/ magazines. The researcher has got long experience of more than 35 years working in education & related field.

Sumaiya Al Sulaimi is a specialist in the Acute Medicine Unit, Department of Medicine, the Royal Hospital, Muscat, Oman.

Ronald Wesonga is Associate Professor at the Department of Statistics, College of Science, Sultan Qaboos University, Oman. He is also founder and chair of Data Science Analytics Lab, a pioneer research lab that conducts high level statistical research. He has taught at various universities, including Islamic University in Uganda and recently, Makerere

University, Kampala, Uganda. He is an expert in statistics, with a specialization in computational statistics. He is a statistical fellow of the Royal Statistics Society, London, UK and the International Statistics Institute, Hague, the Netherlands. He is associate editor of Frontiers Applied Mathematics and Statistics journal, has authored a number of papers, book chapters and peer-reviewed for many journals. And, he has also supervised many postgraduate students' theses at both Master's and Ph.D. levels.

Adhari Al Zaabi is an MD-Ph.D. assistant professor at Sultan Qaboos University's College of Medicine and Health Sciences. She earned a Ph.D. in cancer prevention from Brigham Young University in the USA and was granted a prestigious Fellowship Award in Molecular and Behavioral Cancer Prevention by the National Cancer Institute in 2018. Her area of expertise is in cancer prevention, artificial intelligence in healthcare, and youth well-being. Adhari has received numerous research grants, including the His Majesty Fund for two consecutive years. Recently, she was honored with the Women in Artificial Intelligence Award in Dubai in 2023. She was the first Arab woman to receive the International Brain Research Award from France 2020. She received best poster award in the prestigious European society of medical Oncology conference in Singapore, 2021. Adhari has published tens of articles and book chapters in artificial intelligence in healthcare and in precision oncology.

Abbreviations

ACE2	Angiotensin II-converting Enzyme
ANC	Antenatal Care Visit
APT	Advanced Persistent Threat
ARDS	Acute Respiratory Distress Syndrome
BBB	Big Blue Button
CBDR	Central Birth and Death Registration
CDC	Centers for Disease Control
CoMHSc	College of Medicine and Health Sciences
COVID-19	Coronavirus Disease of 2019
CP	Convalescent Plasma
CPS	Center for Preparatory Studies
CRP	C-Reactive Protein
CT	Computerized Tomography
DM	Diabetes Mellitus
ECCE	Early Childhood Care and Education
ERT	Emergency Remote Teaching
GDP	Gross Domestic Product
GFP	General Foundation Program
GHG	Greenhouse Gases
GP	General Practice
HDL	High-Density Lipoprotein
HEIs	Higher Education Institutions
HFNC	High Flow Nasal Cannula
HIS	Health Information System
HIV	Human Immunodeficiency Virus
IATA	International Air Transport Association

ICN	International Council of Nurses
ICU	Intensive Care Unit
IMV	Invasive Mechanical Ventilation
IT	Information Technology
KPIs	Key Performance Indicators
KSA	Kingdom of Saudi Arabia
LDCs	Least Developed Countries
LDL	Low-density Lipoprotein
LMS	Learning Management Systems
LOS	Length of Stay
MOH	Ministry of Health
MV	Mechanical Ventilation
NCDs	Non-Communicable Diseases
NCSD	National Science Centre, Delhi
NCSM	National Council of Science Museums
NIV	Non-Invasive Ventilation
NPAs	Non-Performing Assets
OCCI	Oman Chamber of Commerce and Industry
OPD	Outpatient Department
OxCGRT	Oxford COVID-19 Government Response Tracker
PR	Promotion Rate
RBS	Red Blood Cells
RMNCH	Reproductive, Maternal, Newborn and Child Health
RT-PCR	Reverse Transcription-Polymerase Chain Reaction Test
SARS-CoV-2	Severe Respiratory Distress Syndrome
SDGs	Sustainable Development Goals
SEM-PLS	Structural Equation Modeling by Partial Least Squares
SOB	Shortness of Breath
SOT	Standard Oxygen Therapy
SpO2	Oxygen Saturation
SQU	Sultan Qaboos University
SSIs	Semi-Structured Interviews
TB	Tuberculosis
UAE	United Arab Emirates
UHC	Universal Health Coverage
UK	United Kingdom
UN	United Nations
UNCTAD	United Nations Conference on Trade and Development
UNDP	United Nations Development Programme
UNESCO	United Nations Educational, Scientific and Cultural Organization
UNICEF	United Nations International Children's Emergency Fund
US	United States

V-LDL	Very Low-Density Lipoprotein
WBC	White Blood Cell
WESP	World Economic Situation and Prospects
WHO	World Health Organization
WTO	World Trade Organization

List of Figures

Chapter 1

Chapter 2

Chapter 3

Chapter 5

Chapter 7

Chapter 8

Chapter 9

Chapter 10

Chapter 11

Chapter 12

Chapter 13

Chapter 14

Chapter 15

List of Tables

Chapter 10

Chapter 13

CHAPTER 1

The Pandemic Effects on Human Capital Development: An Introduction

Ashraf Mishrif

1 Introduction

This chapter provides an introductory overview of the effects of COVID-19 on human capital development. It explains how the pandemic impacted on the operational capacity and function of the health and education sectors and the significant effects that this disruption caused on human development and social well-being. Since late 2019, the spread of the virus has brought a lot of challenges to health, education, labor market, and the economy. Globally, the pandemic has pushed about 70 million people back into extreme poverty, 70% of routine medical tests have not been performed, and more than 168 million young people have been unable to complete their coursework at schools and institutions. It has also raised worries about the global recession and economic calamity due to the disruption of the global value chains, of which the global economy has not yet fully recovered.

A. Mishrif (✉)
Humanities Research Centre, Sultan Qaboos University, Muscat, Oman
e-mail: ashraf.mishrif@gmail.com

A. Mishrif (ed.), *Perspectives on Human Capital Development*,
https://doi.org/10.1007/978-981-97-5246-1_1

On the social and human development levels, immobility, travel limitations, social exclusion, and self-isolation have all contributed to a decrease in the workforce across all economic sectors and countless job losses causing a collapse in human capital (Chaabouni & Mbarek, 2023; Nicola et al., 2020). According to the World Bank (2020), human capital is the knowledge, skills, and health that people accumulate over their lives. It is considered as a key factor in sustainable growth, the eradication of poverty, and the prosperity of societies. Thus, human capital is largely associated with higher income for individuals, greater wealth for nations, and more social cohesiveness. All these factors have been badly affected by the pandemic.

Moreover, if human capital development is defined as the act of providing opportunities to all citizens to develop their potentials via education, health, training, and motivation (Okpata et al., 2021), one could then argue that the capacity of the state to provide the provision of services and access to opportunities has been undermined by the operational capacity and function of institutions during the pandemic. On the one hand, these impediments affected education, which, in the perception of Romer's Growth Model, can increase human capital by enhancing productivity that will lead to a higher growth of output, as well as providing individuals with the required knowledge and skills to thrive and contribute to economic and social development (Islam et al., 2016). On the other hand, the pandemic effects impacted negatively on health, which is essential for human capital since it has a direct impact on workers productivity and performance; hence healthier individuals can perform tasks in a more efficient way (Becker, 2007; Bleakley, 2010).

In this chapter, I argue that health and education are entwined in human development, since higher education is linked to a better health condition through making better health choices, while being healthy contributes to having better access to education and better learning abilities. So, greater investment in health and education can help countries to develop their human capabilities and rapidly recover from the pandemic. To elaborate further on the pandemic of the pandemic on human capital, this chapter explains the impact of the pandemic on health and on education. Then, it will provide a section on the aims, objectives, and structure of this book.

2 Effects of the Pandemic on Health

Health is one of the most affected sectors by the pandemic. The impact has been direct and indirect on health service delivery, causing challenges on the management, human resources, and medical supply. The economic, administrative, and operational costs were severe and even worse in many countries with an overburdened healthcare system (Haileamlak, 2021; WHO, 2023). The human costs of COVID-19 reached almost seven million deaths and more than 700 million confirmed infected cases worldwide by the end of 2023 (WHO, 2023). Table 1 shows that more than 3,791,330 people died from the pandemic between November 2020 and November 2021, a further 1,473,756 deaths in the following 12 months, and another 358,866 deaths from November 2022 to November 2023. Meanwhile, the number of infected cases increased from over 50 million to 253 million in 12 months, between November 2020 and November 2021, and jumped to over 631.9 million in the following 12 months, reaching a total of 771 million by November 2023.

Moreover, the pandemic has significantly altered human behavior due to lockdowns, a prolonged home stay, and social distancing measures, which negatively restricted people's physical activity. This shift in lifestyles resulted in various physical and psychological health complications such as overweight obesity and mental health issues (Di Corrado, 2020). For example, Zheng et al. (2020) found that all types of physical activity have been significantly reduced after the outbreak of the pandemic, with participant's average physical activity level decreasing to 3 min/day of moderate activity and 17 min/day on walking. Time spent on sedentary behavior was much higher during the pandemic compared to pre-pandemic. Daily screen time has not only increased by over 28%, increasing from 5 hours/day to 8 hour/day during lockdowns, but it was also accompanied by

Table 1 Total COVID-19 confirmed cases and deaths (2020–2023)

Year	*Total confirmed cases*	*Total deaths*
November 2020	50,878,707	1,353,071
November 2021	253,323,101	5,144,401
November 2022	631,905,855	6,618,157
November 2023	771,679,618	6,977,023

Source World Health Organization (2023)

uninterrupted periods of inactivity, which have more health detrimental outcomes.

Hamer et al. (2020) found that adverse lifestyle behaviors during the pandemic are associated with COVID-19 infection and that unhealthy behaviors accounted for up to 51% of the population attributable portion of severe COVID-19 hospital admission. Another study found that over 10% of patients who tested positive for COVID-19 developed long-term health conditions that remained for more than 12 weeks after the infection, including physical, cognitive, and mental health-related symptoms (McBride et al., 2021).

In terms of eating pattern, the pandemic also affected people's food consumption pattern, causing a higher consumption of unhealthy and processed food (McBride et al., 2021). There was a noticeable change in eating habits characterized by an increase in snacking frequency and a preference for sweets and highly processed foods over fresh produce and other whole foods like fruits and vegetables. These changes in food habits brought on by the epidemic may have made people less healthy throughout and even after the pandemic (González-Monroy et al., 2021).

Alcohol consumption also increased significantly during the pandemic, which might be related to the pandemic or related mental health issues such as stress and depression. Based on a national survey of over 2200 adults in the UK, almost 30% of participants reported drinking more alcohol during the pandemic than what they usually drink (King's College London, 2020). The causes of higher alcohol consumption are younger age, more children at home, and unemployment. Many studies also found an increase in tobacco use. For example, Rantis et al. (2022) found that about one-third of tobacco smokers, who participated in their study, reported an increase in smoking frequency during the pandemic. This can be related to younger age, lower education, bad living situation, and pandemic-related work situation, social isolation, loneliness, lack of daily structure, and boredom (Vanderbruggen et al., 2020).

When it comes to mental health, increased prevalence of loneliness and social isolation are the main causes of mental health deterioration. A study assessing the psychological effects of the pandemic on 1210 participants in China found that over 50% of participants experienced moderate or severe effects; 29% of participants experienced moderate to severe anxiety symptoms; and 17% of participants reported moderate to severe depression symptoms (Cullen et al., 2020). This confirms the results of the WTO, which found that anxiety and depression prevalence increased by

25% in the first year of the pandemic. This was linked to limitations on people's capacity to work, seek help from loved ones, and participate in their communities, as well as fear of infection, loneliness, death, financial problems, and sadness. In the case of health workers, exhaustion was considered as a major cause of suicidal thoughts.

The pandemic has also had a detrimental effect on the health of the workforce. On the one hand, Downey et al. (2023) argues that the pandemic strained the healthcare system significantly causing immense pressure to the global healthcare workforce. Healthcare workers have had to adjust to various problems with each wave of infection, including longer working hours, heavy workload, new responsibilities, information and work practices, new health policies and guidelines, and massive social shifts within health organizations and the society. It was not surprising, however, that levels of burnout were high, and tales of people wishing to leave the health profession proliferated around the globe (Smallwood et al., 2023). Also, the infection rates and deaths among healthcare providers surged during the pandemic, causing a decline in the health workforce (Stone et al., 2021). For example, the International Council of Nurses reported that over 1.4 million healthcare workers worldwide were infected with COVID-19 in 2020 mainly due to their continual exposure to infected patients, resulting in the death of thousands.

The impact of the pandemic on healthcare providers was severe in developed and developing countries alike. In developed countries, studies conducted in the United States, Italy, and other European countries recorded high rates of infection and mortality among health workers when treating COVID-19 patients (Behera et al., 2020). According to the WHO (2023), about 10% of the confirmed COVID-19 cases were among healthcare providers and nurses occupied the highest percentage among all healthcare providers. In developing countries, a study revealed that over 60,000 nurses were infected with COVID-19 in Iran, this is equivalent to 45% the nurse workforce in the country. Bandyopadhyay et al. (2020) reported that a total of 152,888 infections and over 1400 deaths were reported among healthcare providers as early as May 2020. The study found that the highest infection rate was among female and nurses and the highest death rates were among males and doctors. It also found that general practicians were the highest risk specialty for doctor deaths, whereas mental health was the top risk nursing specialty because there was less personal protective equipment accessible in the community centers. Many mental health nurses work in the community and near patients, increasing their risk of exposure (Shaukat et al., 2020).

Although mental health and psychological factors resulting from the occupational environment of the healthcare providers are considered as hazard (WHO, 2023), the level of risk has significantly increased for mental healthcare providers due to the consistent rise in infection rate and deaths, lack of personal protective equipment, heavy workload, and exposure to extensive media coverage during the pandemic (Vizheh et al., 2020). A survey conducted by WHO (2022a, b) revealed that between 23 and 46% of healthcare workers suffered from anxiety and between 20 and 37% of them experienced depressed symptoms during the pandemic. Overall, the impact of the pandemic on healthcare workforce is multifactorial and led to substantial loss in the healthcare workforce and human capital.

When it comes to public health expenditures, the impact of the pandemic on health and health services created huge pressures on the global economy. The infection and death of hundreds of thousands of medical staff and healthcare workers reduced their productivity and contributed to global health insecurity. High rates of infections that required intensive medical intervention reached over 770 million people globally, resulting in long-term financial burdens on public health organizations. Several studies highlighted the financial costing of the pandemic and its impact on the economy (Wang et al., 2023; World Bank, 2023a, b). For example, a recent study estimated the economic loss in relation to healthcare workers infection of around US$1.3 million (Wang et al., 2023). Table 2 illustrates the total cost and percentage of gross domestic product (GDP) per single COVID-19 infection among healthcare workers in selected developing countries. This table shows that a single healthcare worker infection in Colombia can cost over US$10,000 and go up to US$33,000 in other low-income countries like Kenya, South African, and Eswatini.

A recent study by the World Bank (2023a, b) revealed that governments' spendings on health increased in a line with the growing need of various prevention methods, personal protection equipment, and treatments, bringing total global health expenditure to almost US$9 trillion, the equivalent of 10.89% of global GDP in 2020. The data presented in Fig. 1 shows substantial rise in global health expenditure from 9.83% in 2019 to 10.89% in 2020, about 63% (US$ 5.7 trillion) of the amount

Table 2 Total cost and percentage of GDP per single COVID-19 infection among healthcare workers

Country/region	*Cost (US$)*	*% GDP*
Colombia	10,105	1.54
Eswatini	35,659	9.05
Kenya	33,619	17.98
South Africa—Western cape	33,781	5.7
South Africa—Kwazulu-Natal	34,226	5.77

Source The World Bank (2023a, b)

came from the governments, 36% (US$3.3 trillion) from private sources, and the remaining one percent (US$17 billion) from external sources.

According to WHO (2022a, b), the increase of health expenditure from 2019 to 2020 was substantially higher compared to previous years, with lower-income countries recording the highest increase in health expenditure of 18.6%, followed by 14.9% in lower-middle income countries, and 11% increase in high-income countries. Total spending on COVID-19 accounted for 8% of the overall health spending in 2020. In the following year (2021), the increase in health spending was diverted to COVID-19 vaccination and testing (WHO, 2022a, b). The cost of a single dose of COVID-19 vaccine ranged between US$4 and US$10 (UNICEF, 2023). This extra cost created huge financial challenges for low-income countries, especially when considering that per capita health expenditure is US$41 on average. For these countries to ensure the delivery of the vaccine to 70% of their population over one year, they had

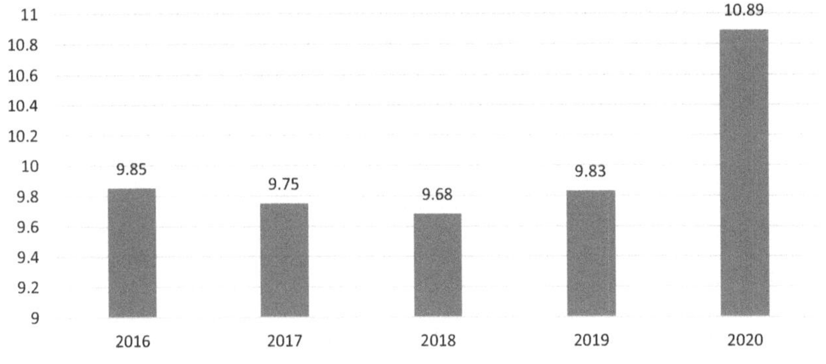

Fig. 1 Global health expenditure (% of GDP) (*Source* World Bank [2023a, b])

to increase their health expenditure by over 56%, unlike 0.8% increase on health expenditure in high-income countries (UNDP, 2023). In fact, COVID-19 vaccination was the most cost-effective intervention to limit and overcome the pandemic, as most studies reported that the efficacy of the vaccine was up to 75% globally.

3 Effects of the Pandemic on Education

The outbreak of the pandemic caused huge disruption to the education system worldwide and forced students and teachers to adopt new educational techniques and methods to continue the process of teaching and learning (Bozkurt et al., 2022). In the first 12 months of the pandemic, about 1.5 billion students in over 180 countries were unable to go to school due to the pandemic-related lockdown (World Economic Forum, 2022). For example, in East Asia and the Pacific region, about 80 million children were not able to learn remotely throughout 2020 (UNICEF, 2020). In Europe, about 45 European countries closed their schools during the peak of the pandemic, which affected over 180 million students, causing a significant gap in learning inequality and learning losses (World Bank, 2021). Despite being unprepared for the transition, most educational institutions were forced to create an emergency remote learning system. This development resulted in long-term consequences for the education system. While it enabled some students to catch up with their education, as much as 40% of students in Liberia dropped out of schools and did not return after they reopened at the end of 2020 (UNICEF, 2020). The introduction of the remote learning system did not prevent the drop off school, which increased from 250,00 in March 2020 to 750,00 in July 2021 in South Africa, while over 45% of students, especially female students in secondary education, dropped schools in Malawi between 2020 and 2021, and about 1 in ten students was missing school in Uganda. This crisis underscores the need for investment in communication and information technology and a more resilience and flexible education system to face similar and unpredicted crises in the future (Ali, 2020).

The sudden and rapid spread of the COVID-19 pandemic forced governments to impose various containment measures such as lockdown, social distancing, and quarantine, forcing physical closure of almost all institutions including schools and colleges. Educational institutions were innovative in developing and using alternative teaching methods to maintain education delivery and minimize the effect of the pandemic on education by shifting to online teaching methods (Rad et al., 2021). Adedoyin and Soykan (2023) defined online learning as "the use of internet and some other important technologies to develop materials for educational purposes, instructional delivery and management of program." Although online learning is not novel for many people, this education method can be challenging and requires technological and cultural adaptations. The rapid shift from regular teaching methods to online teaching created a broad range of challenges for students, teachers, and institutions (Sandars et al., 2020; Schneider & Council., 2021). Among these challenges are:

- **Challenges for Teachers:**

Most educators and instructors had never conducted sessions in an online setting prior to the pandemic, necessitating the acquisition of a diverse set of skills and modifying the content and structure of their services in the best possible methods to engage their learners in a virtual way within a short period (Rad et al., 2021). It took a while until many educators were able to adapt to the digital platforms because of lacking the required knowledge in information technology for carrying out remote teaching (Parkes & Barrs, 2021). Even those instructors who had basic knowledge in IT were taken by surprise of the pandemic and were unable to receive appropriate training to facilitate the remote learning process (Chen et al., 2020). According to Chang and Fang (2020), many teachers were doubting their ability to effectively communicate effectively with student while maintaining the same interaction level as in face-to-face teaching due to tier lacking in technological skills and training. Garbe et al. (2020) found that many teachers did not have the required skills to provide real-time support online such as conducting virtual meeting with students, using new assessment methods for students to achieve proficiency, or to enhance the process of activity completion. Bond et al. (2018) found traces of this problem before the pandemic, when discovering that over 44% of the 941 university teachers surveyed used almost no technology in their etching activities.

Another challenge is the difficulty in assessing and following up with students due to lacking direct communication between teachers and students. According to the findings by Nayir and Sari (2021), 40% of teachers participated in the study reported that they faced challenges in classroom management, since they faced difficulties in the communication and following up with students, while being unable to use some educational materials and involve students in the sessions. Some educators suffered from lack of motivation to develop new IT skills because of their limited knowledge in online teaching and their low self-perception regarding their e-teaching abilities along with lack of confidence in performing lectures online effectively. This makes the adoption of online learning more challenging for educators; some of them refuse to adopt online teaching as an alternative to regular face-to-face teaching methods (Svihus, 2023).

– **Challenges for Students**

Students have also faced considerable challenges in their learning during the pandemic, many of them finding it difficult to adjust to remote learning due to inadequate communication between them and lecturers (Baticulon et al., 2021). Limited access to technology also affected students' learning process. For example, a study conducted in Philippine found that one out of five students did not have a computer, and a huge number of students had to rely on prepaid online data for internet connection. Many students' access to online teaching was limited due to lacking devices, power interruptions, and internet costs. Chang et al. (2020) found that about 70% of the surveyed teachers agreed that the internet speed and stability were poor and teaching platforms were not perfect, while over 50% of the teachers reported that electronic resources were not sufficient to carry out effective online course for students. For online teaching to be successful, technology must be accessible, reliable and user friendly, and technical support with trained faculty must be always readily available (Wallace et al., 2021).

Moreover, younger students are more associated with digital technology than older students, and hence their ability to engage with the online teaching and learning is high due to their exposure to technology and technological devices from smart phones to tablets and computers from the very young age. Hernandez-de-Menendez et al. (2020) found that the surveyed young students, who are known as the "digital generation," spend at least 9 hours per day on digital devices and almost 100% of them believed that they were more proficient in technology than their professors. In fact, this assumption created some sort of delusions and paradoxes that should be considered when applying online teaching because many young students from deprived and disadvantaged backgrounds struggled with online education. Several studies found that many young students showed limitation in their technology usage and a significant number of young people reveal a great difference between their impression and their actual understanding of computer abilities (Ali, 2020; Belay, 2020; The World Bank, 2020).

The pandemic also affected students' social interaction and connections with their beers and faculty, which are critical factors in developing the sense of community at the school and university levels. Remote learning resulted in loneliness and feeling of loss for some students, but others found alternative ways via social media to maintain their social interaction and to engage with each other and faculty. Social media helped in improving this sense of community during remote learning. Instructors offered remote learning tactics that allowed students to communicate using breakout rooms, virtual office hours, video messaging, and regular feedback requests. Other innovative technologies to encourage student-to-student participation included a discussion board for students alone and developing assignments such as think-pair-share, in which students discuss their work with a companion to spot similarities and contrasts. Creating chances for contact is crucial to cultivating a feeling of community and belonging (Wallace et al., 2021). Having acknowledged that, one cannot underestimate the importance of face-to-face teaching when it comes to applied science and laboratory experiments, where students appreciate the benefits of practical experiments, guidance from their instruction, and communication. In this case, online teaching appears to be so limited, restrictive, and demotivating.

In addition to the demotivation to learning that is often caused by external (learning environment) and internal (personal characteristics) factors (Gustiani, 2020), students acknowledged that the pandemic combined stress and anxiety that demotivated and disengaged them in learning (Chiu et al., 2021). Mental health issues such as depression, anxiety, and stress considerably affect students' performance in education (Kotera et al., 2021). For example, Akpinar (2021) found that the increase in mental health issues is attributed to isolation from peers and lecturers, difficulties in the use of online platform, lack of guidance, and lack of counseling. Another study surveyed over 3000 elementary to high school students in Indonesia revealed that 13% of students experienced symptoms that led to stress disorders and depression during the pandemic, particularly during the online learning (Mittal et al., 2021; Nuryana et al., 2023). It also found that approximately 93% of respondents with depressive symptoms were between the ages of 14 and 18, while the remaining 7% were between the ages of 10 and 13. In addition, female students reported a greater negative mental health consequence than males, with females being more likely to experience severe anxiety, sleeplessness, and distress symptoms. These findings reaffirm the fact that poor mental health can reduce productivity and accomplishment, whereas good mental health is associated with improved functioning and achievement. The seriousness of the mental health issue is addressed in the United Nations' 17 sustainable development goals, with the aim of ensuring excellent mental health and well-being (Kotera et al., 2021).

In terms of learning inequality and learning loss, a study by the UNESCO (2022) confirmed that almost 90% of students around the globe were affected by the pandemic lockdown and suspension of traditional teaching methods that severely affected student's learning abilities. Another study found that the suspension of traditional teaching led to an increase in learning inequality and school dropouts (Bartholo et al., 2022). School closure unequally affected students based on different aspects. Dorn et al. (2020) found that students from low-income families were at a higher risk of learning loss due to their limited access to high-quality remote learning tools or to conductive learning environment, showing that only 60% of student form low-income family had access to online course compared to 90% of students from high-income families. The impact of school closure goes far beyond the period of closure. According to the World Bank (2022), students who suffered from learning loss might end up losing about 10% of their future income, which was estimated at US$11 trillion throughout their life. This might also be related to reduced productivity, increased inequality, and social unrest in the future.

4 Aims and Structure of the Book

The aim of this book is to provide a critical analysis of the various effects of the COVID-19 pandemic on human capital development and determine the strategies and policies introduced to minimize the impact of the pandemic on the education and the healthcare sectors. It also aims to explain that education and health are not only fundamental to the broader notion of expanded human capabilities, but they are also vital components of growth and development. It explains how these critical components have been affected by the pandemic and the extent to which low investment in education and health undermined the prosperity and social protection of citizens. Analysis is provided through detailed examination of the impact of the pandemic on the quality of healthcare services, mortality rates, public health policy, and health expenditure. It also assesses the effect of the pandemic on education resources, students and teachers, medical education, and the effectiveness of digital readiness in mitigating pandemic effects on the education system.

While offering a better understanding of varying perspectives on human capital development, this book also provides new insights on the appropriate methods and tools, especially investment in infrastructure and digitalization, to minimize the effect of similar crises in the future. The broader scope of analysis makes this book a unique investigation into the pandemic effects on the two key pillars of human capital—education and healthcare—and appealing to a much wider audience in the Middle East region and globally. It is also important to evaluate human, social, and psychological effects of the pandemic on the wider society and assess the readiness of the education and healthcare sectors to withstand global crises. This evaluation is conducted through detailed examination of the pandemic effects on education, more specifically medical education, physical education, emotional effects on students and teachers, method of communications, learning and teaching, and the extent to which digital readiness has minimized these effects. This book also aims to reveal the severity of the pandemic on human capabilities in terms of loss of lives, illness, vaccinations, knowledge acquisitions, skills development, and productivity, while providing new insights for governments to rapidly recover and deal with similar crises in the future.

Methodologically, this book adopts a variety of research methods, quantitative and qualitative techniques, country case studies, and primary data collected through survey questionnaires, interviews, and official reports to analyze the impact of the pandemic on health and education. The analyses are supported by statistical data and illustrated by tables and figures. Readers, students, researchers, industry practitioners, and policymakers will benefit from the new insights offered by a diverse group of 40 professors, researchers, and industry experts from across the globe.

In terms of structure, this book is organized into two parts. Part one examines the impact of the pandemic on health. Ashraf Mishrif begins with providing an overview of the effects of the pandemic on human capital development, with particular focus on health and education. He evaluates the considerable health risks faced the medical staff with shortage in medical equipment and services and human loss of seven million people died and over 770 million people infected by the virus. He argues that the pandemic caused huge disruption in the medical field, impacted negatively on labor productivity and social well-being, and resulted in huge rise in public health expenditure. Mishrif also explains the impact of the pandemic on education, highlighting the disruptive effects on students, teachers, service delivery, and connectivity. He underscores the capacity of the education institutions to develop alternative modes of delivery, shifting to online education, and adopting new teaching methods and assessments to enable students to acquire the necessary knowledge and skills for their employability. He concludes by stressing that the pandemic effects on human capital development are likely to last for many years.

In Chapter 2, Faryal Khamis et al. explain the epidemiological characteristics of hospitalized patients with moderate versus severe COVID-19 infection. They explain how the success of recognizing factors that cause the progression of COVID-19 from mild to severe diseases is important for the utilization of appropriate resources and improving clinical outcomes. Several clinical, laboratory, and therapeutic factors have been identified as a potential for severity and rapid progression of COVID-19 illness. Early recognition of these factors could facilitate prompt management of hospitalized patients. In Chapter 3, Omar Al-Farsi, Salim Al-Salmi, Raniya Al-Kiyumi, and Yahya Al-Farsi provide an assessment of the impact of COVID-19 on health services utilization in Oman. They provide a cross-sectional analysis of the yearly (outpatient) OPD visits and inpatient volume in health facilities before and during the COVID-19 outbreak using nationwide routine health information system data from January 2019 to December 2020. They found significant reductions in all indicators during the pandemic compared to the pre-pandemic. The average of all-cause outpatient visits per capita was reduced dramatically by 33.9%; the bed occupancy rate was reduced by 21.5%; and the mortality indicators worsened as the crude death rate per 1,000 population increased by 18.5%, indicating a signification decline in Oman health services utilization after the COVID-19 outbreak.

In Chapter 4, Nabeel AlObaidi evaluates the administrative responsibility of the health institution during the COVID-19 pandemic. He discusses the decisions, administrative and directive instructions, and necessity to amend the Law on Combating Infectious Diseases to keep pace with the spread of the virus. While stressing the role of the medical institutions in providing and maintaining health security, he identifies the administrative responsibility is an effective legal tool to contain the pandemic. In Chapter 5, Saira Hafeez, Jibran Hussain, and Rashid Aftab investigate the impact of government stringency in five groups of 22 countries with respect to the timings of policy implementation and the subsequent impact on the mortality rates. The significance of the time frame of policy was analyzed in relation to how early the policy was implemented with respect to other countries and how long the policy was implemented. They conclude that while other factors also contribute to this relationship, government stringency played a significant role in the reduction of COVID-19 mortality rates, relatively better in countries where the percentage of the elderly population is smaller.

In Chapter 6, Said Elhussein Abdelli analyzes the human and social effects of the pandemic in the Arab World, with special focus on education, health, and social interaction. He argues that the social repercussions were directly caused by the pandemic or indirectly by the protective measures imposed by the prevention policies that dictated a certain lifestyle and limited direct social relations. In Chapter 7, Mohd Hussain Kunroo and Mudabera Gulzar explain the socioeconomic, environmental, health, and psychological aspects of the pandemic. They argue that pandemic reaffirmed the interdependence of the global system, where economic recession affects the capacity of the healthcare system, and hence the best effective defense against this pandemic is collective wisdom, coordinated efforts, and a prudent balanced policy mix involving fiscal and monetary measures. They end by concluding that it is dangerous to maintain complacency regarding the rules governing the environment, socioeconomic policies, and the healthcare system.

Part Two focuses on the impact of COVID-19 on education and digitalization. In Chapter 8, Adhari Al Zaabi et al. explain how COVID-19 has re-shaped medical education. They argue that the rapid transition to online learning posed significant challenges for students, educators, and academic institutions during the pandemic. While highlighting the importance of immediate interventions to equip learners and teachers with the essential skills required for continued education, medical schools were probably the most affected due to the critical need for hands-on clinical skill development. They analyzed the perspectives of undergraduate medical students at Sultan Qaboos University in 2020 concerning online teaching and their preferences for the post-COVID era. Results reveal a predominant preference for a combination of synchronous and asynchronous learning. They found that the ability to pause and revisit the sessions was the most perceived benefit of asynchronous lessons, while the ability to connect with professors and peers was very beneficial in synchronous learning. The ended by concluding that while medical students acknowledged the positive aspects of online learning, they did not favor it as the sole mode of education. They expressed a preference for hybrid teaching models beyond the COVID-19 era.

In Chapter 9, N. Ramdas Iyer and Bharat Bhusan Srivastava examine the impact of the pandemic on visitor's footfall at National Science Centre, New Delhi, India, and its impact on educational activities for school children in particular as well as for public in general. They explore the opportunities and challenges experienced by science teachers during the pandemic, as well as the effectiveness of the tools, resources, and support system devised and deployed by the National Science Centre, New Delhi, and how these have now been accepted as the new normal in non-formal free choice science education. They stress the importance of blended learning that is a hybrid form of teaching and holistic learning that involves both classroom and online learning, both structured and free choice learning.

In Chapter 10, Fadi Abdelfattah et al. discuss and identify the influence of digital readiness and perceived stress on higher education students' socio-emotional perceptions in the context of COVID-19. They also aim to define the mediated effect of perceived stress on digital readiness and students' socio-emotional perception during the pandemic crisis. They use a non-probabilistic, purposive sampling strategy approach to collect quantitative data from 300 students in higher educational institutions and analyzed using Partial Least Squares (PLS-SEM). They found a significant positive relationship between digital readiness, perceived stress, and socio-emotional perception, hence offering valuable insights to regulate relevant digital learning authorities.

In Chapter 11, Iyad Abusahloub assesses the awareness levels of Arab students during the initial months of the COVID-19 pandemic in 2020. He delves into the perceptions of Arab students regarding how the pandemic affected their personal lives, academic endeavors, local communities, and the global context through 55 semi-structured interviews, guided by a descriptive-interpretive typology. He uncovered intricate connections between the pandemic and various aspects of life, including global climate, online activities, personal lifestyles, world peace, tourism, global economy, family and society, mental health, specific economic sectors, business models, professional and educational positions, and public health. In Chapter 12, Ramzi Sallem, Hisham Ghunaimi, and Jawaher Al Balushi attempt to develop a teaching model of the entrepreneurship course using the design thinking approach for online teaching in Oman. They draw on the design thinking pedagogical teaching practices and methods to develop a teaching model that highlights the suitable outcomes of the entrepreneurship course. This model is designed for an online teaching method to improve the "creative alertness," self-efficacy, and opportunity evaluation among the students.

In Chapter 13, Sabah Al Balushi and Mohammed Athar Khan assess students' perceptions of emergency remote teaching during the pandemic. They aim to understand the impact of the sudden shift from face-to-face to emergency remote teaching (ERT) on students in Oman using a bottom-up approach. They administered an online survey to Sultan Qaboos University students, where 337 responses were received and analyzed using both descriptive and inferential statistics. The findings are categorized under six different themes: student readiness, communication and interaction with teachers, course materials, online learning and gender ability, students' well-being, and emotions in ERT, and overall ERT experience. These results have significant implications for the students, the teachers, and senior management of higher education institutions in Oman and beyond.

In Chapter 14, Sameer Ahmad Khan and Furqan Qamar assess the learning loss in lockdown and impact of the pandemic on schooling in India, where the education system serves around 265 million students from diverse socioeconomic backgrounds. While nearly 50% of the total students in schools are enrolled in private schools, the authors seek to analyze the effect of the pandemic specifically on the socially and economically disadvantaged groups, which mostly rely on the government for schooling. They also identify the probable causes of massive learning losses among children in government schools and comment on the impact of lockdown and loss of lives and livelihood. The significance of this chapter lies in quantifying and highlighting the extent of the pandemic's impact on the education sector, while helping policymakers address critical issues, reallocate budgets, and make necessary operational and strategic decisions.

5 Conclusion

This chapter provided an overview of the impact of pandemic on human capital development, with particular focus on health and education. It examined various perspectives of the development of human capital, including the pandemic effects on education and healthcare. The disruption of these two critical services sectors affects the entire lifestyle of the individuals, families, students, educators, medical staff and healthcare workers, and their abilities to perform in school or at work.

The share size of the population affected by the pandemic globally was significantly larger than any other crises in the past 50 years. However, the impact of the pandemic varies from region to region and country to country according to their levels of income and quality of their education and healthcare systems. Our analysis revealed that people living in low-income countries were unable to afford the costs of healthcare services to protect themselves and the health of their families during the pandemic, while rural students and individuals from lower-income households invested much less in education than high-income countries.

From the perspectives of human development, the pandemic significantly affected directly the health and well-being of the medical staff and healthcare worker, many of them lost their lives, and those survived were incapable of working in full capacity, causing huge shortage in the human resource in this critical sector. The disruption and lack of healthcare services negatively impacted the well-being of many social groups and reduced labor productivity. Many workers and employees lost their jobs due to the lockdown and closure of business and factories, while others receiving partial income as a result of ill health, absence, or reduction in the number of hours. Reduction in income, together with poor healthcare and education services, pushes many people into poverty (Bartholo et al., 2022). In terms of education, the pandemic disrupted the entire education system globally, resulting in the closure of schools and colleges, loss of learning, shift to online education without training and support services, and huge drops out of schools due to lack of connectivity and cost of internet and equipment in many developing countries. The ability of these countries to increase their investment in health and education is limited in the post-pandemic, which considerably affects human and social development for many years and possibly decades.

References

Adedoyin, O. B., & Soykan, E. (2023). COVID-19 pandemic and online learning: The challenges and opportunities. *Interactive Learning Environments, 31*(2), 863–875.

Akpınar, E. (2021). The effect of online learning on tertiary level students' mental health during the COVID-19 lockdown. *The European Journal of Social & Behavioural Sciences*.

Ali, W. (2020). Online and remote learning in higher education institutes: A necessity in light of COVID-19 pandemic. *Higher Education Studies, 10*(3), 16–25.

Bandyopadhyay, S., Baticulon, R. E., Kadhum, M., Alser, M., Ojuka, D. K., Badereddin, Y., ... & Khundkar, R. (2020). Infection and mortality of health-care workers worldwide from COVID-19: A systematic review. *BMJ Global Health, 5*(12), e003097.

Bartholo, T. L., Koslinski, M. C., Tymms, P., & Castro, D. L. (2022). Learning loss and learning inequality during the COVID-19 pandemic. *Ensaio: Avaliação e Políticas Públicas em Educação, 31*, e0223776.

Baticulon, R. E., Sy, J. J., Alberto, N. R. I., Baron, M. B. C., Mabulay, R. E. C., Rizada, L. G. T., ... & Reyes, J. C. B. (2021). Barriers to online learning in the time of COVID-19: A national survey of medical students in the Philippines. *Medical Science Educator, 31*, 615–626.

Becker, G. S. (2007). Health as human capital: Synthesis and extensions. *Oxford Economic Papers, 59*(3), 379–410.

Behera, D., Praveen, D., & Behera, M. R. (2020). Protecting Indian health workforce during the COVID-19 pandemic. *Journal of Family Medicine and Primary Care, 9*(9), 4541.

Belay, D. G. (2020). COVID-19, distance learning and educational inequality in rural Ethiopia. *Pedagogical Research, 5*(4), em0082.

Bleakley, H. (2010). Health, human capital, and development. *Annual Review of Economics, 2*(1), 283–310.

Bond, M., Marín, V. I., Dolch, C., Bedenlier, S., & Zawacki-Richter, O. (2018). Digital transformation in German higher education: Student and teacher perceptions and usage of digital media. *International Journal of Educational Technology in Higher Education, 15*(1), 1–20.

Bozkurt, A., Karakaya, K., Turk, M., Karakaya, Ö., & Castellanos-Reyes, D. (2022). The impact of COVID-19 on education: A meta-narrative review. *TechTrends, 66*(5), 883–896.

Chaabouni, S., & Mbarek, M. B. (2023). What will be the impact of the COVID-19 pandemic on the human capital and economic growth? Evidence from Eurozone. *Journal of the Knowledge Economy*, 1–17.

Chang, C. L., & Fang, M. (2020, June). E-Learning and online instructions of higher education during the 2019 novel coronavirus diseases (COVID-19) epidemic. *Journal of Physics: Conference Series*, 1574(1), 012166. IOP Publishing.

Chen, T., Peng, L., Yin, X., Rong, J., Yang, J., & Cong, G. (2020, July). Analysis of user satisfaction with online education platforms in China during the COVID-19 pandemic. *Healthcare, 8*(3), 200. MDPI.

Chiu, T. K., Lin, T. J., & Lonka, K. (2021). Motivating online learning: The challenges of COVID-19 and beyond. *The Asia-Pacific Education Researcher, 30*(3), 187–190.

Cullen, W., Gulati, G., & Kelly, B. D. (2020). Mental health in the COVID-19 pandemic. *QJM: An International Journal of Medicine, 113*(5), 311–312.

Di Corrado, D. (2020). *Effects of social distancing on psychological stat....*

Dorn, E., Hancock, B., Sarakatsannis, J., & Viruleg, E. (2020), COVID-19 and learning Loss-disparities grow and students need help. Public and social sector practice. *McKinsey & Company*. https://wasaoly.org/WASA/images/WASA/5.0%20Professional%20Development/4.2%20Conference%20Resources/Winter/2021/COVID-19-and-learning-loss-disparities-grow-and-students-need-help-v3.pdf

Downey, E., Fokeladeh, H. S., & Catton, H. (2023). *What the COVID-19 pandemic has exposed: The findings of five global health workforce professions.*

Garbe, A., Ogurlu, U., Logan, N., & Cook, P. (2020). COVID-19 and remote learning: Experiences of parents with children during the pandemic. *American Journal of Qualitative Research, 4*(3), 45–65.

González-Monroy, C., Gómez-Gómez, I., Olarte-Sánchez, C. M., & Motrico, E. (2021). Eating behaviour changes during the COVID-19 pandemic: A systematic review of longitudinal studies. *International Journal of Environmental Research and Public Health, 18*(21), 11130.

Gustiani, S. (2020). Students' motivation in online learning during COVID-19 pandemic era: A case study. *Holistics (Hospitality and Linguistics): Jurnal Ilmiah Bahasa Inggris, 12*(2).

Haileamlak, A. (2021). The impact of COVID-19 on health and health systems. *Ethiopian Journal of Health Sciences, 31*(6), 1073.

Hamer, M., Kivimäki, M., Gale, C. R., & Batty, G. D. (2020). Lifestyle risk factors, inflammatory mechanisms, and COVID-19 hospitalization: A community-based cohort study of 387,109 adults in UK. *Brain, Behavior, and Immunity, 87*, 184–187.

Hernandez-de-Menendez, M., Escobar Díaz, C. A., & Morales-Menendez, R. (2020). Educational experiences with Generation Z. *International Journal on Interactive Design and Manufacturing (IJIDeM), 14*, 847–859.

Islam, R., Ghani, A. B. A., Kusuma, B., & Theseira, B. B. (2016). Education and human capital effect on Malaysian economic growth. *International Journal of Economics and Financial Issues, 6*(4), 1722–1728.

King's College London (2020). *Nearly a third of the UK public drinking more alcohol than usual during the pandemic*. https://www.kcl.ac.uk/news/nearly-a-third-of-uk-public-drinking-more-alcohol-than-usual-during-the-pandemic

Kotera, Y., Ting, S. H., & Neary, S. (2021). Mental health of Malaysian university students: UK comparison, and relationship between negative mental health attitudes, self-compassion, and resilience. *Higher Education, 81*(2), 403–419.

McBride, E., Arden, M. A., Chater, A., & Chilcot, J. (2021). The impact of COVID-19 on health behaviour, well-being, and long-term physical health. *British Journal of Health Psychology, 26*(2), 259.

Mittal, R., Su, L., & Jain, R. (2021). COVID-19 mental health consequences on medical students worldwide. *Journal of Community Hospital Internal Medicine Perspectives, 11*(3), 296–298.

Nayir, F., & Sari, T. (2021). Identifying parents' home-schooling experience during COVID-19 period. *Asian Journal of Distance Education, 16*(1), 156-170. https://doi.org/10.5281/zenodo.4888516

Nicola, M., Alsafi, Z., Sohrabi, C., Kerwan, A., Al-Jabir, A., Iosifidis, C., ... & Agha, R. (2020). The socio-economic implications of the coronavirus pandemic (COVID-19): A review. *International Journal of Surgery, 78*, 185–193.

Nuryana, Z., Xu, W., Kurniawan, L., Sutanti, N., Makruf, S. A., & Nurcahyati, I. (2023). Student stress and mental health during online learning: Potential for post-COVID-19 school curriculum development. *Comprehensive Psychoneuroendocrinology, 14*, 100184.

Okpata, F. O., Njoku, M. C., & Okpata, O. O. (2021). Human Capital Development (HCD) in COVID-19 pandemic era. *International Journal of Public Administration and Management Research, 7*(2), 39–49.

Parkes, R. S., & Barrs, V. R. (2021). Interaction identified as both a challenge and a benefit in a rapid switch to online teaching during the COVID-19 pandemic. *Journal of Veterinary Medical Education, 48*(6), 629–635.

Rad, F. A., Otaki, F., Baqain, Z., Zary, N., & Al-Halabi, M. (2021). Rapid transition to distance learning due to COVID-19: Perceptions of postgraduate dental learners and instructors. *PLoS ONE, 16*(2), e0246584.

Rantis, K., Panagiotidis, P., Parlapani, E., Holeva, V., Tsapakis, E. M., & Diakogiannis, I. (2022). Substance use during the COVID-19 pandemic in Greece. *Journal of Substance Use, 27*(3), 231–238.

Sandars, J., Correia, R., Dankbaar, M., de Jong, P., Goh, P. S., Hege, I., ... & Pusic, M. (2020). Twelve tips for rapidly migrating to online learning during the COVID-19 pandemic. *MedEdPublish, 9*(1), 82.

Schneider, S. L., & Council, M. L. (2021). Distance learning in the era of COVID-19. *Archives of Dermatological Research, 313*(5), 389–390.

Shaukat, N., Ali, D. M., & Razzak, J. (2020). Physical and mental health impacts of COVID-19 on healthcare workers: A scoping review. *International Journal of Emergency Medicine, 13*, 1–8.

Smallwood, N., Bismark, M., & Willis, K. (2023). Burn-out in the health workforce during the COVID-19 pandemic: opportunities for workplace and leadership approaches to improve well-being. *BMJ Leader, 7*, 178–181.

Stone, K. W., Kintziger, K. W., Jagger, M. A., & Horney, J. A. (2021). Public health workforce burnout in the COVID-19 response in the US. *International Journal of Environmental Research and Public Health, 18*(8), 4369.

Svihus, C. L. (2023). Online teaching in higher education during the COVID-19 pandemic. *Education and Information Technologies*, 1–19.

The World Bank. (2020). *Guidance note: Remote learning & COVID-19.* https://documents1.worldbank.org/curated/en/531681585957264427/pdf/Guidance-Note-on-Remote-Learning-and-COVID-19.pdf

The World Bank. (2020). *Remote learning, EdTech & COVID-19.* https://www.worldbank.org/en/topic/edutech/brief/edtech-COVID-19

The World Bank. (2021). *The impact of COVID-19 on education—Recommendations and opportunities for Ukraine.* https://www.worldbank.org/en/news/opinion/2021/04/02/the-impact-of-COVID-19-on-education-recommendations-and-opportunities-for-ukraine

The World Bank. (2022). *Learning loss, what to do about the heavy cost of COVID-19 on children, youth, and future productivity.* https://thedocs.worldbank.org/en/doc/e52f55322528903b27f1b7e61238e416-0200022022/related/WBG-LearningLosses-flier-10-09-22-e-version.pdf

The World Bank. (2023a). *Current health expenditure (% of GDP).* https://data.worldbank.org/indicator/SH.XPD.CHEX.GD.ZS

The World Bank. (2023b). *The economic burden of COVID-19 infection amongst health care workers.* https://www.worldbank.org/en/topic/health/publication/economic-cost-covid-health-care-workers

UNDP. (2023). *Global dashboard for vaccine equity.* https://data.undp.org/vaccine-equity/

UNESCO (2022). *Education: From disruption to recovery.* https://webarchive.unesco.org/web/20220625033513/https://en.unesco.org/covid19/educationresponse#durationschoolclosures

UNICEF. (2020). *Education and COVID-19 response: Addressing the impact of COVID-19 on education*. https://www.unicef.org/eap/education-and-COVID-19-response

UNICEF. (2023). *COVID-19 vaccine prices*. https://www.unicef.org/supply/media/15861/file/Covid-vaccine-prices-15022023.pdf

Vanderbruggen, N., Matthys, F., Van Laere, S., Zeeuws, D., Santermans, L., Van den Ameele, S., & Crunelle, C. L. (2020). Self-reported alcohol, tobacco, and cannabis use during COVID-19 lockdown measures: Results from a web-based survey. *European Addiction Research, 26*(6), 309–315.

Vizheh, M., Qorbani, M., Arzaghi, S. M., Muhidin, S., Javanmard, Z., & Esmaeili, M. (2020). The mental health of healthcare workers in the COVID-19 pandemic: A systematic review. *Journal of Diabetes & Metabolic Disorders, 19*, 1967–1978.

Wallace, S., Schuler, M. S., Kaulback, M., Hunt, K., & Baker, M. (2021, July). Nursing students experience remote learning during the COVID-19 pandemic. *Nursing Forum*, 56(3), 612–618.

Wang, H., Zeng, W., Kabubei, K. M., Rasanathan, J. J., Kazungu, J., Ginindza, S., ... & Chopra, M. (2023). Modelling the economic burden of SARS-CoV-2 infection in health care workers in four countries. *Nature Communications, 14*(1), 2791.

World Bank. (2020). *The human capital index 2020 update: Human capital in the time of COVID-19*. https://documents1.worldbank.org/curated/en/456901600111156873/pdf/The-Human-Capital-Index-2020-Update-Human-Capital-in-the-Time-of-COVID-19.pdf

World Economic Forum. (2022). *Here's how COVID-19 Affected Education—And how we can get Children's learning back on track*. https://www.weforum.org/agenda/2022/11/covid19-education-impact-legacy/

World Health Organisation. (2022a). *World failing in 'our duty of care' to protect mental health and well-being of health and care workers, finds report on impact of COVID-19*. https://www.who.int/news/item/05-10-2022-world-failing-in--our-duty-of-care--to-protect-mental-health-and-wellbeing-of-health-and-care-workers--finds-report-on-impact-of-COVID-19#:~:text=The%20report%20found%20that%2023,52%20percent%20in%20pooled%20estimates

World Health Organization. (2022b). *Global spending on health: Rising to the pandemic's challenges*. World Health Organization.

World Health Organisation. (2023). *WHO Coronavirus (COVID-19) dashboard*. https://covid19.who.int/

Zheng, C., Huang, W. Y., Sheridan, S., Sit, C. H. P., Chen, X. K., & Wong, S. H. S. (2020). COVID-19 pandemic brings a sedentary lifestyle in young adults: A cross-sectional and longitudinal study. *International Journal of Environmental Research and Public Health, 17*(17), 6035.

PART I

The Impact of COVID-19 on Health

CHAPTER 2

Epidemiology and Risk Factors for Hospitalization of Patients with Moderate Versus Severe COVID-19 Patients

Faryal Khamis, Salah Al Awaidy, Muna Al Shaaibi, Mubarak Al Shukeili, Shabnam Chhetri, Afra Al Balushi, Sumaiya Al Sulaimi, Amal Al Balushi, and Ronald Wesonga

1 Introduction

The emergence of 2019 Coronavirus Disease (COVID-19) pandemic of a novel coronavirus, severe respiratory distress syndrome (SARS-CoV-2), that progressed rapidly worldwide had a disastrous impact on humanity and became a public health emergency of international concern. The end of this international health emergency was announced in May 2023;

F. Khamis · S. Chhetri · A. Al Balushi · S. Al Sulaimi · A. Al Balushi
Department of Medicine, Royal Hospital, Muscat, Oman
e-mail: faryal.k@moh.gov.om

S. Al Awaidy (✉)
Ministry of Health, Muscat, Oman
e-mail: salah.awaidy@gmail.com

A. Mishrif (ed.), *Perspectives on Human Capital Development*,
https://doi.org/10.1007/978-981-97-5246-1_2

however, by that time, the pandemic resulted in more than 766 million infections and 6.9 million deaths globally. The risk of emergence of new variants and new surges of cases remains as long as the virus continues to evolve (World Health Organisation, 2021).

The COVID-19 pandemic created enormous scientific uncertainties in many aspects among understanding the transmissibility, genetic susceptibility, risk factors for disease progression and severity, and the absence of effective therapies (Khamis et al., 2020a). Furthermore, the disease exhibits a broad range of clinical manifestations, which span from mild to severe illness (Khamis et al., 2020b). A growing concern in public health, especially in the context of a new pathogen, is the ability to forecast the progression of the disease (World Health Organization, 2021) severity and the risk factors associated with progression across different clinical spectrums. By using prompt and efficient management strategies, this will not only save individual lives but notably maintain the resilience of the health system in instances when medical resources are limited or nonexistent (Wu Leung et al., 2020).

Various factors that are linked with severe COVID-19 have been incorporated into prediction models for estimating prognosis patients with COVID-19. Comorbidities such as hypertension, diabetes mellitus, chronic respiratory disease, and cardiovascular disease, as well as immune parameters including lymphopenia, leukocyte, and neutrophil elevation, were observed more frequently in patients with severe COVID-19 compared to those with mild cases (Li et al., 2021; Yang et al., 2020).

Some of these risk factors may be more strongly associated with illness severity than others. Thus, identifying risk variables in various clinical settings and populations is critical. Furthermore, understanding the severity of a disease might impact the dispersal and allotment of healthcare personnel, resources, funding, and the prioritizing of vaccines when new cases persistently emerge. The main objective of this chapter is to review

M. Al Shaaibi · M. Al Shukeili · R. Wesonga
Department of Statistics, College of Science, Sultan Qaboos University, Muscat, Oman
e-mail: s29026@student.squ.edu.om

R. Wesonga
e-mail: wesonga@squ.edu.om

the predictors of COVID-19 severity as well as to locate existing literature on epidemiological and clinical features of COVID-19 patients hospitalized with severe cases as opposed to those with mild illness. The following definitions adopted from the World Health Organization (WHO) (World Health Organization, 2021) delineate to describe the clinical severity of illness caused by COVID-19:

Moderate illness: patients who exhibit symptoms suggestive of lower respiratory disease as determined by clinical evaluation or imaging and possess an oxygen saturation reading (SpO2) $\geq$ 94% on room air at sea level. **Severe illness**: patients who have SpO2 < 94% on room air at sea level, a ratio of arterial partial pressure of oxygen to fraction of inspired oxygen (PaO2/FiO2) < 300 mm Hg, a respiratory rate > 30 breaths/min, or lung infiltrates > 50%. **Critical illness**: patients who have respiratory failure, thromboembolism, circulatory shock, myocardial damage, arrhythmias, encephalopathy, septic shock, and/or multiple organ dysfunction (Long et al., 2022; Wang et al., 2020a).

2 Literature Review

Globally, approximately 80% of individuals diagnosed with COVID-19 had mild illness and were able to recuperate without the need for specialized medical intervention, of whom 10–20% could progress and develop more severe symptoms that needed hospitalization and intensive care unit (ICU) management (Huang et al., 2020; Wang et al., 2020b; Vaughan et al., 2021). Recognizing factors associated with moderate versus severe illness is fundament in providing the most effective care for admitted patients especially when resources are scarce. Numerous previous studies have identified risk factors associated with increased risk of death in COVID-19 patients (Shi et al., 2020; Wingert et al., 2021; Zhou et al., 2020), however, little is known about the factors that exacerbate COVID-19 symptoms. In a cohort of 1002 hospitalized patients, whose average age was 54.13 (SD = 16.09) years, 257 (25.7%) died, while the rest were either hospitalized for at least 9 days (n = 477, 47.6%), admitted to ICU (n = 517, 51.6%), or required mechanical ventilation (n = 414, 41.3%) (Fig. 1, A). The majority of these patients had hypertension (n = 513, 51.2%) as the most reported comorbidity, followed by diabetes (n = 499, 49.8%), and the least was liver disease (n = 43, 4.3%). Among the clinical factors bilateral lung consolidation (n = 847, 84.5%) was the most prevalent, followed by shortness of breath ($n = 836$, 83.4%), and the least was sepsis ($n = 174$, 17.4%). The other findings are presented in Table 1 and are similar to those presented by Khamis et al. (2021).

To study the factors associated with severity of COVID-19, an outcome variable was created by categorizing the severity of COVID-19 based on the guidelines recommended by the CDC, which includes the length of stay (LOS) for nine days or more, mortality, and the necessity for intensive care unit (ICU) admission. This categorical classification shows that among the hospitalized patients, COVID-19 was more severe ($n = 839$, 89.1%) than moderate ($n = 163$, 10.9%) Fig. 1, B. The disease severity was statistically tested against the following risk factors: age, nationality, being male, having diabetes, experiencing

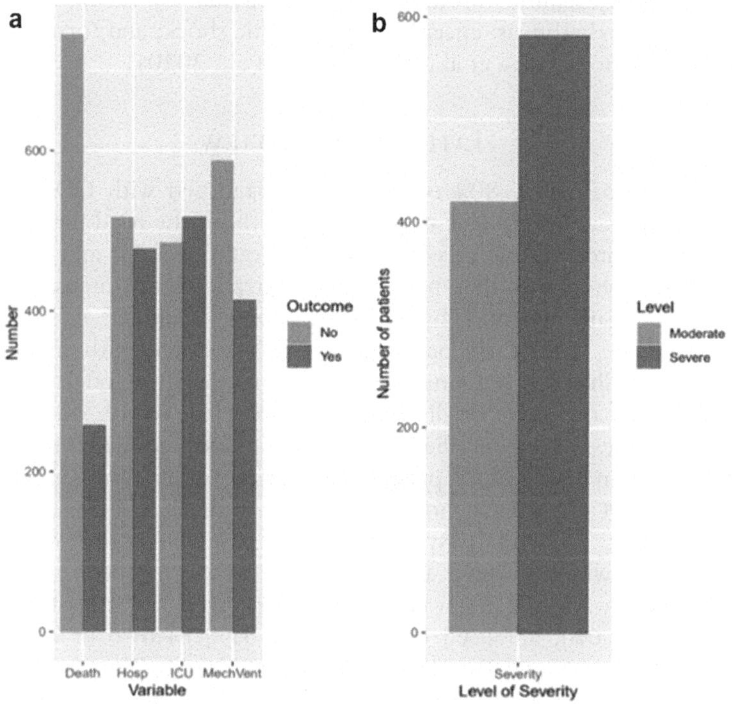

Fig. 1 COVID-19 outcomes (**a**) and Severity Level (**b**) (Figure in permission [Khamis et al., 2021])

Table 1 Description of study variables for the COVID-19 hospitalized patients

Study variable	*Measurement*	*Frequency (n)*	*Percentage*
Demographics			
Gender	Male	355	35.4
	Female	646	64.5
Nationality	Others	231	23.1
	Omani	770	76.8
Comorbidities			
Diabetes Mellitus	Yes	499	49.8
Hypertension	Yes	514	51.3
Dyslipidemia	Yes	216	21.6
Respiratory disease	Yes	116	11.6
Cardiac disease	Yes	209	20.9
Liver disease	Yes	43	4.3
Clinical factors			
Shortness of breath	Yes	836	83.4
Bilateral lung consolidation	Yes	847	84.5
Sepsis	Yes	174	17.4
Acute respiratory distress syndrome	Yes	425	42.4
Non-invasive ventilation requirement	Yes	280	27.9
Therapeutic interventions			
Plasmapheresis	Yes	62	6.2
Convalescent plasma	Yes	393	39.2
Tocilizumab	Yes	325	32.4
Steroids	Yes	649	64.8
Laboratory parameters			

(continued)

Table 1 (continued)

Study variable	*Measurement*	*Frequency* (n)	*Percentage*
Estimated glomerular filtration rate (mL/min/1.73 m^2)	Yes	311	31
Total white cell count (10^9/L)[a]	Mean (SD)	7.7 (4.7)	
Hemoglobin A1c (mmol/L)[a]	Mean (SD)	1.2 (1.1)	
C-reactive protein(mg/L)[a]	Mean (SD)	106.5 (82.1)	
Lactate dehydrogenase (mmol/L)[a]	Mean (SD)	470.65 (536.5)	
Ferritin (ng/mL)[a]	Mean (SD)	1283.45 (2410.2)	
Alanine aminotransferase, (U/L)[a]	Mean (SD)	65.15 (167.1)	
D-dimer (ng/mL)[a]	Mean (SD)	4.45 (13.3)	
Corrected calcium (mmol/L)[a]	Mean (SD)	2.15 (0.2)	
Troponin (pg/mL)[a]	Mean (SD)	159.1 (938.2)	
Vitamin D (IU)[a]	Mean (SD)	69.4 (36.9)	

[a]Numeric variable

shortness of breath (SOB) at presentation, having bilateral chest consolidations, developing acute respiratory distress syndrome (ARDS), sepsis, having high white blood cell count, high C-reactive protein (CRP), high lactate dehydrogenase (LDH), high D-dimer, low corrected calcium, and requiring non-invasive mechanical ventilation (NIV). When adjusted for other factors, severe COVID-19 was significantly associated with non-nationals patients with ARDS, sepsis, elevated CRP, on NIV, and those who required therapy with steroid ($p < 0.05$) (Table 2).

Furthermore, using the logistic regression model, while adjusting for other factors, among hospitalized patients, under the therapeutic interventions, those with severe COVID-19 had 3.28-fold increased likelihood of receiving steroids (1.81–6.07, $p < 0.001$) compared to those with moderate COVID-19. Similarly, increased odds of disease severity were noticed among clinical factors: sepsis (OR = 3.76; 95% CI: 1.35–11.2), ARDS (OR = 27.0; 11.03–82.0), and NIV requirement (OR = 7.09; 95%CI: 2.80–20.7). However, reduced severity was noted among the nationals (OR = 0.43, 95%CI: 0.22–0.83) compared to non-nationals (Table 3).

In a number of earlier studies, gender has been shown to be associated with severity in COVID-19 (Cummings et al., 2020; Du et al., 2020; Galloway et al., 2020; Guan et al., 2020; Li et al., 2020). However, many subsequent researches (Guan et al., 2020; Ya'qoub et al., 2021) have shown that the impact of gender and ethnicity on disease progression is not substantial. The gender disparities in mortality are likely due to a variety of theoretical reasons including hormonal variations and the differences in natural immunological responses. Moreover, societal variations in attitudes and actions among men and women may also influence the spread of infection and subsequent outcomes (Ya'qoub et al., 2021).

Research also has revealed that migrant and ethnic minority populations are more likely to develop severe disease and need hospitalization as a result of COVID-19. In this context, in an earlier report from Oman, almost 98% of the infected hospitalized patients during the Omicron wave were nationals, while the percentage of nationals that required hospitalizations during the first wave caused by the novel Wuhan virus was 77% (Khamis et al., 2022). These variations could be associated with ethnicity and race (Ya'qoub et al., 2021), but also might be related to access health services and the availability of care (Mazzalai et al., 2023). The association between ethnicity and unfavorable outcomes in COVID-19 patients requires further investigation; however, social and economic factors, such

Table 2 Factors associated with severity of COVID-19 among hospitalized patients

Variable	*Level*	*COVID-19 severity*		P *value*
		Moderate (n = *163)*	*Severe* (n = *839)*	
Demographic				
Age	Mean (SD)	51.5 (15.8)	56.0 (16.0)	0.001**
Gender	Male	250 (59.5)	396 (68.2)	0.006**
	Female	170 (40.5)	185 (31.8)	
Nationality	Omani citizen	353 (84.0)	417 (71.8)	0.001**
	Others	67 (16.0)	164 (28.2)	
Comorbidities				
Diabetes Mellitus	Yes	178 (42.4)	321 (55.2)	0.001**
Hypertension	Yes	204 (48.6)	310 (53.3)	0.161
Dyslipidemia	Yes	80 (19.0)	136 (23.4)	0.118
Respiratory disease	Yes	42 (10.0)	74 (12.7)	0.220
Cardiac disease	Yes	76 (18.1)	133 (22.9)	0.080
Liver disease	Yes	13 (3.1)	30 (5.2)	0.153
Clinical				
Shortness of breath	Yes	292 (69.9)	544 (93.8)	0.000**
Bilateral lung consolidation	Yes	297 (70.7)	550 (94.5)	0.000**
Sepsis	Yes	15 (3.6)	159 (27.3)	0.000**
Acute respiratory distress syndrome	Yes	12 (2.9)	413 (71.0)	0.000**
Non-invasive ventilation requirement	Yes	14 (3.3)	266 (45.7)	0.000**
Laboratory				
Total white cell count, (10^9/L)	Mean (SD)	6.2 (3.6)	9.1 (5.9)	0.000**
Hemoglobin A1C, (mmol/L)	Mean (SD)	1.2 (0.7)	1.2 (1.4)	0.207
C-reactive protein(mg/L)	Mean (SD)	81.8 (70.9)	129.1 (91.7)	0.000**
Lactate dehydrogenase, (mmol/L)	Mean (SD)	403.0 (302.5)	534.1 (463.8)	0.000**
Ferritin, (ng/mL)	Mean (SD)	1205.0(1857.3)	1391.9 (3020.1)	0.477
Alanine aminotransferase, (U/L)	Mean (SD)	60.0 (81.7)	71.7 (252.1)	0.576
D-dimer, (ng/mL)	Mean (SD)	2.5 (9.9)	6.4 (16.9)	0.013

Variable	*Level*	*COVID-19 severity*		P *value*
		Moderate (n = *163)*	*Severe* (n = *839)*	
Corrected calcium, (mmol/L)	Mean (SD)	2.1 (0.1)	2.2 (0.2)	0.000**
Troponin, (pg/mL)	Mean (SD)	64.6 (224.7)	227.9 (1532.5)	0.370
Vitamin D, (IU)	Mean (SD)	66.5 (36.3)	72.0 (37.6)	0.382
Estimated glomerular filtration rate (mL/min/1.73 m^2)	Yes	132 (31.5)	179 (30.8)	0.869
Therapeutic interventions				
Plasmapheresis	Yes	2 (0.5)	60 (10.3)	0.000**
Convalescent plasma	Yes	32 (19.6)	361 (43.0)	0.000**
Tocilizumab	Yes	9 (5.5)	316 (37.7)	0.000**
Steroids	Yes	35 (21.5)	614 (73.2)	0.000**

*Significant at 95% CI; **Significant at 99% CI

Table 3 Predictors of COVID-19 severity among hospitalized patient

Independent variables	*Dependent variable: COVID-19 severity*		
Demographics	*Adjusted Odds ratio*	*95% Confidence interval*	p-*value*
Nationality (Omani)	0.43	0.22–0.83	0.012*
Comorbidities			
Clinical factors			
Shortness of breath	–		
Sepsis	3.76	1.35–11.2	0.010*
Acute respiratory distress syndrome	27.0	(11.03–82)	0.000**
Non-invasive ventilation requirement	7.09	2.80–20.7	0.000**
Laboratory parameters			
C-reactive protein (mg/L)	1.00	1.00–1.01	0.045*
Therapeutic interventions			
Steroids	3.28	1.81–6.07	0.001**

*Significant at 95% CI; **Significant at 99% CI

as occupations with risk of direct exposure, crowded living conditions, and barriers in access to healthcare, are potential contributors to the difference in outcomes among certain ethnic groups and minority (Zhang et al., 2023).

The variation in severity of the disease could be based on the five SARS-CoV-2 variants: Alpha (B.1.1.7), Beta (B.1.351), Gamma (P.1), Delta (B.1.617.2), and Omicron (BA.1 and BA.2) (Scovino et al., 2022). A number of studies suggested that some variants are more virulent and transmissible and are associated with severe form of COVID-19 disease (Zhao et al., 2022). The Omicron COVID-19 subtype has been associated with less severe disease in comparison with delta variant (Nyberg et al., 2022). In a cohort of patients from Oman, the most important factors associated with severity were the Delta variant, age, past history of chronic respiratory disease, and the presence of renal impairment on initial presentation (Khamis et al., 2022).

Age has been shown in several reports as the most significant predictor of severity and fatality in COVID-19 patients (Zhou et al., 2020). Furthermore, older patients have a higher tendency to progress rapidly from moderate to severe-stage disease. Inoculating macaques with SARS-CoV have demonstrated that age-dependent functional defects in immune cells can lead to a robust increase of genes associated with inflammation, which in turn causes a decrease in type I interferon beta. This impairs the ability of the immune system to suppress the virus and, ultimately, results in unfavorable outcomes (Bektas et al., 2017; Speranza et al., 2022). Several studies have revealed a relationship between age and illness progression (Cummings et al., 2020). Likewise, patients aged 65 and older constituted a disproportional majority of over 75% of all in-hospital fatalities in the United States. Patients aged 80 years or older had a 16.2-fold increased risk of mortality compared to those aged 18 to 34 years. In addition, the mortality rate among those aged 65 to 79 was 39.2% (Rosenthal et al., 2020).

In the elderly population, the prevalence of comorbidities tend to be common (Patel et al., 2023). Numerous studies have showed that elderly and individuals with chronic diseases such as diabetes, chronic obstructive pulmonary disease (COPD), heart disease, cancer, smoking, chronic kidney disease, cerebrovascular disease, chronic liver disease, immunosuppressive medications, and obesity are more likely to develop severe COVID-19 disease (Patel et al., 2023) (Gallus et al., 2023) (Imam et al., 2020; Price-Haywood et al., 2020; Zhou et al., 2020). Hypertension is among the additional chronic conditions that have been frequently associated with severe clinical outcomes, including hospital admission, intensive care unit admission, and mortality (Khamis et al., 2021). In several other large cohorts, DM was the comorbidity most associated with disease severity (Imam et al., 2020; Patel et al., 2023). Patients with diabetes have a higher chance of developing severe COVID-19 because hyperglycemia may decrease immune system activity, impacting humoral immunity, antioxidant system function, and neutrophil function (Ayelign et al., 2019; Bahendeka et al., 2016) and therefore, increases the susceptibility to nosocomial infections. In a meta-analysis, elevated liver enzymes in infected patients increased the risk of progression to severe disease by 53.5% and the risk of fatality by 23.5% (Yadav et al., 2021). The affinity of SARS-CoV-2 virus to bind to the angiotensin II-converting enzyme (ACE2) receptor on the biliary epithelium increases viral replication and causes biliary dysfunction (Ni et al., 2020).

Severe illness is frequently characterized by pneumonia that may be complicated by respiratory failure and the need for mechanical ventilation

(Chang et al., 2020). On initial presentation, SOB and bilateral consolidations on chest radiography can be suggestive of significant viral effects, indicating that patients with these aberrant findings are likely to progress from moderate to severe conditions. Nevertheless, during the initial stages of illness, radiographic examinations may reveal normal results in 15% of patients who undergo CT imaging and in 40% of patients who undergo chest radiography (Jalaber et al., 2020; Khamis et al., 2021).

Viral sepsis a condition characterized by multisystem dysregulation of cytokines, hyperinflammation, and altered mitochondrial metabolism is a common finding in patients with critical COVID-19 illness and it is an indicative of disease progression and unfavorable clinical outcomes (Herrera-Van Oostdam et al., 2021).

Similarly, ARDS is an indicator for critical and potentially deadly COVID-19. ARDS develops in 42% of individuals with COVID-19 pneumonia and in 60%-80% of those who need ICU care. ARDS in COVID-19 patients has a predictable temporal course across days, with a median time to intubation of 8.5 days after symptom starts (Xu et al., 2020). Hence, in order to prevent the progression of the disease, it is crucial to monitor respiratory rate and SpO2 in order to identify patients at an early stage. If admission to the intensive care unit is necessary, the mortality rate for COVID-19 patients with ARDS is between 26% and 61.5%; for those who are managed with mechanical ventilation, the mortality rate ranges from 65.7% to 94%. COVID-19 ARDS is distinguished by the characteristic pathological finding of diffuse alveolar injury in the lung, which may advance to lung fibrosis as scar tissues gradually substitute cellular components. In fatal instances, there is diffuse microvascular thrombosis, indicating thrombotic microangiopathy and disseminated intravascular coagulation (Xu et al., 2020). Thus, early monitoring of alterations in the coagulation cascade, including D-dimer, is critical and can be predicator of progression to severe disease.

In a retrospective, multicenter research conducted in Wuhan, China, 191 laboratory-confirmed COVID-19 patients who died by January 31, 2020, were analyzed. The study found that sepsis was the most often reported cause of death, followed by respiratory failure, ARDS, and heart failure. Similarly, national data from the USA reported that the most frequent cause of fatality was acute respiratory failure, accounting for 30.8% ($n = 19{,}960$) of cases, followed by acute renal failure at 18.8% ($n = 12{,}181$), and sepsis at 18.6% ($n = 12{,}039$) (Contou et al., 2020). Sepsis is a frequently occurring consequence that may be directly induced by SARS-CoV-2 infection. This is supported by various publications that have shown a low occurrence of bacterial co-infection (Contou et al., 2020; Pandak et al., 2023).

In terms of laboratory predictors, abnormalities in various hematological and biochemical biomarkers have been linked with progression to severe COVID-19. Increase in level of white blood cells, elevated CRP, high LDH, high D-dimer and ferritin levels, increased corrected calcium, CD3 + CD8 + T-cells $\leqslant 75$ cells μL^{-1}, and high cardiac troponin I $\geqslant 0.05$ ng mL^{-1} have been predictors for severe disease in patients admitted with COVID-19 pneumonia. These parameters are also indicative of cytokine storm, a marker of severe disease (Ragab et al., 2020) when the immune system in response to the virus triggers a dysregulated hyperactive inflammatory reaction that results in uncontrolled release of cytokines (Mo et al., 2021). In other reports, lymphopenia and high inflammatory markers such as CRP, procalcitonin, and interleukin-6 were associated with progression to severe disease (Lacap Jr et al., 2022). Additional research is needed to establish the role of these laboratory variables in disease progression.

Studies have shown that hypocalcemia predicts a poor clinical outcome in critically ill patients in the hospital setting. Calcium is an important element in the viral fusion of enveloped viruses such as SARS-CoV, MERS-CoV, and Ebola viruses, which enhances reproduction (Nathan et al., 2019). Similarly, COVID-19 patients have shown a significant occurrence of hypocalcemia, which has been proposed as a dependable indicator for hospitalization need and disease advancement. The deleterious consequence of hypocalcemia in COVID-19 patients may be attributed to its adverse influence on heart function, which might result in fatality if it becomes severe or acute (Straus et al., 2020) and its roles in coagulation and inflammation cascades. COVID-19 patients have increased levels of fatty acids both saturated and unsaturated that have a pro-inflammatory function with high affinity to bind calcium, and can result in cytokine storm, multisystem organ failure, and acute lung damage (Osman et al., 2021).

Elevated CRP has been observed in patients with severe COVID-19 disease as a result of overproduction of inflammatory cytokines and cell destruction (di Filippo et al., 2021). High CRP potentially can predict disease progression in patients with moderate COVID-19, therefore, aiding in early diagnosis of severe COVID-19.

Several investigations revealed that during COVID-19 hospitalization, elevated levels of cardiac troponin I were seen in over half of the deceased (Salvatici et al., 2020). Patients with COVID-19 pneumonia also were reported to have coagulation derangement, characterized by increased D-dimer levels (Milbrandt et al., 2009) and pro-inflammatory cytokines (Corrales-Medina et al., 2012) causing ischemia and thrombosis. In addition, angiotensin converting enzyme 2 receptor, the receptor for SARS-CoV-2, is expressed on myocytes and vascular endothelial cells (Mendoza-Torres et al., 2015). Thus, at least theoretically, direct cardiac involvement by the virus is conceivable.

In a retrospective research on the early detection of laboratory-confirmed COVID-19 individuals who were prone to advance to severe illness, a clinical score web application constitutes of eight variables was developed and validated in order to identify the clinical and laboratory parameters associated with disease progression and the need for ICU care to guide the management and to optimize the use of the available medical resources Fig. 2. The cohort included 313 COVID-19 patients from Oman that were hospitalized between March 9, 2020, and July 20, 2020, among whom 45% were admitted in an ICU facility either on initial presentation or later during hospitalization. About 58% of the patients were in the age group between 41 and 70 years, 67% were male patients, and 64% were Omani nationals. The mortality rate was 15%. About 72% were low risk on initial admission, based on CURB-65 score and 81 of these 225 were eventually admitted to an ICU, representing more than half (81/151, 57%) of total ICU patients (Lacap et al., 2022). Furthermore, a long hospitalization period and high CURB-65 score were also risk factors for ICU admission (Satici et al., 2020). Numerous studies have shown similar findings to the importance of clinical scores in determining severity of COVID-19 in patients (Oktariani et al., 2019).

Among 1096 patients from Kuwait who were enrolled between February and April 2020, the risk factors that predicted death were asthma, smoking, and high procalcitonin (Almazeedi et al., 2020). Researchers from KSA reported fatality rate of 32.1% among 352 critically ill patients. Age, smoking, history of pulmonary embolism, reduced SpO2/FiO2 ratio, high lactate and D-dimers, and decreased SpO2/FiO2 ratio were mortality predictors in multivariate regression analysis (Alharthy et al., 2021). A national study of 64,781 patients with confirmed COVID-19 who were discharged between April 1, 2020, and May 31, 2020, from 592 hospitals in the United States revealed

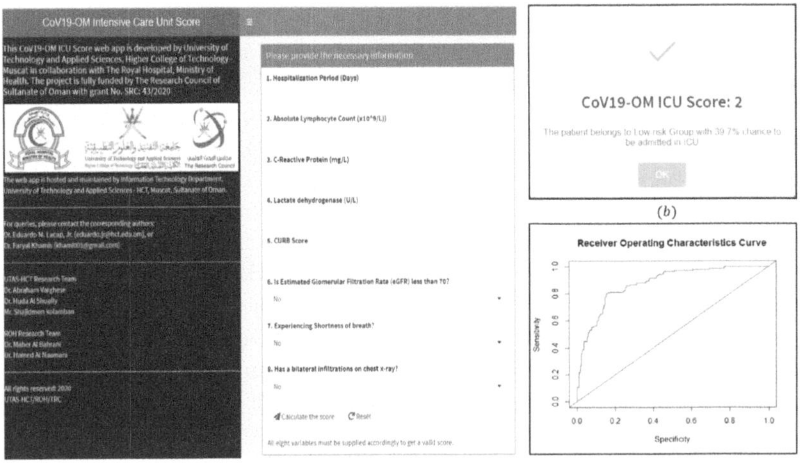

Fig. 2 COVID-19 OM ICU score web application (Permission from Authors)

that almost 19% of patients with COVID-19 needed intensive care unit care, 16% required invasive mechanical ventilation, and 20.3% perished. However, in a study from Oman, 47% of COVID-19 patients required intensive care unit care, 41% of patients needed invasive mechanical ventilation, and 26.0% of patients died, with ICU mortality reaching 42%. Significantly associated with mortality were preexisting hypertension, moderate to severe ARDS, lymphocyte counts below 0.5, albumin below 22, procalcitonin above 0.2, D-dimer above 1200, and the requirement for continuous renal replacement therapy (Rastad et al., 2020).

Furthermore, in comparison with moderate COVID-19, the odds ratio of disease severity was 7.09 (2.80–20.77, $p < 0.001$) times greater in patients with severe COVID-19 on NIV. Wendel Garcia and colleagues compared NIV against various respiratory support techniques, including standard oxygen treatment (SOT), high flow nasal cannula (HFNC), and invasive mechanical ventilation (IMV), in their sub-analysis of a prospective global registry of critically sick COVID-19 patients. An increased overall ICU mortality (SOT: 18%, HFNC: 20%, NIV: 37%, IMV: 25%, $p = 0.016$) was linked to the use of NIV. The NIV group had a higher median length of stay in the ICU and a longer in-hospital stay until intubation than the other three groups. These results, which have been documented in ARDS patients, provide evidence that NIV should be avoided because of the higher risk of ICU mortality (Wendel Garcia et al., 2021). In ARDS of viral etiology, the use of NIV is associated with high failure rates up to 85% (Zhao et al., 2021).

Therapeutics including convalescent plasma (CP), tocilizumab, and steroids were administered early on in moderate and severe COVID-19 patients to prevent further progression. Another cohort of patients from Oman, in the bivariate analysis, all the proposed therapies had significant association with severity and had an impact on disease progression.

Approximately 35% of patients in the moderate group received steroids, compared to 73% in the severe group. Steroids were 3.28 (95% CI: 1.81–6.07, $p < 0.05$) times more likely to be utilized as an intervention in severe than mild COVID-19 hospitalized patients to prevent further deterioration. Studies both observational and RCTs revealed a favorable benefit of utilizing low dosage steroids in severe COVID-19 pneumonia on mortality, progression of disease, requirement for MV, and LOS (Balcells et al., 2021; Bhimraj et al., 2021).

The use of CP from infected individuals and passively transferring antibodies to others to protect or treat has been used in the past. Previous studies on coronavirus epidemics caused by MERS and SARS have shown that CP is safe and may have therapeutic advantages, such as accelerating viral clearance, especially when given early in the course of the illness (Van Paassen et al., 2020). In some recent studies, early use of CP has been shown to decrease progression of COVID-19 (Janiaud et al., 2021); however, the reports on the benefit of CP in COVID-19 have been inconsistent (Agarwal et al., 2020).

Treatment with tocilizumab promptly when there are indicators of increased oxygen need was shown to be useful in avoiding disease progression. In the EMPACTA study, nonventilated hospitalized patients needing oxygen who received tocilizumab during the first two days of admission had a reduced probability of progression to MV or death by day 28 than those who were not treated with tocilizumab (12% vs. 19.3%, respectively) (Salama et al., 2021). Furthermore, in the Recovery study, among those not receiving IMV at baseline, patients who received tocilizumab were less likely to attain the composite objective of IMV or death (35% vs. 40%) (Salama et al., 2021).

3 Conclusion

Multiple studies have investigated the risk variables associated with the course of illness in hospitalized COVID-19 patients. These studies included patients who had been verified by RT-PCR and were undergoing identical investigations and treatment procedures. As a result, it was possible to accurately determine the proportions of moderate and severe cases.

However, the relatively large sample size of cohorts and the wide spectrum of clinical disease identified risk factors for severity with great precision. The retrospective nature of the study and missing data preclude detailed analyses of other significant factors associated with disease progression. Furthermore, some important risk factors such as comorbidities showed contradictory results in different studies and larger sample sizes are needed to show the differences. Nevertheless, the risk factors for developing moderate versus severe COVID-19 illness among hospitalized patients are important. Factors including age, gender, nationality, DM, SOB and/or bilateral lung consolidation on admission, ARDS, and sepsis are associated with severe COVID-19 among hospitalized patients. Moreover, high WBC, CRP, LDH, D-dimer, low corrected calcium, and need for NIV are parameters significantly associated with severe COVID-19. These individuals need vigilant monitoring and early treatment even in the absence of severe illness, since the risk of progression is high. Early detection of severity variables may not only improve the care of hospitalized COVID-19 patients, but it may also minimize case mortality and medical costs. Further large-scale multicenter trials are required.

Acknowledgements The authors acknowledge the re-use of data from a prior Open Access publication https://www.mdpi.com/2079-9721/10/1/1.

Author Contributions Conceptualization: S.A.A., F.K. and R.W. Formal analysis: S.A.A., F.K., R.W. and M.A.S. (Muna Al Shaaibi). Investigation: F.K., S.A.A., M.A.S. (Muna Al Shaaibi), M.A.S. (Mubarak Al Shukeili), S.C., A.A.B. (Afra Al Balushi), S.A.S., A.A.B. (Amal Al Buloshi) and R.W. Methodology: F.K., S.A.A., R.W. and M.A.S. (Muna Al Shaaibi). Project administration: S.A.A., F.K., R.W. and M.A.S. (Muna Al Shaaibi). Supervision: F.K., S.A.A., R.W. and M.A.S. (Muna Al Shaaibi). Visualization: F.K., S.A.A. and R.W. Writing, review and editing: F.K., S.A.A., R.W. and M.A.S. (Muna Al Shaaibi). All authors have read and agreed to the published version of the manuscript.

Funding: This research received no external funding.

Institutional Review Board Statement: The study was conducted according to the guidelines of the Declaration of Helsinki and approved by the Royal Hospital Ethical and Research Committee (SR #26/2020).

Informed Consent Statement: Patient consent was waived as we used anonymized data. Furthermore, we have not conducted any patient interviews, and thus, the written informed consent information was not required. The data included in the manuscript were based on secondary data extracted from the hospital surveillance system.

Data Availability Statement The data will be shared upon reasonable request.

Conflicts of Interest The authors declare no conflict of interest.

References

Agarwal, A., Mukherjee, A., Kumar, G., Chatterjee, P., Bhatnagar, T., & Malhotra, P. (2020). Convalescent plasma in the management of moderate COVID-19 in adults in India: open label phase II multicentre randomised controlled trial (PLACID Trial). *BMJ*, *371*.

Alharthy, A., Aletreby, W., Faqihi, F., Balhamar, A., Alaklobi, F., Alanezi, K., Jaganathan, P., Tamim, H., Alqahtani, S. A., & Karakitsos, D. (2021). Clinical characteristics and predictors of 28-day mortality in 352 critically ill patients with COVID-19: A retrospective study. *Journal of Epidemiology and Global Health, 11*(1), 98.

Almazeedi, S., Al-Youha, S., Jamal, M. H., Al-Haddad, M., Al-Muhaini, A., Al-Ghimlas, F., & Al-Sabah, S. (2020). Characteristics, risk factors and outcomes among the first consecutive 1096 patients diagnosed with COVID-19 in Kuwait. *EClinicalMedicine*, *24*, 100448.

Ayelign, B., Negash, M., Genetu, M., Wondmagegn, T., & Shibabaw, T. (2019). Immunological impacts of diabetes on the susceptibility of Mycobacterium tuberculosis. *Journal of Immunology Research*, *2019*, 1–8.

Bahendeka, S., Wesonga, R., Mutungi, G., Muwonge, J., Neema, S., & Guwatudde, D. (2016). Prevalence and correlates of diabetes mellitus in Uganda: A population-based national survey. *Tropical Medicine and International Health*, *21*(3). https://doi.org/10.1111/tmi.12663

Balcells, M. E., Rojas, L., Le Corre, N., Martínez-Valdebenito, C., Ceballos, M. E., Ferrés, M., Chang, M., Vizcaya, C., Mondaca, S., & Huete, Á. (2021). Early versus deferred anti-SARS-CoV-2 convalescent plasma in patients admitted for COVID-19: A randomized phase II clinical trial. *PLoS Medicine, 18*(3), e1003415.

Bektas, A., Schurman, S. H., Sen, R., & Ferrucci, L. (2017). Human T cell immunosenescence and inflammation in aging. *Journal of Leukocyte Biology, 102*(4), 977–988.

Bhimraj, A., Shumaker, A. H., & Lavergne, V. (2021). *COVID-19 guideline, Part 1: Treatment and management*. https://www.idsociety.org/practice-guideline/COVID-19-guideline-treatment-and-management/

Chang, M. C., Park, Y. K., Kim, B. O., & Park, D. (2020). Risk factors for disease progression in COVID-19 patients. *BMC infectious diseases, 20*(1), 445.

Contou, D., Claudinon, A., Pajot, O., Micaëlo, M., Longuet Flandre, P., Dubert, M., ... & Plantefève, G. (2020). Bacterial and viral co-infections in patients with severe SARS-CoV-2 pneumonia admitted to a French ICU. *Annals of intensive care, 10*(1), 119.

Corrales-Medina, V. F., Musher, D. M., Wells, G. A., Chirinos, J. A., Chen, L., & Fine, M. J. (2012). Cardiac complications in patients with community-acquired pneumonia: Incidence, timing, risk factors, and association with short-term mortality. *Circulation, 125*(6), 773–781.

Cummings, M. J., Baldwin, M. R., Abrams, D., Jacobson, S. D., Meyer, B. J., Balough, E. M., ... & O'Donnell, M. R. (2020). Epidemiology, clinical course, and outcomes of critically ill adults with COVID-19 in New York City: A prospective cohort study. *Lancet, 395*(10239), 1763–1770.

di Filippo, L., Doga, M., Frara, S., & Giustina, A. (2021). Hypocalcemia in COVID-19: Prevalence, clinical significance and therapeutic implications. *Reviews in Endocrine and Metabolic Disorders*, 1–10.

Du, R.-H., Liang, L.-R., Yang, C.-Q., Wang, W., Cao, T.-Z., Li, M., Guo, G.-Y., Du, J., Zheng, C.-L., & Zhu, Q. (2020). Predictors of mortality for patients with COVID-19 pneumonia caused by SARS-CoV-2: a prospective cohort study. *European Respiratory Journal*, *55*(5), 2000524.

Galloway, J. B., Norton, S., Barker, R. D., Brookes, A., Carey, I., Clarke, B. D., Jina, R., Reid, C., Russell, M. D., & Sneep, R. (2020). A clinical risk score to identify patients with COVID-19 at high risk of critical care admission or death: An observational cohort study. *Journal of Infection, 81*(2), 282–288.

Gallus, S., Scala, M., Possenti, I., Jarach, C. M., Clancy, L., Fernandez, E., Gorini, G., Carreras, G., Malevolti, M. C., & Commar, A. (2023). The role of smoking in COVID-19 progression: A comprehensive meta-analysis. *European Respiratory Review, 32*(167), 220191.

Guan, W. J., Liang, W. H., Zhao, Y., Liang, H. R., Chen, Z. S., Li, Y. M., ... & He, J. X. (2020). Comorbidity and its impact on 1590 patients with COVID-19 in China: A nationwide analysis. *The European Respiratory Journal, 55*(5), 2000547.

Herrera-Van Oostdam, A. S., Castañeda-Delgado, J. E., Oropeza-Valdez, J. J., Borrego, J. C., Monárrez-Espino, J., Zheng, J., Mandal, R., Zhang, L.,

Soto-Guzmán, E., & Fernández-Ruiz, J. C. (2021). Immunometabolic signatures predict risk of progression to sepsis in COVID-19. *PLoS ONE, 16*(8), e0256784.

Huang, C., Wang, Y., Li, X., Ren, L., Zhao, J., Hu, Y., ... & Cao, B. (2020). Clinical features of patients infected with 2019 novel coronavirus in Wuhan, China. *The Lancet*, *395*(10223), 497–506.

Imam, Z., Odish, F., Gill, I., O'Connor, D., Armstrong, J., Vanood, A., Ibironke, O., Hanna, A., Ranski, A., & Halalau, A. (2020). Older age and comorbidity are independent mortality predictors in a large cohort of 1305 COVID-19 patients in Michigan, United States. *Journal of Internal Medicine, 288*(4), 469–476.

Jalaber, C., Lapotre, T., Morcet-Delattre, T., Ribet, F., Jouneau, S., & Lederlin, M. (2020). Chest CT in COVID-19 pneumonia: A review of current knowledge. *Diagnostic and Interventional Imaging, 101*(7–8), 431–437.

Janiaud, P., Axfors, C., Schmitt, A. M., Gloy, V., Ebrahimi, F., Hepprich, M., Smith, E. R., Haber, N. A., Khanna, N., & Moher, D. (2021). Association of convalescent plasma treatment with clinical outcomes in patients with COVID-19: A systematic review and meta-analysis. *JAMA, 325*(12), 1185–1195.

Khamis, F., Al Rashidi, B., Al-Zakwani, I., Al Wahaibi, A. H., & Al Awaidy, S. T. (2020a). Epidemiology of COVID-19 infection in Oman: analysis of the first 1304 cases. *Oman Medical Journal*, *35*(3), e145.

Khamis, F., Al-Zakwani, I., Al Naamani, H., Al Lawati, S., Pandak, N., Omar, M. B., ... & Al Awaidy, S. T. (2020b). Clinical characteristics and outcomes of the first 63 adult patients hospitalized with COVID-19: An experience from Oman. *Journal of Infection and Public Health*, *13*(7), 906–913.

Khamis, F., Al Awaidy, S., Ba'Omar, M., Osman, W., Chhetri, S., Ambusaid, Z., Al Fahdi, Z., Al Lawati, J., Al Sulaimi, K., & Al Bulushi, S. A. (2022). The impact of demographic, clinical characteristics and the various COVID-19 variant types on all-cause mortality: A case-series retrospective study. *Diseases, 10*(4), 100.

Khamis, F., Al Awaidy, S., Shaaibi, M. A., Shukeili, M. A., Chhetri, S., Balushi, A. A., Sulaimi, S. A., Balushi, A. A., & Wesonga, R. (2021). Epidemiological characteristics of hospitalized patients with moderate versus severe COVID-19 infection: A retrospective cohort single centre study. *Diseases, 10*(1), 1.

Lacap, E. M., Jr., Varghese, A., Khamis, F., Al Bahrani, M., Al Naamani, H., Kolamban, S., Al Dowaiki, S., & Al Shuaily, H. S. (2022). Development and validation of the CoV19-OM intensive care unit score: An early ICU identification for laboratory-confirmed SARS-CoV-2 patients from a retrospective cohort study in Oman. *International Journal of Infectious Diseases, 117*, 241–246.

Li, J., He, X., Yuan, Y., Zhang, W., Li, X., Zhang, Y., ... & Dong, G. (2021). Meta-analysis investigating the relationship between clinical features, outcomes, and severity of severe acute respiratory syndrome coronavirus 2 (SARS-CoV-2) pneumonia. *American Journal of Infection Control, 49*(1), 82–89.

Li, X., Xu, S., Yu, M., Wang, K., Tao, Y., Zhou, Y., Shi, J., Zhou, M., Wu, B., & Yang, Z. (2020). Risk factors for severity and mortality in adult COVID-19 inpatients in Wuhan. *Journal of Allergy and Clinical Immunology, 146*(1), 110–118.

Long, B., Carius, B. M., Chavez, S., Liang, S. Y., Brady, W. J., Koyfman, A., & Gottlieb, M. (2022). Clinical update on COVID-19 for the emergency clinician: Presentation and evaluation. *The American Journal of Emergency Medicine, 54*, 46–57.

Mazzalai, E., Giannini, D., Tosti, M. E., D'Angelo, F., Declich, S., Jaljaa, A., Caminada, S., Turatto, F., De Marchi, C., & Gatta, A. (2023). Risk of COVID-19 severe outcomes and mortality in migrants and ethnic minorities compared to the general population in the European WHO region: A systematic review. *Journal of International Migration and Integration, 24*, 1–31.

Mendoza-Torres, E., Oyarzún, A., Mondaca-Ruff, D., Azocar, A., Castro, P. F., Jalil, J. E., Chiong, M., Lavandero, S., & Ocaranza, M. P. (2015). ACE2 and vasoactive peptides: Novel players in cardiovascular/renal remodeling and hypertension. *Therapeutic Advances in Cardiovascular Disease, 9*(4), 217–237.

Milbrandt, E. B., Reade, M. C., Lee, M., Shook, S. L., Angus, D. C., Kong, L., Carter, M., Yealy, D. M., Kellum, J. A., & Investigators, G. (2009). Prevalence and significance of coagulation abnormalities in community-acquired pneumonia. *Molecular Medicine, 15*, 438–445.

Mo, P., Xing, Y., Xiao, Y., Deng, L., Zhao, Q., Wang, H., Xiong, Y., Cheng, Z., Gao, S., & Liang, K. (2021). Clinical characteristics of refractory coronavirus disease 2019 in Wuhan, China. *Clinical Infectious Diseases, 73*(11), e4208–e4213.

Nathan, L., Lai, A. L., Millet, J. K., Straus, M. R., Freed, J. H., Whittaker, G. R., & Daniel, S. (2019). Calcium ions directly interact with the Ebola virus fusion peptide to promote structure–function changes that enhance infection. *ACS Infectious Diseases, 6*(2), 250–260.

Ni, W., Yang, X., Yang, D., Bao, J., Li, R., Xiao, Y., Hou, C., Wang, H., Liu, J., & Yang, D. (2020). Role of angiotensin-converting enzyme 2 (ACE2) in COVID-19. *Critical Care, 24*(1), 1–10.

Nyberg, T., Ferguson, N. M., Nash, S. G., Webster, H. H., Flaxman, S., Andrews, N., Hinsley, W., Bernal, J. L., Kall, M., & Bhatt, S. (2022). Comparative analysis of the risks of hospitalisation and death associated with

SARS-CoV-2 omicron (B. 1.1. 529) and delta (B. 1.617. 2) variants in England: a cohort study. *The Lancet, 399*(10332), 1303–1312.

Oktariani, N. R., Pitoyo, C. W., Singh, G., & Mansjoer, A. (2019). CURB 65 score as a predictor of early mortality in hospital-acquired pneumonia. *The Egyptian Journal of Chest Diseases and Tuberculosis, 68*(2), 231–235.

Osman, W., Al Fahdi, F., Al Salmi, I., Al Khalili, H., Gokhale, A., & Khamis, F. (2021). Serum calcium and vitamin D levels: Correlation with severity of COVID-19 in hospitalized patients in Royal Hospital, Oman. *International Journal of Infectious Diseases, 107*, 153–163.

Pandak, N., Khamis, F., Al Balushi, Z., Chhetri, S., Al Lawati, A., AbouElhamd, H., ... & Al Dowaiki, S. (2023). Low rate of bacterial coinfections and antibiotic overprescribing during COVID-19 pandemic: A retrospective study from Oman. *Oman medical journal, 38*(4), e525.

Patel, R., Kooner, J. S., & Zhang, W. (2023). Comorbidities associated with the severity of COVID-19, and differences across ethnic groups: A UK Biobank cohort study. *BMC Public Health, 23*(1), 1566.

Price-Haywood, E. G., Burton, J., Fort, D., & Seoane, L. (2020). Hospitalization and mortality among black patients and white patients with COVID-19. *New England Journal of Medicine, 382*(26), 2534–2543.

Ragab, D., Salah Eldin, H., Taeimah, M., Khattab, R., & Salem, R. (2020). The COVID-19 cytokine storm; what we know so far. *Frontiers in Immunology, 11*, 1446.

Rastad, H., Karim, H., Ejtahed, H.-S., Tajbakhsh, R., Noorisepehr, M., Babaei, M., Azimzadeh, M., Soleimani, A., Inanloo, S. H., & Shafiabadi Hassani, N. (2020). Risk and predictors of in-hospital mortality from COVID-19 in patients with diabetes and cardiovascular disease. *Diabetology & Metabolic Syndrome, 12*(1), 1–11.

Rosenthal, N., Cao, Z., Gundrum, J., Sianis, J., & Safo, S. (2020). Risk factors associated with in-hospital mortality in a US national sample of patients with COVID-19. *JAMA Network Open, 3*(12), e2029058.

Salama, C., Han, J., Yau, L., Reiss, W. G., Kramer, B., Neidhart, J. D., Criner, G. J., Kaplan-Lewis, E., Baden, R., & Pandit, L. (2021). Tocilizumab in patients hospitalized with COVID-19 pneumonia. *New England Journal of Medicine, 384*(1), 20–30.

Salvatici, M., Barbieri, B., Cioffi, S. M. G., Morenghi, E., Leone, F. P., Maura, F., Moriello, G., & Sandri, M. T. (2020). Association between cardiac troponin I and mortality in patients with COVID-19. *Biomarkers, 25*(8), 634–640.

Satici, C., Demirkol, M. A., Altunok, E. S., Gursoy, B., Alkan, M., Kamat, S., Demirok, B., Surmeli, C. D., Calik, M., & Cavus, Z. (2020). Performance of pneumonia severity index and CURB-65 in predicting 30-day mortality in patients with COVID-19. *International Journal of Infectious Diseases, 98*, 84–89.

Scovino, A. M., Dahab, E. C., Vieira, G. F., Freire-de-Lima, L., Freire-de-Lima, C. G., & Morrot, A. (2022). SARS-CoV-2's variants of concern: A brief characterization. *Frontiers in Immunology, 13*, 834098.

Shi, S., Qin, M., Shen, B., Cai, Y., Liu, T., Yang, F., ... & Huang, C. (2020). Association of cardiac injury with mortality in hospitalized patients with COVID-19 in Wuhan, China. *JAMA Cardiology*, *5*(7), 802–810.

Speranza, E., Purushotham, J. N., Port, J. R., Schwarz, B., Flagg, M., Williamson, B. N., Feldmann, F., Singh, M., Pérez-Pérez, L., & Sturdevant, G. L. (2022). Age-related differences in immune dynamics during SARS-CoV-2 infection in rhesus macaques. *Life Science Alliance*, *5*(4), e202101314.

Straus, M. R., Tang, T., Lai, A. L., Flegel, A., Bidon, M., Freed, J. H., Daniel, S., & Whittaker, G. R. (2020). Ca2+ Ions promote fusion of middle east respiratory syndrome coronavirus with host cells and increase infectivity. *Journal of Virology, 94*(13), e00426-20.

Van Paassen, J., Vos, J. S., Hoekstra, E. M., Neumann, K. M. I., Boot, P. C., & Arbous, S. M. (2020). Corticosteroid use in COVID-19 patients: A systematic review and meta-analysis on clinical outcomes. *Critical Care, 24*, 1–22.

Vaughan, L., Veruttipong, D., Shaw, J. G., Levy, N., Edwards, L., & Winget, M. (2021). Relationship of socio-demographics, comorbidities, symptoms and healthcare access with early COVID-19 presentation and disease severity. *BMC Infectious Diseases*, *21*, 1–10.

Wang, D., Hu, B., Hu, C., Zhu, F., Liu, X., Zhang, J., ... & Peng, Z. (2020a). Clinical characteristics of 138 hospitalized patients with 2019 novel coronavirus–infected pneumonia in Wuhan, China. *JAMA*, *323*(11), 1061–1069.

Wang, W., Tang, J., & Wei, F. (2020b). Updated understanding of the outbreak of 2019 novel coronavirus (2019-nCoV) in Wuhan, China. *Journal of Medical Virology*, *92*(4), 441–447.

Wendel Garcia, P. D., Aguirre-Bermeo, H., Buehler, P. K., Alfaro-Farias, M., Yuen, B., David, S., Tschoellitsch, T., Wengenmayer, T., Korsos, A., & Fogagnolo, A. (2021). Implications of early respiratory support strategies on disease progression in critical COVID-19: A matched subanalysis of the prospective RISC-19-ICU cohort. *Critical Care, 25*(1), 175.

Wingert, A., Pillay, J., Gates, M., Guitard, S., Rahman, S., Beck, A., ... & Hartling, L. (2021). Risk factors for severity of COVID-19: A rapid review to inform vaccine prioritisation in Canada. *BMJ Open*, *11*(5), e044684.

World Health Organisation. (2021). *WHO COVID-19 dashboard*. https://covid19.who.int/?adgroupsurvey=\{adgroupsurvey\}&gclid=CjwKCAjw9aiIBhA1EiwAJ_GTSnCYhzmUZLYFXSiPFfmpjX89RdB5Xv-1LORycQso81Wu5VTT8Mk81hoCZLgQAvD_BwE

World Health Organization. (2021, October 6). A clinical case definition of post COVID-19 condition by a Delphi consensus (No. WHO/2019-nCoV/Post_COVID-19_condition/Clinical_case_definition/2021.1). World Health Organization.

Wu, C., Chen, X., Cai, Y., Zhou, X., Xu, S., Huang, H., Zhang, L., Zhou, X., Du, C., & Zhang, Y. (2020). Risk factors associated with acute respiratory distress syndrome and death in patients with coronavirus disease 2019 pneumonia in Wuhan, China. *JAMA Internal Medicine, 180*(7), 934–943.

Xu, Z., Shi, L., Wang, Y., Zhang, J., Huang, L., Zhang, C., Liu, S., Zhao, P., Liu, H., & Zhu, L. (2020). Pathological findings of COVID-19 associated with acute respiratory distress syndrome. *The Lancet Respiratory Medicine, 8*(4), 420–422.

Yadav, D. K., Singh, A., Zhang, Q., Bai, X., Zhang, W., Yadav, R. K., Singh, A., Zhiwei, L., Adhikari, V. P., & Liang, T. (2021). Involvement of liver in COVID-19: Systematic review and meta-analysis. *Gut, 70*(4), 807–809.

Yang, J., Zheng, Y. A., Gou, X., Pu, K., Chen, Z., Guo, Q., … & Zhou, Y. (2020). Prevalence of comorbidities and its effects in patients infected with SARS-CoV-2: A systematic review and meta-analysis. *International Journal of Infectious Diseases*, *94*, 91–95.

Ya'qoub, L., Elgendy, I. Y., & Pepine, C. J. (2021). Sex and gender differences in COVID-19: More to be learned! *American Heart Journal Plus: Cardiology Research and Practice*, *3*, 100011.

Zhang, J. J., Dong, X., Liu, G. H., & Gao, Y. D. (2023). Risk and protective factors for COVID-19 morbidity, severity, and mortality. *Clinical Reviews in Allergy & Immunology, 64*(1), 90–107.

Zhao, C., Bai, Y., Wang, C., Zhong, Y., Lu, N., Tian, L., Cai, F., & Jin, R. (2021). Risk factors related to the severity of COVID-19 in Wuhan. *International Journal of Medical Sciences, 18*(1), 120.

Zhao, Y., Huang, J., Zhang, L., Chen, S., Gao, J., & Jiao, H. (2022). The global transmission of new coronavirus variants. *Environmental Research, 206*, 112240.

Zhou, F., Yu, T.; Du, R., Fan, G., Liu, Y., Liu, Z., Xiang, J., Wang, Y., Song, B., Gu, X. et al. (2020). Clinical course and risk factors for mortality of adult inpatients with COVID-19 in Wuhan, China: A retrospective cohort study. Lancet, 395, 1054–1062

CHAPTER 3

Assessment of the Impact of COVID-19 Pandemic on Health Services Utilization in Oman: A Cross-Sectional Study

Omar Al-Farsi, Salim Al-Salmi, Raniya Al-Kiyumi, and Yahya Al-Farsi

1 Introduction

The COVID-19 pandemic has led to significant disruptions in the delivery of essential health services (Moynihan et al., 2021). Healthcare utilization was observed to decline during pandemics because of the fear of contracting COVID-19 within health facilities (Ekman et al., 2021). Several health institutions postponed non-urgent health services like elective operations, OPD visits, medical examinations, and premarital counselling (Al-Marhoon, 2020). Some health centers at primary healthcare level were closed to focus on the admitted cases (Al Ghafri et al., 2021). In addition, some essential health services were disrupted for several months due to shortage of health workers while they quarantined (Singh et al., 2021). However, a variation of impact of the pandemic was

O. Al-Farsi (✉) · S. Al-Salmi · R. Al-Kiyumi · Y. Al-Farsi
Oman College of Health Sciences, Mutrah, Oman
e-mail: omaralfarsi24102@gmail.com

A. Mishrif (ed.), *Perspectives on Human Capital Development*,
https://doi.org/10.1007/978-981-97-5246-1_3

observed due to type of facility, location, and type of healthcare service (Xiao et al., 2021).

The possible effect of the COVID-19 creates concern among health decision makers toward the progress of achieving Universal Health Coverage (UHC) due to increase in mortality cases caused by the pandemic (Amos et al., 2021). The UHC service coverage index is a composite indicator that consists of four domains which are: reproductive, maternal, newborn and child health (RMNCH), infectious diseases, non-communicable diseases (NCDs), and service capacity and access (Hussain & Arif, 2021). It has been established to monitor the progress of coverage of essential health services. COVID-19 pandemic affected the main coverage of essential health services such as vaccination, infectious diseases, chronic diseases, maternal health, and child health (Rachamin et al., 2021). More than 40% of the 129 countries reported disruptions in these kinds of services (WHO, 2022).

2 Literature Review

The same scenario of COVID-19 pandemic was observed in some countries in West Africa due to Ebola virus disease outbreak from 2014 to 2016 (Rezapour et al., 2022). Some essential health services disrupted such as HIV program, tuberculosis testing, and malaria treatment (Xiao et al., 2021). As a result, this disruption led to 10,000 excess preventable mortality due to infectious diseases (Xu et al., 2021).

Due to COVID-19 pandemic, medicine delayed giving to the patients against some infectious diseases by more than 30 days (WHO, 2020). Around 65 countries reported disruptions to HIV testing, TB diagnosis, and hepatitis B and C treatment, whereas approximately 43 countries reported disruptions to one or more malaria services (WHO, 2022).

Some vaccinations were postponed such as cholera, polio, yellow fever, measles, and meningitis due to the COVID-19 (Kotlar et al., 2021). It was estimated that 117 million children had risk to be affected with measles in 37 countries (WHO, 2022). The number of children vaccinated in Lebanon declined by 31% in 2019 compared to 2020 (Mansour et al., 2021). Similar reduction was reported in England (McDonald et al., 2020) and USA (Santoli, 2020). Chandir et al. (2020) found that 52.5% decrease in average daily vaccinations administered during COVID-19 pandemic in Pakistan where also 40 million children did not get polio vaccination in April 2020. Nepal has confronted a high prevalence of maternal deaths, child deaths, and different forms of malnutrition (Singh et al., 2021). It was reported a decline by 51.4% of the accessibility of health services, besides a significant rise in maternal and child mortality (Ashish et al., 2020). One systematic review showed a 38% global reduction in antenatal care (ANC) appointments (Townsend et al., 2021). In addition, scoping reviews indicated a decrease in prenatal care visits during the pandemic (Kotlar et al., 2021).

Some countries have reported a considerable decline in diagnosis, treatment, and admissions for various health conditions related to chronic diseases such as stroke and cancer during the COVID-19 pandemic (Yamaguchi et al., 2022). Italy faced horrible days during COVID-19 pandemic period; it was found a high rise in hospital deaths related to cardiovascular, neoplasms, and metabolic and endocrine diseases, besides corona virus deaths (Santi et al., 2021). A decline in the number of new diabetic cases and an increase in type 2 diabetes-related deaths were observed in the UK (Carr et al., 2021). Furthermore, a reduction and delay in the diagnosis of new cancer cases were observed. Similarly, neoplasms are not treated in a timely manner (Patt et al., 2020).

Many factors resulted in disruptions in access to essential health services, such as staff shortages, a decrease in the number of hospital inpatients, and the cancellation of elective surgeries (Hung et al., 2022). Surgery interruptions were reported in 129 countries affecting 38% of major and minor operations (WHO, 2022). A study conducted in the USA (Birkmeyer et al., 2020) reported a remarkable decline in utilization of many elective procedures and preventive care, besides hospital admissions from March to April in 2020. According to a global study conducted to investigate the effect of the COVID-19 pandemic on surgical services in 190 countries (Nepogodiev et al., 2020), the findings indicated that more than 2 million surgeries were cancelled per week during the 12 weeks of peak period in 2020. Additionally, a systematic review of 81 studies found that over 17.9 million services were provided in 20 countries, representing a significant reduction in healthcare utilization during the pandemic period of 2020 (Moynihan et al., 2021).

A health system cannot neglect the health requirements for people, such as vaccinations, maternal health, infectious disease, chronic diseases, and mental health (Rezapour et al., 2022). Ignoring these health requirements would cause a broad catastrophe. In spite of the Supreme Committee's efforts to alleviate the impact of COVID-19 pandemic in Oman, it has significantly affected the healthcare system (Al Khalili et al., 2021). Little is known about how the COVID-19 affected health services utilization among population in Oman. To the best of the researcher's knowledge, no study has been conducted to examine the impact of the COVID-19 pandemic on healthcare services utilization. Therefore, this chapter aims to evaluate the impact of the COVID-19 pandemic on healthcare services utilization by observing OPD visits, hospital admissions, and surgical and radiological procedures across Oman. Further analysis of trends in utilization was carried out according to governorates, specialities, and types of healthcare services.

3 Methodology

3.1 Study Design

A cross-sectional study was conducted between 2019 and 2020 to find out the impact of COVID-19 on health services utilization from health facilities under the supervision of MOH at all levels in all governorates. Primary, secondary, and tertiary healthcare services are provided through eleven governorates in 262 health facilities.

3.2 Data Collection

Data from the routine health information system data at MOH were used and analyzed to compare monthly all-cause health facility visits, inpatient volume, and surgical and radiological procedures in health facilities in 2019 to those in 2020 before and during the COVID-19 pandemic. These are the main health services provided by MOH so it has been selected for comparison purpose. In this chapter, all health institutions across the country included. Data from routine health information system were extracted via Annual Health Report 2019 (MOH, 2019) and 2020 (MOH, 2020). As data were collected using two different methods in 2019 and 2020, both approaches will be discussed.

Healthcare services in Oman are provided by the government in collaboration with the private sector. MOH is the main healthcare provider, and it covers around 90% of health services (Elhadi et al., 2007).

It implements health policies, health development plans, and health strategies. Other governmental non-MOH health sectors also provided health services such as Sultan Qaboos University Hospital, Armed Forces Hospital, Royal Oman Police, Petroleum Development Oman Clinics, and Medical Services of Diwan of Royal Court. The government support all these health institutions financially. In addition, there are 27 private hospitals and 1230 private clinics that provide health services as well (MOH, 2020).

Health information system (HIS) is a comprehensive integrated information system established to manage the process of the medical, administrative, and financial in a health institution (Al-Gharbi et al., 2015). HIS is responsible to provide reliable, relevant, up-to-date, and health-related information to decision makers at MOH central level or at the governorate level for use in planning and evaluation. HIS collects and publishes different types of data, health indicators, including morbidity, mortality, health services utilization, and human resource data. MOH disseminates a 5th year's developmental health plan every five years; health information is used to monitor the key performance indicators (KPIs) to ensure the implementation of health plans over five years. Measuring burden of diseases, identifying the requirements of health care, and monitoring sustainable development goals (SDGs) are the main tasks of HIS as well.

The strength of any health system depends on the six building blocks. One of these blocks is supported by health information. Oman health vision 2050 relied on strong health information to identify the current health situation and report the appropriate intervention for the future (MOH, 2020). Different reports published to enrich the vision by evidence-based such as "ATLAS" and Synopsis (Ministry of Health, 2012).

There are two main sources of health data at MOH which are routine HIS data and research articles. Statistical forms have been designed by HIS in collaboration with other stakeholders such as primary and secondary health care. Routine HIS data have been collected monthly from 1990s till 2019 by a statistician at the wilayat level in public and private health institutions. At the beginning of each month, the statisticians collected and completed the statistical forms data that have been generated during the previous month in collaboration with the nurses. After revision of the data by a statistician in the wilayat, it was electronically sent to a regional health information statistician, who reviews the data at the regional level. The compiled data are sent to the department of information and statistics at MOH headquarters, which compiles the data at the national level, and subjects it to deep analysis as shown in Fig. 1. This information is used for planning, monitoring, and identifying the requirements and evaluation purposes. The compiled data provide trends for a decade in health service utilization, human resources, and expenditures to plan for the future and identify health needs.

HIS depends on various health data sources including census data, births and deaths notification system, health facility registers, human resources, and national health surveys. Research articles are also used to know the health status for specific diseases.

Nowadays, HIS depends on electronic health records, geographical information system (GIS), and web-based platform such as birth and death registration. *Al-Shifa system* has been established to have quick information rather than using the manual forms. *Al-Shifa system* is a comprehensive healthcare services management system automating most

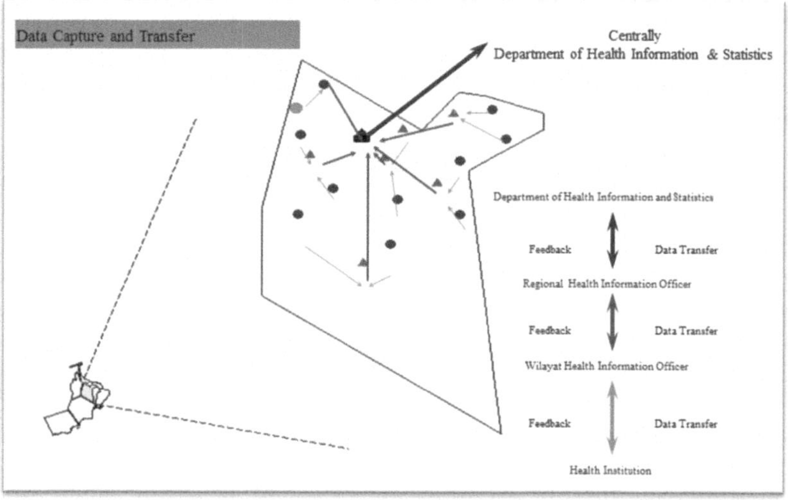

Fig. 1 Method of transferring the national health data at MOH (*Source* Al Muzahmi SNK. Mortality Patterns in Oman: Demographic and Epidemiological Review; 2015 [cited January 31, 2021] http://espace.library.uq.edu.au/view/UQ:369205)

processes of healthcare delivery at MOH in the health institutions (Khan & Ismail, 2017).

Ministry of Health has developed a central data warehouse, "Nabd Al-Shifa," to collect the historical data generated by the HIS. Nabd Al-Shifa is an electronic system use artificial intelligence analytics to display statistical dashboards to boost data visualization using data from Al-Shifa system (WHO, 2021).

HIS data have been collected from the health institutions using different platforms. There are two programs extracted from Al-Shifa system which are the Central Birth and Death Registration (CBDR) and Nabd Al-Shifa. Data have been captured from Nabd Al-Shifa since 2020 such as OPD visits, admissions, and radiological and surgical procedure. All these kinds of data are reported in total and disaggregated by sex, nationality, types of procedures, department (surgery, medicine, maternity, pediatric), and hospital type (regional, wilayat, or local). CBDR is computerized nationwide birth and death registry. All vital events happening within or reported to healthcare facilities (public and private) are recorded into a single registry. All the mortality indicators have been calculated based on CBDR since 2016.

3.3 *Data Analysis*

Comparative analysis has been conducted to find out the impact of COVID-19 pandemic on the health service utilization. One year before the pandemic (2019) was selected as a reference period and the year when it has started in 2020 as the observation period.

Descriptive statistics were reported for health service utilization such as OPD visits, hospitalization, and surgical and radiological procedures. Pearson's chi-square test was used for categorical data. Monthly trend has been utilized to report health service utilization throughout a year. Since we have used published routine health data from HIS, this study does not need an ethical approval. Also, there was no need for consent form.

4 Result

Table 1 shows the comparison of OPD visits between 2019 and 2020 according to the type of health institution, age group, clinics, and governorates. Overall, all four variables were highly statistically significant

(*P*-value = 0.0001) in 2019 compared to 2020, after weighted the OPD cases. The total number of OPD visits decreased by around 5.1 million visits (−33%) in 2020 compared to 2019. Most of the reduction in visits was in the health centers and polyclinics, with a reduction of 76.5% compared to the hospitals. Since the MOH is the main healthcare provider in Oman, most of the Omani people visit governmental health institutions while expatriates visit the private sector. Therefore, the percentage of Omani population to OPD visits was around 95% in 2020. Adult people in Oman (15–59 years) constituted about 56% of the total population. Thus, around half of the reduction of OPD visits was in this age group. All the patients should visit the General Practice (GP) clinics as a first visit, so it is made up of 57% of the total OPD visits. The findings shows that most of the reduction in the GP, then surgery clinic due cancellation or postpone the elective operations. North Batinah Governorate has the largest reduction by 18%, followed by Muscat Governorate (16%), and then South Batinah Governorate (13%).

Figure 2 displays the number of confirmed cases from March to December 2020. The first case was registered on February 24, 2020. We conducted a 7-day moving average for confirmed cases to have the overall shape in 2020. The new cases were gradually raised till reached a peak in the middle of July 2020. Then, the cases dropped down with some fluctuations after August 2020. At the end of 2020, the registered cases were very few.

Figure 3 represents the number of inpatients who have been discharged (including deaths) from the MOH hospitals in 2019 and 2020 according to the governorates. The healthcare system in Oman has three types of care: primary, secondary, and tertiary care. Muscat Governorate has the four main tertiary care hospitals in the country. All cases from other governorates are referred to these hospitals. Therefore, most of the admitted cases are in Muscat Governorate which indicated the highest reduction with 26.7% among other governorates, followed by Ad Dakhiliyah and then North Al-Batinah.

Figures 4 and 5 illustrate the surgical and radiological procedures in 2019 and 2020 distributed by months. According to the two graphs, the number of procedures declined sharply after February, when the first cases were confirmed. In April, healthcare system has adapted to deal with COVID-19 cases, so the number of procedures stayed stable. After May, the number of procedures increased especially the radiological one. Although the number of COVID-19 cases reached the peak in July, the

Table 1 Number of OPD visits in 2019 and 2020

Variables		*2019 N (%)*	*2020 N (%)*	*Rate of change (2019–2020)*	*P-value*
Type of health institution	Hospital	4,477,653 (28.6)	3,266,424 (31.1)	−23.5	0.0001
	HC\EHC	11,182,556 (71.4)	7,250,551 (68.9)	−76.5	
Age group	0–4	3,392,888 (22.7)	1,776,914 (17.9)	−32.3	0.0001
	5–14	2,186,975 (14.6)	1,083,927 (10.9)	−22.1	
	15–59	7,780,606 (52.1)	5,756,205 (57.9)	−40.5	
	60+	1,586,899 (10.6)	1,331,855 (13.4)	−5.1	
Clinics	General Practice Clinic	8,927,784 (57)	5,981,988 (65.5)	−45.1	0.0001
	Accident and Emergency Clinic	845,110 (5.4)	667,418 (7.3)	−2.7	
	Medicine Clinic	1,864,457 (11.9)	936,274 (10.3)	−14.2	
	Surgical Clinic	1,427,159 (9.1)	178,238 (2)	−19.1	
	Gynaecology Clinics	1,035,583 (6.6)	603,946 (6.6)	−6.6	
	Child Health & Immunization	1,029,040 (6.6)	457,257 (5.0)	−8.8	
	Dental	531,076 (3.4)	307,953 (3.4)	−3.4	
Governorates	Muscat	2,588,150 (16.5)	1,765,822 (16.8)	−16.0	0.0001
	Dhofar	1,786,175 (11.4)	1,209,513 (11.5)	−11.2	
	Musandam	281,363 (1.8)	181,840 (1.7)	−1.9	
	Al-Buraymi	456,140 (2.9)	304,885 (2.9)	−2.9	
	Ad Dakhiliyah	1,757,938 (11.2)	1,195,146 (11.4)	−10.9	
	North Al-Batinah	2,936,021 (18.7)	1,968,236 (18.7)	−18.8	

(continued)

Table 1 (continued)

Variables		*2019* *N (%)*	*2020* *N (%)*	*Rate of change (2019–2020)*	*P-value*
	South Al-Batinah	1,796,573 (11.5)	1,123,969 (10.7)	−13.1	
	South Ash Sharqiyah	1,679,345 (10.7)	1,126,175 (10.7)	−10.8	
	North Ash Sharqiyah	1,203,942 (7.7)	826,367 (7.9)	−7.3	
	Ad Dhahirah	885,691 (5.7)	580,789 (5.5)	−5.9	
	Al-Wusta	288,871 (1.8)	234,233 (2.2)	−1.1	

Source Annual Health Report 2020, MOH

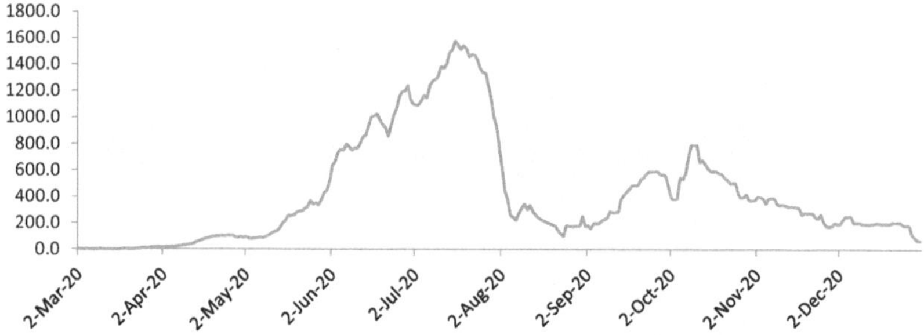

Fig. 2 Number of confirmed cases (7-days moving average) with COVID-19 in 2020 (*Source* WHO website https://covid19.who.int/region/emro/country/om)

procedures raised up till the end of the 2020. However, it did not reach rates seen from 2019, by the end of December 2020.

5 Discussion

In Oman, healthcare services were analyzed during the COVID-19 pandemic based on routine health information system data. This chapter indicated that the pandemic affected healthcare service utilization in significant way, particularly at the beginning of the outbreak. Findings

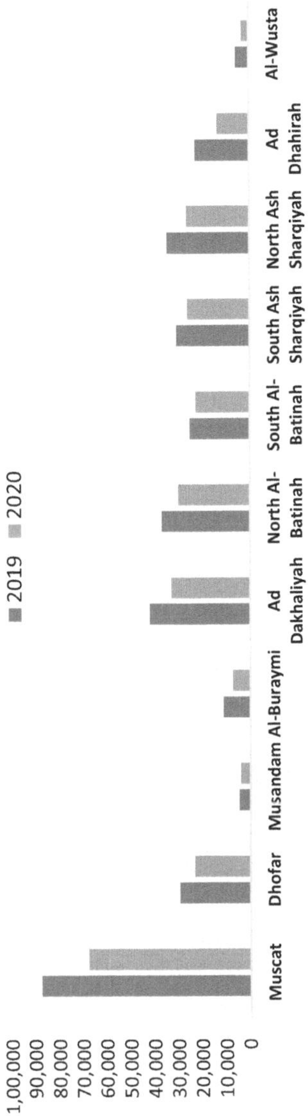

Fig. 3 Hospitalization cases in 2019 and 2020 distributed by Governorates (*Source* Annual Health Report 2020, MOH)

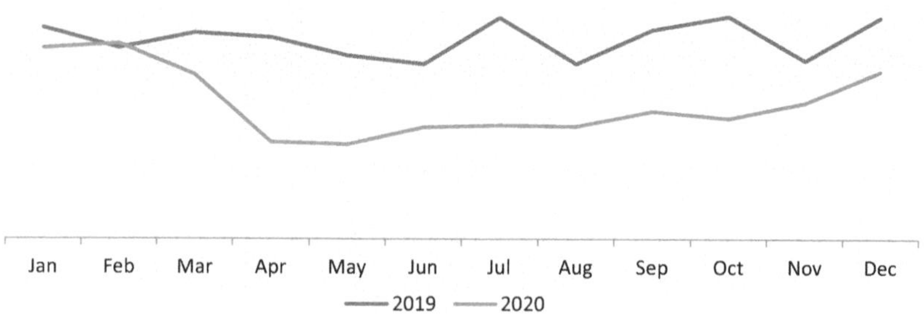

Fig. 4 Surgical procedures in 2019 and 2020 distributed by months (*Source* Annual Health Report 2020, MOH)

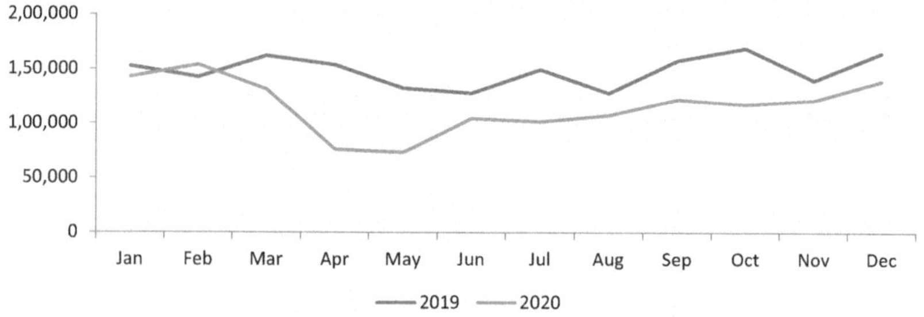

Fig. 5 Radiological procedures in 2019 and 2020 distributed by months (*Source* Annual Health Report 2020, MOH)

showed that the number of admissions, OPD visits, and surgical and radiological procedures declined significantly.

The largest decline in the OPD visits, hospitalizations, and surgical and radiological procedures was during the initial two months (March and April 2020) of the COVID-19 pandemic in Oman. The main reasons for decreasing the number of essential services provided in the early period of COVID-19 pandemic were restrictions applied to the public such as quarantine and curfew, fears to have virus infection inside the health institutions, and postpone elective procedures. By May 2020, all kinds of health service had been adapted to the pandemic. Thus, a steady increase was observed in the number of OPD visits, admissions, and procedures.

Findings of analysis of 262 health institutions in Oman revealed that the COVID-19 pandemic has negative consequences on essential health services, particularly at the primary healthcare institutions. Some studies revealed a decline in the utilization of health services, especially in the primary healthcare such as in China (Xiao et al., 2021), Japan (Kumagai, 2021), the United States (Jeffery et al., 2020), the UK (Howarth et al., 2021), Iran (Rezapour et al., 2022), Switzerland (Rachamin et al., 2021), Italy (Santi et al., 2021), and Sweden (Ekman et al., 2021) revealed a decline in the utilization of health services, especially in the primary health care. This study revealed that OPD visits in health institutions at all levels decreased concurrently with the COVID-19 outbreak. Despite MoH's rapid action to manage and control the pandemic, most health service utilization has not rebounded before May 2020.

Health services utilization was found to be affected by some socio-demographic factors such as age, sex, and governorates. Based on national data, the number of OPD visits declined from 37% in 2019 to 28.8% in 2020 among children younger than 14 years. It is consistent with Yamaguchi et al. (2022), who showed that the number of patients for non-COVID-19 significantly declined in patients aged less than 16 years. This finding may be explained by parents' fears that their children will contract Coronavirus.

In 2020, respiratory diseases, especially common cold diseases, decreased by 63.3% compared to 2019 in the OPD visits, despite a high number of COVID-19 confirmed as new cases. There was a decrease in communicable diseases from 31.5% in 2019 to 24.6% in 2020. Respiratory diseases have had the greatest reduction compared to other types of diseases. As well as USA (Lauer et al., 2020), Singapore (Tan et al., 2020) found a reduction in respiratory diseases. This reduction could be attributed to the public commitment to follow the instructions set by the MOH authorities during the pandemic, such as wearing face masks, social distancing, and washing hands properly.

The total OPD visits decreased more in General Practice, followed by surgery clinics in 2020. However, compared to other specialized clinics, the surgery clinic was the most affected. In 2020, it represents only 2% of the OPD visits, compared to 9% in 2019. Possible explanations for the decline in 2020 are the cancellation of several elective operations and postponement of others. Many patients postponed their visits to avoid transmission of the coronavirus, or they fear being infected with the COVID-19 virus. In the initial phase of the pandemic, MOH policies restricted the attendance of OPD patients, which resulted in a substantial decline in attendance. In general, the country's response to the pandemic was similar to that of other countries; health service utilization declined at the onset of the pandemic (Xiao et al., 2021). Some health services postponed such as elective surgeries and non-urgent appointments. Future research is needed to assess the long-term impacts of these delays. It is imperative that non-COVID-19 patients receive reliable and safe healthcare services.

The reduction of surgical and radiological procedures due to the pandemic may have negative consequences in the future. Therefore, there is a need to measure the effects of the reduction in healthcare service utilization. WHO conducted a quick evaluation in 163 countries (WHO, 2020); the reduction in the OPD visits was presented in 25% of responding countries. NCD programs were disrupted because of suspending screening programs and the cancellation of elective operations. Nowadays, patients around the world continue to visit health institutions for routine examinations and follow-ups.

As a consequence of COVID-19, maternity care and other essential health services are impacted. Therefore, the maternal mortality ratio increased sharply from 14.1 per 100 thousand live births in 2019 to 29.4 in 2020 and 45.7 in 2021 for Omani women due to direct or indirect deaths caused by COVID-19 (MOH, 2020). The number of antenatal visits decreased in 2020 compared to 2019 due to closing of some primary care health institutions (MOH, 2020). Almost one-third of the women had missed at least one antenatal care visit (ANC) appointment during their follow-up for the pregnancy period (Rabbani et al., 2021). Half of the pregnant women were fear of infections as the main reason for missing appointments in health institutions.

Some mothers lost their lives due to COVID-19 as a direct cause of death in Oman. A study conducted by Riley et al. (2020) reported that a decline of 10% in the maternal care during COVID-19 caused terrible consequences for the lives of mothers. Another study in India indicated a substantial raise during the pandemic in inpatient deaths among pregnant women and number of still-birth because of a 43% reduction in hospital admissions and a decline of 66% in the emergency obstetric visits as well (Kumari et al., 2020).

The child mortality indicators in Oman improved significantly over the last four decades with high coverage of immunization and an increase in antenatal services. The coverage of all kinds of vaccination reached about 99.9% and the number of antenatal first visit increased by 73.2% in 2018 compared to 1990 (MOH, 2020). In addition, infant and under five years mortality decreased from 103 and 149 per 1000 live births in 1975 to 7.6 and 9.3 in 2020, respectively. However, the infant mortality rate increased to 8.1 and less than five years mortality rate increased to 10.1 in 2021 (NCSI, 2022) as a possible result of the pandemic. These indicators contributed to reduce the life expectancy at birth from 77.2 in 2019 to 74.1 in 2021 (NCSI, 2022). Based on Ashish et al. (2020)'s study, preterm birth and institutional stillbirths in Nepal were higher by 30% and 46%, respectively, during the pandemic.

COVID-19 could cause excess mortality either directly or indirectly by raising the mortality cases from other diseases (Al Wahaibi et al., 2021). The main leading cause of death in Oman is ischemic heart disease in the last decade (MOH, 2020). The number of deaths due to non-COVID-19 was 9023 in 2020 compared to 8325 in 2019, an increase of 8.4%. Total deaths due to cardiovascular diseases were 2477 in 2020 while it was 1955 in 2019, which increased by 26.7%. An increase in deaths due to cardiovascular diseases in 2020 could be attributed to a decrease in hospitalizations for those patients who would need admission during the pandemic. It has been observed a decline by 28.4% in hospitalizations of cardiovascular disease in Oman. Consistent with previous studies, it has been reported a significant decrease in admissions for cardiovascular diseases during the pandemic in Italy (Filippo et al., 2020), Switzerland (Rachamin et al., 2021), USA (Bhatt et al., 2020), and Japan (Morishita et al., 2022).

At the beginning of the outbreak, MOH decided to prepare a field hospital for admitted COVID-19 cases. Some health centers temporarily closed to provide services related to COVID-19 diseases in the regional hospitals. A significant reduction in admissions was reported during the pandemic in other countries as well as USA (Birkmeyer et al., 2020) and Italy (Filippo et al., 2020). Moreover, the causes of the decline in hospitalizations were not clear. This reduction could be explained by minimizing the bed capacity for non-COVID-19 patients due to conversion to COVID-19 wards.

The resilience of the health system is a crucial lesson that should be learnt from this pandemic to minimize the negative consequences of such disruptions (Ekman et al., 2021). Access to healthcare services should be simplified by conducting alternative approaches such as telemedicine, especially for those patients with chronic diseases and elderly patients who require routine visits and general guidance without the need for physical examination. The equity of delivery of the health services for all areas in the country should be facilitated particularly for those patients in rural and remote places where it may help them to save money and avoid waiting time. The use of technology in the era of COVID-19 facilitated access to the health services in Oman. Telemedicine has been rapidly used in the initial peak of the pandemic particularly for those patients with chronic diseases in the primary health care in the Netherlands (Auener et al., 2020). Unfortunately, telemedicine services statistics have not been captured during the pandemic to investigate the real reduction in OPD visits in Oman.

The response to COVID-19 in Oman has begun with the establishment of a Supreme Committee, which includes all relevant stakeholders from various sectors (Al Ghafri et al., 2021). Guidelines and short-term strategies were implemented by MOH. Among these were multi-sectorial strategies, public–private partnership, and technology reinforcement use (Al Khalili et al., 2021). Although the private sector supported MOH during the pandemic by admitting some COVID-19 patients, conducting tests (PCR), and giving COVID-19 vaccinations, continued efforts are required to sustain and strength the health system. It is also important to note that other countries have implemented health policies to reduce disruptions of the pandemic and warrant the provision of essential health services (WHO, 2022). It has been verified by countries with a strong UHC, such as Singapore, Japan, and South Korea (WHO, 2022). In developing countries such as Nepal, the government has implemented public health prevention programs and hospital-based interventions to combat the pandemic. As a result of these interventions, the pandemic has been effectively combated and essential health services have been returned (Hussain & Arif, 2021).

Preparedness to respond to pandemics and public health threats is essential to mitigate the impact on the health system. It is vital for health systems to guarantee the accessibility for non-COVID-19 patients to have safe health care, especially for vulnerable people, disabled patients, emergency cases, and chronic diseases. Also, it is important to communicate with the public through the media to reassure the availability of health services even during the pandemic. Resilient healthcare systems are essential to minimize the negative consequences of such disruptions along with responding more rapidly and effectively to protect the patients.

5.1 *Limitations*

The strength of this study is that it provides an overview of the effect of the COVID-19 pandemic on healthcare service utilization that covers outpatient visits and admissions along with surgical and radiological procedures. However, this study had some limitations. First, this is a descriptive study to have an overview of the impact of the pandemic on a specific time period and without more information in relation to possible confounding variables, a depth analytic one is required in the future. Second, health data were collected through two different approaches in 2019 and 2020 so the methodology could cause some discrepancies in the two years. Third, some patients were treated via telemedicine during the pandemic, but the system did not monitor such data. Therefore, these numbers should be taken into consideration in the future to investigate the actual decline.

6 Conclusion

In conclusion, the present study assessed the impact of the COVID-19 pandemic on the utilization of health services, based on the OPD visits, procedures, and inpatient data from 262 health institutions in Oman. Overall, healthcare utilization decreased among patients during the COVID-19 pandemic that was affected essential health services by reducing the access to the services, particularly in the first 3 months.

6.1 *Practical Implications*

The findings of this chapter can be used as a basis for future planning, construction guidelines, and protocols that could facilitate access to essential health services in the possible occurrence of future pandemics. MOH staff gained a practical experience in dealing with such pandemic at different level. Decision makers would have effective interventions to control the pandemic. Monitoring should be conducted in a sustainable manner to realize the trend and changes in providing essential health services. It is necessary to conduct a cohort analysis in order to investigate the economic impact of COVID-19 and its effects on disease-specific healthcare services. Additionally, patient satisfaction should be measured in order to identify vulnerable patient groups.

Acknowledgements The authors would like to acknowledge the support provided by the team in the Information and Statistics Department at the Ministry of Health.

Competing Interests The authors declare that they have no competing interests.

References

Al Ghafri, T., Al Ajmi, F., Al Balushi, L., Mohan Kurup, P., Al Ghamari, A., Al Balushi, Z., Al Fahdi, F., Al Lawati, H., Al Hashmi, S., Al Manji, A., & Al, S. A. (2021). Responses to the pandemic COVID-19 in primary health care in Oman: Muscat experience. *Oman Medical Journal, 36*(1), e216. https://doi.org/10.5001/omj.2020.70

Al-Gharbi, K., Gattoufi, S., Al-Badi, A., & Al-Hashmi, A. (2015). Al-Shifa health care information system in Oman: A debatable implementation success. *The Electronic Journal of Information Systems in Developing Countries, 66*(1), 1–17. https://doi.org/10.1002/j.1681-4835.2015.tb00471.x

Al Khalili, S., Al Maani, A., Al Wahaibi, A., Al Yaquobi, F., Al-Jardani, A., Al Harthi, K., Alqayoudhi, A., Al Manji, A., Al Rawahi, B., & Al-Abri, S. (2021). Challenges and opportunities for public health service in Oman from the COVID-19 pandemic: Learning lessons for a better future. *Frontiers in Public Health, 9*, 770946. https://doi.org/10.3389/fpubh.2021.770946

Al-Marhoon, M. (2020). The impact of COVID-19 on urology practice in Oman. *Sultan Qaboos University Medical Journal, 20*, 404–405. https://doi.org/10.18295/squmj.2020.20.04.023

Al Wahaibi, A., Al-Maani, A., Alyaquobi, F., Al Harthy, K., Al-Jardani, A., Al Rawahi, B., & Al-Abri, S. (2021). Effects of COVID-19 on mortality: A 5-year population-based study in Oman. *International Journal of Infectious Diseases, 104*, 102–107. https://doi.org/10.1016/j.ijid.2020.12.054

Amos, O. A., Adebisi, Y. A., Bamisaiye, A., Olayemi, A. H., Ilesanmi, E. B., Micheal, A. I., Ekpenyong, A., & Lucero-Prisno, D. E. (2021). COVID-19 and progress towards achieving universal health coverage in Africa: A case of Nigeria. *International Journal of Health Planning Management, 36*, 1417–1422. https://doi.org/10.1002/hpm.3263. Epub 2021, June 23.

Ashish, k, Gurung, R., Kinney, M. V., Sunny, A. K., Moinuddin, M., Basnet, O., et al. (2020). Effect of the COVID-19 pandemic response on intrapartum care, stillbirth, and neonatal mortality outcomes in Nepal: a prospective observational study. *The Lancet Global Health, 8*(10), e1273–e1281. https://doi.org/10.1016/S2214-109X(20)30345-4

Auener, S., Kroon, D., Wackers, E., Dulmen, S. V., & Jeurissen, P. (2020). COVID-19: A window of opportunity for positive healthcare reforms. *International Journal of Health Policy Management, 9*(10), 419–422. https://doi.org/10.34172/ijhpm.2020.66

Bhatt, A. S., Moscone, A., McElrath, E. E., et al. (2020). Fewer hospitalizations for acute cardiovascular conditions during the COVID- 19 pandemic. *Journal of the American College of Cardiology, 76*, 280–288. https://doi.org/10.1016/j.jacc.2020.05.038

Birkmeyer, J. D., Barnato, A., Birkmeyer, N., Bessler, R., & Skinner, J. (2020). The impact of the COVID-19 pandemic on hospital admissions in the United States. *Health Affairs, 39*(11), 2010–2017. https://doi.org/10.1377/hlthaff.2020.00980

Carr, M. J., Wright, A. K., Leelarathna, L., et al. (2021). Impact of COVID-19 on diagnoses, monitoring, and mortality in people with type 2 diabetes in the UK. *Lancet Diabetes Endocrinology, 9*, 413–415. https://doi.org/10.1016/S2213-8587(21)00116-9

Chandir, S., Siddiqi, D. A., Setayesh, H., & Khan, A. J. (2020). Impact of COVID-19 lockdown on routine immunisation in Karachi, Pakistan. *The Lancet Global Health, 8*(9), e1118–e1120. https://doi.org/10.1016/S2214-109X(20)30290-4

Ekman, B., Arvidsson, E., Thulesius, H., Wilkens, J., & Cronberg, O. (2021). Impact of the COVID-19 pandemic on primary care utilization: Evidence from Sweden using national register data. *BMC Research Notes, 14*, 424. https://doi.org/10.1186/s13104-021-05839-7

Elhadi, M., Al-Hosni, A., Day, K., Al-Hamadani, A., Al-Toqi, A., Al-Shamli, N., & Al-Hashmi, A. (2007). Review of health information systems in Oman. *Sultan Qaboos University Medical Journal, 12*(2), 101–120. https://doi.org/10.24200/squjs.vol12iss2pp101-120

Filippo, O., D'Ascenzo, F., Angelini, F., et al. (2020). Reduced rate of hospital admissions for ACS during COVID-19 outbreak in northern Italy. *New England Journal of Medicine, 383*, 88–89. https://doi.org/10.1056/NEJMc2009166

Howarth, A., Munro, M., Theodorou, A., et al. (2021). Trends in healthcare utilisation during COVID-19: A longitudinal study from the UK. *British Medical Journal Open, 11*, e048151. https://doi.org/10.1136/bmjopen-2020-048151

Hung, K., WallineEmily, J., Chan, Y., Huang, Z., Siu, E., Yeoh, E., & Graham, C. (2022). Health service utilization in Hong Kong during the COVID-19 pandemic—A cross-sectional public survey. *International Journal of Health Policy Management, 11*(4), 508–513. https://doi.org/10.34172/IJHPM.2020.183

Hussain, R., & Arif, S. (2021). Universal health coverage and COVID-19: Recent developments and implications. *Journal of Pharmaceutical Policy and Practice, 14*, 23. https://doi.org/10.1186/s40545-021-00306-x
Jeffery, M., D'Onofrio, G., Paek, H., Platts-Mills, T., Soares, W., Hoppe, J., Genes, N., Nath, B., & Melnick, E. (2020). Trends in emergency department visits and hospital admissions in health care systems in 5 states in the first months of the COVID-19 pandemic in the US. *JAMA International Medicine, 180*(10), 1328–1333. https://doi.org/10.1001/jamainternmed.2020.3288
Khan, S., & Ismail, M. (2017). Al-Shifa: Case study on Sultanate of Oman's national healthcare information system. *Indian Journal of Science and Technology, 10*, 17. https://doi.org/10.17485/ijst/2017/v10i17/113060
Kotlar, B., Gerson, E., Petrillo, S., Langer, A., & Tiemeier, H. (2021). The impact of the COVID-19 pandemic on maternal and perinatal health: A scoping review. *Reproductive Health, 18*, 10. https://doi.org/10.1186/s12978-021-01070-6
Kumagai, N. (2021). The impact of the COVID-19 pandemic on physician visits in Japan. *Frontiers in Public Health, 9*, 743371. https://doi.org/10.3389/fpubh.2021.743371
Kumari, V., Mehta, K., & Choudhary, R. (2020). COVID-19 outbreak and decreased hospitalisation of pregnant women in labour. *Lancet Global Health, 8*, e1116–e1117. https://doi.org/10.1016/S2214-109X(20)30319-3
Lauer, S. A., Grantz, K. H., Bi, Q., et al. (2020). The incubation period of coronavirus disease 2019 (COVID-19) from publicly reported confirmed cases: Estimation and application. *Annals of Internal Medicine, 172*(9), 577–582. https://doi.org/10.7326/m20-050423
Mansour, Z., Arab, J., Said, R., Rady, A., Hamadeh, R., Gerbaka, B., et al. (2021). Impact of COVID-19 pandemic on the utilization of routine immunization services in Lebanon. *PLoS ONE, 16*(2), e0246951. https://doi.org/10.1371/journal.pone.0246951
McDonald, H. I., Tessier, E., White, J. M., Woodruff, M., Knowles, C., Bates, C., et al. (2020). Early impact of the coronavirus disease (COVID-19) pandemic and physical distancing measures on routine childhood vaccinations in England, January to April 2020. *Euro-Surveillance, 25*(19), 2000848. https://doi.org/10.2807/1560-7917.ES.2020.25.19.2000848. PMID: 32431288.
Ministry of Health. (2012). *Oman health vision 2050, Synopsis of strategic studies.*
Ministry of Health. (2019). *Annual health report*. Directorate General of Health Services.
Ministry of Health. (2020). *Annual health report*. Directorate General of Health Services.

Morishita, T., Takada, D., Shin, J.-H., et al. (2022). Trends, treatment approaches, and in-hospital mortality for acute coronary syndrome in Japan during the coronavirus disease 2019 pandemic. *Journal of Atherosclerosis and Thrombosis, 29*(5), 597–607. https://doi.org/10.5551/jat.62746

Moynihan, R., Sanders, S., Michaleff, Z., Scott, A., Clark, J., Emma, J., Jones, M., Kitchener, E., Fox, M., Johansson, M., Lang, E., Duggan, A., Scott, I., & Albarqouni, L. (2021). Impact of COVID-19 pandemic on utilisation of healthcare services: A systematic review. *British Medical Journal Open, 11*, e045343. https://doi.org/10.1136/bmjopen-2020-045343

National Centre of Information & Statistics. (2022). *Statistical Yearbook.*

Nepogodiev, D., et al. (2020). Elective surgery cancellations due to the COVID-19 pandemic: Global predictive modelling to inform surgical recovery plans. *British Journal of Surgery, 107*(11), 1440–1449. https://doi.org/10.1002/bjs.11746. Epub 2020, June 13.

Patt, D., Gordan, L., Diaz, M., et al. (2020). Impact of COVID-19 on cancer care: How the pandemic is delaying cancer diagnosis and treatment for American seniors. *Journal of Clinical Encology, 4*, 1059–1071. https://doi.org/10.1200/CCI.20.00134

Rabbani, U., Saigul, A., Sulaiman, A., et al. (2021). Impact of COVID-19 on Antenatal Care Utilization among Pregnant Women in Qassim, Saudi Arabia. *Cureus, 13*(11), e19554. https://doi.org/10.7759/cureus.19554

Rachamin, Y., Senn, O., Streit, S., Dubois, J., Deml, M. J., & Jungo, K. T. (2021). Impact of the COVID-19 pandemic on the intensity of health services use in general practice: A retrospective cohort study. *International Journal of Public Health, 66*, 635508. https://doi.org/10.3389/ijph.2021.635508

Rezapour, R., Dorosti, A., Farahbakhsh, M., Azami-aghdash, S., & Iranzad, I. (2022). The impact of the COVID-19 pandemic on primary health care utilization: An experience from Iran. *BMC Health Services Research, 22*, 404–412. https://doi.org/10.1186/s12913-022-07753-5

Riley, T., Sully, E., Ahmed, Z., & Biddlecom, A. (2020). Estimates of the potential impact of the COVID-19 pandemic on sexual and reproductive health in low-and middle-income countries impacts of the pandemic on SRH outcomes. *International Perspectives on Sexual and Reproductive Health, 46*, 73–76.

Santi, L., Golinelli, D., Tampieri, A., et al. (2021). Non-COVID-19 patients in times of pandemic: Emergency department visits, hospitalizations and cause-specific mortality in northern Italy. *PLoS ONE, 16*, e0248995. https://doi.org/10.1371/journal.pone.0248995

Santoli, J. M. (2020). Effects of the COVID-19 pandemic on routine pediatric vaccine ordering and administration—United States. *The Morbidity and Mortality Weekly Report, 69*. https://doi.org/10.15585/mmwr.mm6919e2 PMID: 32407298.

Singh, D., Sunuwar, D., Shah, S., Karki, K., Sah, L., Adhikari, B., & Kumar, R. (2021). Impact of COVID-19 on health services utilization in Province-2 of Nepal: A qualitative study among community members and stakeholders. *BMC Health Services Research, 21*, 74–188. https://doi.org/10.1186/s12913-021-06176-y

Tan, J. Y., Conceicao, E. P., Sim, X. Y. J., Wee, L. E. I., Aung, M. K., & Venkatachalam, I. (2020). Public health measures during COVID-19 pandemic reduced hospital admissions for community respiratory viral infections. *Journal of Hospital Infection, 106*(2), 387–389. https://doi.org/10.1016/j.jhin.2020.07.023

Townsend, R., Chmielewska, B., Barratt, I., et al. (2021). Global changes in maternity care provision during the COVID19 pandemic: A systematic review and meta-analysis. *E Clinical Medicine, 37*, 100947. https://doi.org/10.1016/j.eclinm.2021.100947

Xiao, H., Dai, X., Wagenaar, B. H., Liu, F., Augusto, O., Guo, Y., et al. (2021). The impact of the COVID-19 pandemic on health services utilization in China: Time-series analyses for 2016–2020. *Lancet Regional Health Western Pacific, 9*, 100122. https://doi.org/10.1016/j.lanwpc.2021.100122

Xu, L., Zhuo, L., Zhang, J., Yang, W., Liu, G., Zhan, S., Wang, S., & Xiao, H. (2021). Impact of the COVID-19 pandemic on outpatient service in primary healthcare institutions: An inspiration from Yinchuan of China. *International Journal of Health Policy and Management*, 1–8. https://doi.org/10.34172/IJHPM.2021.119

Yamaguchi, S., Okada, A., Sunaga, S., Kurakawa, K., Yamauchi, T., Nangaku, M., & Kadowaki, T. (2022). Impact of COVID- 19 pandemic on healthcare service use for non- COVID- 19 patients in Japan: Retrospective cohort study. *British Medical Journal Open, 12*, e060390. https://doi.org/10.1136/bmjopen-2021-060390

World Health Organization (WHO). (2020). *Rapid assessment of service delivery for NCDs during COVID-19 pandemic*. Geneva.

World Health Organization (WHO). (2021). *Comprehensive assessment of Oman's health information system 2019*.

World Health Organization (WHO). (2022). *World Health Statistics Report. Monitoring health for the Sustainable Development Goals*.

CHAPTER 4

Administrative Responsibility of the Health Institution During the COVID-19 Pandemic

NABEEL ALOBAIDI

1 Introduction

Administrative responsibility is a legal situation in which the state, institutions, public utilities, and administrative public institutions are obligated to take legal actions or illegal actions of others due to moral errors, administrative errors, or errors of illegal actions.

The general principle of this type of responsibility is that the responsibility of the administrative authority is based on the occurrence of the error. For unless the administrative authority is at fault, it cannot be forced, pressured, or threatened in any way to compensate or correct the damage. The existence of a violation of the principle of equality before the public burdens or the activities of the administration have special risks and the damages cannot be compensated because the administrative department benefits from the activities and in return bears compensation for the resulting damages.

N. ALOBAIDI (✉)
Faculty of Law and Political Science, Swedish Crown University, Gothenburg, Sweden
e-mail: nabeel.alobaidi@bnu.edu.iq

A. Mishrif (ed.), *Perspectives on Human Capital Development*,
https://doi.org/10.1007/978-981-97-5246-1_4

Medical institutions are among the facilities that have a large and effective role in society, especially since health and security are among the most important activities that the state provides to individuals who are in dire need of them. They are institutions of public interest and play a major role in implementing the state's general policy. And its health activity is linked to the direct life of the human being and its permanence.

This leads us to find a balance in administrative responsibility that sends individuals a kind of calmness when reviewing health institutions and obtaining services, in addition to protecting employees of health institutions in all their functions to have a motive for health work when protecting them.

Hence, administrative responsibility is an effective legal tool and at the same time a guarantee and can contain the situation in which the management of health institutions can keep pace with the developments surrounding health institutions for this right. This protection is usually through legal means stipulated in administrative law and health legislation after the increase in population numbers and the complexity of modern life, as diseases and epidemics have taken the form of real social disasters and this is what we have seen in the shadow of the Corona pandemic (COVID-19) and its direct impact on the destruction of human power on the demographic, economic, commercial, political, and scientific level.

Health departments resort to using their authority to issue binding administrative decisions that include general rules aimed at protecting public order in general and public health in particular. Since the beginning of the spread of the Corona pandemic, the countries of the world have become aware of the danger of this epidemic that has restricted the entire world and imposed its will on society. Therefore, the Sultanate of Oman needed to be ready to take preventive and precautionary measures to confront COVID-19. Indeed, the Sultanate was quick to issue decisions, administrative and directive instructions, and amend the Infectious Disease Control Act to keep up with this virus.

Based on the foregoing mentioned above, we have the idea to discuss the issue of the administrative responsibility of government health institutions regarding their health activities, especially in the current period of the spread of the Coronavirus and its disruption to all areas of life.

First: The Importance of Research:

1. The medical aspect communicates directly with the person who deals with health institutions through receiving treatment, and this happens with all members of society.
2. The medical activity of the health institution of all its different types has important privacy.

Second: Research Objectives:

1. Clarifying all obstacles facing health workers and enact laws that guarantee protection for workers in health institutions.
2. Proposing the necessary solutions and guarantees for those who work in health institutions.
3. Working on developing medical awareness for all individuals working in health institutions and spreading a culture of legality among employees in health institutions.
4. Searching for appropriate solutions, especially those related to the responsibility for the burden of proof. To find protection for the affected.

Third: The Research Problem:

- What is the strength of the legal rules for the administrative responsibility of health institutions for their medical activity in protecting the rights of individuals who have been harmed by this activity?
- To what extent have health laws kept pace with technological developments that have emerged in the field of medicine?

Fourth: Research Methodology:

Follow the analytical approach to analyze the general rules of administrative responsibility for health institutions, as well as the comparative approach.

Fifth: Research Structure:

The first topic: What are health institutions and their legal nature?

The second topic: Determining the administrative responsibility of health institutions.

Recommendations:

First: Working on developing the work of health institutions that provide health services to the general public, aiding these institutions, and protecting their employees.
Second: Drafting a law that keeps pace with technological developments in the health field.

First: The Importance of Research:

1. The medical aspect communicates directly with the person who deals with health institutions through receiving treatment, and this happens with all members of society.
2. The medical activity of the health institution of all its different types has important privacy.

2 The First Topic

2.1 *What Are Health Centers (Institutions) and Their Legal Nature?*

Public health is a basic requirement for all members of society, and being preoccupied with its images and upgrading them to the maximum extent possible are of great importance to all countries, especially at present as a result of the increase in population numbers and the ease of spread of infectious diseases and epidemics. It is the protection of citizens against threats to their health from epidemics, infection risks, and risks arising from health sciences.[1]

For this reason, since ancient times, man has been targeting the state of health for himself and others from his relatives, friends, and relatives, because he realized that without health, he would become in a state of weakness that makes him unable to resist the hardships of life.[2]

But with the progress of life, there has been a noticeable development, and there has been a dedication to public health and interest in what is related to it.[3]

It can be said that the health institution is a human group of specialists and various medical professions and material inputs that are organized in a specific style to serve patients and meet their needs. It is also defined as a human social structure aimed at achieving and meeting certain goals, and it consists of professionals and specialists in health and medical fields who provide healthcare services.

2.2 We Will Divide This Study into Two Sections

The first requirement: is the definition of the health institution.
The second requirement: is the nature of the legal health institution.

3 The First Requirement

3.1 Definition of a Health Institution

Health institutions are institutions that provide a variety of services, each of which has its specialty. The institutions begin their work by exploring, examining, and scrutinizing to detect diseases. Then, health institutions are provided, each according to its exact specialization. These health institutions are provided by a specialized medical staff, each according to its specialization, using advanced medical equipment and keeping pace with the technological development taking place. Right now, these devices constitute an important and indispensable part of the necessary medical services.

A healthcare facility provides treatment to patients by specialized medical and nursing staff and medical equipment. The best-known type of hospital is the general hospital, which usually has an emergency department to treat urgent health problems ranging from fire and accident victims to heart attacks. A district hospital is usually the main healthcare facility in its area, with a large number of beds for intensive or intensive care and extra beds for patients who require long-term care. Specialized hospitals include trauma centers, rehabilitation hospitals, children's hospitals, hospitals for the elderly, and hospitals to deal with special medical needs such as psychiatric treatment and some categories of diseases. Specialized hospitals can help reduce healthcare costs compared to general hospitals.

The World Health Organization defined the hospital in general, on the occasion of issuing the first report of the technical committee on the organization of health care in hospitals, as the integrated part of the social health organization and its function to provide full preventive and curative care to the entire population... in addition to being a center for training health workers and sociobiological research.

And some defined the general hospital or the government hospital (Public Hospital) as a hospital that is managed by the state or one of its public bodies as a person of public law, so the hospital is described as publicly owned.[4]

Public health institutions are classified according to[5]:

1. General hospitals according to medical specialties, which are hospitals in which there are major medical specialties represented in the Department of Internal Medicine, General Surgery, Pediatrics, Obstetrics and Gynecology, and may include specialized medical services such as ophthalmology, otolaryngology, and orthopedics. In addition, it also includes the outpatient clinics of the general hospital, a special section for pharmaceutical services, radiology departments, laboratories, laboratories, and other departments.
2. The public hospital according to ownership, as it is part of the public utilities—the health facility—which is affiliated with the state in terms of management, supervision, and budget.[6]

These hospitals are divided into two types[7]:

The first type: is public hospitals that provide services to all citizens, which are hospitals affiliated with the Ministry of Health.

The second type: is public hospitals that provide services to the sector or a specific group of society, such as military hospitals. Accordingly, the general hospital is a public institution, owned by the state, supervision, control, financing, and management, and contains four main medical specialties (internal, general surgery, children, obstetrics, and gynecology), in addition to other health services in most cases, and public hospitals—providing treatment and medical services under a set of principles, including the principle of continuity in the implementation of the public service regularly and permanently, the principle of the quality of the service that is provided, and the principle of equality of all before the service provided by the public hospital, which is a constitutional principle and one of the general constitutional principles.[8]

The composition of the general hospital includes technical devices, medical and non-medical equipment, as well as highly skilled and trained technical and technical workforce, technical and medium-skilled workforce, administrative cadres, and unskilled workforce, and each type of them plays a different role from the other type, but in the end, everyone joins hands to serving the patient, providing treatment and prevention.

Departments in hospitals are divided into technical departments, which include doctors and members of the health team, including pharmacists, nurses, and auxiliary professionals. This is in addition to services of a medical-administrative nature that is based on services related to patient files, medical social services, and admission and discharge services for patients. The administrative department in the hospital includes personnel of administration, financial management, and public relations with maintenance services.

As for the technical department, which includes doctors, it includes trained doctors, known as interns, and recent graduates. They work for one year in hospitals after graduating and completing their studies in the Faculty of Medicine, under the supervision of specialized doctors and they are not responsible for patients. This is in addition to the resident physicians who spent the training period and were selected to work in the hospital, in preparation for their qualification as physicians specializing in one or more of the various medical specialties, and they are responsible for treating patients, in addition to the specialized physicians who bear direct responsibility for the treatment of patients and may work as full-time physicians or also part-timers, and there are also consultant doctors who provide advice and advice to specialized doctors when they need to.[9]

4 The Second Requirement

4.1 The Nature of the Legal Health Institution

Health institutions, by their nature, are institutions characterized by an administrative nature, and one of their goals that they seek to achieve is to provide a service to members of society, whether it is in return for money or free of charge, and they bear responsibility for the injured or sick.

Error is the basis for the administration's responsibility for its actions that cause harm to others. The exception is its responsibility based on risk or liability. The responsibility of the state is based on an error by the availability of three pillars of error and damage and a causal relationship between them. The injured person cannot claim compensation unless he proves the administration's mistake or one of its employees or during the performance of work or because of it, but to apply this theory requires a distinction between the personal error that is attributed to the employee and bears compensation for the damage caused by his mistake out of his own money, and the accompanying error that is attributed to the administration, which bears compensation permanently.[10]

The origin for the injured party is his obligation to prove the error attributed to the administration, the damage, and the causal relationship, that is, the burden of proof falls on the injured, unlike liability based on risk.[11]

The rules that regulate the functioning of public or private health institutions are administrative, and they bear responsibility in case of failure to provide services.[12]

Therefore, it is the legal nature of health institutions that allows us to know the type of lawsuits filed by the person affected by legal medical work to obtain compensation as a result of negligence in medical work.[13] Accordingly, the jurisdiction in these cases belongs to the administrative judge, which is known as the public utility system.[14]

What distinguishes the health institution from others is that it has a legal personality and an independent financial system, and in the application of this, the injured patient from the health institution as a result of the medical work it provided to him can dispute these institutions before the courts to claim compensation.[15]

The damage caused by health pandemics is the result of a personal error, which is far from true because personal errors are the cause of them. It was an accompanying error, because the state did not maintain health or did not take the necessary precautions to provide the necessary care for the injured, and then there was a slowdown in maintaining public health, which helped in the spread of the Corona epidemic (COVID-19).

5 The Second Topic

5.1 *Determining the Administrative Responsibility of Health Institutions*

The role that the health facility plays in the lives of individuals, no one can dispute, given the great service it provides to the citizen in the field of health care and treatment, which made the state, through laws and legislation, attach great importance to this sensitive facility. Public health institutions are administrative institutions, and during their usual activity, they make mistakes, intentionally or unintentionally, that cause harm to their users, and they must be redressed. Accordingly, the system of administrative responsibility for public health institutions was established, thanks to the jurisprudence and the judiciary to protect the injured party, and to enable it to file a lawsuit against it before the administrative court to demand appropriate compensation to redress the damage suffered by it. While the administrative responsibility is established against the public health facility, the injured person or his representative is in a state of disorder, especially in terms of proving the error. The causation is to obtain the appropriate compensation, which is estimated at the time of the judicial pronouncement, and this is a consecration of the principle of justice. Hence, it is necessary to protect the right of the injured person who was exposed to a mistake in it, as well as the right of the public health facility, which in turn was established to provide a noble service related to the life of the individual.

Public health is one of the greatest concerns that falls on the shoulders of the state, which has established various public facilities, which are not far from administrative responsibility like other public facilities and are affected by the same principles of administrative responsibility in general, and this applies to health institutions in general because their management bears all responsibility.

Determining the administrative responsibility of the health institution is through the actions that the institution provides to members of society because of the administrative responsibility (legal responsibility that takes place in the administrative legal system and relates to the responsibility of the executive authority for its harmful actions).[16]

Administrative responsibility was also defined as: the obligation that falls on a person, finally, to compensate for damage caused to another person.[17]

And the fact that health institutions, whether public or private, are supervised by the Ministry of Health, and it has the competence to follow up on their supervisory progress.

Administrative responsibility is considered the most distinguished because the administration is responsible for any error within the health institution. What is meant here is not the wrong behavior of the administration that draws attention, but the damage generated and the feeling of unfairness of the situation embodied in the person affected by the administrative work inside the health institution, which bears its consequences, and the solution to this problem does not pass through the idea of error, but by passing through the idea of fairness to the affected individual as a result of infection from an infection within the health institution as a result of negligence or negligence on the part of the health institution employees.[18]

Concerning the administrative responsibility of the health institution for the harm, it causes to others due to its harmful actions, as decided by the French Council of State, which is based on error and is supplemented by exception with the idea of responsibility based on risks and bearing the liability (i.e., responsibility without fault). Therefore, the administration must take great efforts, including protecting public employees.

About the corner of the error that must be available to say the responsibility of the administration, the French Council of State has made a distinction between each of the personal errors that is attributed to the employee himself and arranges his responsibility and thus bears the payment of compensation for the damage suffered by others, and the accompanying error that is attributed to the facility and is asked by the state alone from her money.

Error as a condition for the responsibility of the public authority raises several problems, foremost of which is defining the idea of error that necessitates this responsibility and how to prove it, and whether it is possible to assume this error.[19]

Based on this, the responsibility of the state in France was not decided at once. After the state was not asked about its actions, even if they caused harm, it began to ask about these actions when they resulted in harm, but this responsibility was based at first based on error, and then in A later stage, the administrative judiciary eased the liability system and established it based on the assumption of error due to the difficulty of proving error in some of the administration's work, especially works of a technical nature that are difficult for the aggrieved to prove. The absence of error in the actions committed by the administration avoids administrative liability.[20]

The error in administrative responsibility has an innovative feature, as we have previously emphasized, which is the distinction between an accompanying error and a personal error. In the first case, the responsibility rests with the public utility, which bears the burden of compensation, and the jurisdiction is the administrative judiciary. In the second case, the responsibility lies with the employee in a personal capacity, the judgment for compensation is executed from his funds, and the jurisdiction is vested in the ordinary judiciary.

Within the scope of the responsibility of the medical public facilities, a distinction can be made between two types of work that may be the subject of accompanying errors, which are medical work and the work of organizing and running the facility.

Medical work is considered one of the activities that are difficult to accomplish on the part of the medical facility, so the administrative judiciary stresses, as a general principle, the degree of error committed in these actions.

Although the content of the obligation is the same in both the medical error that complicates the responsibility of the medical facility and its counterpart in private law, which is the obligation to exercise care, it is not possible to estimate the medical error attributed to the public facility according to the objective criterion in force in civil law, which is based on the usual behavior of the average person. Since the medical error punishable by law is the result committing a serious error. Therefore, the administrative judge estimates this error in each case separately, using the criteria that seem familiar to him, such as the means available at the facility, the circumstances of the time and place, the state of urgency, and the position of the victim.

As for the work of organizing and running the medical facility, it includes, in addition to the administrative and organizational work of the facility, the ongoing care work.

The error in these actions includes many forms, such as the error in diagnosing the disease, or the lack of commitment to the patient's insight or obtaining his consent. The judiciary of the French Council of State has expanded the scope of the error in the organization and management of the medical facility, no longer limiting it to the fixed error, but rather applying the idea of the supposed error, in cases in which the patient suffers severe harm that is not at all commensurate with the reason for his stay in the hospital or with treatment subject to him, without at the same time being able to establish evidence of an error on the part of the medical facility.

But the origin of medical liability at present, according to the general rules of liability, is that the burden of proof falls on the plaintiff and he has to prove the elements of responsibility and its pillars, including error, damage, and causation.

For a medical facility's liability to be held, a causal relationship must be established between the facility's activity and the damage, but this relationship can be negated, which consequently leads to the denial of liability when the damage is caused by a foreign cause beyond the facility's control.

If the responsibility of the medical facility meets its obligations—whether it is based on fault or without fault—the facility bears the burden of obligation to compensate the damages incurred by the injured party. Compensation is the main goal that the injured person seeks to achieve to compensate for the damage he has suffered. However, compensation is subject to general principles that must be observed and rules governing its assessment.[21]

The system of administrative responsibility for transmission of infection, especially in light of the spread of the COVID-19 epidemic, is included in two forms for which the health institution is responsible, which are:

1. Responsibility due to lack of isolation procedures or violation of isolation systems in light of the spread of COVID-19: Here the error committed results from breaching the services provided by the health institution and this leads to the spread of infection inside it, whether due to late diagnosis or delay in completing examination procedures or errors preventing antibiotics, giving the patient appropriate treatment for infection, or eliminating isolation activity in symptoms of infectious diseases.[22]
2. The responsibility of the health institution as a result of its failure to sterilize and fumigate during the spread of infectious diseases, as is the case during the spread of the Coronavirus: There is a fact that it is not possible to blame administrative failure on the health institution by not sterilizing or fumigating. But in light of the Corona

pandemic, this was possible, as not paying attention to the cleanliness of the health institution could help the spread of infectious diseases.[23]

Accordingly, the health institution should take the necessary preventive measures to avoid the institution from getting infections or not caring for patients so that it does not fall under liability and show its deliberate negligence, and it is also necessary to isolate people who suffer from or are likely to have infectious diseases, especially COVID-19 is fast spreading. The institution can take a complete or partial closure if it finds it impossible to respond to preventive measures or measures related to the safety of patients, and this is what happened in one of the hospitals of the Arab Republic of Egypt (Al-Salam Hospital).[24]

After diagnosing and defining the responsibility of the health institution from an administrative point of view, we must search for ways for health departments to use their authority to issue binding administrative decisions that include general rules aimed at protecting public order in general and public health in particular, because the duty to preserve the lives of members of society rests on the responsibility of everyone, and it is an existing responsibility that does not absolve the health institution or any other individual from his responsibility toward society.

There are several methods that the health administration resorts to in dealing with critical health conditions, including:

First: The administrative and organizational decisions taken by the health institution in addressing the aggravating health conditions, which are:

1. Imposing a health ban: The ban means to forbid or prevent a certain action or procedure when practicing a specific individual activity, whether that prevention is in terms of purpose, time or place,[25] and accordingly, the ban may be absolute or it may be relative and the first is represented in preventing certain acts with harmful effects on the public health system, while the other is to prevent some activities at a specific time or place because they harm public health.[26]
2. Health license: Health licensing is defined as obligating individuals to obtain a permit, permission, or approval from the health authorities to allow them to practice the activity, before starting

it. By enabling the health authorities to impose what they deem appropriate precautions that would prevent this harm.[27]

3. Health notification: Notification in general that informs the administration about the practice of a certain activity or certain freedom to obtain permission to practice it in connection with the public order,[28] the notification is not a request or a solicitation of approval to practice the activity but includes data submitted to the competent administrative authority to be informed in advance of what is intended. It is an activity, and the authority of the administration is limited to verifying the validity of the data contained therein and the fulfillment of the procedures established by law.[29]

Second: Unilateral administrative decision: Individual administrative decisions are called those decisions that address a particular individual or individuals so that they exhaust their subject as soon as they are implemented,[30] and in the field of public health, these decisions take two forms: the health order and the health prohibition. There are three forms for individual administrative decisions:

1. Health orders issued by the competent authority: Individual seizure orders are one of the most widely used methods by administrative control authorities since many administrative control measures are carried out using seizure orders, and examples in the field of public health are the health inspection teams directing shop owners, restaurants, and vendors. Itinerant people follow legal procedures to protect public health.[31]
2. Health prohibition order: What is meant by health prohibition here is the order to refrain from doing something such as preventing the introduction of drugs and medical narcotics, as well as preventing a person with a contagious disease such as the Coronavirus from working for a specified period until his recovery.[32]
3. Direct execution: Direct execution is generally defined as the right of the administration to implement its orders on individuals by force without the need for prior permission from the judiciary.[33] In other words, it is the ability of the administration if it takes an executive decision to implement it by itself forcibly using public force. Against the individual refraining from implementation,[34] the direct implementation that the administration resorts to is in normal and exceptional circumstances.

Based on what was mentioned above regarding administrative responsibility toward procedures in light of the Corona pandemic, the countries of the world have harnessed all possibilities to control the Coronavirus and limit the infection that has spread at an abnormal speed, and most countries of the world have taken administrative and other legal measures and restrictions have been imposed. Administrative measures have been imposed on dealing with COVID-19 patients or suspects, as well as imposing administrative measures on health institutions, and among these countries is the Sultanate of Oman, under a royal order issued on March 10, 2020, which included the formation of a higher committee to manage to deal with the Corona pandemic. Since the Sultanate, like other countries, has not declared a state of emergency, a higher committee is formed to examine the mechanism for dealing with developments resulting from the spread of the Coronavirus "COVID-19," in light of the emerging health data and indicators and what is issued by the World Health Organization in this regard.

After the Royal Decree regarding the formation of the Supreme Committee, Royal Decree No. 6/21 was issued, which complements the previous decree in taking quick precautionary measures and measures in the face of COVID-19, as Article 49 stipulates (.....take quick measures to confront any danger threatening The safety of the State, its territorial integrity, the security and interests of its people, or hindering State institutions from performing their tasks.[35]

And since there is a royal decree from His Majesty to form a supreme committee, whose work is to monitor and follow up on the developments of the Corona pandemic and the speed of its spread among members of society, the orders issued by His Majesty stipulated monitoring all the developments left by the Coronavirus and the efforts made at the regional and international levels to contain the crisis, find solutions, adopt proposals and recommendations, and authorize the Supreme Committee to use all the tools that contribute to the success of the committee's tasks.

The Supreme Committee also directed a way to deal with the Corona pandemic through the sixth point, which states (that it called on all institutions in the public and private sectors to provide an environment of physical distancing and to monitor the commitment of all its employees and beneficiaries to precautionary measures, and to monitor violators to subject them to the procedures it adopted in this regard).

It also included the statement issued by the Supreme Committee, which is in charge of examining the mechanism for dealing with developments resulting from the spread of the Coronavirus (COVID-19), issued by meeting No. 39 on 30/11/2020 AD, in the fourth paragraph of it that states: "The Supreme Committee emphasized the general orientation In dealing with the effects of this pandemic, it balances the deliberate openness of various activities within the framework of the recovery process in various fields, to ensure the continuation of the state's performance of its duties and the continuation of the work of the private sector on the one hand, and the precautionary requirements necessary to prevent all members of society from contracting this disease on the other hand."

Perhaps the fifth paragraph of the same statement states that: "The epidemiological situation of this pandemic is the basic criterion upon which decisions will continue to be taken in the future regarding opening various activities or returning to closing them, which calls for putting all the precautionary controls approved into effect by public sector individuals and institutions, and private."

The Sultanate of Oman addressed the direction of health institutions by authorizing the Minister of Health to continuously follow up on all hospitals and health centers and to deal with extreme precision to limit the rapid spread of the Corona pandemic, and thus issued an amendment to the Law on Combating Infectious Diseases by Royal Decree to deal with infectious diseases such as the Coronavirus, according to Law No. 73/92 regarding the control of infectious diseases, as amended according to Royal Decree No. 32/2020.

At the beginning of the legislation of the Infectious Diseases Control Law 73/92, there were no serious and contagious diseases, as there had been no outbreaks for a long period. Therefore, the Omani legislator did not pay any prior attention to the development of penal provisions punishing the deliberate transmission of infection or non-compliance with the laws and the regulations and instructions that are taken to reduce the transmission of infectious diseases. The fact that these diseases have effects on society, and this was the reason for enacting the Law on Combating Infectious Diseases to protect the Omani society and foreign residents on its land.

When considering the Omani Infectious Disease Control Law, which contains twenty articles, attached to a table that identified infectious diseases and divided them into three sections, each section of it contains several diseases of an infectious nature, and for this, we find that COVID-19 has been mentioned in the category of syndromes, and therefore the state, in this case, applies what is stated in the texts of the law regarding exceptional circumstances in this dangerous period.

One of the most important things that the law touched on is determining who is responsible for reporting when an infectious disease is infected or suspected of infection by any individual.

1. The doctor who examined the patient.
2. The official of the health institution in which the disease appeared.
3. The official of the laboratory in which the sample that indicates the presence of the disease was examined.
4. The head of the patient's family, or whoever supports him, takes him in or serves him.
5. The responsible employer or manager if the injury appears in an industrial or commercial establishment or public place.
6. The driver of the means of transport if the disease appears or is suspected while the patient is there.
7. A representative of the administrative authority (the governor, the sheik, or the police).[36]

When looking at the second paragraph, we find that the legislator obliged the health institution official to report any infectious disease, which is an administrative responsibility for the head of the institution to take urgent administrative measures as drawn up by the law and authorized by him, and here the notification must include the name of the infected person consisting of three sections: His title, place of work, and address to facilitate the access of the competent authority to him, and also the responsibility lies with the injured or suspected person that he must go to the nearest health institution for detection and taking the necessary precautions. All of this was regulated by Article (5) bis, which states: "A person infected with one of the infectious diseases listed in the first section of the table attached to this law has the right to receive health care and treatment in governmental treatment homes by the rules and procedures determined by the Minister of Health." Article (5) bis (7) also stipulates: A person infected or suspected of having one of the infectious diseases mentioned in the first section of the table attached to this law shall abide by the instructions and instructions issued to him by the health institution that treats him, and a person infected with one of these diseases is prohibited from—as soon as he becomes aware of his infection—performing any behavior that leads to the transmission of the infection to others.[37]

As for the prevention and safety measures against infectious diseases regarding those coming from outside the borders, safety measures are applied to them, and the infected person must inform the authorities upon arrival immediately and avoid mixing permanently. Isolation and quarantine procedures in the places are designated by the Ministry of Health, as is the case in countries of the world.

It is noted that the legislator in the amended law gave full powers to the Ministry of Health to take administrative and preventive measures and measures about to maintain the safety of the country from the outbreak of infectious diseases, especially what we are dealing with as COVID-19.

When we return to the amended Royal Decree, we find a clear indication that it is forbidden for all persons to obstruct or refrain from implementing any measure that would prevent the spread of diseases or epidemics, and this is what was stipulated in Article (5) bis (8) of the amended Royal Decree No. 32/2021, which stipulates that it is prohibited for any person to disrupt or refrain from implementing the procedures and measures established to prevent the spread of infection or to transmit it to others.

Given the development of the epidemiological health conditions in the Sultanate of Oman and the exacerbation of the infection rate in various countries of the world, the Sultanate of Oman has taken it upon itself to harness all administrative and legal capabilities to limit the spread of COVID-19 and follow up on the implementation of those measures about the health of individuals in Omani society as well as maintaining facilities, especially health and commercial, and imposing sanctions. Those who do not adhere to the imposed curfew hours. Increasing inspection campaigns and issuing the correct instructions that help maintain the health of community members. Especially since the Omani legislator gave the administrative authorities powers to confront this epidemic on an exceptional basis, and one of these powers is to authorize the Minister of Health to take appropriate measures to prevent diseases, whether they are contagious or not.

The Omani Ministry of Health has taken a set of administrative decisions against health institutions in the Sultanate of Oman, which is an administrative responsibility taken by the Ministry in light of the Corona pandemic—temporarily another private health facility.

The Ministry withdrew clinical privileges from some medical staff, suspended two specialized private health institutions, and issued warnings to 66 private health institutions while warning 34 private health institutions for publishing some advertisements on social media without obtaining the necessary permits.[38]

That is why we believe that the administrative responsibility of health institutions for all their activities should be characterized by great interest by the employees of health institutions of all kinds and that there should be restriction and impartiality in the follow-up of the affairs of these health institutions, especially as they receive the lives of members of society, and the thing is that the Sultanate of Oman has taken strict measures. It provided great support to members of society as well as every foreigner residing on its lands to preserve the country from infectious diseases.

6 Conclusion

Based on what was mentioned in the above research (Administrative Responsibility of the Health Institution in the Light of the COVID-19 Pandemic). About a stone ball we touched. However, it is the responsibility of the government to try to combat the virus once and for all Antivirus.

At the end of the research, it reached several results and recommendations:

7 Results

1. This COVID-19 pandemic has spread worldwide, and no one has ever been spared from it, whether it is a developed country or a backward country, whether it is poor or rich countries. That is why it is necessary to cooperate at an international level for prevention, protection, and limiting the scale of this epidemic. Because many countries lack effective health means to combat the epidemic.
2. Health is considered a natural right of the human being and is proven in all laws, religions, and constitutions.
3. There was great interest from the authorities of the Sultanate of Oman, and this was through taking preventive and procedural measures to contain the spread of COVID-19.

4. The administrative responsibility of health institutions is a very important real responsibility because the health institution considers a cure disease and the contraindication to it for individuals to obtain treatment.
5. The error of the health institutions is an administrative error, the consequences of which are borne by the administration in the health institution, whether it is public or private.
6. There is a great responsibility on health institutions in case of neglect or failure to treat any case of infectious diseases.

8 Recommendations

1. It is necessary to work on the development of laws related to public health to know the causes and develop appropriate and rapid solutions in taking preventive measures and keeping abreast of developments affecting them.
2. The necessity of developing health legislation and prevention measures by identifying the causes, developing appropriate solutions, and developing public health.
3. Activating the supervisory role of the health and environmental preventive agency on health and environmental activities.
4. Training and developing the capabilities of health administration staff in the field of health crises and how to deal with them.
5. We call for holding electronic educational seminars specialized in determining the methods in the hands of health departments to confront the epidemic in general and the Corona pandemic in particular so that there is great acceptance among the citizen in applying these methods and not violating them.
6. Follow-up by the Ministry of Health directly on all health institutions and not be lenient in imposing the maximum penalties if health institutions do not comply with health and safety conditions.

After our research, we hope that there will be interest in the issue of legal regulation of health institutions to achieve its goals for all members of society, considering not to underestimate or any violation of human rights and the balance between preserving the health of the individual and observing his basic rights stipulated in human rights constitutions and declarations.

Notes

1. Adel Al-Saeed Abu Al-Khair (2009, p. 285).
2. M. Sankale (1969, p. 18).
3. Mohammed Melhaoui (2005, p. 151 et suivants).
4. Najeeb Khalaf Ahmed (2006, p. 245).
5. Saja Hussein Alawi (2017, p. 14).
6. Thamer Yasser Al-Bakri (2005, p. 27).
7. Muhammad Abdel Moneim Shuaib (2014, p. 105).
8. Saja Hussein Alawi (2017, p. 1).
9. Saja Hussein Alawi (2017, p. 13).
10. Fouad Al-Attar (1972/1963, p. 678).
11. Abdel Raouf Hashem Bassiouni (2008, p. 112).
12. Marc Dupont (2001, p. 7).
13. Ahmed Mahiou (1979, p. 430).
14. Bernard Bomicir (1998, p. 23).
15. Bernard Kiyours (1994, p. 180).
16. Maha Abdul Rahim Al-Zahrani (2017, p. 51).
17. Suad Al Sharqi (1973, p. 100).
18. Michel Paillet (1996, p. 127).
19. Abdel Raouf Hashem Bassiouni (2007, p. 10).
20. Hamdi Ali Omar (1995, p. 256).
21. Loi n° 2002-303 du 4 mars 2002 relative aux droits des malades et à la qualité du système de santé, NOR: MESX0100092L. Version consolidée au 30 mai 2020: https://www.legifrance.gouv.fr/affichTexte.do?cidTexte=JORFTEXT000000227015 22/8/2022 p.m. 1345.
22. Marcello Albini (Risarcimento danni da Infezioni Ospedaliere), Ultime news di Diritto Sanitario: https://www.studiolegalealbini.it/infezioni-ospedaliere.
23. Noel Emmanuel Essomba, Infections nosocomiales et expertises judiciaires, Memoire online: https://www.memoireonline.com/08/11/4684/Infections-nosocomiales-etexpertises-judiciaires.html.
24. Quanto all'Italia, sono state adottate già da tempo –sia a livello nazionale che a livello regionale – misure di buone pratiche cliniche in tema di prevenzione delle ICA. Ricordiamo, in particolare, due risalenti circolari del Ministero della Sanità.
25. Hamdi Al-Qubeilat (2008, p. 32).

26. Eid Muhammad Manahi (2009, p. 467).
27. Adel Abu al-Khair (1995, p. 223).
28. Hanan Muhammad Al-Qaisi (2013, p. 36).
29. Hamdi Hamouda (2008, p. 77).
30. Adel Al-Saeed Abu Al-Khair (2009, p. 66).
31. Khaled Jaber Khudair (2014, p. 125).
32. Khaled Jaber Khudair (2014, p. 129).
33. Adel Abu al-Khair (2007, p. 262).
34. Issam Abdel-Wahab Al-Barzanji et al. (1993, p. 459).
35. Royal Decree No. 6/2021 issuing the Basic Law of the State.
36. Law on Combating Infectious Diseases amended by Royal Decree No. 32/2020.
37. Royal Decree No. 32/2020 amending some provisions of the Law on Combating Infectious Diseases.
38. https://www.omandaily.om/, Oman Newspaper, date of visit 22/ 8/2022.

References

The Legal Literature

Al-Attar, F. (1972/1963). *Administrative judiciary*. Arab Renaissance House.

Al-Bakri, T. Y. (2005). *Hospital administration*. Al-Yazuri Scientific Publishing and Distribution House.

Al-Barzanji, I. A.-W., Badir, A. M., & Al-Salami, M. Y. (1993). *Principles and provisions of administrative law*. Dar Al-Kutub for Printing and Publishing.

al-Khair, A. A. (1995). *Administrative control, and its limits*. General Egyptian Book Organization.

al-Khair, A. A. (2007). *Administrative police* (1st ed.). Dar Al-Fikr Al-Jamii.

Al-Khair, A. A.-S. A. (2009). *Administrative law*. n.p.

Al-Qubeilat, H. (2008). *Administrative law* (Vol. 1, 1st ed.). Wael Publishing House.

Al Sharqi, S. (1973). *Administrative responsibility* (3rd ed.). Dar Al Maaref.

Al-Zahrani, M. A. R. (2017). *The administration's responsibility for the failure to execute judicial judgments in the Saudi system (comparative study)* (1st ed.). Dar Al-Kitab Al-Jaami Publishing and Distribution.

Bassiouni, A. R. H. (2007). *Presumption of error in the field of administrative responsibility, a comparative study*. Arab Thought House.

Bassiouni, A. R. H. (2008). *Presumption of error in the field of administrative responsibility*. Arab Thought House.
Bomicir, B. (1998, October 15). *L'hôpital, Documentation francaise*.
Dupont, M. (2001). *Droit hospitalier* (3rd ed.). Dalloz.
Hamouda, H. (2008). *The licensing and notification system, a comparative applied study on the freedom of issuing newspapers in Egypt, France, and the United Kingdom*. Dar Al-Nahda Al-Arabiya.
Kiyours, B. (1994). *Soigner l'hôpital (pour l'autonomie au nquotidien)*. Erés.
Mahiou, A. (1979). *Lectures in administrative institutions* (2nd ed.; M. A. Sasila, Trans.). Diwan of University Publications.
Manahi, E. M. (2009). *Administrative protection of the environment—A comparative study*. Dar Al-Nahda Al-Arabiya.
Melhaoui, M. (2005). *Peste, contagion et martyre, Histoire du fléau en Occident musulman medieval*. édition PUBLISUD.
Omar, H. A. (1995). *Liability without fault for public medical facilities*. Dar Al-Nahda Al-Arabiya.
Paillet, M. (1996). *la Responsabilité Administrative*. Dalloz.
Sankale, M. (1969). *Médecins et action sanitaire en Afrique noire*. Présence Africaine Édition.
Shuaib, M. A. M. (2014). *Management of health organizations/hospitals* (1st ed., 3rd part). Universities Publishing House.

Letters and Theses

Alawi, S. H. (2017). *Civil liability for medical errors in public hospitals* (Master's thesis). Birzeit University.
Khudair, K. J. (2014). *The duty of administration to achieving and protecting public health in Iraqi law* (Master's thesis). College of Law, University of Baghdad.

Newspapers and Magazines

Ahmed, N. K. (2006). The general hospital's responsibility for its doctors' mistakes. *Journal of Legal Sciences, 21*. University of Baghdad.
Al-Qaisi, H. M. (2013). Freedom of demonstration between notice and permission. Research published in the *Journal of Legal Studies* (35). Department of Legal Studies, House of Wisdom, Baghdad.

The Laws

Law on Combating Infectious Diseases 73/92.
Royal Decree No. 6/2021, the Basic Law of the State.
Royal Decree No. 32/2020 amending some provisions of the Law on Combating Infectious Diseases.

CHAPTER 5

Understanding the Effectiveness of Stringent Governmental Policies Against Mortality Rates in the Case Study of COVID-19: A Comparison of Twenty-Two Countries

Saira Hafeez, Jibran Hussain, and Rashid Aftab

1 Introduction

In December 2019, the first case of Coronavirus (SARS-CoV-2) was detected in Wuhan, China, and the virus had hit almost every country around the globe within months due to its rapid spread. The World Health Organization (WHO) officially declared it a pandemic in March 2020, and even more than three years later, researchers are still finding out new information about various aspects of this novel virus such

S. Hafeez (✉)
Department of Political Science, Colorado State University,
Fort Collins, CO, USA
e-mail: hafeez7@colostate.edu

J. Hussain · R. Aftab
Riphah Institute of Public Policy, Riphah International University, Islamabad,
Pakistan

A. Mishrif (ed.), *Perspectives on Human Capital Development*,
https://doi.org/10.1007/978-981-97-5246-1_5

as scientific comparison of variants of the virus, the lasting impact of COVID-19 pandemic on the global economy, and the impact of varying response of different states for containment and treatment of this virus, etc. COVID-19 now has more than 6.9 million deaths globally ("WHO coronavirus disease (COVID-19) dashboard," 2023); however, the death count and the curve of the transmission vary greatly from state to state as each country's government was observed to enact containment strategies with varying stringency and response time. The sweeping impact of the COVID-19 pandemic reverberated across the world, leading to disruption in nearly every country, spanning all continents (De Giusti, 2020). Its socioeconomic implications can be seen across the world, particularly in developing countries, and the way the COVID-19 pandemic has forced the world governments to make stop-gap arrangements to keep the system running has exposed the underlying weaknesses in the health sector and the vulnerability of existing fragile systems. As the global health sector was directly hit by the pandemic without any exception, the health systems of even the most developed countries like the United States of America, Russia, France, Germany, and the United Kingdom could not bear the brunt of the deadly virus. Particularly, the third wave caused a huge surge in the number of affected patients and the virus has been seen to mutate into several variants, for example, the deadly UK variant (Sharma et al., 2021).

Unprecedented steps were taken by governments around the world as well as health officials across the countries to manage the increasing number of COVID-19 patients and provide required treatment to critical patients. Measures like large-scale quarantine/isolation centers, smart lockdowns, crowd management through early shop closures, safe days, etc., were taken which helped contain the spread. Although the fatality of COVID-19 also depends on an individual's age or pre-existing health conditions, nevertheless, the government plays a significant role in implementing public health policies, like funding for testing, enforcing lockdowns, and providing its people with reliable information about the virus. Therefore, this chapter emphasized the significance of presenting a quantitative analysis of the impact that government-imposed stringent measures had on COVID-19 mortality worldwide, in order to pinpoint the most effective measures to reverse or slow both the transmission of the virus and its corresponding death rate. The primary objective was to identify the most efficacious measures in mitigating the virus's transmission and its associated fatality rate. Due to the limited scientific knowledge about this novel virus, the enactment of stringent policies was the only option in the early days of the virus outbreak to help keep transmission rates in check before the possible rollout of the vaccine and save countless lives. The quantitative analysis of those policies was aimed at generating the debate to pinpoint the policies that were most effective in decreasing the COVID-19 infection rates and supporting a declining global economy.

The objective of this chapter is to comprehend if the non-pharmaceutical government interventions in terms of the stringent policies adopted by various governments addressed the COVID-19 mortality rates. If yes, by how much? How did the timing of the policy implementation affect the mortality rate trend? Were the governments' stringent measures reflected in the physical mobility of people within the country? To answer these research questions, this research relied upon the Stringency Index, which calculates the varying degrees of strictness of the measures put in place by countries to control the spread of COVID-19. The research encompassed a range of measures, such as school closures, the prohibition of large gatherings, the enforcement of mask mandates, the imposition of curfews, and the implementation of comprehensive lockdowns. These lockdowns also entailed the closure of various businesses, including restaurants, bars, gyms, studios, movie theaters, arcades, etc. Not all intervention forms had the same effectiveness, and therefore, the government stringency variable was employed to measure the collective effectiveness of these interventions. In addition, governments faced the decision to balance economic interests with health-related interests, and thus, some interventions were not worth the trade-off of economic loss. The chapter also discusses the mobility of people as it relates to the transmission of COVID-19 and this mobility of people was analyzed as the movement of people as a whole, rather than the movement to specific categories of location. For example, if a government imposed a lockdown, how did the mobility patterns of people change regarding this mandate? In this way, the mobility data provided insight into how strictly the government mandate was enforced or adhered to. Since this chapter analyzes the timing of policy as well, what is considered to be the appropriate timeline for policy implementation could be defined in relation to the pandemic as a whole. This research defined 'early' as the timeframe in which the first five cases of COVID-19 were reported in any said country to assess when the country began implementing policies against this pandemic.

2 Literature Review

The twenty-first century is familiar with contagions such as severe acute respiratory syndrome (SARS), Middle East Respiratory Syndrome, and Ebola outbreaks. These contagions are different from other health threats because of their virulence, transmissibility, and invisible nature. The literature on the subject of COVID-19 (SARS-CoV-2) may be considered in its early stages of maturity with respect to long-term implications, nevertheless, De Larochelambert et al. (2020) showed that a high level of government effectiveness could not alleviate higher COVID-19 death rates in countries that were already in the midst of a static or decreasing life expectancy paired with high income and a high rate of non-communicable diseases. Therefore, the authors relied on variables of average life expectancy, average income, and rate of non-communicable diseases to supplement their findings on government effectiveness and concluded that due to the nature of the virus, COVID-19 mortality was predetermined by inherent factors and not by public decisions. Furthermore, the study professed that the government response was measured by three indices (measured on a scale of 1–100) to reflect the level of the government action using the Oxford COVID-19 Government Response Tracker: Containment and Health Index (lockdown restriction, testing policies, investment in healthcare and vaccines), Stringency Index (strictness of policies), and Economic Support Index (income support and debt relief). On the other hand, the study calculated mortality rates as a ratio between the total number of deaths and the population size of each country, with an endpoint of August 31, 2020. However, their analysis differs from the research in this chapter as the different timeframes of data sets show different policy effectiveness depending on the severity of COVID-19 transmission at the time. Since by the end of 2020, some countries had claimed to have been hit by 3 separate waves of COVID-19, it must be considered whether the data used in the research was from the peak time of COVID-19's mortality rate or another specified time.

Conversely, Dergiades et al. (2020) while focusing primarily on government policies and stringencies found that the strength of government interventions and the timing of government action at the early stages of the COVID-19 outbreak had a significant impact on reducing the growing COVID-19 mortality rate. This research used daily data from 32 countries, differing from the previously mentioned study which used 188 countries, partially accounting for discrepancies between findings. The study also used the Oxford University data source to analyze the impact of government interventions on a country's daily trends of COVID-19-related deaths and accounted for changes within government response, concluding that governments that began with a low-strength policy measure but increased the strength of their response were successful in slowing down or reversing the growth rate of deaths. Flaxman et al. (2020) rendered that the lockdown in Europe from May 2020 to June 2020 had a considerable impact on the reducing transmission of the virus. This study reported that the various government intervention methods were implemented in rapid succession, making it difficult to analyze the individual effects of each intervention. Thus, only the effect of lockdown was identifiable, but it has had a 'substantial effect.' Even within analysis between countries, the impressive effect of lockdown remained consistent. Their research compared a model country with no interventions with models that had interventions and calculated that across 11 countries included in the report, concluding that 2.8–3.5 million deaths were averted because of these government interventions, and therefore, the implemented measures seemed to control the pandemic during the selected timeframe.

Brauner et al. (2021) analyzed the impact of non-pharmaceutical government interventions on first-wave COVID-19 spread in the case study of 41 countries and concluded that some interventions were robustly more effective than others, such as the closure of educational institutions and banning gatherings remained highly effective; closure of businesses like restaurants, bars, night clubs and delivery of personal services had a small-to-moderate effect; and with these restrictions already in place, stay-at-home mandate had a small impact. Clyde et al. (2021) added to the evidence, simulation studies, and clinical experience of the COVID-19 pandemic by analyzing the impact of stringent policies on mortality growth rate in the case study of 37 OECD (Organization for Economic Cooperation and Development) countries. This study used the timeframe of 70 days after implementation of containment policies from March 2020 to October 2020 and analyzed their impact till January 2021. The findings of this research showed school closure and restrictions on public transport to have a persistently significant influence on mortality rates while the stay-at-home mandate was seen as effective after the span of 70 days with a 90% significance level. The closure of workplaces and restrictions on internal travel were observed to have no significant impact.

The research yielded valuable insights into maintaining public life with reduced restrictions rather than resorting to more stringent measures at all levels. Xiu et al. (2022) also contributed to the global evidence by assessing the impact of strict containment policies against COVID-19 spread and revealed that policies involving the restriction of international travel and the closure of public transportation consistently proved effective in mitigating the disease's spread within one week of implementation. Moreover, the policy impact was observed to be strong in countries with higher population density and countries with cultural tightness. The other policies were shown to have little to no impact according to this study.

Brodeur et al. (2021) discussed mobility measures and the differences between four different mobility data providers in their methodology including Google LLC Community Mobility Reports, 'Unacast,' 'Safegraph,' and 'Baidu' Maps. The review showed that mobility data could not explain everything about social distancing and transmission. For example, mobility data was limited to people with smartphones or GPS locators. Moreover, this data was insufficient to determine the risk of transmission. To understand the trade-off between different levels of interventions, specifically in the United States, Agrawal et al. (2023) stated '... a small decrease in mobility reduces the number of deaths; however, after registering a 40% drop in mobility, the benefits of restrictions diminish,' meaning the reduction of the number of deaths was not as significant after a certain cut-off. The authors showed that a decrease in mobility did not automatically correlate to a decrease in COVID-19 transmission, and therefore, deaths. Likewise, an increase in mobility restrictions by the governments did not correlate to a slowing or reversing of the COVID-19 mortality rate. Instead, the authors seemed to believe that lifting the most severe of mobility restrictions might actually have reduced the death rate due to COVID-19 in the U.S., but this claim is highly debatable. However, various studies on COVID-19-induced anxiety and depression supported this opinion of lifting the strict restrictions. These studies used different scales to make the case that the stricter measures prompted fear in public and disturbed their mental health, such as Amin (2020) employed the Likert scale for measuring coronaphobic responses to healthcare workers while Lee (2020) used a 5-item screener for clinical levels of anxiety related to COVID-19 which is known as the Coronavirus Anxiety Scale, and Collins (2021) developed a 10-item scale to measure the COVID-19-induced anxiety (Kachanoff et al., 2020).

Within the existing research on governments' policy interventions in relation to COVID-19, there are discrepancies between its correlation to COVID-19 mortality rates and these inconsistencies exist mainly due to varying data collection methods and different definitions of government effectiveness. Although there is still much to be learned about this pandemic, the evidence in the form of literature on this subject has been gaining ground. The review of existing literature clarifies where the existing research focused its attention, what research has not already been looked at, and where arguments within the field lie. Even within a single correlation such as government effectiveness, these studies disagree about one, if the correlation and COVID-19 transmission in a country have a relationship, and two, to what extent.

3 Research Methodology

The existing literature portrays a weak consensus on the degree to which government effectiveness alleviated the COVID-19 mortality rates at the peak of this pandemic. This chapter takes into account the WZB Berlin Social Center's project called 'Dashboard: Social and Political Correlates of COVID-19.' After studying multiple measures, the variable 'Government Effectiveness' was selected for analysis using the Government Effectiveness Index by the World Bank Group. It measured the quality of public service, policy formulation, policy implementation, and the credibility of governments' commitment as these factors hypothetically played a vital role in the outcome of the pandemic. To validate this hypothesis, the R Studio was employed for data visualization and analysis. Consequently, in the graphs, there were many outliers and a very weak correlation with the mortality rate as the Government Effectiveness Index value could not reflect the changes made in policies on the onset of the COVID-19 pandemic or the subsequent change in the number of cases or deaths in that country respectively. Moreover, it did not take into account the improvement of services in response to COVID-19. Therefore, government effectiveness was measured by taking into view the varying stringency of policies enacted by governments around the world. This research hypothesized that the countries that implemented stringent policies in response to this pandemic earlier were able to keep the COVID-19 death rates low, and the countries that did implement stringent policies but were not able to lower the COVID-19 mortality rates had internal movement within the country as it was not reduced by much, and therefore, the policies were not either followed or enforced or both. Mobility, thus, was used as a way of analyzing the outliers. These outliers were countries that seemed to have stringent government interventions, yet no resulting reduction in the COVID-19 mortality rates as Agrawal et al. (2023) suggested that there is an important trade-off for government entities to consider whether the intervention's effectiveness against COVID-19 transmission mattered more or the economic downturn it caused did.

Stringency was calculated using the Stringency Index published by the Oxford COVID-19 Government Response Tracker (OxCGRT). It collected the latest available information on indicators of government response by enacting policies, such as school closures and travel bans, and also by recording them on a common scale. The composite measure from 0 to 100 is an additive score of the 9 indicators: school closures, workplace closures, cancelation of public events, restrictions on gatherings, closure of public transport, public information campaigns, stay-at-home mandate, restrictions on internal movement, and international travel controls. This stringency data measured government lockdown mandates and this chapter provides evidence for the positive side of government lockdowns as an effective form of intervention that averted COVID-19-related deaths. The OxCGRT tracker warns that it should 'not be interpreted as a rating of the appropriateness or effectiveness of a country's response.' Mobility was determined through the Mobility Index measured by Google as it provided insight into physically measurable change resulting from policy changes in order to assess if the lockdown policies implemented by the government resulted in a change in people's movement trends over time or not. The COVID-19 Community Mobility Reports by Google separated movement trends into different categories of places: retail and recreation, groceries and pharmacies, parks, transit stations, workplaces, and residences. The aggregated data was collected from anonymized individuals who turned on their 'Location History' settings. However, this setting is off by default and that is why the data trend had some gaps because of the users whose movements could not be tracked due to their 'Location History' being disabled. Considering how the mobility data was used in this chapter, at what point mobility stops factoring into COVID-19 mortality was not necessarily focused keeping in mind that mobility and COVID-19 do not necessarily have an automatic correlation.

After analyzing the mortality data files of the World Health Organization (WHO) Coronavirus (COVID-19) Dashboard, 22 countries were chosen from the list of countries most affected by COVID-19. As shown in Fig. 1, these countries were then divided into five groups based on the percentage of the population with 65+ age recorded before the pandemic hit, keeping in view the significance of age as a factor contributing to a higher number of deaths caused by COVID-19 infections. Using this grouping technique, the age factor-related variations in COVID-19 mortality were minimized and the effects of stringent policies and the time when these policies were implemented on COVID-19 mortality rates were observed more accurately. In countries like Germany where 65+ people make up more than 20% of the total population and the United Arab Emirates (UAE) where 65+ people make up only about 2% of the total population, the cumulative deaths in the former would be much higher than in a country like the UAE where there are fewer people over the age of 65. Since this chapter focused specifically on the effectiveness of stringency and mobility on COVID-19 mortality, the grouping attempted to factor out the age to the extent possible. In order to make fair comparisons, there were no comparisons between a country with a lower elderly population and a country with a higher elderly population. The following plot shows the breakdown of the share of the population that is above the age of 65, from the countries with the least share to the greatest share in ascending order.

Data was analyzed in the timeframe of four months, starting from February 2020 till the end of May 2020, against each country's mortality rate and Stringency Index. This timeframe was chosen because the scientific knowledge about the nature of this virus at that time was very limited and no pharmaceutical interventions were available to prevent the infection, so the governments only had the option to enact containment policies to curb the spread of COVID-19. Later on, other factors such as elaborate scientific knowledge on the transmission patterns of Coronavirus, availability of immunity boosters, awareness campaigns, and the provision of advanced healthcare facilities, more ventilators, and vaccines also started to affect the COVID-19 mortality rates and studying the impact of a factor in isolation became more difficult in the real-world setup. Therefore, the mean Stringency Index was calculated to analyze the stringency of policies during the timeframe with the sharp increasing trend to the point where it was maintained at a certain level or started decreasing.

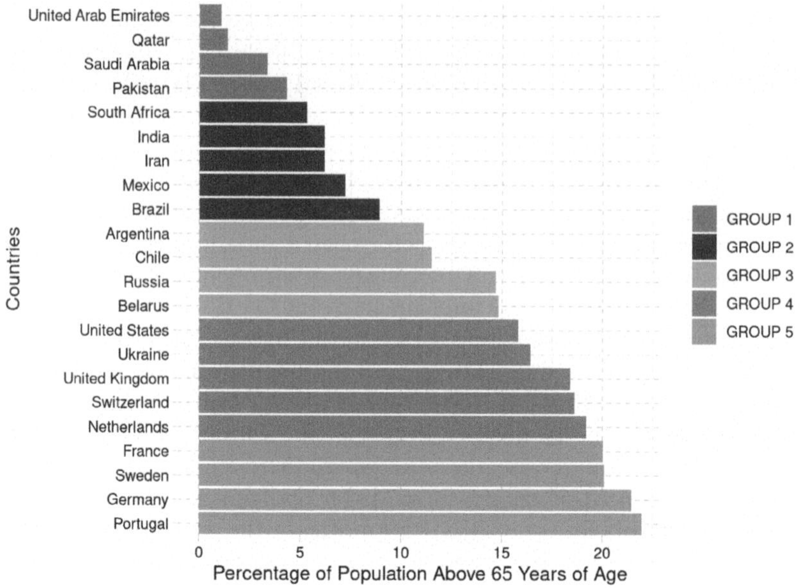

Fig. 1 Classification of selected countries according to the percentage of the population with 65+ age (*Source* Author's calculations)

In the analysis of selected 22 countries, at least five confirmed cases were reported by the first 10 days of March 2020, and COVID-19-related deaths were recorded to begin as early as the beginning of March. Therefore, the impact of the strength of stringent policies in these months on COVID-19 mortality was observed to be reflected in the mortality rates which kept increasing in the first few months. This timeframe is also significant because the changes in stringent policies and mobility in the starting months of the COVID-19 outbreak affected the morality in upcoming months as well because it is quite possible that some deaths occurred very soon after the transmission of the virus but in many cases, death was not an immediate reaction to the infection. Quality of healthcare also sped up or delayed deaths influencing the mortality rate curve. For instance, the use of ventilators increased the time between getting infected and dying. Therefore, it seems reasonable to say that the mortality rate in the month of May 2020 could have been affected greatly by the changes in Government Stringency and the Mobility Index of the preceding month. Again, the 'early' stage was determined as the time before or equal to the day when at least the first five confirmed COVID-19 cases were reported.

4 Results and Discussion

As illustrated in Figs. 2 and 3, the overall analysis of the average infection rate and the average mortality rate, respectively, against the average stringency for all 22 countries showed a negative correlation implying that with the increasing stringency, a decrease in the spread of disease and disease-induced deaths was observed. However, the analysis of the average mortality rate against the average stringency had many outliers where the death count kept rising even after the enactment of stringent policies but that can be justified by the fact that the already infected patients in the preceding months could not recover from the disease and died. Moreover, this trend can also be attributed to other factors such as timely diagnosis and treatment of the infection or fragile healthcare infrastructure of countries under study that couldn't handle the outbreak of the pandemic. The combined analysis of all countries, however, did not address the differences in the population of the elderly who were more likely to get infected and less likely to recover from the disease due to weaker immunity as compared to the other age groups. Therefore, the countries were grouped based on the percentage of the elderly population in order to make a fair comparison and rule out the age factor to the extent possible.

4.1 Group 1 Analysis

Among the 22 selected countries, the countries with a percentage of elderly population ranging from 0 to 5% included Pakistan, Qatar, Saudi Arabia, and the United Arab Emirates. The dates (MM/DD/YYYY) for all the countries in this group with at least five confirmed cases of COVID-19 officially reported were March 4, 2020 for Pakistan, March 4, 2020 for Qatar, March 6, 2020 for Saudi Arabia, and January 27, 2020 for the United Arab Emirates. As shown in Fig. 4, the variations in the Stringency Index for all four countries from the start of February 2020 to the end of May 2020 indicated that there was a sharp increase in the value of the Stringency Index for all four countries after the start of March 2020. This trend suggested that Pakistan started implementing

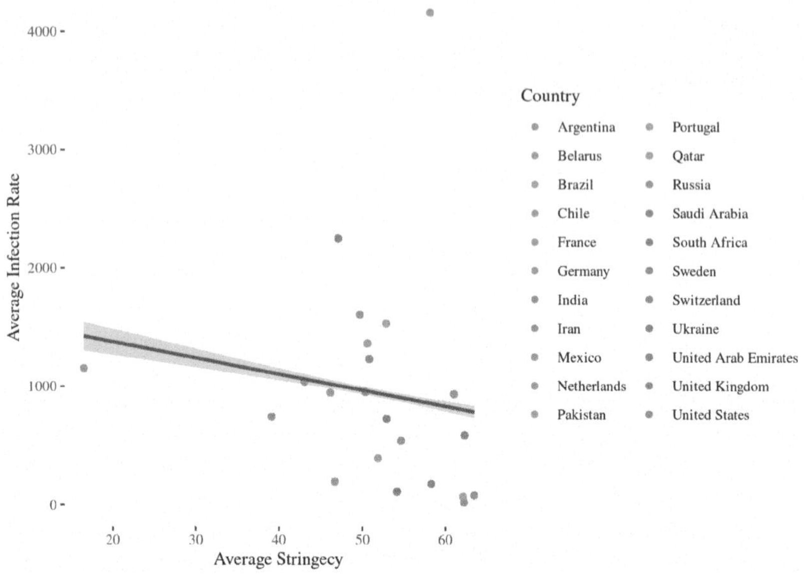

Fig. 2 The correlation between the mean Stringency Index and the mean infection rate of all 22 countries (*Source* Author's calculations)

stringent policies earlier as compared to the other three countries in the group. The dates when at least five confirmed cases of COVID-19 were reported in Pakistan, Qatar, and Saudi Arabia were very close together, i.e., the first week of March. Additionally, the value of the Stringency Index for Pakistan was observed at over 25 at the start of March and for the other three countries, it was observed below 15 where the United Arab Emirates started implementing stringent policies almost a month after the first five confirmed cases were reported. Moreover, the value of the Stringency Index for Qatar was slightly higher than that of Saudi Arabia at the start of March but after the start of April, Saudi Arabia and UAE gained the lead over Qatar. Despite these differences, it can be concluded that these three countries were not too late in implementing stringent policies.

Figure 5 represents the infection rate (per 100,000 people) for each of these same four countries from February 2020 to the end of May 2020, and Fig. 6 shows the variations in mortality rate (per 100,000 people) for each of these same four countries from February 2020 to the end

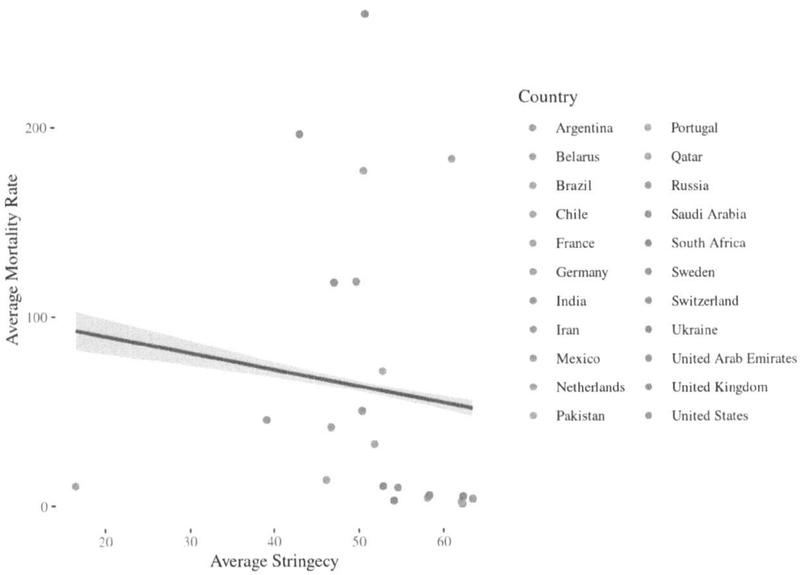

Fig. 3 The correlation between the mean Stringency Index and the mean mortality rate of all 22 countries (*Source* Author's calculations)

of May 2020. According to the curve shown in Fig. 5, the infection rate of Pakistan remained the lowest among all four countries as Pakistan was the first country to enact lockdown policies, mitigating the spread of COVID-19. The infection rate of Qatar, which had the lowest stringency measures among the group, can be observed increasing exponentially by mid-April and holding the leading position till the end of May with about 20,000 infections per 10,000 population. On the other hand, the infection rates of Saudi Arabia and the UAE can be seen increasing hand in hand after mid-May with the UAE in the lead, however, both of these states remained below 5,000 infections per 100,000 population by the end of May 2020.

As illustrated in Fig. 6, the death rates in Pakistan remained the lowest in the group throughout the timeframe while that of the UAE (from mid-April to the end of May 2020) were much higher than the other three countries in the group as Pakistan started implementing stringent policies quite earlier, unlike the UAE. Thus, these two plots support the hypotheses that countries that acted early in response to COVID-19 were

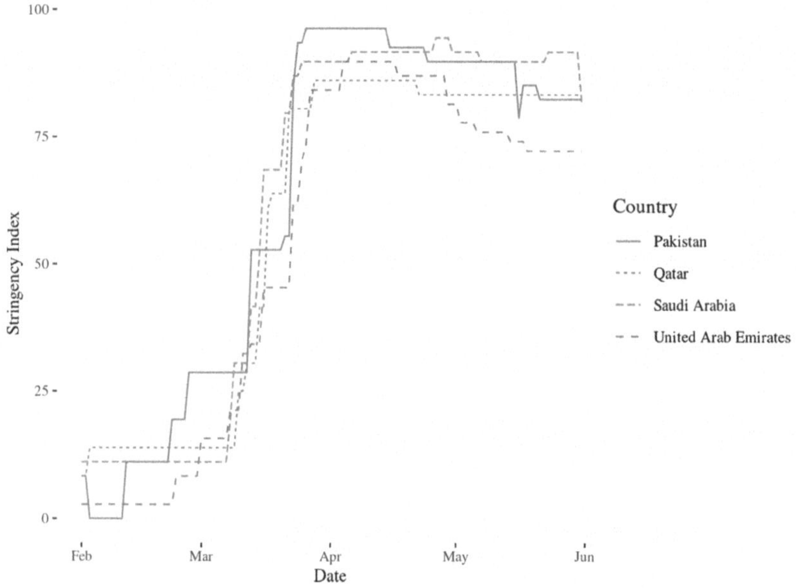

Fig. 4 Stringency Index of Group 1 countries from the start of February to the end of May 2020 (*Source* Author's calculations)

more successful in keeping the COVID-19 mortality rates lower at the start of the pandemic as compared to countries that acted late.

Figure 7 shows the relationship between the mean Stringency Index from the start of February to the end of May 2020 against the mean infection rate for all four countries of Group 1, and Fig. 8 shows the relationship between the mean Stringency Index from the start of February to the end of May 2020 against mean mortality rate for all four countries of Group 1.

It can be observed from the data represented in Figs. 7 and 8 that Pakistan has the second-highest value of mean stringency and the lowest mean infection rate as well as mean mortality rate, supporting the hypothesis that the countries that acted earliest in response to the COVID-19 outbreak and enacted stringent policies were able to curb the transmission rates and COVID-19-related deaths. The Kingdom of Saudi Arabia had the highest Stringency Index, lower infection rate, and an average of five deaths per 100,000 population, mildly supporting the hypotheses.

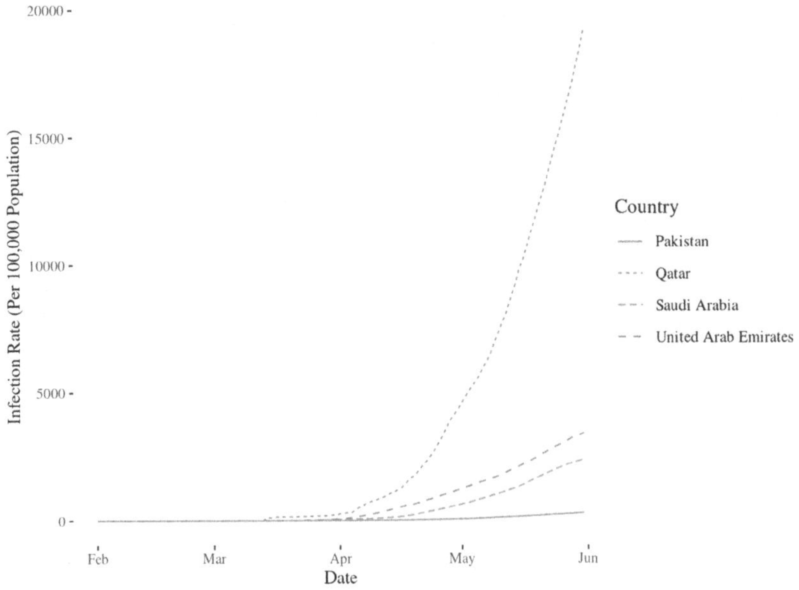

Fig. 5 Infection rates of Group 1 countries from the start of February to the end of May 2020 (*Source* Author's calculations)

The UAE, on the other hand, had the lowest mean stringency value in the group, the mean infection rate exceeding that of Saudi Arabia and Pakistan, and the highest mean mortality rate, supporting the hypothesis that countries with lower stringency and a late response had higher spread and death rates. The mean infection rate of Qatar was recorded as the highest which can be justified by the fact that Qatar had lower stringency as compared to that of Pakistan and Saudi Arabia, however, the mortality rate of Qatar was lesser than that of Saudi Arabia due to unknown factors. The lower percentage of the elderly population in Qatar might be the reason behind this trend.

The overall trend line represents a weak negative correlation between the mean stringency and the mean infection rate of Group 1 countries, showing that the stringent measures did not fully curb the infection rates. However, the trendline of mean stringency and mean mortality rate represents a strong negative correlation, implying that the stringent measures significantly reduced COVID-19-related deaths. It can be

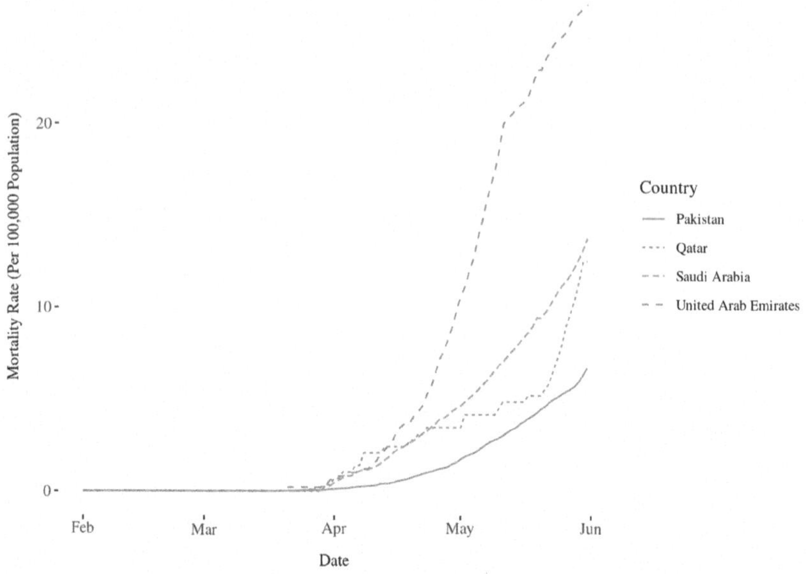

Fig. 6 Mortality rates of Group 1 countries from the start of February to the end of May 2020 (*Source* Author's calculations)

concluded using the linear models that the data for this group supported the theory that implementing stronger stringent policies in relation to the first five reported cases allowed countries to keep the COVID-19 infection rates and mortality rates lower, the latter more significantly than the former. Figure 9 displays the relationship between Mobility Index and Stringency Index for all countries in the group.

The graphs in Fig. 9 portrayed the strong negative correlation highlighting that the people in all of the four countries followed their government's COVID-19 mandates as the Mobility Index can be observed falling with the rising Stringency Index. Since significant differences can be seen in the correlation coefficient values of the Stringency Index against the Mobility Index graphs of the four countries, it is reasonable to state that there is a strong relationship between people adhering to a government's stringent policies and the country's mortality rate. Therefore, the overall data for Group 1 suggested that the countries that implemented stringent policies earlier in response to COVID-19 did better in terms of keeping the COVID-19 mortality rates low.

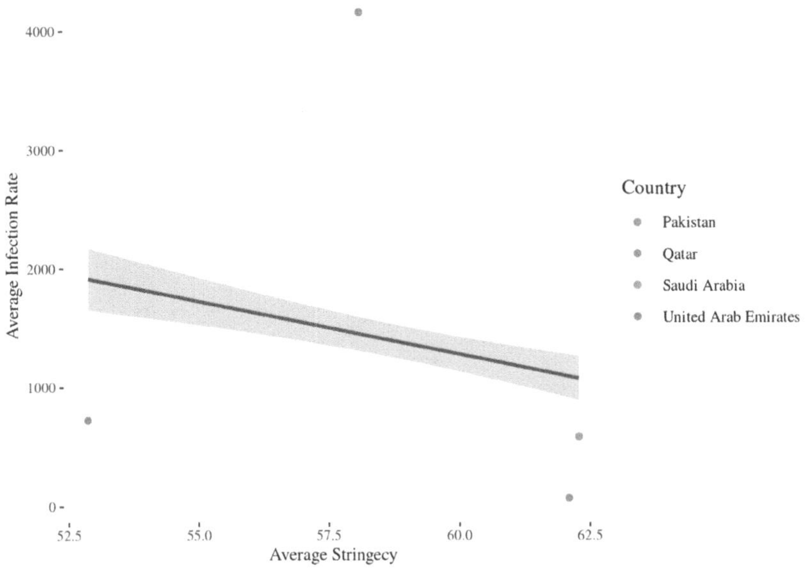

Fig. 7 The correlation between Group 1's mean Stringency Index and mean infection rate (*Source* Author's calculations)

4.2 Group 2 Analysis

The second group consisted of Brazil, India, Iran, Mexico, and South Africa, where the percentage of older people ranged from 5 to 10%. The dates (MM/DD/YYYY) for all the countries in this group with at least five confirmed reported cases of COVID-19 were March 6, 2020 for Brazil, March 3, 2020 for India, February 21, 2020 for Iran, February 25, 2020 for Mexico, and March 10, 2020 for South Africa. Figure 10 represents variations in the Stringency Index for all five countries from the start of February to the end of May 2020.

According to data shown in Fig. 10, an increase in Stringency Index values for all the countries except Mexico started somewhere near the date when at least five confirmed cases of COVID-19 were reported. It is important to notice that Mexico was very late in responding to COVID-19 as compared to the other countries in the group and while Iran started enhancing stringency to combat the pandemic earlier than other group members, it had the lowest stringency by the end of April 2020 which

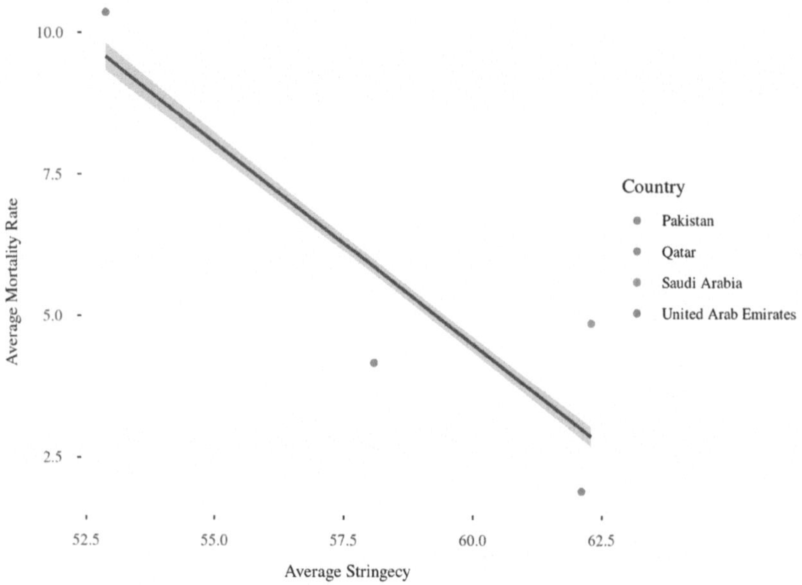

Fig. 8 The correlation between Group 1's mean Stringency Index and mean mortality rate (*Source* Author's calculations)

kept the decline proceeding further. Figure 11 displays the infection rate (per 100,000 people) for each of these five countries from February 2020 to the end of May 2020, whereas Fig. 12 shows variations in the mortality rate (per 100,000 people) for the same countries and timeframe.

It can be observed that the spread rate of COVID-19 infections, as well as deaths due to COVID-19 in Iran, started occurring by the start of March and these rates were quite higher as compared to the rest of the countries till the start of May which can be attributed to lower stringency value of the preceding month. For Brazil and Mexico, the infection rate as well as COVID-19-related deaths continued to increase rapidly in May 2020 where the infection rate of Mexico was lower, and the mortality rate was higher than that of Brazil. The infection and mortality rates of South Africa and India can however be observed as quite lower than that of other group members toward the end of May 2020. The delayed response to the COVID-19 outbreak with a comparatively lower Stringency Index can be inferred as the reason for the higher mortality rate in Brazil and

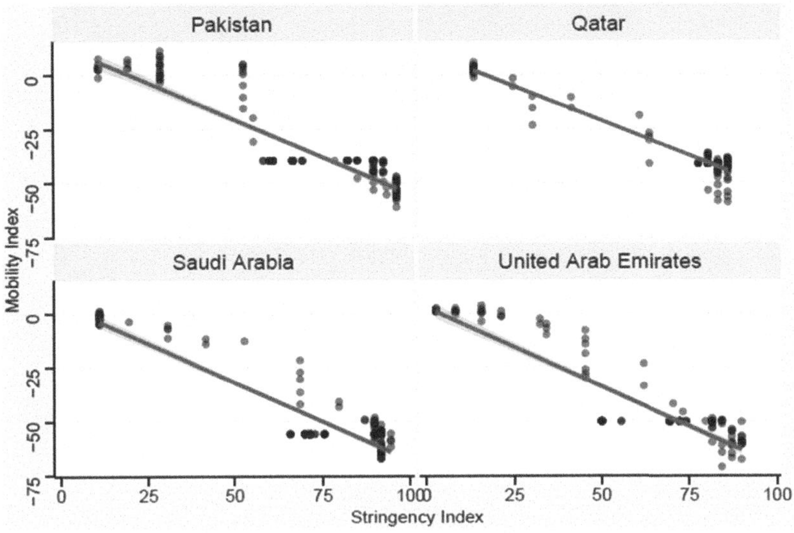

Fig. 9 The correlation between Stringency Index and Mobility Index of Group 1 countries (*Source* Author's calculations)

Mexico. Figure 13 shows the relationship between the mean Stringency Index from February to May and the mean infection rate for all four countries in Group 2 and Fig. 14 illustrates the relationship between the mean stringency and the mean mortality rate for the same countries and timeframe.

It is worth noting that Iran had the lowest mean value for the Stringency Index and the highest mean infection and mortality rates. Mexico, on the other hand, due to acting late in response to COVID-19 as compared to other countries and having the second lowest value for the mean Stringency Index, managed to keep the mean COVID-19 infection rate lower than that of Brazil as shown in Fig. 13; but mean COVID-19 mortality rate was quite higher like Iran as shown in Fig. 14. The trends of India and South Africa also support the hypothesis that countries with more stringent policies had significantly lower infection and mortality rates amid the COVID-19 pandemic. In general, the linear models in these graphs depict a strong negative correlation of the mean Stringency Index with the mean infection rate as well as the mean mortality rate. This type of trend suggests that the overall data for Group 2 supports the

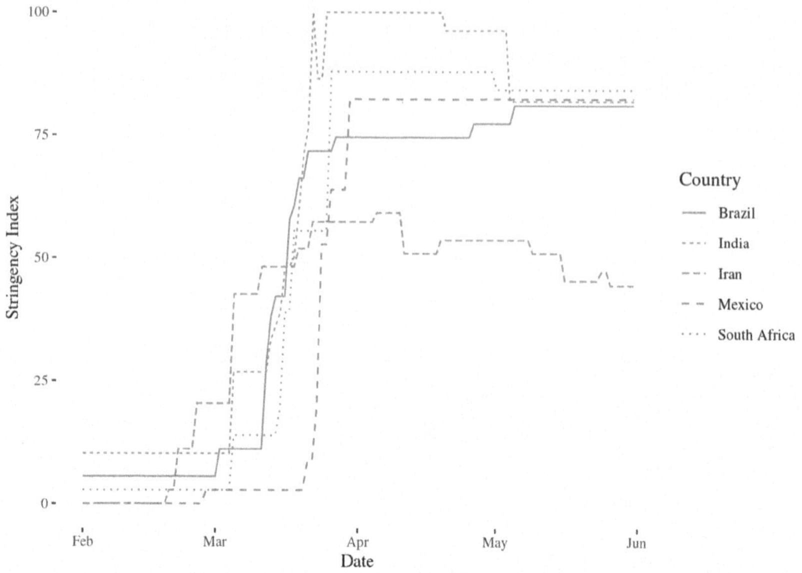

Fig. 10 Stringency Index of Group 2 countries from the start of February to the end of May 2020 (*Source* Author's calculations)

theory that implementing stronger stringent policies for a longer time period helped countries keep the COVID-19-related death rate lower. Figure 15 illustrates the relationship between Mobility Index and Stringency Index for the countries in the second group. Note that the mobility data of Iran by Google was not available due to strict regulations on data provision.

Figure 15 highlighted the existence of a negative correlation with a strong coefficient for all the graphs which means the stronger the stringent measures, the lower the mobility of people. However, the negative correlation for Brazil's graph was comparatively weaker than that of other countries in the group which can be inferred as comparatively lower adherence of people to stringent public policies. The general trend in the data for Group 2 suggested that the countries that implemented strong stringent policies for a longer time period were more successful in keeping the mortality rates low in comparison with the countries that didn't. Moreover, the data for this group supported the theory that the countries that had more stringent policies in response to COVID-19 did

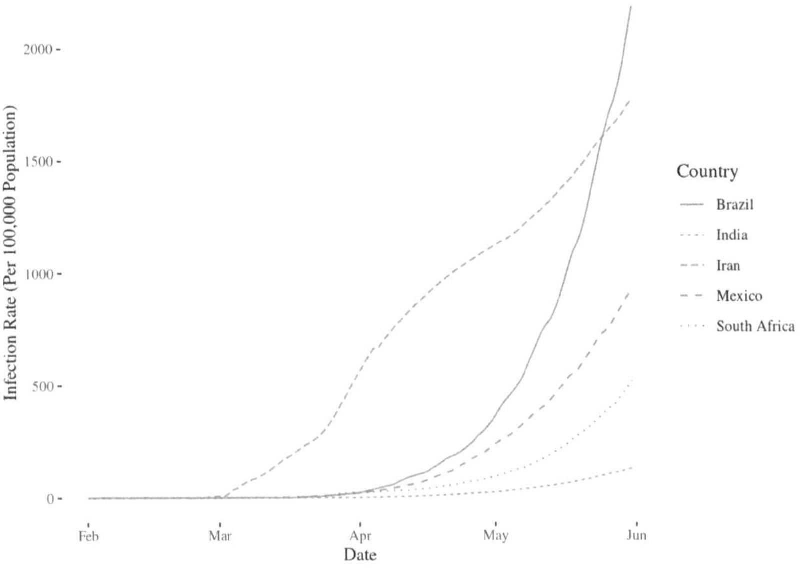

Fig. 11 Infection rates of Group 2 countries from the start of February to the end of May 2020 (*Source* Author's calculations)

better in terms of keeping the mortality rate low. Mexico had a lower mortality rate than that of Brazil, but higher than that of India and South Africa due to the late enactment of containment policies. Moreover, the correlation between Brazil's Mobility Index and Stringency Index graph is the weakest in the group and the mean mortality rate is the second highest. However, this evidence is not enough to draw the conclusion that people's adherence to their government's mandate aided in keeping the COVID-19 mortality rate in check.

4.3 Group 3 Analysis

Countries in the selected list where the percentage of older people lies between 10 and 15% are Argentina, Belarus, Chile, and Russia. The dates (MM/DD/YYYY) for all the countries in this group with at least five confirmed reported cases of COVID-19 were March 7, 2020 for Argentina, March 5, 2020 for Belarus, March 7, 2020 for Chile, and

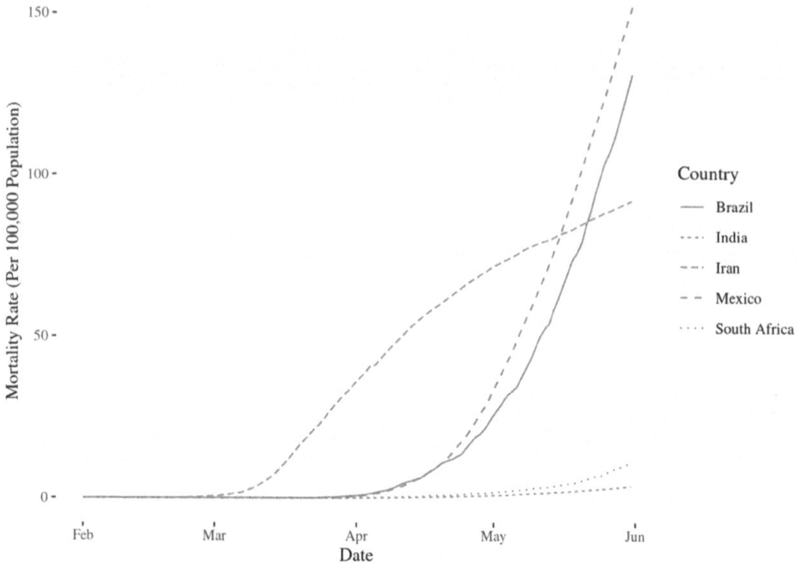

Fig. 12 Mortality rates of Group 2 countries from the start of February to the end of May 2020 (*Source* Author's calculations)

March 7, 2020 for Russia. Figure 16 illustrates the variations in the Stringency Index for all four countries from the start of February to the end of May 2020.

Considering both Fig. 16 and the dates when at least five cases were reported, Russia can be observed to have acted early in response to the COVID-19 outbreak followed by Argentina. Chile and Belarus had the Stringency Index value at zero till mid-March and the values for Belarus remained lowest throughout the timeframe of this study. However, the Stringency Index values of Chile rose sharply afterward but did not go as high as those of Argentina and Russia. Figure 17 shows the infection rate (per 100,000 people) for all four countries from February 2020 to the end of May 2020, whereas Fig. 18 displays variations in mortality rate (per 100,000 people) for the same countries and timeframe.

As illustrated in Figs. 17 and 18, Chile was the leading member in terms of COVID-19 infection rate as well as mortality rate by the end of May 2020, mainly due to the delay in responding to the COVID-19 outbreak through policy interventions. Belarus led the list of infection

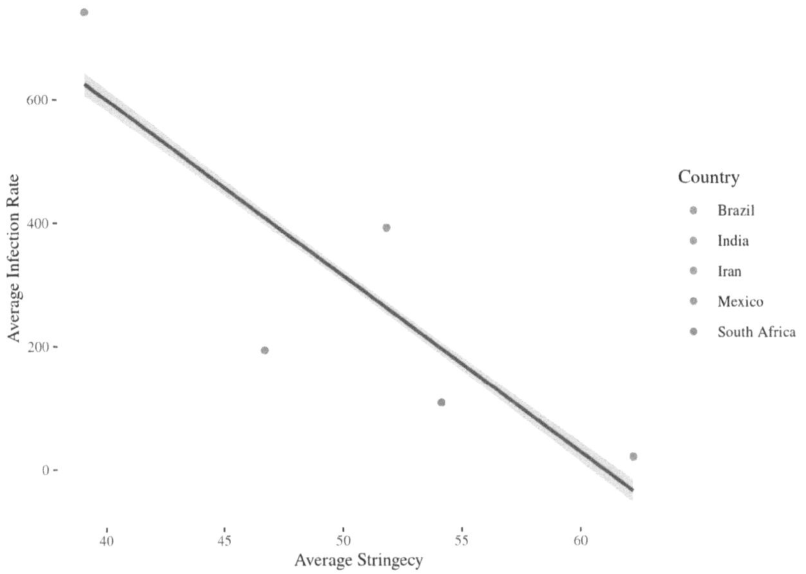

Fig. 13 The correlation between Group 2's mean Stringency Index and mean infection rate (*Source* Author's calculations)

rates from mid-April to mid-May and remained the second highest in terms of mortality till the beginning of May. Argentina, acting earlier as compared to Chile and Belarus, was successful in keeping the infection and mortality rates lowest till the end of May. Russia was the earliest to enact containment policies against COVID-19 spread with the highest stringency almost throughout the selected timeframe, however, the spread and death rates rose sharply toward the end of April. Figures 19 and 20 illustrate the relationship between the mean Stringency Index from February to the end of May against the mean infection rate and mean mortality rate for all four countries in Group 3, respectively.

The trends in the graphs for Group 3 suggested that the enactment of strict policies for a longer time period helped countries keep the COVID-19 infection rate as well as mortality rate significantly lower referring to the case of Russia and Argentina. Russia was a very good example in terms of response time as it started enacting policies earlier than others. The outlier nature of Chile cannot be ignored for having a higher value for both mean infection rates and mean mortality rates despite having

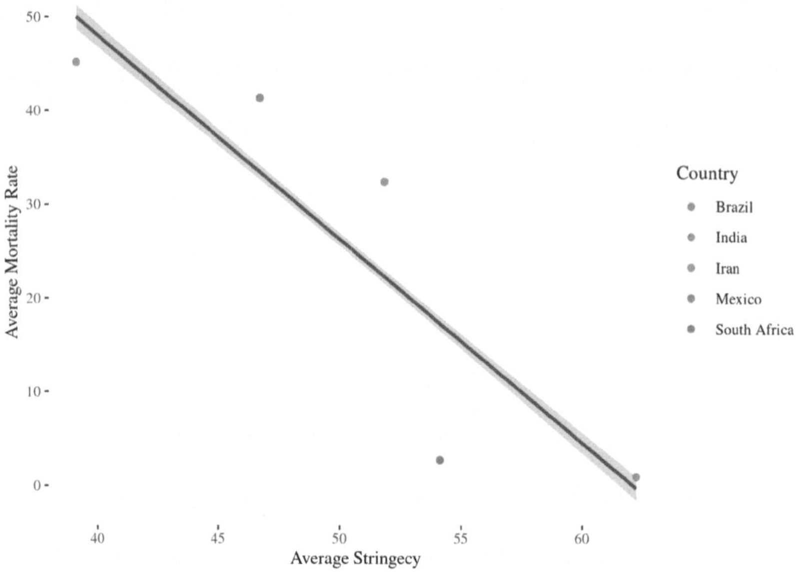

Fig. 14 The correlation between Group 2's mean Stringency Index and mean mortality rate (*Source* Author's calculations)

a comparatively higher value than Belarus for the Stringency Index. The trend line for the mean COVID-19 infection rate against mean stringency showed a stronger negative correlation than the trend line for the mean mortality rate, however, both trends supported the hypothesis that the stricter the containment policies, the lower the spread and mortality of the COVID-19 pandemic. Figure 21 demonstrates the relationship between the Mobility Index and Stringency Index for three countries of Group 3. Note that the mobility data of Russia by Google was not available publicly.

Keeping in view the abovementioned correlation coefficient values, people in both Chile and Argentina followed the lockdown orders issued by their respective governments rigidly in response to the COVID-19 outbreak. By observing the overall data for group 3, trends suggested that the countries that implemented stringent policies early in response to COVID-19 were successful in keeping the mortality rates lower. It can also be observed from the data of this group that the countries that maintained stricter policies for a longer time period were more successful in terms of keeping the COVID-19 mortality rate low. The mean mortality

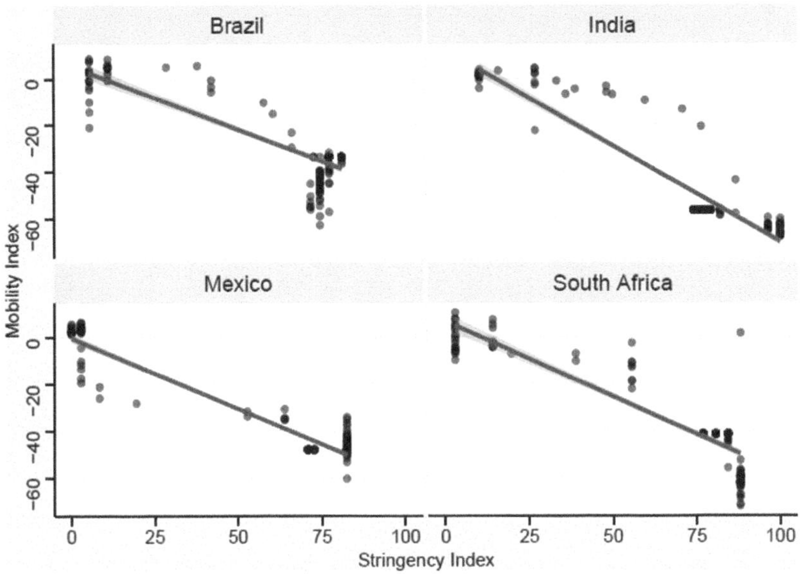

Fig. 15 The correlation between Stringency Index and Mobility Index of Group 2 countries (*Source* Author's calculations)

rate of Chile, being the highest despite the strong negative correlation coefficient value of the Mobility Index against the Stringency Index, and the unavailability of mobility data in Russia made it difficult to draw out any concrete conclusion on whether the people's adherence to their government's policy interventions affected the COVID-19 mortality rate in these countries or not.

4.4 *Group 4 Analysis*

The fourth group comprised countries where the percentage of the elderly population ranges from 15 to 20%. These countries included the Netherlands, Switzerland, Ukraine, the United Kingdom, and the United States. The dates (MM/DD/YYYY) with at least five confirmed officially reported cases of COVID-19 were March 1, 2020 for the Netherlands, February 28, 2020 for Switzerland, March 17, 2020 for Ukraine, February 10, 2020 for the United Kingdom, and January 27, 2020 for

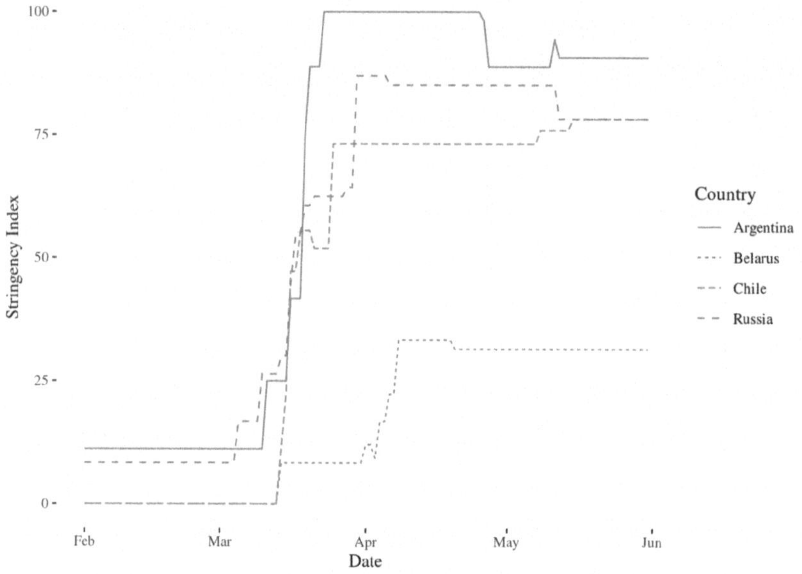

Fig. 16 Stringency Index of Group 3 countries from the start of February to the end of May 2020 (*Source* Author's calculations)

the United States. Figure 22 illustrates the variations in the Stringency Index for all five countries from February to the end of May 2020.

As demonstrated by Fig. 22 and the dates when at least five cases were reported, the United Kingdom was very late in actively responding to the COVID-19 outbreak as compared to other countries of this group. The United States also started acting almost a month after at least five cases were reported. The Netherlands, on the other hand, started enacting containment policies almost a week after at least five cases were reported. Ukraine was the only country that started acting in response to COVID-19 half a month before at least five cases were reported and brought about a sharp rise in terms of stringency with the detection of the first few cases, maintaining the highest value for the Stringency Index during the selected timeframe. The stringency values of all five states were observed at peaks approaching mid-March, residing above 70. Figure 23 illustrates the infection rate (per 100,000 people) for each of these five countries from February 2020 to the end of May 2020, whereas Fig. 24 shows

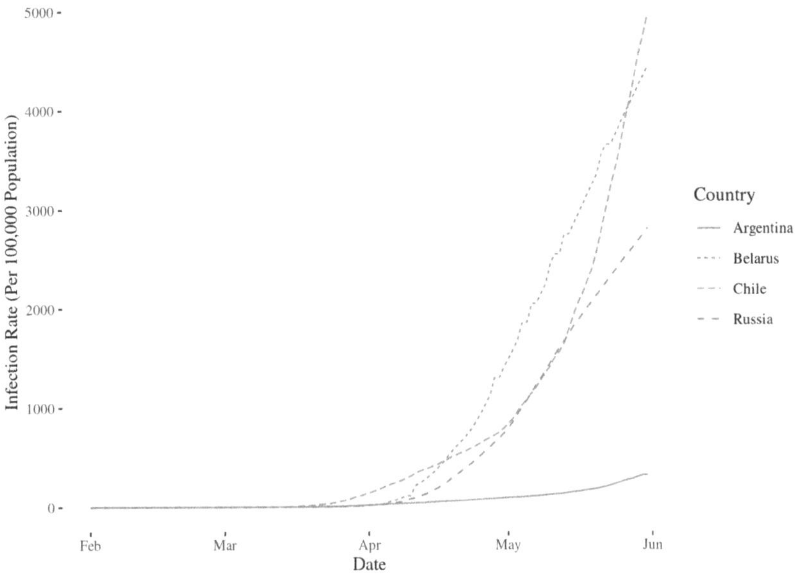

Fig. 17 Infection rates of Group 3 countries from the start of February to the end of May 2020 (*Source* Author's calculations)

variations in the mortality rate (per 100,000 people) for the same states and timeframe.

As shown in Figs. 23 and 24, the infection rate in Switzerland rose rapidly approaching mid-March till the end of April 2020 despite earlier policy interventions. However, the mortality rate was managed by the start of May and then it stayed second to the lowest by the end of May. The infection rate in the United States rose rapidly in April and was recorded to be the highest among the group reaching the end of May 2020, whereas the mortality rate remained lower than that of the United Kingdom and the Netherlands. Moreover, the surge in the COVID-19 infection and mortality rates in the United Kingdom was observed starting from April till the end of May where the transmission rates remained lower than those of Switzerland and the United States. However, the rate of deaths was recorded to be the highest, over 600 per 100,000 population, which can be attributed to a delayed response to the COVID-19 outbreak.

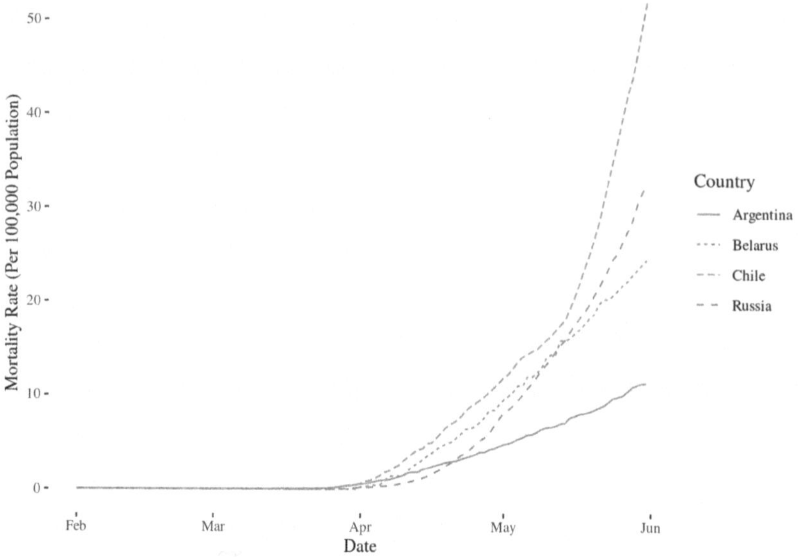

Fig. 18 Mortality rates of Group 3 countries from the start of February to the end of May 2020 (*Source* Author's calculations)

The Netherlands started enacting its containment policies within a week of the first five reported cases and was observed with a mortality rate lower than that of the United Kingdom and higher than that of the United States, Switzerland, and Ukraine by the end of May. Ukraine was the only country to put in place the containment policies to curb transmission of COVID-19 a month before the first five reported cases and maintained the highest stringency value throughout the timeframe, and therefore, had the lowest mean infection and mortality rates. Figures 25 and 26 display the relationship between the mean Stringency Index from February to the end of May 2020 against the mean infection rate and mean mortality rate for all five countries in Group 4, respectively.

Both graphs above illustrated a strong negative correlation between mean stringency and mean infection rate as well as mean stringency and mean mortality rate. The United Kingdom did worst in terms of keeping the mean mortality rate lower as compared to the United States, Switzerland, and the Netherlands despite having a relatively higher value of mean stringency than these three. However, the mean infection rate

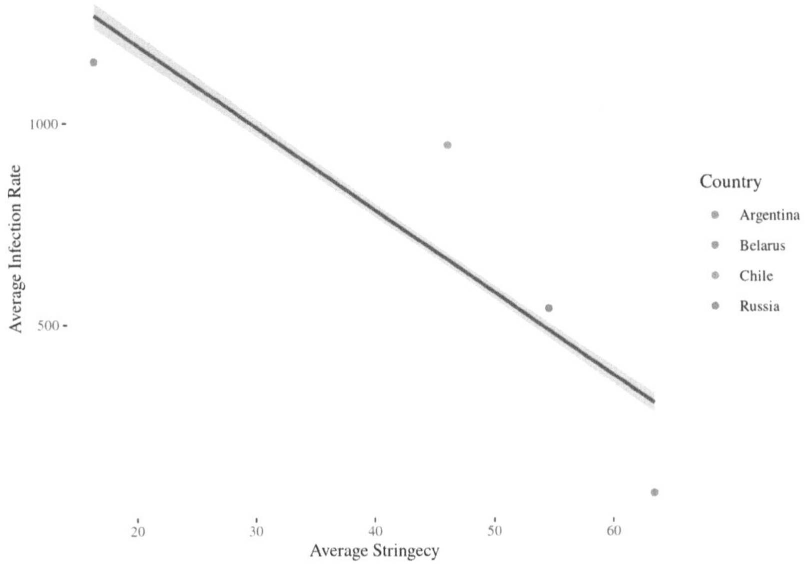

Fig. 19 The correlation between Group 3's mean Stringency Index and mean infection rate (*Source* Author's calculations)

was observed to be significantly lower than that of Switzerland and a little lower than that of the Netherlands and the United States. The Netherlands was observed to have a moderate stringency value with the third-highest average COVID-19 infection rate and the second-highest mean mortality rate. On the other hand, Switzerland was observed to have the lowest mean stringency with the highest mean transmission rate, however, the mean mortality rate was relatively lower than that of the United Kingdom and the Netherlands and the same as the United States. Ukraine had a peak value for mean stringency, with the lowest mean infection and death rates. The overall linear model in the graphs for this group supported the theory that the stricter policies enacted earlier and implemented for a fair amount of time helped countries keep the COVID-19 spread and mortality rates in check. Figure 27 illustrates the relationship between the Mobility Index and Stringency Index for all countries in Group 4 from February 2020 to the end of May 2020. Note that the mobility data for Ukraine by Google was not available publicly.

The figures and the correlation coefficient values indicated that many people in the Netherlands did not strictly follow the stringent policies implemented by their respective governments as compared to people in

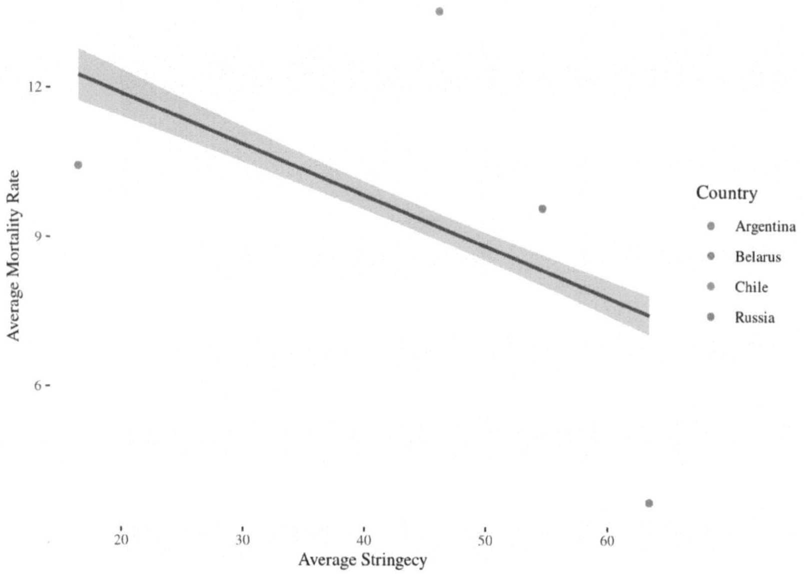

Fig. 20 The correlation between Group 3's mean Stringency Index and mean mortality rate (*Source* Author's calculations)

the other countries of Group 4. This explains higher values for spread and death rates. Moreover, the graph for Switzerland and the United States had a weaker negative correlation than that of the United Kingdom which explains the highest infection rates of both countries, respectively, despite putting in place stringent policies a week before the first five reported cases. The mobility data for the United Kingdom showed rigid adherence of the public to the stringent containment policies, however, the highest mortality rates can be attributed to the late response to tackle the pandemic. Observing the overall data for Group 4, the trends supported the theory that countries that started acting early in response to COVID-19 were successful in terms of keeping the COVID-19 mortality rate low, such as Ukraine. Furthermore, the data also suggested that the countries where people did not adhere to the stringent policies put in place by their governments, faced dire consequences in terms of mortality rate, for instance, the Netherlands.

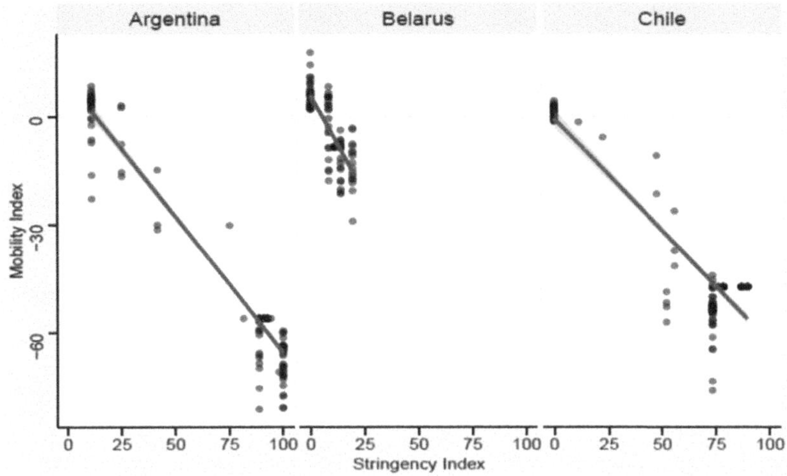

Fig. 21 The correlation between Mobility Index and Stringency Index for countries in Group 3 (*Source* Author's calculations)

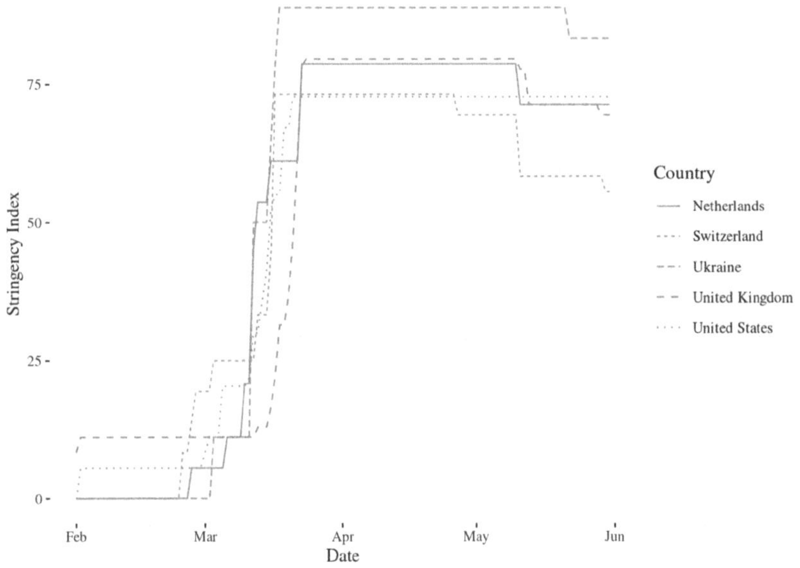

Fig. 22 Stringency Index of Group 4 countries from the start of February to the end of May 2020 (*Source* Author's calculations)

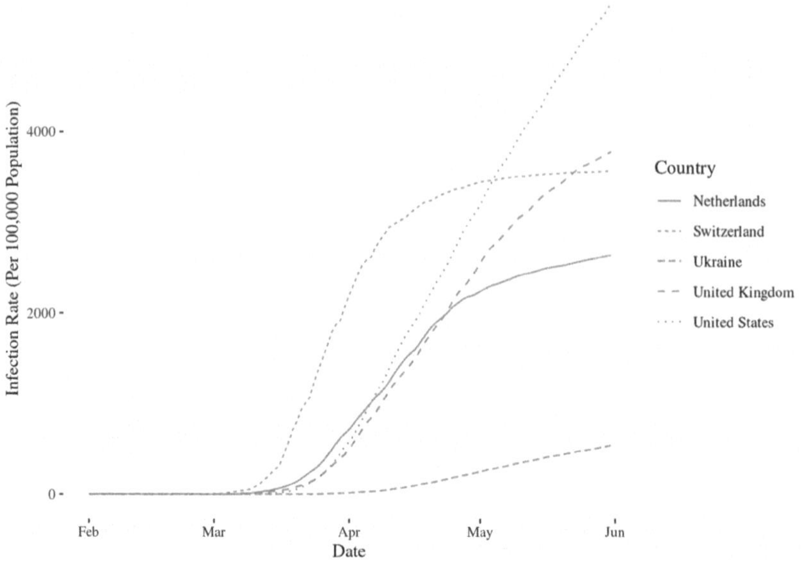

Fig. 23 Infection rates of Group 4 countries from the start of February to the end of May 2020 (*Source* Author's calculations)

4.5 *Group 5 Analysis*

The last group of countries, where the percentage of the elderly population lies between 20 and 25%, included France, Germany, Portugal, and Sweden. The dates (MM/DD/YYYY) with at least five confirmed reported cases of COVID-19 were January 30, 2020 for France, January 31, 2020 for Germany, March 5, 2020 for Portugal, and February 29, 2020 for Sweden. Figure 28 portrays the variations in the Stringency Index for these countries over the time from February to the end of May 2020.

As illustrated in Fig. 28, Portugal was the only country to respond to COVID-19 sometime around the date when at least five confirmed cases were reported. The other three countries were late to implement stringent policies. It is also important to note that Germany took more time to reach the peak value for the Stringency Index after it first started implementing stringent policies in comparison with the other countries in this group. France was about 3 weeks late in responding to the pandemic

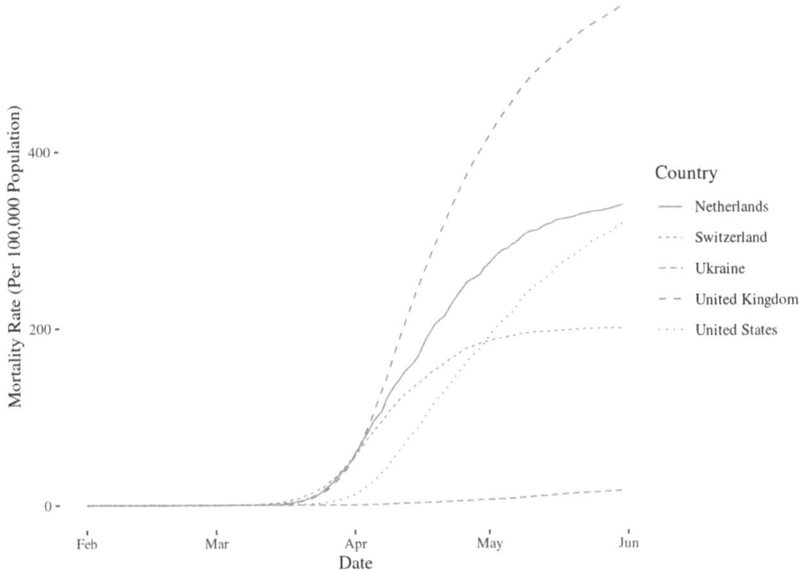

Fig. 24 Mortality rates of Group 4 countries from the start of February to the end of May 2020 (*Source* Author's calculations)

by putting in place stringent policies, however, it had the highest value for the Stringency Index for the remaining time period till May 2020. Figure 29 represents variations in infection rate (per 10,000 people) for all four countries from February to the end of May 2020 and Fig. 30 shows variations in mortality rate (per 100,000 people) for the same countries and timeframe.

The graphs in Figs. 29 and 30 illustrate that Germany and France started acting late in response to COVID-19 and Germany took more time to reach the peak Stringency Index value as compared to other group members. However, they managed to keep the mean infection rates lower than that of Portugal and Sweden, but the mean mortality rate of France was recorded as the highest and that of Germany was recorded as the lowest in the group. On the other hand, Sweden was the last among group members in terms of policy interventions and remained at the lowest value of stringency till mid-May and thus, ended up having the highest COVID-19 infection rate and second-highest mortality rate by the end of May 2020. However, Portugal responded earlier and enacted

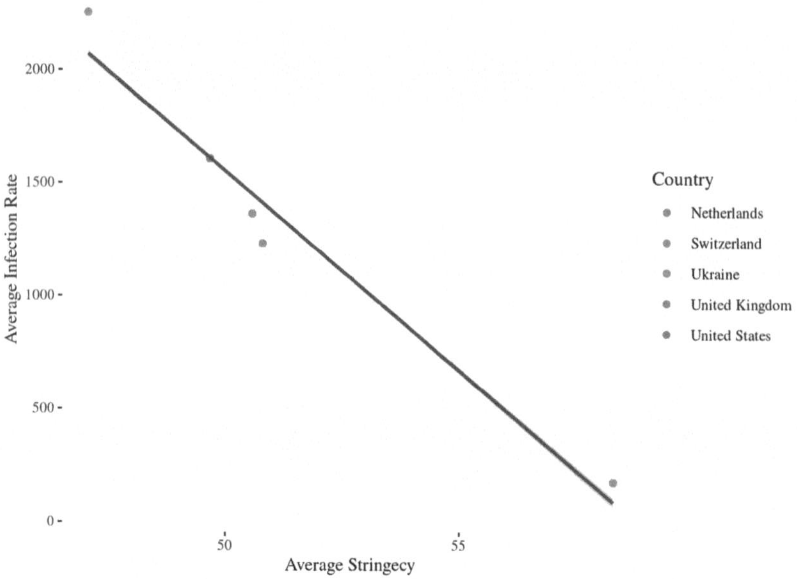

Fig. 25 The correlation between Group 4's mean Stringency Index and mean infection rate (*Source* Author's calculations)

highly stringent policies to tackle the COVID-19 outbreak but the infection rate was recorded as the highest in April and the second highest by the end of May 2020. Figures 31 and 32 show the relationship between the mean Stringency Index from February to the end of May 2020 against the mean infection rate and the mean mortality rate for all four countries in Group 5, respectively.

As illustrated in Figs. 31 and 32, the linear correlation trends exhibited a very weak negative correlation. Sweden was observed to have the second-highest mean infection rate and the highest mean mortality rate attributed to the lowest value of mean stringency in the group. On the other hand, Portugal was observed to have the highest mean infection rate despite having a higher value of mean stringency. France and Germany, however, had the lowest mean infection rates against the highest value of mean stringency for France and a relatively medium value for Germany. France had the highest values for the mean Stringency Index, and yet, the mean mortality rate of France was the second highest in the group. These

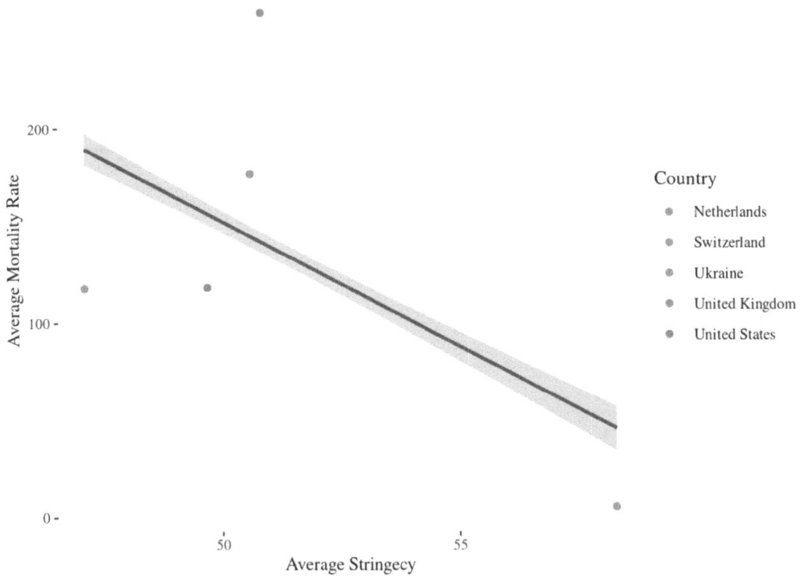

Fig. 26 The correlation between Group 4's mean Stringency Index and mean mortality rate (*Source* Author's calculations)

trends did not fully support the hypothesis that the countries with stricter containment policies and earlier responses to COVID-19 were able to keep mortality rates in check. Figure 33 shows the relationship between the Mobility Index and Stringency Index for all countries in Group 5 from February to the end of May 2020.

Sweden's relationship between the Mobility Index and Stringency Index was observed to have little to no correlation and the mean mortality rate in Sweden was the second highest in the group suggesting that the public's high mobility might have caused the surge in COVID-19 mortality rates. Portugal, on the other hand, showed a very strong negative correlation, and the mean mortality rate in Portugal was the second lowest in the group suggesting that people's adherence to stringent measures mitigated the death rate. However, the relationship for France represented the strongest negative correlation but the second-highest mean mortality rate. The graph for Germany had a weaker negative correlation as compared to France and Portugal and yet, Germany managed to

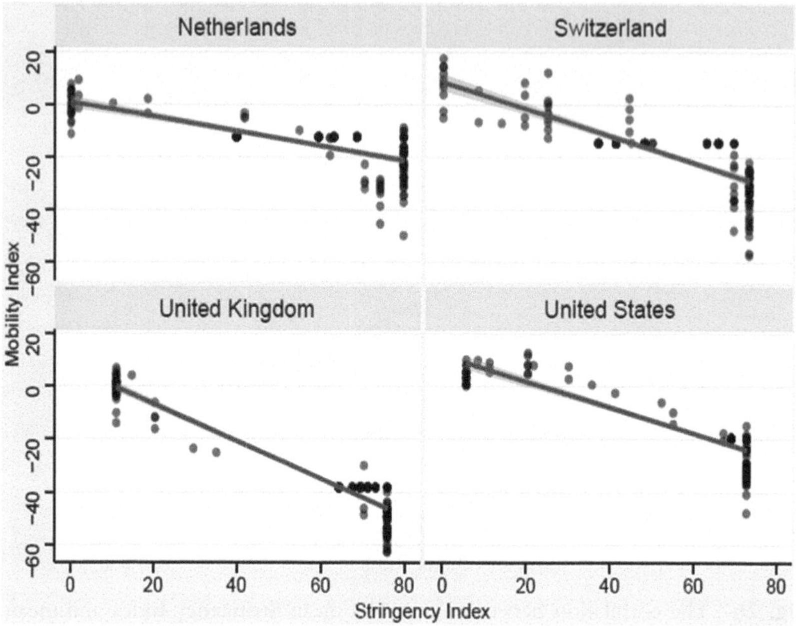

Fig. 27 The correlation between Mobility Index and Stringency Index for countries in Group 4 (*Source* Author's calculations)

keep the death rate lowest in the group. The overall data for Group 5 suggested that the inconsistencies in the trends for France, Portugal, and Germany did not support the theory that the countries who implemented stringent policies early in response to COVID-19 and those who maintained the stricter policies for a longer time period did better in terms of keeping the COVID-19 mortality rate low. However, these inconsistencies can be explained considering the higher percentage of the elderly population in these states who are more likely to catch the infection and less likely to recover from it, depending on the strength of their immunity and pre-existing health conditions.

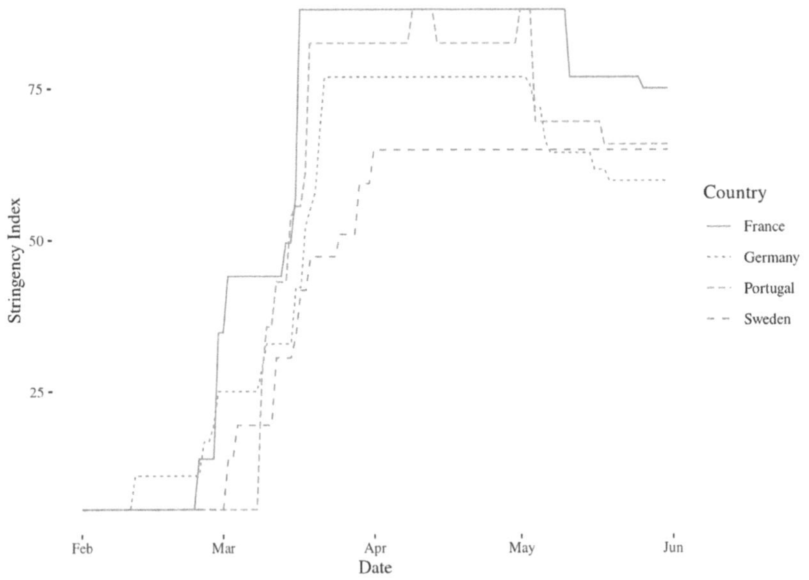

Fig. 28 Stringency Index of Group 5 countries from the start of February to the end of May 2020 (*Source* Author's calculations)

4.6 *Significance and Limitations*

This chapter is significant as it explores government stringency measures and their effectiveness in mitigating COVID-19 mortality rates comprehensively. By scrutinizing the interplay between government stringency and public adherence to measures, the chapter sheds light on the complex dynamics of pandemic management. Furthermore, it underscores the importance of policy timing, both in terms of early implementation relative to other countries and the duration of implementation. These insights hold significant implications for future pandemic preparedness and response strategies, emphasizing the role of government interventions in safeguarding public health.

This research acknowledges the room for error in the calculation of COVID-19 mortality as there is a disparity between the actual number of COVID-19 infections and the reported number of infections. Not everyone with COVID-19 could be included in government reports within their country as the virus was asymptomatic in many people

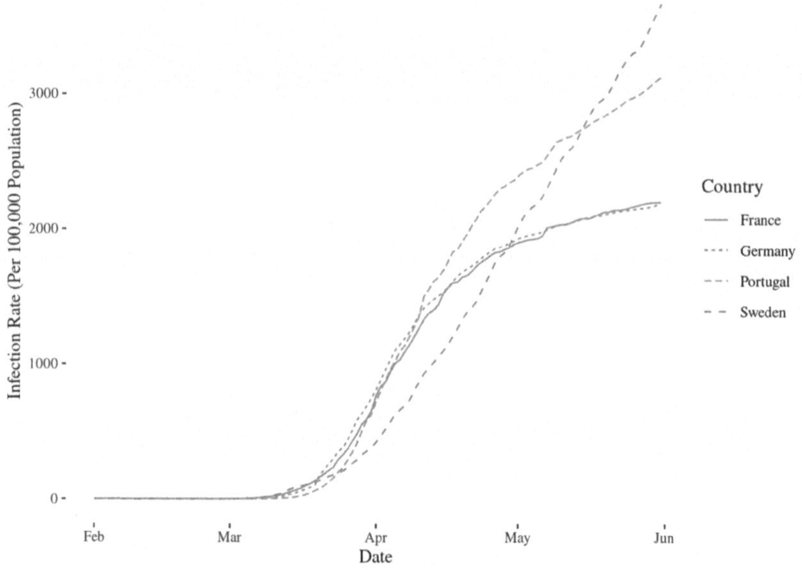

Fig. 29 Infection rates of Group 5 countries from the start of February to the end of May 2020 (*Source* Author's calculations)

and also, not everyone who had symptoms reported this information. The possible underestimation of infection count is due to testing in official locations and hospital settings which did not include milder or asymptomatic cases in the community and the deaths outside hospitals might not have been included in official reports. In addition, the Google Mobility Index used in this study provided limited information with gaps as it only measured people owning smart devices with location services and data sets were not available for some countries, like Iran and Russia.

Additional studies could analyze how long a policy needed to be kept in place in order to have a significant impact on the COVID-19 mortality rate. Moreover, further studies could also break down the Stringency Index in order to see how different measures: school closures, business closures, mask mandates, etc. measured up to each other. The questions like, which interventions were the most/least effective or for which specific policy does the timing of the intervention matter could be asked. Also, this research includes only 22 countries, but with more case studies

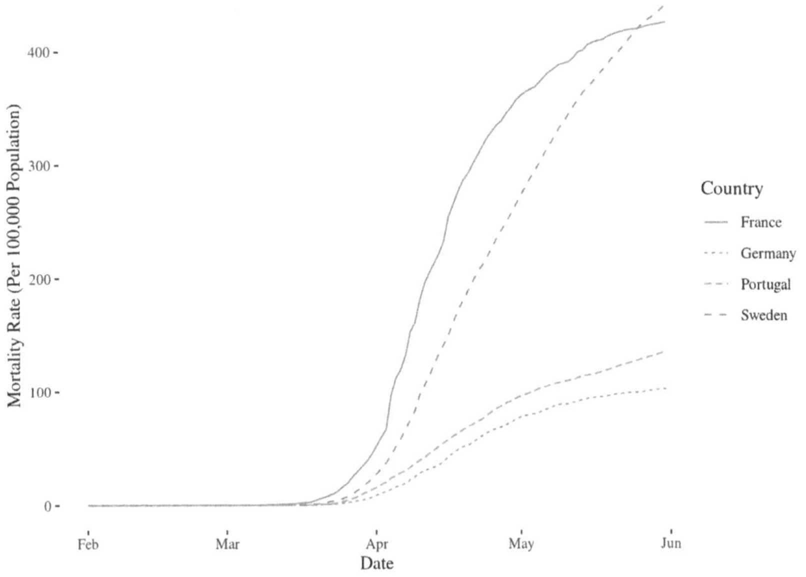

Fig. 30 Mortality rates of Group 5 countries from the start of February to the end of May 2020 (*Source* Author's calculations)

the relationship between Government Stringency Index and COVID-19 mortality rate could be more accurately determined.

5 Conclusion and Policy Recommendations

While government stringency does play a significant role in the COVID-19 transmission and mortality rates, other factors also contribute to this relationship. This chapter assesses the effectiveness of government stringency against the COVID-19 spread and mortality rates, determined by the people's adherence to their respective government's policy measures. Additionally, the timeframe of the policy was observed to matter in terms of early response to the first five reported cases. The calculation of mean stringency took into account both the strength of the government mandates and how long the policy was implemented. An overall significant negative correlation was found to determine that the countries with more stringent policies, quick response time, and a longer period of policy enforcement did way better in keeping the COVID-19-related infection

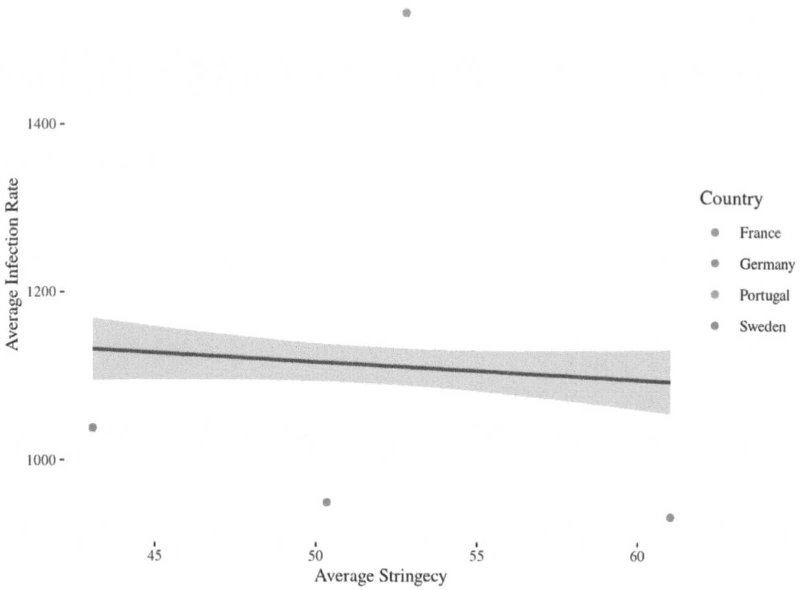

Fig. 31 The correlation between Group 5's mean Stringency Index and mean infection rate (*Source* Author's calculations)

and death rates in check, significantly better in countries with relatively less percentage of the elderly population. Therefore, it concluded that stringency policies can be considered effective tools to curtail pandemics. Nevertheless, other factors like healthcare quality, population density, belief in the virus, and wealth all play crucial roles in determining how a nation reacts to the virus and how none of these factors can be studied in isolation.

This chapter opens up avenues for multifaceted policy perspectives that are crucial for effective pandemic preparedness and response. First and foremost, governments should consider the importance of early and stringent policy implementation in curbing the spread of infectious diseases. As observed in this research, countries that acted promptly and decisively experienced better outcomes in terms of COVID-19 mortality rates. Therefore, it is imperative for nations to develop clear and adaptable response strategies that can be swiftly activated in the face of emerging infectious threats. Furthermore, fostering public adherence to these

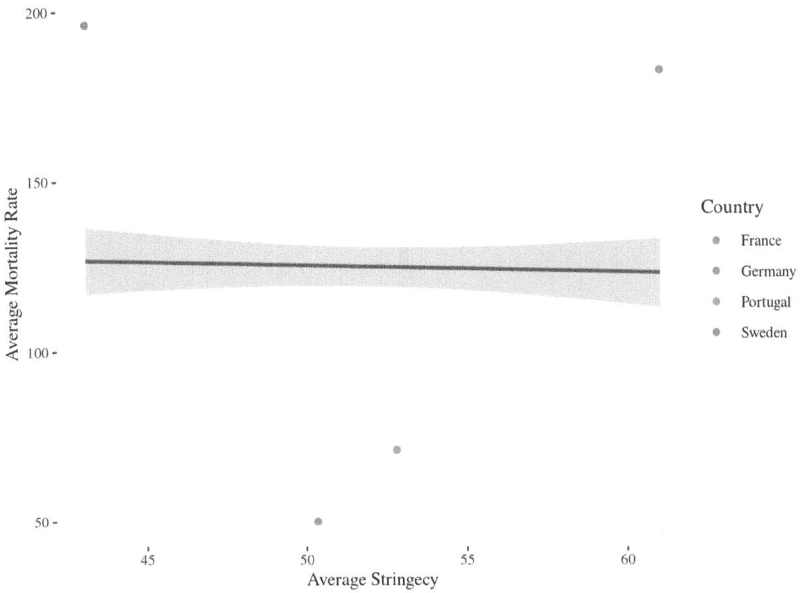

Fig. 32 The correlation between Group 5's mean Stringency Index and mean mortality rate (*Source* Author's calculations)

measures is paramount. Communication strategies should be designed to effectively convey the necessity of compliance to the general population. It is also vital to address the specific needs and concerns of different demographic groups to ensure a cohesive response. Additionally, this chapter underscores the significance of considering the demographic composition of a country. As indicated, countries with a smaller percentage of elderly populations appeared to benefit more from stringent government policies. Future policies should take into account the unique vulnerabilities of different age groups, particularly the elderly, and tailor interventions accordingly. Strengthening healthcare systems, especially in countries with aging populations, is essential. This includes ensuring adequate medical resources, increasing healthcare accessibility, and enhancing the capacity for critical care. Moreover, international collaboration and data sharing are pivotal for a coordinated global response to pandemics. Governments should work together to share knowledge, experiences, and best practices to collectively combat infectious diseases. The research findings highlight

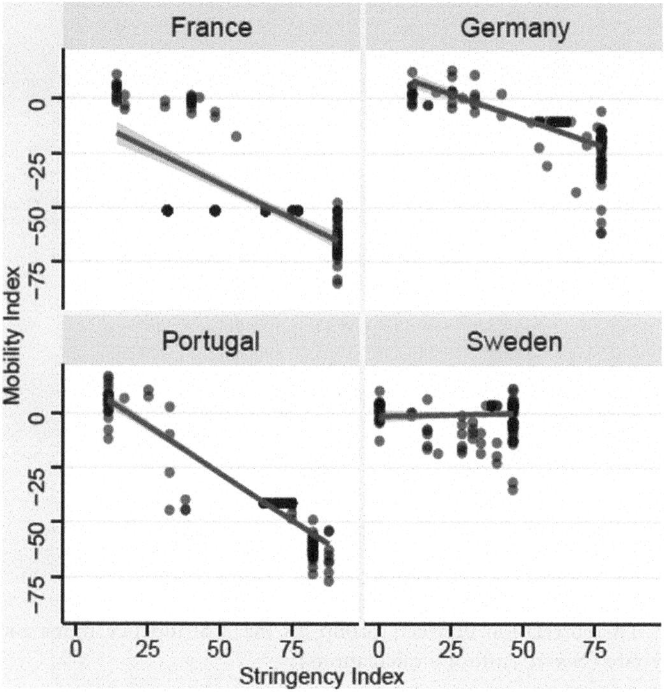

Fig. 33 The correlation between Mobility Index and Stringency Index for countries in Group 5 (*Source* Author's calculations)

the need for a united front in the face of global health crises, emphasizing that the effectiveness of government stringency measures is interconnected with the actions of neighboring and distant nations. In conclusion, the recommendations and implications derived from this chapter provide valuable guidance for policymakers and public health authorities in their endeavors to safeguard public health during pandemics.

References

Agrawal, V., Cantor, J., Sood, N., & Whaley, C. (2023). The impact of the COVID-19 shelter-in-place policy responses on excess mortality. *Health Economics, 32*(11), 2499–2515. https://doi.org/10.1002/hec.4737

Amin, S. (2020). The psychology of coronavirus fear: Are healthcare professionals suffering from corona-phobia? *International Journal of Healthcare Management*, 1–8. https://doi.org/10.1080/20479700.2020.1765119

Brauner, J. M., Mindermann, S., Sharma, M., Johnston, D., Salvatier, J., Gavenčiak, T., Stephenson, A. B., Leech, G., Altman, G., Mikulik, V., & Norman, A. J. (2021). Inferring the effectiveness of government interventions against COVID-19. *Science, 371*(6531). https://doi.org/10.1126/science.abd9338

Brodeur, A., Gray, D., Islam, A., & Bhuiyan, S. (2021). *A literature review of the economics of COVID-19*. IZA Institute of Labor Economics, June 2020. http://ftp.iza.org/dp13411.pdf

Clyde, W., Kakolyris, A., & Koimisis, G. (2021). A study of the effectiveness of governmental strategies for managing mortality from COVID-19. *Eastern Economic Journal, 47*(4), 487–505. https://doi.org/10.1057/s41302-021-00202-x

Collins, F. E. (2021). Measuring COVID-19-related fear and threat in Australian, Indian, and Nepali university students. *Personality and Individual Differences, 175*, 110693, August 2020. https://doi.org/10.1016/j.paid.2021.110693

Dergiades, T., Milas, C., Mossialos, E., & Panagiotidis, T. (2020, May 15). *Effectiveness of government policies in response to the COVID-19 outbreak*. https://doi.org/10.2139/ssrn.3602004

De Giusti, A. (2020). Policy brief: Education during COVID-19 and beyond. *Revista Iberoamericana de Tecnología En Educación y Educación En Tecnología, 26*, e12. https://doi.org/10.24215/18509959.26.e12

De Larochelambert, Q., Marc, A., Antero, J., Le Bourg, E., & Toussaint, J. F. (2020, October 26). COVID-19 mortality: A matter of vulnerability among nations facing limited margins of adaptation. *Frontiers*. https://doi.org/10.3389/fpubh.2020.604339/full

Flaxman, S., Mishra, S., Gandy, A., Unwin, H. J. T., Mellan, T. A., Coupland, H., Whittaker, C., Zhu, H., Berah, T., Eaton, J. W., & Monod, M. (2020). Estimating the effects of non-pharmaceutical interventions on COVID-19 in Europe. *Nature, 584*, 257–261. https://doi.org/10.1038/s41586-020-2405-7

Humanitarian Data Exchange. (n.d.). *OXFORD COVID-19 Government Response Stringency Index*. UN-OCHA. Retrieved November 3, 2023, from https://data.humdata.org/dataset/oxford-COVID-19-government-response-tracker

Kachanoff, F. J., Bigman, Y. E., Kapsaskis, K., & Gray, K. (2020). Measuring realistic and symbolic threats of COVID-19 and their unique impacts on well-being and adherence to public health behaviors. *Social Psychological and Personality Science*. https://doi.org/10.1177/1948550620931634

Lee, S. A. (2020). Coronavirus Anxiety Scale: A brief mental health screener for COVID-19 related anxiety. *Death Studies, 44*(7), 393–401. https://doi.org/10.1080/07481187.2020.1748481

Sharma, M., Mindermann, S., Rogers-Smith, C., Leech, G., Snodin, B., Ahuja, J., Sandbrink, J. B., Monrad, J. T., Altman, G., Dhaliwal, G., & Finnveden, L. (2021). Understanding the effectiveness of government interventions against the resurgence of COVID-19 in Europe. *Nature Communications, 12*(1), 1–13. https://doi.org/10.1038/s41467-021-26013-4

United States, Department of Health and Human Services, Centers for Disease Control and Prevention. (2020, September 1). *About COVID-19*. Centers for Disease Control and Prevention. https://www.cdc.gov/coronavirus/2019-ncov/cdcresponse/about-COVID-19.html

World Bank Data. Accessed from https://data.worldbank.org/indicator/SP.POP.TOTL?locations=PK

World Health Organization. (2023). *WHO coronavirus disease (COVID-19) dashboard*. Geneva. https://covid19.who.int/

Xiu, Z., Feng, P., Yin, J., & Zhu, Y. (2022). Are stringent containment and closure policies associated with a lower COVID-19 spread rate? Global evidence. *International Journal of Environmental Research and Public Health, 19*(3). https://doi.org/10.3390/ijerph19031725

CHAPTER 6

Social Effects of the COVID-19 Pandemic in the Arab World: The Trinity of Education, Health, and Social Interactions

Said Elhussein Abdelli

1 Introduction

From the point of view of sociology, society is just a field of social interactions and the interweaving of its various components, resulting in phenomena that can be measured and studied. Some of these phenomena have a cosmic dimension, that is, they are a common denominator between different societies despite their spatial difference and differing structural and cultural characteristics. The same applies to the COVID-19 pandemic, which has acquired a global character, as it is a phenomenon that has swept all societies and generated many problems from it, and has been the subject of social sciences, including sociology in particular.

The COVID-19 pandemic is nothing more than a sociological question par excellence in order to know its social effects, and in fact it is many. Especially since this pandemic reaches countries that are already suffering

S. E. Abdelli (✉)
Sultan Qaboos University, Muscat, Oman
e-mail: s.abdelli@squ.edu.om

A. Mishrif (ed.), *Perspectives on Human Capital Development*,
https://doi.org/10.1007/978-981-97-5246-1_6

from humanitarian crises caused by conflicts, natural disasters, and climate change. These are countries where bombs, violence, or floods have forced people to flee their homes, living under plastic sheeting in the open, or crammed into refugee camps or informal settlements. They do not have homes where they practice social distancing or isolation. They also lack clean water and soap to wash their hands, as this is the simplest way to protect themselves from the virus. But if they get sick, they have no way to reach health care facilities that can provide them with a bed and a respirator (António Guterres).

With the spread of the virus, visual media and social media began broadcasting and transmitting news of the new virus, which caused the spread of a lot of information, both true and false, in addition to the resort of many countries to total or partial quarantine in an attempt to remedy the rapid spread of the virus. With the passage of time, several psychological consequences were recorded resulting from the random transmission of information on the one hand, and the quarantine that led to the isolation of people from each other on the other hand. For isolation resulting from quarantine, and for panic caused by people's fear of getting sick or infecting people close to them.

The educational sector, with its institutions, is one of the most important sectors influencing the structure and environment of societies and has a clear impact on their economy. It is the mainstay of countries in progress, growth, and achieving goals. It is worth noting and as is well-known that the institutions of the educational sector are not separated from any global or local variables, as the future of societies is the future of the sustainability of this sector, and due to this strong interconnection between the education sector and its institutions and the local environment, higher education institutions, including universities and institutes, have been affected greatly. Concrete with the problem of the times, which is the COVID-19 pandemic. The same thing happened in the health sector, where there is aversion by many individuals to the vaccine against this virus, as well as the problem of distancing, which sometimes seems difficult, especially in public transportation, specifically in countries that are not prepared for this, meaning that they do not have a developed fleet that allows the implementation of procedures Safety and always on the health side. There are many rumors about this epidemic. The Arab collective imagination has emerged with its multiple connotations, providing conflicting interpretations and scientific perception, which has repercussions on social interactions, and by this we mean the nature of the relationship between individuals affected by this pandemic, which we will address through the nature of relations between individuals and the reduction of the intensity of traditional communication, especially with the closure of cafes, universities, and places of worship. Whatever space allows for assembly, all of this resulted in resorting to alternative solutions that we will reveal in the body of this work: *The Social Effects of the COVID-19 Pandemic in the Arab World: The Trinity of Education, Health and Social Interactions.*

2 Theoretical and Methodological Foundations

2.1 The Problem of Studying

The study of social phenomena primarily requires considering the interrelationship between a number of variables in order to reach an objective understanding of the nature of the phenomenon under study, and in this context, the COVID-19 epidemic has many effects on all sectors of society, and in this article, we will limit ourselves to the trinity of education, health, and social interactions. These three sectors were directly affected by the epidemic, giving rise to new forms of social work. What are the most prominent social impacts resulting from the COVID-19 pandemic through the three areas referred to?

Such a central question can be disassembled according to the following:

- What are the effects of the pandemic on education in the Arab world?
- What are the most prominent health measures to confront the pandemic in the Arab world through the question of limits and contradictions?
- What is the relationship between the pandemic and the new forms of social relations that have prevailed in our Arab societies?
- How can the effects of the pandemic on Omani society be assessed and the methods adopted to confront it?

2.2 *Objectives*

This study aims to highlight the following main objectives:

- Exposing the effects of the pandemic on Arab society, including Omani society
- Highlighting the health effects of COVID-19 and how to deal with it.
- Knowing the repercussions of the pandemic on the education sector in the Arab world and ways to deal with it through many examples, especially from the Omani society.
- Knowing the features of social interactions imposed by the pandemic.

2.3 *The Importance of the Study*

The importance of this study is reflected in its convergence between several social variables and a major variable, which is the COVID-19 pandemic in the Arab world in general and the Sultanate of Oman in particular. Therefore, its importance can be summarized in the following points:

- Awareness of the social dimensions of the COVID-19 pandemic.
- Highlighting the readiness of Arab countries, including the Sultanate of Oman, for such sudden challenges.
- Reading on the subject of structures and jobs in Arab society.
- Uncovering new manifestations of social relations and interactions caused by the epidemic.
- Knowing the social effects of the pandemic and ways to deal with it.

2.4 *Study Methodology*

Given that this study is a theoretical work that does not depend on field work, we will follow the descriptive analytical approach based on studies on the COVID-19 pandemic, as well as relying on the methodology of studying the content and observation.

3 The Effects of the COVID-19 Pandemic in Arab Countries

In this element, we will discuss the effects of the COVID-19 pandemic on Arab societies, as they are inevitably not separated from the social dimensions, whether at the level of structures or jobs. Society will therefore undergo several transformations and produce new phenomena that are the product of this influence. Through this research paper, we will focus on three main dimensions, namely education, health, and social relations, but we will examine through our analysis the Omani example without neglecting the Arab world in general.

3.1 The COVID-19 Pandemic and the Educational Issue, What Is the Relationship?

Education in Arab society in general is considered a national priority that various governments have bet on since their independence. It was even considered a national priority, prompting a huge amount of funding. The Sultanate of Oman, for example, is one of the pioneering countries in the education reform that Sultan Qaboos bet on since the beginning of the Renaissance in 1970.

There have been profound changes that have confused the educational process due to the COVID-19 pandemic, so all Arab countries hastened to take urgent and preventive measures represented in the following:

- After the closure of schools and universities, the importance of education and study increased in order to achieve social and physical distancing.
- Converting academic curricula into electronic curricula for dynamic and effective communication with students, whether in schools or universities.
- Universities began to create platforms for virtual rapprochement between departments and learners, and to raise electronic courses, exams, study activities, and assignments on electronic platforms.

The pandemic has confused and separated learners from their normal school environment. For example, in the member states of the Organization of Islamic Cooperation, 432.6 million learners have dropped out of school. However, even if school closures of this magnitude are considered temporary measures, they are likely to have long-term multiplier effects on the level of human capital development in societies with a predominantly child and youth population. The first reason is that the increase in the number of learners who have dropped out of school or may not return to it, as a result of disrupting their education may be the catalyst for these effects. In this context, "the disruption of education poses a risk of a decline in the educational level of the most vulnerable children, whose basic education was not strong at first, and children are often from disadvantaged social and economic backgrounds, and minority groups" (Organization of Islamic Cooperation Center for Statistical, 2020, p. 41).

The educational system in all its stages has benefited from the tremendous development in the field of technology, especially information networks, computers, and the Internet, which contributed to the ease of the spread of information and its transmission between different individuals regardless of geographical distances. Such a matter resulted in the development of knowledge. The educational and educational field benefited from the tremendous technological revolution that is used in the educational process, especially what is known as "*E-learning technologies such as computers and their various programs, educational television, video, cassette recorder, data projector, smart board, calculator, smartphones, distance education, and other innovations in educational technologies in the educational process. All of which is an urgent necessity to keep pace with the cognitive, scientific, and technical development and meet the needs and requirements of the times*" (Organization of Islamic Cooperation Center for Statistical, 2020).

It turns out that COVID-19 has reshaped the education sector by revolutionizing learning, but it is not always inclusive of marginalized students, especially in developing countries with sub-standard technological infrastructures (UNESCO, 2020). One of the challenges in this area is the fact that modern communication technologies are not available to all social strata, and here it is necessary to consider the financial situation of students, as well as the availability of the Internet in rural and remote areas.

The Sultanate of Oman is among the most prominent Arab countries that have succeeded in confronting the pandemic due to the measures and measures it has taken and the capabilities allocated for that. It worked on finding alternative solutions to ensure the success of the educational process in its various stages so that there would be no rupture and continuity would be achieved. So educational platforms were sent to ensure the continuity of the distance learning process, so mechanisms were developed to provide remote lectures, and the same was true for the tests, which were mostly conducted electronically.

The pandemic will have an impact on the level of learning despite the solutions that have been found. For example, students who do not have the ability to attend distance education will be in an unsafe situation. This is proven by one of the studies: "*Our analysis shows that the impact of the pandemic on K–12 student learning was significant, leaving students on average five months behind in mathematics and four months behind in reading by the end of the school year. The pandemic widened pre-existing opportunity and achievement gaps, hitting historically disadvantaged students hardest. In math, students in majority Black schools ended the year with six months of unfinished learning, students in low-income schools with seven. High schoolers have become more likely to drop out of school, and high school seniors, especially those from low-income families, are less likely to go on to postsecondary education. And the crisis had an impact on not just academics but also the broader health and well-being of students, with more than 35 percent of parents very or extremely concerned about their children's mental health*" (Dorn et al., 2021).

On the other hand, many countries have noticed the weakness of their educational structure, which necessitated the need to review and reform it. In this way "Produced *by the Commonwealth Secretariat and South Africa-based JET Education Services, the report urges governments to build more resilient education systems that can withstand future crises and ensure continuity of educational provision and access to education services, especially for marginalized populations*" (Commonwealth, 2022).

This pandemic has also revealed how Arab countries need to review their development plans, especially in keeping pace with modern technologies that will develop the educational process. "*This crisis has exposed the many inadequacies and inequities in our education systems – from access to the broadband and computers needed for online education, and the supportive environments needed to focus on learning, up to the misalignment between resources and needs*" (Andreas Schleicher). Indeed, several Arab countries have rushed to develop their educational infrastructure and move toward digitization, shortening effort and time, and thus developing the educational process. Some studies believe that COVID-19 has caused an economic crisis for a number of countries, which means that spending on education will be low in the coming years, and this in itself is a threat to the future of education. "However, the current crisis may affect education budgets more quickly as public revenues decline sharply and governments review the prioritisation of education in national budgets. Forecasts predict that the pandemic will lead to slower growth in government spending in the coming year, and that if the share of government spending devoted to education were to remain unchanged, education spending would continue to grow but at significantly lower rates than before the pandemic" (Andreas Schleicher).

3.2 *The Impact of the Pandemic on the Health Situation in the Arab world*

The health sector is the most affected by the pandemic in the Arab world, especially those countries that suffer from problems in their health institutions in terms of number, quality, and equipment. As soon as the number of the injured increased, the difficulty became apparent in embracing them and providing them with treatment, despite the efforts made. While there are other Arab countries that have harnessed enormous potential to confront the pandemic, including the Sultanate of Oman, it has been able to face the challenges of the pandemic thanks to the compulsory vaccination campaigns that included Omani citizens and expatriates.

The general health situation in the world was to address the epidemic with all available capabilities, and even support the health effort through spending, receiving aid, and harnessing all the capabilities of the state for this. The COVID-19 outbreak has contributed to creating emergency health response mechanisms at the global and national levels to protect people's health and avoid a sharp rise in infection rates. All over the world, health facilities, facilities, and equipment have been redeployed to cope with the influx of patients suffering from this disease (Organization of Islamic Cooperation Center for Statistical, 2020, p. 32).

With the spread of the virus, the visual media and social media began broadcasting and transmitting news of the new virus that has spread in the world, and which caused the spread of a lot of information, whether correct or incorrect, in addition to the resort of many countries. To total or partial quarantine, in an attempt to treat the rapid spread of the virus. On the other hand, the mystery surrounding the pandemic in terms of its source and the treatments to cure it was one of the things that made the health situation more complicated, which gave way for false news to be transmitted about this virus. Such a matter has several psychological effects on the residents of the Arab region, especially with the beginning of the quarantine application (Pazzanese, 2021 October 20).

Over time, several psychological consequences were recorded resulting from the random transmission of information on the one hand, and the quarantine that led to the isolation of people from each other on the other hand, so the rate of registration of symptoms of depression and anxiety increased, all because of the isolation resulting from the stone, and panic caused by people's fear of illness or harm to those close to them, in addition to the emergence of occupational pressures such as severe physical exhaustion or fear of death among medical personnel working in high-risk health facilities, or losing a job in some other professions.

Social sciences have been widely concerned with studying the phenomenon and its consequences, this means, its social effects. In this context, several field studies have appeared that presented a number of facts and explanations. Perhaps the most prominent of these results can be summarized in the following points:

- High levels of despair and frustration were observed in the presence of the pandemic and exacerbation of mental illness in people with a previous history of mental illness, which eventually led to an increase in the use of alcohol and drugs in some people, which usually causes exacerbation of anxiety states and thus entering into a flawed vicious cycle. The persistence of these problems for a long period of time, in turn, led to an increase in the rates of suicidal thoughts and suicide (Abbott, 2021 November 3).
- At the age level, we found that younger people (less than 31 years) in the Arab community are the most vulnerable to anxiety, which may lead to disruption and decline in the quality of work in state institutions and companies, which negatively affects the economy, and anxiety becomes a negative factor. In addition, it affects the economy of countries and the stability of some types of social relations (Vahratian et al., 2021 November 4).
- Anxiety levels increased among members of the Arab world in general after the outbreak of the COVID-19 pandemic, and female and younger individuals were the most affected by the consequences of COVID-19, which directly or indirectly affects the mental health of individuals along with its direct impact on physical health (Bassel Abdel-Hadi Soufan et al., winter 2022, p. 124).

- Elderly patients in long-term care settings have represented the true face of fragility in the pandemic; in Western countries, the media paid attention to them and highlighted their real-life conditions: too much isolation, few social and cultural activities, dilapidated or inadequate buildings, a lack of nursing staff, and also weak administrative organization, which reflects a chronic lack of staff. Funding of these centers, with a lack of system functioning, a lack of means to conduct regular inspections, and a decrease in services (Marie-Helene Parizeau, winter 2021, p. 124).

According to the World Health Organization, health workers in most countries with high COVID-19 infection have had problems accessing protective equipment to protect themselves and their patients from infection and infecting others. Thus, this case has caused a steady increase in the transmission of infection to health workers around the world (Organization of Islamic Cooperation Center for Statistical, May 2020, p. 34).

3.3 Social Relations Following the COVID-19 Pandemic

Social distancing and the imposition of quarantine are among the issues imposed by the pandemic, which necessitated new standards of life that changed the social lifestyle. Such a situation will inevitably have negative repercussions because it contradicts the nature of the human self in its social aspect based on the flexibility of social relations such as interaction, integration, and communication. In this context, many institutions in which rapprochement occurs between individuals have been closed, so telephone communications have replaced face-to-face meetings between people, and other precautionary measures that ensure the protection of citizens within each country. Based on this definition of the World Health Organization, social distancing cannot be considered a tool of social marginalization or social exclusion, but rather a pattern of precautionary measures taken by countries in order to preserve public health and the lives of citizens. In this way, social distancing has become a positive concept that includes containment, not exclusion, but crisis containment in order to survive natural crises (Fatima Al-Zahraa Salem Mahmoud, July 2020). Social relations under quarantine will take on new colors that accompany the nature of the stage, such as virtual convergence through virtual social media via the Internet, and information and communication technology. What distinguishes this virtual convergence is the realization of the idea of social inclusion of peoples in order to achieve community development within the framework of social distancing. The process of social distancing and physical isolation in order to survive an imminent danger that destroys humanity, and this imminent danger is not seen with the naked eye and spreads in a continuous manner that does not allow convergence in the accepted sense, but rather the inevitability of distance with the presence of virtual convergence.

We note here that the idea of social distancing has negative effects through the quarantine process and the reduction of rapprochement between humans. It also has positive dimensions, especially on the family, as it began to restore its balance and began to unite in order to survive in a healthy and better social life. Especially the average families who found staying at home a great value to rediscover and correct many of the behavioral practices of their children and parents as well. The family has begun to witness psychological and social calm within it instead of the hustle and bustle of daily life. Social distancing has also contributed to creating a kind of collective commitment and calm societal dialogue between peoples and governments, which made the inevitability of compliance with authoritarian decisions indisputable, as authoritarian commitment has turned into a collective and synergistic commitment to help countries get out of the Corona pandemic. This collective commitment despite social distancing stems from the mental will, the inherent humanity within individuals to survive. Social responsibility infiltrated the hearts of children, youth, and adults alike in a few months.

In general, social relations have become more fragile and violent due to social distancing, and individuals have felt tightness and siege in their transactions, which were dominated by a social nature, which they are accustomed to through their daily work or the various relationships that they establish within the groups to which they belong. The social impact of Corona appears in the dimensions of awareness of the importance of mental and social health and conviction in the application of social distancing measures. There are also effects on the behavior of individuals in terms of the prevalence of anxiety and varying levels of social affiliation among individuals, which caused a disparity in the adoption of social responsibility by increasing social distancing(Oosterhoff et al., 2020).

The results of a study showed that the effects of Corona, from the social angle, are causing radical changes in the behavior of society as a result of the effects resulting from quarantine and the complexity of the psychological state of the injured and isolated. Individuals, and the effects on marital life as a result of separation and feelings of frustration, which increases the views and behaviors of societal violence and changes the personality of individuals as a result of closing the manifestations of public life and the negative psychological effects that follow (Mazza et al., 2020).

In general, the nature of social relations has become characterized by a rupture with those that were in the list of social relations that turned entirely to electronic communication, and the relations became dry, which affected the low quality of joint benefits despite the intensity of communication, which is what we noticed in the majority of distance education experiences, through complaints. All parties, i.e., parents, students, teachers, and administrators alike. In this context, it cannot be denied that a large segment of society denied the dangers of the epidemic and kept preserving the nature of social relations to which they are accustomed, bypassing all preventive measures and quarantine. Whereas, emotional and social feelings diminished in other types of relationships, and electronic communication or telecommunication dominated in this type of relationship, while another group accepted the new situation and tried to adapt to it, as the owners of this type tried to adhere to prevention and physical distance, with many solutions to establish positive relationships from a distance, through multiple activities, both electronic and direct, with the aim of avoiding social isolation and activating human communication (Fatima Fattouni, 2021).

The pandemic affected religious practices in various ways, including canceling worship (Prayer), pilgrimages, observance of religious holidays, and closing religious schools. The drop in travel is likely to persist even after the virus's impact wears off and alter social dynamics such as spending more time with family, staying close to one's home and hanging out with close friends. This is one of the most prominent changes that affected social relations, which have become based on caution, superficiality, distance, and tendencies toward the virtual dimension.

It is not surprising that the pandemic caused social effects that affected various fields, including education, health, and social relations. Society at the level of its structures and functions is affected by everything that is external factor, especially if it was an epidemic with multiple risks. The COVID-19 pandemic has raised several questions, the most important of which is: What is the ability of Arab societies to deal with such an emergency?

These three sectors: education, health, and social relations are, in our opinion, among the most important areas affected by the pandemic. Arab societies, including the Sultanate of Oman, are characterized by the abundance and strength of social ties that are the product of the strength of social solidarity and the strength of social relations. Therefore, the quarantine imposed by the pandemic was not easy for individuals to accept.

4 Findings and Recommendations

4.1 Results

The most important recommendations it reached are:

- The COVID-19 pandemic has affected Arab societies to varying degrees according to the capacity of each country, especially in terms of the capabilities and experiences available to it.
- The pandemic has brought about major transformations in the educational process, the most important of which is the closure of educational institutions and the opening up of distance education.
- The decline in educational efficiency, especially for weak students.
- Most of the Arab countries suffered from weak health infrastructure and their inability to confront the epidemic, while other countries were able to do so, especially the Gulf countries, including the Sultanate of Oman.
- The epidemic represented a health catastrophe that caused many damages to the health aspect in Arab countries, especially those that suffer from the fragility of their health infrastructure.
- The epidemic has affected the nature of social relations, especially since the imposition of quarantine and physical distancing.
- As a result of the difference, new patterns of hypothetical social relationships have emerged, as well as impaired social communication due to fear.

4.2 Recommendations

The study recommends the following:

- The need for Arab countries, especially those that have suffered from many development failures, to review their development policies.
- The development of the health infrastructure has become more urgent than before.
- Developing technologies adopted in education in order to keep pace with existing challenges.
- The study also recommends consolidating cooperation between the components of society and launching a donation campaign in order to support the efforts of the state in building public projects, especially in the health and educational fields.
- The necessity of continuing health and psychological care for some victims of the epidemic, especially due to anxiety and stress.

5 Conclusion

This paper tried to answer the social effects of the Corona pandemic through the educational and health reality and social ills. The pandemic has severely affected social relations, which has resulted in new patterns of interaction between individuals and group. On the other hand, the health and educational status of the Arab countries varied according to the readiness of the infrastructure to confront the existing situation. However, this does not prevent the Arab countries from reviewing their development policy based on the results recorded by the pandemic and working to reform and develop various sectors, especially the educational health aspect.

References

Abbott, A. (2021). COVID's mental-health toll: How scientists are tracking a surge in depression. *Nature* [Internet]. 3 February 2021 [cited 2021 November 3], *590*(7845), 194–195. https://doi.org/10.1038/d41586-021-00175-z

Andreas Schleicher. *The impact of COVID-19 on education*. https://www.oecd.org/

António Guterres. *COVID-19 is a threat to all of humanity—And therefore all of humanity must act to eradicate it.* https://www.un.org/ar/coronavirus/articles

Bassel Abdel-Hadi Soufan, Bassel Omar Bayrakdar, & Iyad Abdel-Hadi Soufan. (2022). *Studying the impact of COVID-19 on mental health in Syria compared to a sample of Arab countries: A study of anxiety level variables before and during the outbreak of the COVID-19 pandemic.* QScience, Hamad Bin Khalifa University House for Publication.

Commonwealth. (2022, January 24). *The impact of COVID-19 on education systems in the Commonwealth.* https://reliefweb.int/

Dorn, E., Hancock, B., Sarakatsannis, J., & Viruleg, E. (2021, July 27). *US states and districts have the opportunity to not only help students catch up on unfinished learning from the pandemic but also tackle long-standing historical inequities in education.* https://www.mckinsey.com/

Fatima Al-Zahraa Salem Mahmoud. (2020). Social distancing and its educational effects in the time of the emerging Covid 19 (Corona). *Educational Journal, 75.* Faculty of Education, Ain Shams University, Egypt.

Fatima Fattouni. (2021, March 9). *How did physical distancing in the time of Corona affect the change in social relations?* Al-Mayadeen. https://www.almayadeen.net/

Marie-Helene Parizeau. (2021). The COVID–19 pandemic: Between social vulnerabilities and technical logics. *Tabayyun, 9*(35).

Mazza, M., Marano, G., Lai, C., Janiri, L., & Sani, G. (2020). Danger in danger: Interpersonal violence during COVID-19 quarantine. *Psychiatry Research, 289*, 113046.

Oosterhoff, B., Palmer, C. A., Wilson, J., & Shook, N. (2020). Adolescents' motivations to engage in social distancing during the COVID-19 pandemic: Associations with mental and social health. *Journal of Adolescent Health.*

Organization of Islamic Cooperation Center for Statistical, Economic and Social Research and Training for Islamic Countries. (2020). Social and economic effects of the COVID-19 pandemic in OIC member countries: Prospects and challenges, Ankara, Turkey.

Pazzanese, C. (2020, May 8). *Battling the 'pandemic of misinformation'* [Internet]. [cited 2021 October 20]. https://news.harvard.edu/gazette/story/2020/05/social-media-used-to-spread-create-COVID-19-falsehoods/

UNESCO. (2020, May 4). *Empowering students with disabilities during the COVID-19 crisis.* https://bit.ly/3bRDSRu

Vahratian, A., Blumberg, S. J., & Terlizzi, E. P. et al. (2021). *Symptoms of anxiety or depressive disorder and use of mental health care among adults during the COVID-19 pandemic—United States*, August 2020–February 2021. Centers for Disease Control and Prevention [Internet]. [cited 2021 November 4]. https://doi.org/10.15585/mmwr.mm7013e2

CHAPTER 7

Socioeconomic, Environmental, Health, and Psychological Aspects of COVID-19 Pandemic: Lessons Learnt and Future Directions

Mohd Hussain Kunroo and Mudabera Gulzar

1 Introduction

Pandemics have never stopped threatening the very human existence on earth down the lines of history and ruining it on a massive scale. The impact is vast, and the threat is devastating. Natural disasters and wars are not even close to this threat. Look at the statistics. The last century witnessed two unfortunate worst world wars (WW). The number of human lives lost in World War I was about 16 million. In World War II,

M. H. Kunroo (✉)
Department of Economics & Business Environment, Indian Institute of Management Sirmaur, Sirmaur, India
e-mail: mhkunroo@iimsirmaur.ac.in

M. Gulzar
MMINSR, Sher-i-Kashmir Institute of Medical Sciences, SKIMS, Soura, Srinagar, Jammu and Kashmir, India

A. Mishrif (ed.), *Perspectives on Human Capital Development*,
https://doi.org/10.1007/978-981-97-5246-1_7

it stood at around 60 million deaths (ignoring the unrecorded deaths). In contrast, the Spanish flu, popularly known as the 1918 influenza pandemic, resulted in 17 to 50 million deaths worldwide. Some have even reported this human loss as high as 100 million. Such pandemics have been witnessed repeatedly throughout the timeline of history. For instance, the plague of Justinian was a pandemic that afflicted the Byzantine (Eastern Roman) Empire. It took place as early as the 6th Century AD and killed almost half of the globe's population (50 to 100 million people). Similarly, The Black Death of the fourteenth century—a great plague of pandemic magnitude, killed as many as 200 million lives. The influenza A virus H2N2 of 1957, a pandemic that broke out in Guizhou (China) and killed 1 to 4 million people.

The latest virus is SARS-CoV2, and the disease caused by it is popularly named COVID-19 (Coronavirus disease 2019). It started in Wuhan, a city in the Hubie Province of China, towards the end of 2019. It developed as a cluster of pneumonia cases in Wuhan and spread at a very rapid pace. It is not like the world did not caution about the occurrence of such a pandemic. On the one hand, the recent viral health hazards in the form of severe acute respiratory syndrome—coronavirus or SARS-CoV (2002–2003), Human CoV NL63 (2004), HKU1 (2005), H1N1 influenza (2009), Middle East respiratory syndrome or MERS-CoV (2012), and the mini-outbreaks such as West Nile virus, Bird flu, Zika virus, and Nipah virus were raising the alarm for the occurrence of such pandemics like COVID-19; on the other hand, over the past two decades, there has been no dearth of research articles that warned the world about odds in favour of occurrence of a pandemic. For instance, Cheng et al. wrote as early as 2007 that "…the presence of a large reservoir of SARS-CoV-like viruses in horseshoe bats, together with the culture of eating exotic mammals in southern China, is a time bomb. The possibility of the re-emergence of SARS and other novel viruses from animals or laboratories and, therefore, the need for preparedness should not be ignored."

These repeated calls from nature and researchers went unheard. These unheard voices added more to the state of despair and grief as we live in a world of globalization. See the case of the COVID-19 pandemic. It started in China and spread across the globe. With more than 697.63 million Coronavirus cases and around 230 countries, dependencies, and territories affected, the world cried in helplessness. The United States, India, Brazil, South Korea, Russia, the UK, France, Turkey, Italy, Japan, Spain, Germany, Australia, Vietnam, Taiwan, Columbia, Argentina,

Portugal, Mexico, Poland, South Africa, Iran, Ukraine, Peru, Chile, Malaysia, Belgium, Qatar, Indonesia, the Netherlands, Canada, DPRK, Thailand, Switzerland, Philippines, Denmark, Hong Kong, Sweden, Singapore, Serbia, New Zealand, Iraq, Hungary, Bangladesh, Slovakia, Romania, Georgia, Jordan, Pakistan, Ireland, Finland, Norway, Kazakhstan, Slovenia, Lebanon, Lithuania, Bulgaria, Tunisia, Croatia, Cuba, Belarus, Saudi Arabia, Nepal, Sri Lanka, Kuwait, Myanmar, Cyprus, Qatar, Palestine, Libya, Armenia, Egypt, Oman, and many more countries recorded lakhs of positive coronavirus cases. Moreover, the world lost more than 69.37 lakh human lives (until November 10, 2023; Worldometer, 2023). In the initial years, the number of positive coronavirus cases was growing exponentially with each passing day. Sadly, the numbers kept on piling up hour after hour. Rising patterns of Corona positive cases were witnessed by the countries under the "second-wave." Figs. 1, 2, 3 and 4 gives the complete picture of the COVID-19 infection development across the globe. With more than 70% of world population administered with at least one dose of a COVID-19 vaccine, the hope is to flatten the curve of new severe cases. There is a need to develop a "universal vaccine" that can cure all the coronavirus variants.

Another primary concern is that this pandemic affected every social fabric and every sector of the economy. The situation led to social distancing, isolation, transportation shutdown, boundary closure, home quarantine (of the infected), and economic lockdowns (partial or complete) in almost all the affected countries. In most countries, the

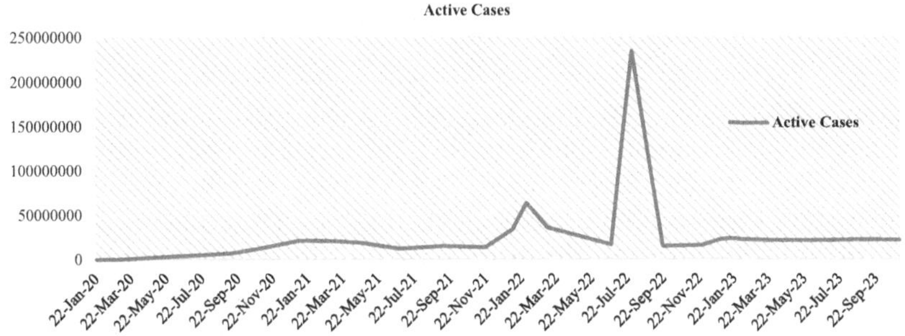

Fig. 1 Active COVID-19 positive cases (*Source* Authors' Calculation based on Worldometer Data. COVID—Coronavirus Statistics—Worldometer [worldometers.info])

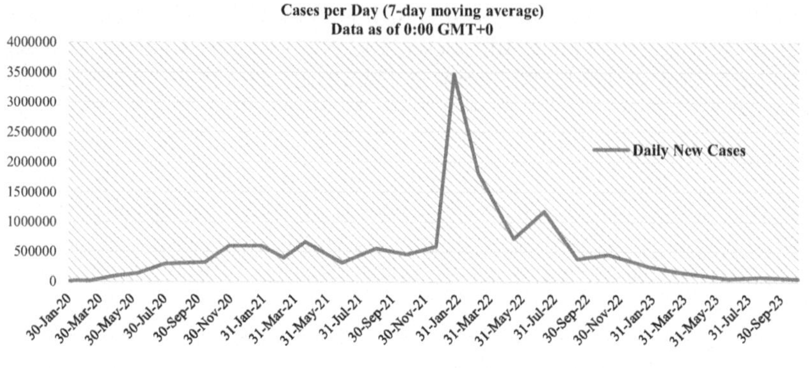

Fig. 2 Daily new cases (*Source* Authors' Calculation based on Worldometer Data. COVID—Coronavirus Statistics—Worldometer [worldometers.info])

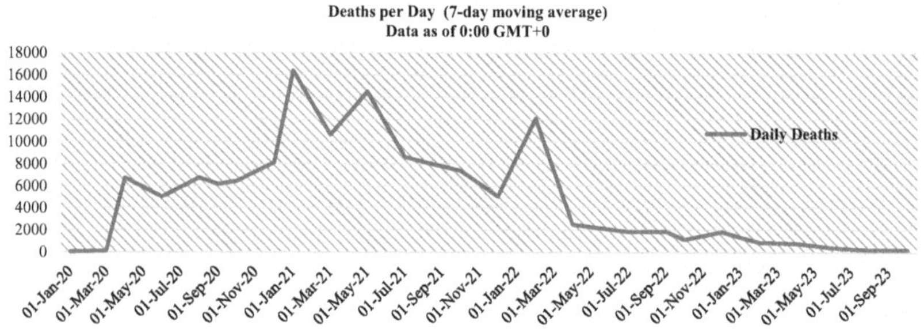

Fig. 3 Daily deaths (*Source* Authors' Calculation based on Worldometer Data. COVID—Coronavirus Statistics—Worldometer [worldometers.info])

summer 2021 saw a second wave of partial lockdowns and night curfews. The economic shutdown led to a catastrophe, with consequences far and wide. Emergencies of COVID-19 intensity aggravate the pre-existing socioeconomic problems such as poverty, economic disparities, discrimination against the marginalized, political subjugation, drastic decline of income generation, hunger, starvation, job loss and migration, family disintegration, disruption of social networks, gender discrimination, community breakdown, stigmatization, loss of trust, and the like (Joshi, 2021; Zacharias et al., 2019). No doubt, vulnerable sections are more likely to be disproportionately affected (IASC, 2015).

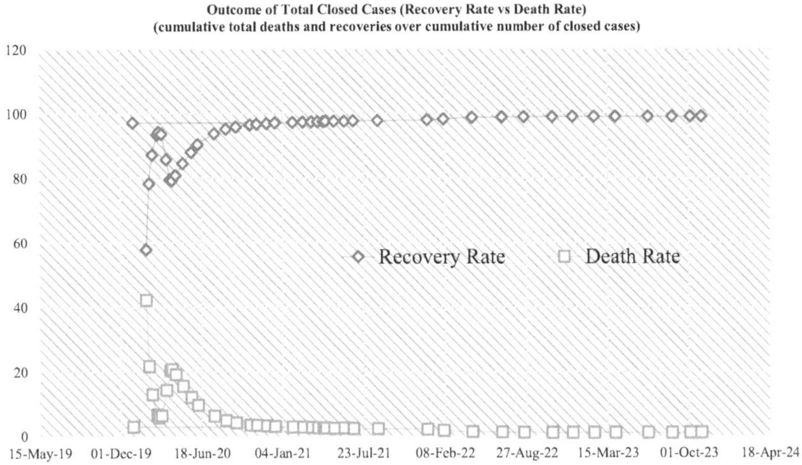

Fig. 4 Outcome of cases (Recovery or Death) (*Source* Authors' Calculation based on Worldometer Data. COVID—Coronavirus Statistics—Worldometer [worldometers.info])

Such socioeconomic consequences create other problems, diseases, and vicious circles. Unfortunately, the world started investing in borders and nuclear armaments but neglected the health sector. To quote Bill Gates in his 2015 TED Talk, "…the disaster that we worried about earlier was a nuclear war. Today, the greatest risk of global catastrophe is a highly infectious virus rather than a war. Not missiles, but microbes. The saddest part is that we have invested a huge amount in nuclear deterrents, but we have invested very little in a system to stop a pandemic. We are not ready for the next epidemic. And this is a big global failure. We need global preparedness. We need strong health systems." The bitter reality is that the situation of the health sector is dismal across the globe. This only added more to the despair.

2 Literature Review

Pandemics leave an ever-lasting impact and affect every social fabric and every sector of the economy. For instance, the situation of COVID-19 led to social distancing, isolation, transportation shutdown, boundary closure, home quarantine (of the infected), and economic lockdowns (partial or complete) in almost all the affected countries. In most countries, the summer of 2021 saw a second wave of partial lockdowns and night curfews. The economic shutdown led to a catastrophe, with far-reaching consequences (Chinazzi et al., 2020). It also led to misinformation dissemination, thereby manifesting ostracism, discrimination, and death. The greatest challenge of the COVID-19 crisis was to curb the pandemic of infodemics (Joshi, 2021).

By the coming of 2023, the emergency of the COVID-19 pandemic disease started receding. The main reason behind the slowing down of the contagious spread of COVID-19 virus variants is the achievement of herd immunity and medical research developments related to the COVID-19 vaccine invention. However, even towards the end of 2023, the pandemic is far from over.

There is a least doubt that the global healthcare crisis creates widespread negative effects because preventive steps related to curbing the spread and occurrence of such pandemic diseases are largely missing. In addition, the earlier literature related to the pandemics is generally ignored until the next contagious disease occurs or is largely overlooked. There is a sufficient amount of theoretical and empirical research related to the pandemics. Callegari and Feder (2022) provide an extensive literature review of studies discussing the long-term effects of pandemics. The authors present the pandemic effects on long-term economic development via theoretical and empirical economic and historical research on diseases. Cipolla (1974) reflects on the scholarly contributions directed towards exploring the relationship among three important variables, namely growth in population, economic growth, and magnitude and/or spread of diseases. Such scholarly ideas were developed as early as 1798 by Thomas Malthus in his book "An *Essay on the Principle of Population*" (Malthus, 1798). Weil (2014) and Costa (2015) write about health and economic growth. Bloom et al. (2022) reviewed the long-term economic effects of modern pandemics.

According to the World Bank's Global Economic Prospects Report (2020) and Basco et al. (2021), pandemics could affect growth in productivity, aggregate supply, and aggregate demand. Other effects of pandemics and epidemics include impacts on human capital (Acemoglu & Johnson, 2007; Meyers & Thomasson, 2021; Odugbesan & Rjoub, 2019), demographic effects (Delfino & Simmons, 2005; Acemoglu & Johnson, 2007), impact on land and physical capital (Acemoglu & Johnson, 2007), impact on the real return of capital (Basco et al., 2021), social capital distribution across different social strata (Hallegatte et al., 2020; McCannon & Rodriguez, 2019), impact on consumption, investment, and income (Jinjarak et al., 2021), socioeconomic effects (Garrett, 2008), financial effects (Keerthiratne & Tol, 2017), income inequalities versus sustainable development (Odugbesan & Rjoub, 2019), role of and/or changes in the government institutions during a pandemic (Alfani, 2013; Cavallo et al., 2013), knowledge, innovation, research and development (Hopkins, 1988; Jinjarak et al., 2021; Pamuk, 2007), market failure in the provision of a vaccine as a public good and research related to the vaccine invention (Kremer, 2000; Levenson, 2016), labour and human capital effects (Pamuk, 2007; Stiglitz & Guzman, 2021; Young, 2005). Research works such as Jinjarak et al. (2021), Stiglitz and Guzman (2021), and Pamuk (2007) have explored the investment and physical capital effects of earlier diseases.

3 COVID-19 and the Global Economy

COVID-19 did not come as an alarm of a health emergency only. However, it came with the financial and economic crisis when the world economy was already facing a recessionary situation. According to The United Nations (UN) World Economic Situation and Prospects (WESP) 2020 report, the global growth slowed to a 10-year low of 2.3% in 2019, with 1/5th of the global countries seeing a decline in their per capita income. European Union has seen a staggering growth; least developed countries (LDCs) are far away from realizing the 7% target annual growth rate of GDP; falling per capita GDP growth rates of the Latin American and the Caribbean countries; slowed GDP growth rate of East Asia and South Asia[1]; and, the falling growth rate of GDP in the African

[1] COVID-19 came when India was going through hard times, as it was in the middle of an economic slowdown. With 75% of the workforce in casual and self-employed jobs; looming banking, credit, and financial crisis; soaring public debt; the drastic demonetization experiment and its aftermath; poorly executed GST; rising unemployment; and continuous depreciation of the Indian rupee, the situation demands a much-crafted approach from India to mitigate all ill-effects of COVID-19 disease on its people and the economy. Given the severity of the pandemic and the sufferings of vulnerable (people), the situation demands a more proactive, inclusive, active, prolonged, and extensive approach. There is a need for a ***long-term multi-pronged approach*** to recover the Indian Economy from the ill consequences of the COVID-19 pandemic disease.

countries keeps them at an arms distance to realize sustainable development goals.[2] Besides, the growing trade tensions reduced the global trade growth to 0.3% in 2019 compared to 3.9% in 2018. The best example of such trade disputes was the recent US-China trade war. There is an ongoing prolonged and widespread global economic slowdown that arose from the situations of bilateral and multilateral trade disputes, growing inward-looking policies, ever-rising poverty and unemployment rates across economies, aggravating and deepening political polarization, high horizontal and vertical inequalities among and within the countries, unsustainable global climatic crisis associated with over-depleting of world's natural resources, and widespread global policy uncertainties.

The onset of the COVID-19 pandemic worsened the economic slowdown (see, for instance, Goodell & Huynh, 2020). The global economy has come to a standstill (Anderson et al., 2020). According to the UN WESP (2023) report, it is premature to comment on the final impacts of COVID-19 disease. The situation is worsened due to the war in Ukraine, the war in Gaza, multiple interconnected world crisis, volatilities in food and energy markets, high global inflation, wildfires, floods, other natural calamities, and the humanitarian crisis in Gaza and many other countries. The Report projects a decelerated world output growth rate from an estimated 3% in 2022 to 1.9% in 2023. Such a growth rate would be one of the lowest growth rates in recent decades. The world economy may take a longer time to recover. The consequences are profound and painful. We discuss these consequences under two categories: (i) the demand-reducing factors; and (ii) the supply-impeding factors.

3.1 Demand—Reducing Factors

- The beginning of this century witnessed the worst socioeconomic damage caused by the global financial crisis of 2007–2009, the Euro sovereign-debt crisis of 2009–2012, and the commodity price downturn of 2014–2016 (UNCTAD, 2019). This damage got aggravated in the presence of volatile oil prices, deteriorating real estate sector, falling international trade flows, slowing global manufacturing activity, unaddressed macroeconomic and structural issues, and growing geopolitical tensions. All this ended in years

[2] Ethiopia, Rwanda, and Cote D'Ivoire are the only African countries that are performing relatively better.

of a continued economic slowdown. COVID-19 added more to this slowdown. There occurred a reduction in the consumption demand. Eventually, it led to one of the worst economic recessions. The situation warranted that the global economy was unprepared to bear another external shock. No doubt, COVID-19 generated far-reaching, widespread, and long-lasting negative economic consequences. Furthermore, no country on the globe, not even India, saved itself from such consequences. Given high global macroeconomic challenges faced, the UN hopelessly forecasts world growth rate of 2.7% in 2024. The UN cautioned that the world economy might contract if adequate fiscal responses are not taken on time. According to Fillippini and Yayati (2022) and Pitterle and Niermann (2022), higher vaccination rates and generous fiscal support measures reduced the output losses in developed economies.

- Impaired financial sectors and financial instability created by high levels of debt arising from prolonged loose monetary policies in developed countries and easy-credit conditions in emerging economies reduced the economy's ability to cope with external shocks like COVID-19.
- The COVID-19 crisis emulated business uncertainties, and uncertainties made firms and investors pessimistic about prospects. The bearish sentiments, along with already falling business confidence, further curtailed investments.[3]
- COVID-19 revived the teachings of Keynesian economics—popularly known as the economics of recession or depression—that the role of the government is indispensable, and markets cannot deliver optimally in every situation. The declining economic activities hit the tax revenue collections. This pandemic demanded an increase in the governments' expenditures. However, the challenge lies in the fact that up to 2019, much fiscal easing has already occurred, and

[3] Business confidence index (BCI) monitors the growth in production and output; forecasts the turning points in the economic activities; thereby serving as a leading indicator of future economic developments in a country. It is based upon regular opinion surveys dealing with production, sales, orders, and stocks of finished goods in the industry sector. A number above 100 indicates increased confidence in business performance shortly, and a number below 100 suggests a decrease in confidence towards the future business performance. Business confidence fell sharply during the year 2019, even below 100 for most countries such as the United States, the Euro area, and China. It deteriorated further since the beginning of 2020 (OECD, 2020).

there is a huge burden of fiscal deficits on the global economies. Be it the aggressive fiscal expansions of some East Asian economies or the sizeable, elevated budget deficits and substantial public debts of India, Italy, Japan, or the US, the scope for a generous fiscal easing policy is significantly more minor (IMF WEO, 2019). The world economy started showing signs of recovery in early 2023. However, inflation reduction targeted tight policies are expected to hamper economic activity going forward (International Monetary Fund, 2023).

- Kumar (2020) wrote as early as 2020 that overcoming economic consequences of COVID-19 pandemic will require a series of fiscal austerity steps and political will. In 2023, even after a slight recovery, the countries cannot go for total production shortly. Moreover, exports, which play a crucial role in promoting economic growth, piling the stocks of foreign exchange reserves, and adding surplus to the economy's balance-of-payments situation, can re-define the business cycles and growth and development trajectories of the economies across the globe.
- This COVID-19 disease promoted economic inequalities. COVID-19 has led to a sudden economic stop. Because of this, workers working on consolidated salaries, temporary contracts, or daily wage basis lost their jobs. This widened the gap of economic division. Subsequently, it hampered the growth of economies. It led to a decrease in consumer demand. Not only the economic crisis, it also led to social discrimination, societal crises, food crisis, and humanitarian crises. For instance, unskilled labourers, private-sector employees, women, migrant workers, footloose labourers, wage hunters and gatherers, marginalized groups, homeless people, and workers from lower-skilled and lower economic occupations were much vulnerable to the economic crisis and health risks. The rising tension due to the economic losses led to a spike in domestic violence and other collateral effects of this pandemic. The pandemic developed chances of bridging the gap between large Asian countries and the rich global economies and created speculations of changes in the world order. For instance, the disease exposed the disastrous health system and weak social justice prevailing in the United States. To put it in the words of public intellectual Noam Chomsky, "…the damage from the pandemic was rooted in a colossal market failure, exacerbated by the capitalism of the neoliberal era." There is not a

single speck of doubt that neoclassicals ridiculed warnings of people like Garrett as "alarmist & Malthusian." This disease has proven them wrong. There are high chances that we are heading towards a world of absolute uncertainties and possibilities.

3.2 Supply—Impeding Factors

- The advent of COVID-19 has debunked the idea that we are immune to external global shocks. Countries across the globe adopted the policy of lockdown—mild to complete restrictions on the movement of people and goods, excluding the essentials and essential services—to either stop the community spread of this contagious viral disease or at least delay its spread till some vaccine or treatment of choice was discovered. This primarily affected the production units within the countries, production networks across economies, and global supply chains. There were cases where it led to a complete shutdown of production units. Already, the global economy was limping as the world industrial production recorded almost zero percentage change in 2019, attributed mainly to weaker trade and investment activities (UN WESP, 2020). The situation developed difficult and grave.
- Towards the end of 2019Q2, the Global Manufacturing Purchasing Managers' Index (PMI)[4] fell to its lowest level of 49.5 since 2012. In March 2020, it deteriorated for almost all the countries of the world. In 2022, it declined. In the second half of 2022, the PMI remained in contraction number. This low value raises the alarm for global leaders. It demands serious concern because manufacturers serve as the backbone of the world economy. Since the value of PMI is less

[4] The Purchasing Managers Index (PMI) generates the prevailing direction of economic trends in the manufacturing sector. Thus, it indicates the economic health of this vital sector of an economy. It is based on a monthly survey of 19 industries' 400 supply chain managers. The PMI survey covers the upstream and the downstream activity of five major areas: new orders, inventory levels, supplier deliveries, employment, and production. The headline PMI is a number from 0 to 100. A PMI value of more than 50 represents an improvement compared with the previous month, and a value of less than 50 represents deterioration. A number equal to 50 indicates no change. PMI can be used to represent goods and services sectors as well. Note that IHS Market, in association with ISM and IFPSM, produces the J. P. Morgan Global Manufacturing PMI.

than 50 which signals contraction in the global economy, COVID-19 'only added more salt to this wound as it extended and intensified this economic shrink.

- Except for South Asian and East Asian countries, there has been a reduction in the average labour productivity growth in all the economies of West Asia, Latin America, the Caribbean, Africa, Europe, Japan, Western Europe, and the United States, between the period 2016–2019 (UN WESP, 2020). Much of the reason lies in low investments and slow capital formation, low contributions from capital-deepening, and total factor productivity. COVID-19 further declined it and impeded countries' long-term economic development prospects via reduced labour productivity.
- This global shock shattered the already looming banking and financial sector. With banks being saddled by non-performing assets (NPAs) partly driven by crony capitalism, lackadaisical demand for bank credit and bank loans, credit losses, reduced capacities, the moratorium on re-payment of term loans and re-payment holidays, etcetera, leaves this sector on the verge of crisis.
- E-commerce is another sector that bore the brunt of lockdown calls worldwide. Some e-commerce businesses survived the brutal hit. It is surprising and exciting to note that COVID-19 had a tremendous influence on consumer behaviour. Companies needed to survive in the flexible digital workplace to meet the unprecedented demands of customers. Experts suggested that the survival of e-commerce businesses depended on what they were selling and how they adapted to the situation. It is quite possible that in the post-coronavirus world, people may have shifted priorities. These shifted priorities could pave the way for a more humane economy.
- The Labour market is the one that remained largely insulated from the persistent slowdown of the global economy over the years. ILO (2019) estimates suggested that the world unemployment rate fell to less than 5% in 2019. Nevertheless, the shock of COVID-19 did not warrant curtailment of unemployment globally. COVID-19 led to partial or total lockdowns across the countries. Informal workers, contractual labourers, hand-to-mouth people, daily wagers, men and women, unorganized workers, poor and downtrodden, hawkers, vendors, migrant workers, commuters, shopkeepers, and the uneducated youth faced dismal pain. Private employees suffered high risks of losing their jobs. Fear of facing retrenchment prevailed

widespread in the job market. This was aggravated by the ill-panned and ill-executed government policies. Even the formal sector suffered enormous challenges. Stagnant real wage growth existed in most countries, incentiveless productivity gains, rising productivity-pay gaps, increasing wage-inequalities, and gender pay gaps, both within and across economies (UN WESP, 2020). This, along with pay cuts and stay on recruitment policies, may prevail longer in the post-COVID-19 era. According to World Employment and Social Outlook: Trends (2023), the recovery from the COVID-19 crisis is incomplete even by the end of 2022, and the total recovery to pre-COVID-19 pandemic levels is not possible soon.

The situation does not stop here. These demand-reducing and supply-impeding factors are interwoven, interplay, and lead to multiplier effects. It generates a vicious circle across sectors and economies. Perhaps, the global economy may head towards one more world recession. The worst consequence can be another Great Depression. This may end in altering the patterns of production and consumption altogether. The coming years can pose a considerable challenge to the world leaders. The need is to save the lives, livelihood, rural economy, and the global economy. Moreover, to minimize the pandemic loss, governments must adopt a balanced policy mix in the coming years. Easy fiscal and monetary policy can offset the damage. Governments must infuse substantial resources into the economy, and a significant fiscal stimulus is imperative to deal with the problem. Central banks around the world have once again become mainline of defence. At the same time, social crisis needs to be minimized. Curtail non-essential expenses, increase healthcare outlays, and maximize social benefits. Public distribution of essentials will have to be expanded to fulfil basic needs. Governments must adopt inclusive ways to transfer incomes to the people experiencing poverty. In sum, all the marginalized and vulnerable people need to be cared for longer.

4 COVID-19 and the Environment

According to the United Nation's environment chief, Inger Anderson, "nature is sending us a message with the coronavirus pandemic and the ongoing climate crisis." She said that taking care of nature means caring for us as humans, who are highly interconnected with nature. The global health crisis of COVID-19 resulted in the closure of factories, cancellation of transportation facilities, and reduction of other destructive human activities. This economic shutdown led to a significant drop in greenhouse gases (GHG) emissions. As a result, nature has started healing. For instance, Gautam (2020) estimated that air pollutants in New York City reduced by 50%, and coal use in China decreased by 40% in early 2020 compared to 2019 estimates. Overall, GHG emissions recorded a 25% drop in the initial three months of COVID-19 (Gautam, 2020). Subsequently, this healing touch of nature demanded proper disposal of medical and other wastes arising from the pandemic (Bashir et al., 2020; Hellewell et al., 2020). The WHO (World Health Organization) published a report in 2022 on "Global analysis of healthcare waste in the context of COVID-19: status, impacts and recommendations." According to the report, COVID-19 generated 1.44 lakh tonnes of waste from 8 billion vaccine doses, 2.6 thousand tonnes of plastic from 140 million test kits, 7.31 lakh litres of chemical waste, and a 10-fold increase in healthcare waste loads at facilities.

COVID-19 exposed the need for better medical waste management at healthcare disposal facilities. The WHO Report (2022) recommends reforms related to the disposal of medical waste. It seems that nature is bouncing back the pressure human have put on it over years. The rising outbreak of epidemics like Ebola, MERS-CoV, Bird flu, West Nile virus, Zika virus, Nipah virus, and COVID-19 serve as an alarm that human beings are not maintaining a balance with nature/animals. The statement of Professor Andrew Cunningham, Zoological Society of London, was an eye-opener in which he quoted that it was predicted that there would be another viral epidemic from wildlife. It is quite inhuman, unfortunate, and ironic that there are live wild animal markets across the world in which animals are being transported over large distances. People in large numbers come in direct contact with such animals' bodily fluids, thereby maximizing the transmission of pathogens from such animals to humans.

John Scanlon, the former secretary-general of the Convention on International Trade of Endangered Species of Wild Fauna and Flora, said that illegal wildlife trade has indirectly caused this problem. The materialism in humans is soaring up and up. Humans are being reciprocated in the form of such outbreaks.

Looking at the statistics before the outbreak of COVID-19, all the indexes showed that our planet is sick. For instance, it has been estimated that indoor and outdoor air pollution caused 7 million deaths in 2016 alone (World Health Organization, 2018). The undying want of money, urbanization, consumerism, industrialization, and sophisticated lifestyle have brought drastic environmental changes. It looked impossible for the nations to change their ways before the COVID-19 pandemic. However, the outbreak of this global health crisis made it clear to the inhabitants of planet Earth that even the slightest positive change has a substantial positive impact on the environment. The world witnessed the improved quality of air, water, and soil. The emissions of air pollutants and greenhouse gases decreased significantly.

It is pretty ridiculous to separate human health from nature. It is impossible and dangerous at the same time to talk about human health and ignore the health of planet earth. These two things are inextricable. In sum, this pandemic debunked many notions of the environment. New horizons are opening for reframing the environmental policies and treaties. It has offered us a unique opportunity to rethink our environment, wildlife, health, and policies. Deep down, we are connected to nature for our existence. If we would not take lessons from the COVID-19 pandemic, then new pandemics are inevitable.

5 COVID-19, Health, and Positive Psychology

Several frameworks and models conceptualize and record responses to emergencies and disasters' mental health and psychosocial impacts (Ventevogel, 2018; Weiss et al., 2003). COVID-19 is a disaster. The latest disaster faced by the entire world.[5] This pandemic has claimed many precious lives, and people are so much scared about it. Understanding the gravity of this pandemic situation, one can easily discern the devastation caused by it at multiple levels and layers across the globe. The pandemic is not still over. This is a pandemic of fear, economic disruption, disorganization, stigmatization, confusion, and death. After World War II, the psychological bruises were harsher than the physical ones. The psychological wounds were complex and took much time to heal. The eminent psychologists and their works (see, for instance, Seligman & Csikzentmihalyi, 2000; Sheldon & King, 2001; Lopez & Snyder, 2009, among others) recommended taking lessons from the victims of World War II

[5] Disasters are as old as humans. Disasters are sudden calamitous situations that disrupt a community's functioning in a short time and cause damage to the community in all dimensions to an extent beyond the capacity of that community.

for regaining everyday life. Post catastrophe coping is vital for regaining normalcy and health, which follows the psychosocial approach and goes beyond the absence of disease or symptomatic illness (Sytema, 2006). The pandemic witnessed the practice of physical distancing, bullying, vilifying, petrifying, demonizing, religious abuse, expletives, abandonments, ostracism, and social stigmatization.

It was customary to get scared about the novel virus. Look at the death statistics of the affected countries. However, it was illogical to succumb to the fear of the virus. The situation warranted channelize this fear healthily by taking proper care of health, eating lots of fruits as they are stress relievers, doing some physical activity and practicing meditation at home, voicing love, care, and compassion, spending time with family, spreading authentic news and protecting oneself from information overload, enhancing emotional stability and learning to turn adversity into opportunity, helping the vulnerable and taking care of needy people, and encouraging "virtual touch" in today's circumstances.

According to the cognitive psychologist Richard Lazarus, the way people think about and appraise a stressor is one of the significant factors determining the impact of such a stressor. So, the pandemic demanded targeting the cognitive appraisal approach of people towards the crisis. To enhance the coping strategies of people. To encourage people to discover new ways of responding to the situation maturely and healthily. Resilience was one such way. A personal attribute or ability to bounce back. Only resilient ones overcome the loss. Non-resilient ones need to learn this. Psychologists advocate that resilience is a skill, so there is a provision for improvement. It is high time to embrace the concept of psychological well-being. Understand the fragilities of the human psyche. In short, to bring positive changes in one's life.

6 Conclusions

The COVID-19 pandemic made us realize that our lives are shared beyond the national borders. We live in a world of cosmopolitanism, meaning it is high time to acknowledge and awaken the desire for co-existence. It is high time to rethink and reframe our laws, policies, and values to identify the cracks that made us susceptible to this global health crisis. We must weave a new canopy of warmth, care, compassion, security, love, interdependence, coordination, and upliftment for all of us. The world leadership must assemble the people of all ages, genders, races, cultures, ethnicities, and regions, and dissolve the tangles and differences to protect humankind. It is nerve-wrenching to see the mosaic of death and dying created by an invisible virus. However, our coordinated efforts and indomitable spirits can get us immense collective triumph.

The COVID-19 pandemic was diabolical as it destroyed lives and livelihoods. COVID-19 is still not over. It may take some time to access the overall, inevitably large, economic damage to the global economy. The review mirror shows the recent global economic recession 2008 and how the world economy rose again. Thus, it is a silver lining that can guide the world today in combating the current recession. On the economic front, specific measures can be employed. The global economy can be resuscitated and revived only by coordinated global efforts. The common slogan should be: "whatever it takes will be done to stop the crisis." Countries with fewer resources in reserve must be aided to recover. Global civil bodies and corporations must work in tandem to reduce the sufferings arising as collateral effects of the pandemic. Undoubtedly, countries must see this crisis through the prism of coordination rather than competition. Emphasis must be on efficiency in policymaking. The need is to set up long-term fiscal goals. Deep fiscal-monetary coordination is required to scale down the macroeconomic risks and uncertainties.[6] It is high time to make a global call towards addressing the issues related to the deep climatic crisis, environmental hazards, food insecurities, undernourishment, economic inequalities, and lack of opportunities in education, employment, and health.

On the social front, there is not an iota of doubt in the statement of WHO that the greatest threat to the global economy and security is pandemics, health emergencies, and weak health systems. Lack of access to effective public health measures makes a pandemic worse. So, the need of the hour is to propagate and adopt the concept of "global health security." It can act as a shield and armour against health impact and social disruption caused by epidemic and pandemic outbreaks (Zowalaty & Järhult, 2020). Global health security, in harmony with International Health Regulations, includes a range of measures to protect the world from infectious diseases. To put it clearly, one can say that it is a set

[6] In this crisis time, cutting the interest rates is of utmost importance because interest payments divert resources away from development finance. The share of public revenue spent on interest payments increased in over 70% of developing countries between 2010 and 2019 (UN WESP, 2020).

of shared "labor and wisdom" of countries, organizations, communities, agencies, and individuals which nudges them towards greater awareness, cooperation, and collaboration. The basic unit of global health security is preparedness. The onus lies on all of us to shape the global research, which will focus on preparing vaccines and treatments for such pandemics. Framing valid public health policies can become a guiding force in enhancing the health of communities worldwide. All this can be achieved by focusing on proper planning, preparation, training, and coordination. The efficient management of such pandemics can never be achieved without the integration and collaboration of medical science, social science, natural sciences, technology, ecology, law, economics, and politics. Community participation is akin to the prevention and management of such pandemics.

That human health, animal health, and wildlife sectors are inextricable entities, a more umbrella term of "one health approach" must be encouraged. It should be noted and accepted that globalization, urbanization, and technology are the means of development and sources of the fastest and furthest transmission of diseases.

References

Acemoglu, D., & Johnson, S. (2007). Disease and development: The effect of life expectancy on economic growth. *Journal of Political Economy, 115*(6), 925–985.

Alfani, G. (2013). Plague in seventeenth-century Europe and the decline of Italy: An epidemiological hypothesis. *European Review of Economic History, 17*(4), 408–430.

Anderson, R. M., Heesterbeek, H., Klinkenberg, D., & Hollingsworth, T. D. (2020). How will country-based mitigation measures influence the course of the COVID-19 epidemic? *The Lancet, 395*(10228), 931–934. https://doi.org/10.1016/S0140-6736(20)30567-5

Bashir, M. F., Ma B., Bilal., Komal, B., Bashir, M. A., Tan, D., & Bashir, M. (2020) Correlation between climate indicators and COVID-19 pandemic in New York, USA. *Science of The Total Environment, 728*(138835). https://doi.org/10.1016/j.scitotenv.2020.138835

Basco, S., Domènech, J., & Rosés, J. R. (2021). The redistributive effects of pandemics: Evidence on the Spanish flu. *World Development, 141*, 105389.

Bloom, D. E., Kuhn, M., & Prettner, K. (2022). Modern infectious diseases: Macroeconomic impacts and policy responses. *Journal of Economic Literature, 60*(1), 85–131.

Callegari, B., & Feder, C. (2022). A literature review of pandemics and development: The long-term perspective. *Economics of Disasters and Climate Change, 6*(1), 183–212.

Cavallo, E., Galiani, S., Noy, I., & Pantano, J. (2013). Catastrophic natural disasters and economic growth. *Review of Economics and Statistics, 95*(5), 1549–1561.

Cheng, V. C. C., Lau, S. K. P., Woo, P. C. Y., & Yuen, K. Y. (2007). Severe acute respiratory syndrome coronavirus as an agent of emerging and reemerging infection. *Clinical Microbiology Reviews, 20*(4), 660–694.

Chinazzi, M., Davis, J. T., Ajelli, M., Gioannini, C., Litvinova, M., Merler, S., et al. (2020). The effect of travel restrictions on the spread of the 2019 novel coronavirus (COVID-19) outbreak. *Science, 368*(6489), 395–400. https://doi.org/10.1126/science.aba9757

Cipolla, C. M. (1974). The plague and the pre-Malthus Malthusians. *Journal of European Economic History, 3*(2), 277.

Costa, D. L. (2015). Health and the Economy in the United States from 1750 to the Present. *Journal of Economic Literature, 53*(3), 503–570.

Delfino, D., & Simmons, P. J. (2005). Dynamics of tuberculosis and economic growth. *Environment and Development Economics, 10*(6), 719–743.

Fillippini, F. & Yayati, E. L. (2022). *Pandemic divergence: A short note on COVID-19 and global income inequality* (Working Paper No. 168). Global Economy and Development Program, Brookings Institution.

Garrett, T. A. (2008, March/April). Pandemic economics: The 1918 influenza and its modern-day implications. *Federal Reserve Bank of St. Louis Review, 90.*

Gautam, S. (2020). COVID-19: Air pollution remains low as people stay at home. *Air Quality, Atmosphere, & Health, 13*(7), 853–857. https://doi.org/10.1007/s11869-020-00842-6

Goodell, J. W., & Huynh, T. L. D. (2020). Did congress trade ahead? Considering the reaction of U.S. industries to COVID-19. *Finance Research Letters, 36*(101578). https://doi.org/10.1016/j.frl.2020.101578

Hallegatte, S., Vogt-Schilb, A., Rozenberg, J., Bangalore, M., & Beaudet, C. (2020). From poverty to disaster and back: A review of the literature. *Economics of Disasters and Climate Change, 4*, 223–247.

Hellewell, J., Abbott, S., Gimma, A., Bosse, N. I., Jarvis, C. I., Russell, T. W., Munday, J. D., Kucharski, A. J., Edmunds, W. J., & Sun, F. (2020). Feasibility of controlling COVID-19 outbreaks by isolation of cases and contacts. *The Lancet Global Health, 8*(4), e488–e496. https://doi.org/10.1016/S2214-109X(20)30074-7

Hopkins, J. W. (1988). The eradication of smallpox: Organizational learning and innovation in international health administration. *The Journal of Developing Areas, 22*(3), 321–332.

IASC (Inter-Agency Standing Committee), Reference Group on Mental Health and Psychosocial Support in Emergency Settings. (2015). *Mental health and psychosocial support in Ebola virus disease outbreaks: A guide for public health programme planners*. Geneva.

ILO. (2019). *World employment and social outlook: Trends 2019*. International Labour Office. https://www.ilo.org/wcmsp5/groups/public/---dgreports/---dcomm/---publ/documents/publication/wcms_670542.pdf. Viewed on 4 December 2020

IMF WEO. (2019). *World economic outlook databases*. https://www.imf.org/en/Publications/SPROLLs/world-economic-outlook-databases#sort=%40imfdate%20descending. Viewed on 12 June 2021.

International Monetary Fund. (2023, October). *World economic outlook: Navigating global divergences*. Washington, DC.

Jinjarak, Y., Noy, I., & Ta, Q. (2021). Pandemics and economic growth: Evidence from the 1968 H3N2 influenza. *Economics of Disasters and Climate Change*, 1–21.

Joshi, A. (2021). COVID-19 pandemic in India: Through psycho-social lens. *Journal of Social and Economic Development*, 1–24. https://doi.org/10.1007/s40847-020-00136-8

Keerthiratne, S., & Tol, R. S. (2017). Impact of natural disasters on financial development. *Economics of Disasters and Climate Change, 1*(1), 33–54.

Kremer, M. (2000). Creating markets for new vaccines. Part I: Rationale. *Innovation Policy and the Economy, 1*, 35–72.

Kumar, A. (2020, August 4). Impact of COVID-19 and what needs to be done. *Economic and Political Weekly, 14*(55).

Levenson, K. G. (2016). *Capital and the common good: How innovative finance is tackling the world's most urgent problems*. Columbia University Press.

Lopez, S. J., & Snyder, C. R. (Eds.). (2009). *The Oxford handbook of positive psychology*. Oxford University Press.

Malthus, T. R. (1798). *An essay on the principle of population as it affects the future improvement of society, with remarks on the speculations of Mr. Godwin, M. Condorcet, and other writers*. J. Johnson in St. Paul's churchyard, London.

McCannon, B. C., & Rodriguez, Z. (2019). Orphans and pro-social behaviour: Evidence from Uganda. *Journal of International Development, 31*(6), 495–515.

Meyers, K., & Thomasson, M. A. (2021). Can pandemics affect educational attainment? Evidence from the polio epidemic of 1916. *Cliometrica, 15*(2), 231–265.

Odugbesan, J. A., & Rjoub, H. (2019). Relationship among HIV/AIDS prevalence, human capital, good governance, and sustainable development: Empirical evidence from Sub-Saharan Africa. *Sustainability, 11*(5), 1348.

OECD. (2020). *Business confidence index (BCI) (indicator)*. https://doi.org/10.1787/3092dc4f-en. Viewed on 12 January 2021.

Pamuk, Ş. (2007). The black death and the origins of the 'great divergence' across Europe, 1300–1600. *European Review of Economic History, 11*(3), 289–317.

Pitterle, I., & Niermann, L. (2022). *The COVID-19 crisis: What explains cross-country differences in the pandemic's short-term economic impact*. United Nations Department of Economic and Social Affairs. United States of America. Retrieved November 6, 2023, from https://policycommons.net/artifacts/4462532/the-COVID-19-crisis/5259803/. CID: 20.500.12592/xnjpbc.

Seligman, M. E. P., & Csikzentmihalyi, M. (2000). Positive psychology: An introduction. *American Psychologist, 55*(1), 5–14. https://doi.org/10.1037/0003-066X.55.1.5

Sheldon, K. M., & King, L. (2001). Why positive psychology is necessary. *American Psychologist, 56*(3), 216–217. https://doi.org/10.1037/0003-066X.56.3.216

Stiglitz, J. E., & Guzman, M. M. (2021). The pandemic economic crisis, precautionary behavior, and mobility constraints: An application of the dynamic disequilibrium model with randomness. *Industrial and Corporate Change, 30*(2), 467–497.

Sytema, S. (2006). Mental health at the crossroads: The promise of the psychosocial approach. *International Journal of Integrated Care*. https://doi.org/10.5334/ijic.149

UN WESP. (2020). *The world economic situation and prospects*. United Nations New York https://unctad.org/en/PublicationsLibrary/wesp2020_en.pdf. Viewed on 11 April 2021.

UN WESP. (2023). Report (United Nation's World Economic Situation and Prospects, 2023). World Economic Situation and Prospects 2023 | UNCTAD. Viewed on 2 November 2023.

UNCTAD. (2019). *Trade and development report 2019: Financing a global green new deal*. Sales No. E.19.II.D.15. https://unctad.org/en/PublicationsLibrary/tdr2019_en.pdf. Viewed on 28 June 2021.

Ventevogel, P. (2018). Interventions for mental health and psychosocial support in complex humanitarian emergencies: Moving towards consensus in policy and action? In N. Morina & A. Nickerson (Eds.), *Mental health of refugee and conflict-affected populations*. Springer. https://doi.org/10.1007/978-3-319-97046-2_8

Weil, D. N. (2014). Health and economic growth. In P. Aghion & S. Durlauf (Eds.), *Handbook of economic growth* (1st ed., vol. 2, Chapter 3, pp. 623–82). Elsevier.

Weiss, M. G., Saraceno, B., Saxena, S., & van Ommeren, M. (2003). Mental health in the aftermath of disasters: Consensus and controversy. *The Journal of Nervous and Mental Disease, 191*(9), 611–615. https://doi.org/10.1097/01.nmd.0000087188.96516.a3

WHO. (2018). *Global health estimates 2016: Deaths by cause, age, sex, by country and by region, 2000–2016.* Geneva, World Health Organization. https://www.who.int/healthinfo/global_burden_disease/estimates/en/index1.html. Viewed on 30 December 2020.

WHO Report. (2022). *Global analysis of healthcare waste in the context of COVID-19: status, impacts and recommendations.* World Health Organization. Licence: (CC BY-NC-SA 3.0 IGO). Accessed on 10 November 2023 at 9789240039612-eng.pdf (who.int)/Global analysis of health care waste in the context of COVID-19 (who.int).

World Employment and Social Outlook: Trends. (2023). Geneva: International Labour Office, 2023. Accessed on 04 November 2023 at wcms_865332.pdf (ilo.org)/Report: World Employment and Social Outlook: Trends 2023 (ilo.org).

World Bank, Global Economic Prospects Report. (2020, June). World Bank, Washington, DC.

Worldometer. (2023). https://www.worldometers.info/coronavirus/

Young, A. (2005). The gift of the dying: The tragedy of AIDS and the welfare of future African generations. *The Quarterly Journal of Economics, 120*(2), 423–466.

Zacharias, L., Harikrishnan, U., Jayakumar, C., & Sekar, K. (2019). Psychosocial perspective of Nipah virus outbreak in Kerala, India. https://doi.org/10.17354/ijss/2018/30

Zowalaty Mohamed, E. El., & Järhultc, J. D. (2020, June). From SARS to COVID-19: A previously unknown SARS-related coronavirus (SARS-CoV-2) of pandemic potential infecting humans—Call for a One Health approach. *One Health, 9*. https://doi.org/10.1016/j.onehlt.2020.100124

PART II

The Impact of COVID-19 on Education

CHAPTER 8

How Is COVID-19 Re-shaping Medical Education?

Adhari Al Zaabi, Hamed Al Sinawi, Thamra Al Ghafri, Ahmed Al Harthi, and Abdulraman Al Mirza

1 Introduction

The coronavirus disease (COVID-19) pandemic led to unexpected interruptions across all sectors (WHO, 2020). With restrictions such as social distancing, self-isolation and quarantine, universities across the world started to re-structure their academic agendas. According to UNESCO,

A. Al Zaabi (✉)
College of Medicine and Health Science, Sultan Qaboos University, Muscat, Oman
e-mail: Adhari@squ.edu.om

H. Al Sinawi
Sultan Qaboos University Hospital, Seeb, Oman
e-mail: senawi@squ.edu.om

T. Al Ghafri
Ministry of Health, Muscat, Oman

A. Al Harthi · A. Al Mirza
College of Medicine, Sultan Qaboos University, Seeb, Oman

A. Mishrif (ed.), *Perspectives on Human Capital Development*,
https://doi.org/10.1007/978-981-97-5246-1_8

more than 188 countries enforced educational institutes closure in the first quarter of 2020 due to the COVID-19 pandemic while others suspended or postponed academic activities and substituted face-to-face classes with online classes in what was called emergency remote learning (ERT) (P, 2020). The online learning became the main mode of teaching in most medical schools and educational institutes introduced different online platforms and to adopt better training and evaluation strategies. It is worth mentioning that online learning is not a new concept. In fact radio, DVDs and interactive Web-based programs were used in different countries during wars, violence and natural disasters for remote learning (Davies, 2011; Shraim & Khlaif, 2010). Fortunately, with the current digital technology, there are various interactive tools available to smooth the remote learning experience and ensure the continuation of learning.

Despite the availability of several interactive platforms, many challenges have been reported to negatively affect the online learning experience such as poor technical skills of learners and educators, lack of solid institutional strategies and a general negative attitude toward online learning (Molodynski et al., 2021). The main challenges reported by the students were related to time management, lack of communication with peers and teachers, poor internet connection, unavailable gadgets to facilitate online learning process and lack of confidence about dealing with computer hardware and software (Rajab et al., 2020). Therefore, the transition to online learning was not a simple digitization of learning content. Instead, it requires acquiring technical skills such as rewriting content to fit the online delivery method and finding strategies to keep the students engaged in online sessions. It is even more challenging to shift a skill-based session with hands-on learning from face-to-face to online (Dedeilia et al., 2020).

During the pandemic, the college of Medicine and Health Sciences (CoMHSc) at Sultan Qaboos University (SQU) in Oman introduced rapid re-configuration of the teaching curriculum, education systems and hospital facilities to ensure continuity of clinical care, contain the spread of COVID-19 without interrupting students learning. This rapid transformation of system and re-allocation of services was not without challenges, and it carried with it important lessons. The aim of this study is to describe how online learning was implemented at the CoMHSc and develop an understanding the students' perspectives during the online learning and how their preference for the post-COVID-19 era can influence the quality and quantity of online learning in the future and help policymakers evaluate the current medical curriculum. This study adds to the emerging literatures on how the COVID-19 pandemic reshaped medical education.

2 Method

2.1 *Context*

Before COVID-19 pandemic, the standard curriculum in the college of Medicine and health Sciences at Sultan Qaboos University was conducted fully on campus. The curriculum consists of three phases, phases I and II are both pre-clinical while phase III is a clinical phase. Phase I is a foundational phase where discipline-based courses are taught, while the main bulk of phase II was multidisciplinary organ system-based courses. During phase III the students start their clinical clerkships at the university hospital and other affiliated ministry of health institutions. The student intake is around 130 students each year and the average duration of the MD program is 7 years.

2.2 *Transformation to Remote Teaching*

During spring 2020, SQU announced emergency remote learning where all theoretical classes, practical and assessment were conducted remotely for both clinical and pre-clinical students. Some courses were entirely conducted either in a synchronous or asynchronous format while others adopted a blended synchronous and asynchronous mode. Synchronous learning is a learning strategy, where the course is conducted virtually in a fixed time with both learners and educators in the live classroom and can have real time discussion and communication. While in the asynchronous learning, the course is virtual but not live. The sessions are usually recorded, and the discussion happens through emails or other social networking tools.

2.3 *Staff Development*

The emergency shift to online learning was not planned and the majority of medical curriculum were not designed for remote learning. Furthermore, not all educators and learners have good familiarity with interactive online platforms and the use of online assessment tools. Therefore, to aid the transition to remote learning, several workshops have been conducted to train faculty on the use of digital platforms and on the utilization of different online tools to deliver teaching and assessment. Many of the workshop sessions and learning material were recorded and were made available to the faculty on the College website (https://www.squ.edu.om/medicine).

2.4 *Study Instruments*

The Questionnaires was designed by four investigators after a comprehensive literature review. The team constituted 2 assistant professors from the CoMHSc and a clinical consultant from Sultan Qaboos University Hospital. All investigators were involved in the emergency transition to remote learning. The questionnaire underwent multiple rounds of revision by the research team till the final version was agreed upon. It consisted of 3 subscales: sociodemographic (10 items), perception of online learning (9 item) and perception of remote learning of clinical skills (2 items) subscales. Questions were multiple choice questions, 5-point Likert scale ranging from 1 = Strongly disagree to 5 = Strongly agree with a blank left for any other comments. For the qualitative part, three general questions were added at the end of the survey with "explain" options for each. The questions are: "How much of the curriculum you wish to continue as online? 1–10%, 10–25%, 25–50%, 50–75%, 75–80%", "How do you rate your satisfaction with online learning? Very satisfied, satisfied, mixed opinion, not satisfied, not very satisfied", and the last question was "What are the major challenges if resolved would make your online learning experience be more satisfactory?" The questions from the survey aimed to evaluate the overall perception of students toward remote learning and to uncover the main benefits and challenges perceived by them. They also evaluate the overall satisfaction and their view regarding implementation of remote learning in medical education in the future.

Ethical approval was obtained from the medical research ethics committee at the College of Medicine and Health Sciences, SQU. All participants consented and were provided with an information sheet about the project. The questionnaire was anonymous, and confidentiality of information was assured.

2.5 Survey Implementation and Validation

The survey was piloted on 30 participants. The questions were reviewed by the researchers and modified accordingly. A Cronbach analysis was conducted on the "Perception of online learning" and "remote learning for clinical skills" subscales of the survey. It was found that the subscales' alpha score was 0.78 and 0.81, respectively, which indicates that the subscales have an adequate level of inter-item reliability. All medical students registered at the CoMHSc were invited to participate in the study through an online link sent by institutional emails between 27th July 2020 and 27th August 2020.

2.6 Statistical Analysis

Descriptive statistics of mean, standard deviations, frequencies and percentages to describe participants were implemented for analysis. An independent-samples t-test was used to investigate if the subscale scores differed significantly by participants' demographics.

3 Results

3.1 Demographics of Participants

One hundred and eighty-five medical students responded to the survey out of 750 registered students (response rate of 24%). The demographics of the participants are shown in Table 1. The mean age was 20.3 years, with a male-to-female ratio of 1.4:1. The majority of the participants were Omanis (173, 93.5%). Majority of the students were in their pre-clinical years (158, 85.9%) compared to clinical year students (26, 14.1%). One hundred and four students had GPA $\geq$ 3 and 81 (57%) had GPA < 3 (43%). Almost all students reported good overall IT abilities such as emailing skills, word processing, PowerPoint use and browsing the internet. About half of the participants reported not having good typing skills.

Majority of courses were conducted online through the use of video-conferencing tools. Majority of the participants reported that at least one course was conducted in a combined synchronous and asynchronous format during the pandemic. Half of students showed more preference toward a combined synchronous and asynchronous learning (n = 92, 50%) followed by a preference toward asynchronous learning (n = 47,

Table 1 Demographics of participants

Category		*Number (%)*
Age	Mean	20.3
	Median	20
Gender	Female	77 (41.6%)
	Male	108 (58.4%)
Nationality	Omani	173 (93.5%)
	Non- Omani	12 (6.5%)
Marital status	Single	184 (99.5%)
	Married	1 (0.5%)
Academic Phase	Phase 1	64 (34.8%)
	Phase 2	94 (51.1%)
	Phase 3	26 (14.1%)
Cumulative GPA	1.00–1.99	2 (1.1%)
	2.00–2.99	79 (42.7%)
	3.00–3.49	68 (36.8%)
	3.50–4.00	36 (19.5%)
IT abilities	Emailing skills	147 (79%)
	Word processing	108 (58.4%)
	PowerPoint	134 (72%)
	Browsing the internet	145 (78%)
	Keyboard skills	102 (55%)
	Using media software	127 (69%)

25%). Only 26 (14%) students prefer synchronous only learning over other learning modalities.

3.2 *Benefits and Challenges of Synchronous and Asynchronous Learning*

The most reported benefit of the asynchronous learning was the ability to pause, revisit or stop the sessions as needed (n = 125, 67.6%) followed by the flexibility of the sessions (where, when and how to access content) (n = 116, 62.7%) Fig. 1. While the most perceived benefit of the synchronous learning was the connection with professors and peers followed by accountability and the ability to manage time since sessions are scheduled and attendance is considered Fig. 2.

On the other hand, the most perceived challenges of asynchronous learning were difficulty in time management and completion of all coursework on time (n = 112, 60.5%) followed by the feeling of disconnection from instructors (n = 94, 50.8%) Fig. 3. Finding a reliable and stable

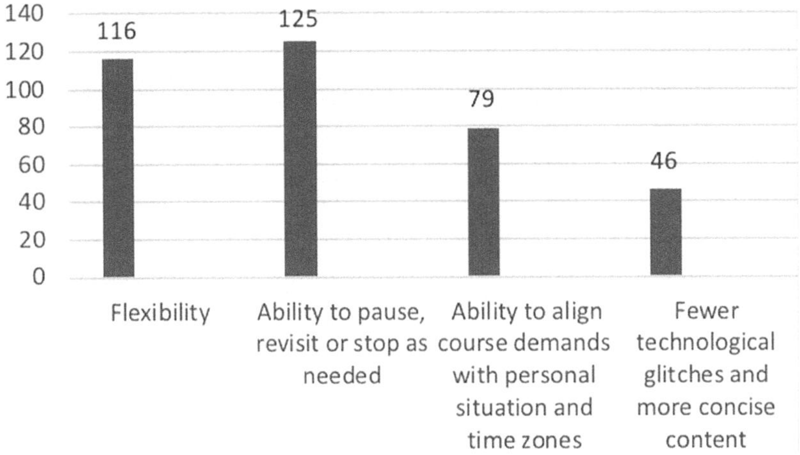

Fig. 1 Perceived benefits of asynchronous learning

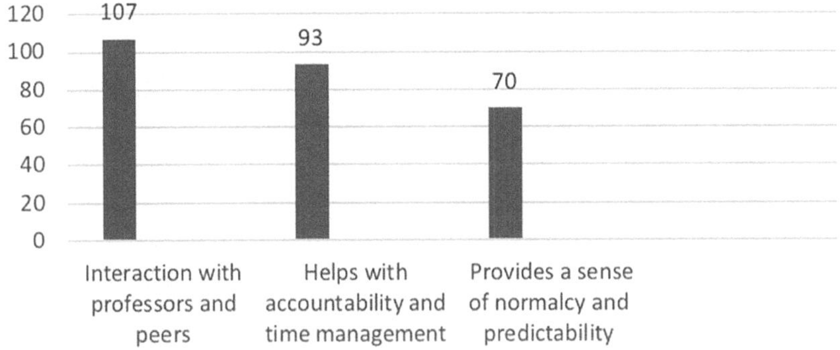

Fig. 2 Perceived benefits of synchronous learning

internet connection was not a challenge for the majority of the participants in asynchronous learning. Instead, it was the most perceived challenge in synchronous learning (n = 85, 45.9%). The second most perceived challenge in synchronous learning was distraction by their families followed by unclear communications or expectations from instructors about attending classes and assessment (n = 71, 38.4%) Fig. 4.

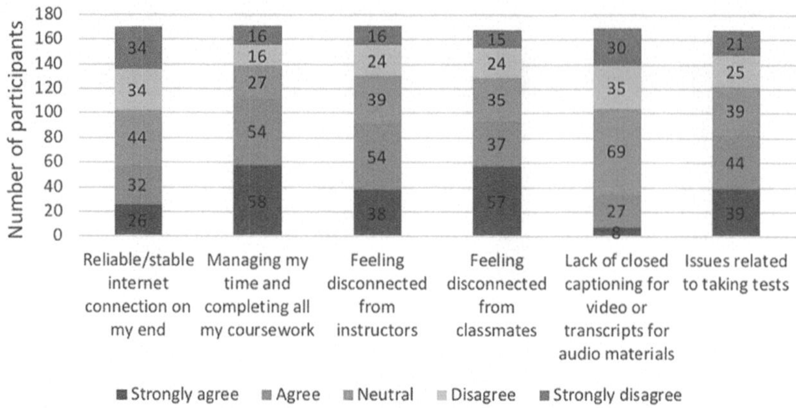

Fig. 3 Perceived challenges of asynchronous learning

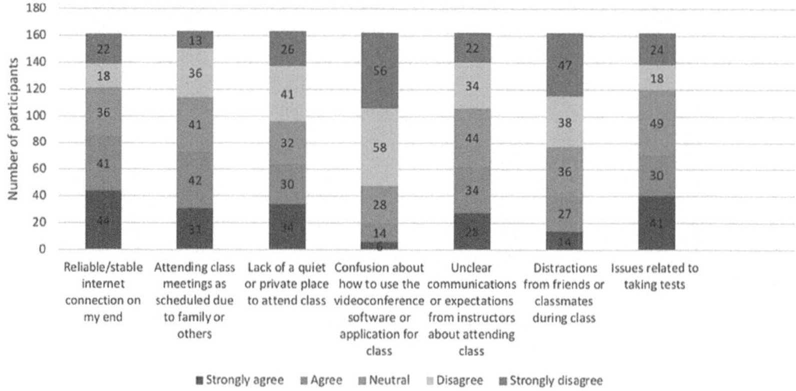

Fig. 4 Perceived challenges of synchronous learning

When asked to compare their learning experience during the study period to that of the first week of emergency remote learning, the majority of the students reported feeling more comfortable with remote learning compared to the first week of online learning. In fact, some even highly recommended a hybrid curriculum in the future.

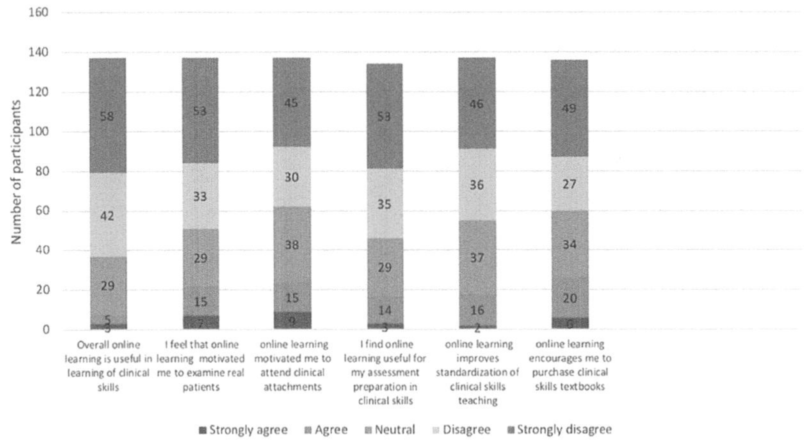

Fig. 5 Perception of the usefulness of online learning for learning clinical skills

3.3 Perception of Online Learning for Clinical Skills Education

The vast majority of the participants agreed that online learning did not help them learn clinical skills nor it helped in standardization of clinical teaching, motivate students to attend clinical attachments, or encouraged them to purchase clinical skills textbooks. Very few students found it useful to motivate them to examine real patients ($n = 24$, 13%) Fig. 5.

When asked to rate various e-learning mediums in term of their usefulness for clinical skills learning, students rated online demonstrative videos, images and descriptive text as the most beneficial media ($n = 123$; 66.5%, $n = 116$; 66.7%, $n = 75$;40.5%, respectively) Fig. 6. Moderated hyperlinks appeared not to be beneficial for majority of the students in clinical skills learning.

There was no significant statistical association between the challenges perceived in online clinical skills learning and either the GPA, gender or academic year ($p > 0.05$).

3.4 Satisfaction and Future Expectation

Majority (45%) of students were highly satisfied and supportive of online education especially for theoretical sessions in the pre-clinical years Fig. 7. Almost half of the students expressed their wish to have most of the

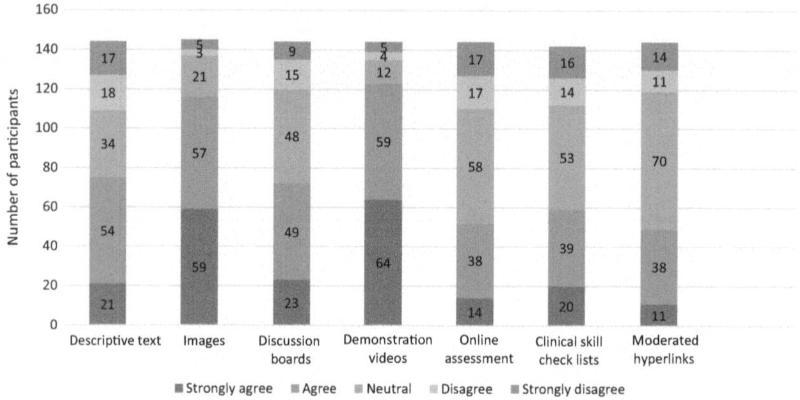

Fig. 6 The media tools that were found to be useful in my learning of clinical skills

theory classes online in the future in a recorded format so they can have a flexibility in their learning. They reported preference for face-to-face session only for discussion and application exercises. Almost 75% of the student who reported preference for online learning to continue in the future were from pre-clinical years.

Almost third of the students (36%) wish that 25–50% of the curriculum continue as online Fig. 8. In the "explain" section they reported their preference for didactic lectures to be made available online. Some students don't support online learning and they reported that face-to-face interaction is vital for their understanding and communications with peers and tutors is part of the learning process. Regarding the challenges question, the reported challenges were arranged in themes as in the Table 2.

4 Discussion

Despite the emergency shift during the COVID-19 pandemic and the lack of readiness, online learning has provided an opportunity for many students to continue learning without interruption. It is thought to be a real test for the agility of educational institutes and resilience of educators and learners to adapt changes (Yurttas et al., 2020). The transition was not without obstacles and challenges along the three main learning perspectives: educator, students and contents. Educators need

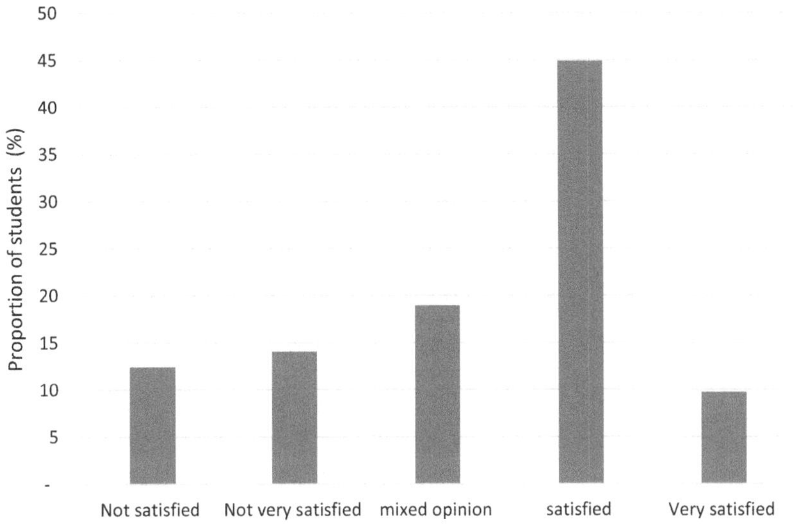

Fig. 7 Overall satisfaction with online teaching

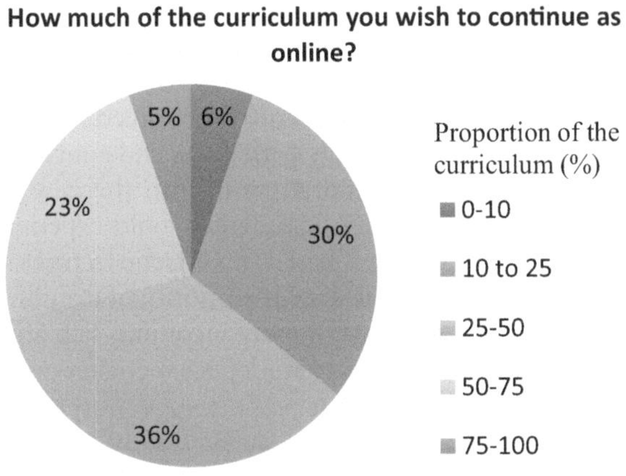

Fig. 8 The proportion of students who wish online learning to continue in the future

Table 2 Themes of challenges of online learning that if resolved will improve satisfaction

Challenge theme	*Sample of student quotes*
Technical issues	"It would be better if we have better and cheaper internet connection" "Technical support should be readily available for both students and teachers"
Communication	"To have a meeting at least once a month, between the students and course coordinators to discuss problems faced" "One virtual meeting about the strategy of online learning instead of many emails and confusion "
Decision making	"More collaboration between students and tutors in decision making"
Readiness	"Training the professors and teachers to be well-versed with technology"
Psychosocial issues	"Understanding that both students and faculty needs extra support during online learning are struggling with this transition
Synchronous/ asynchronous	"Eliminating live/synchronous lectures as they are a waste of time"

to be equipped with the needed skills and tools to facilitate the continuation of the learning process through the use of several interactive learning resources and platforms. Students were forced to be independent learners and to communicate virtually with peers and educators. Contents and assignments needed to be tailored to fit into the new platforms. It has been argued that the pre-clinical students would experience minimal disruption since their curriculum is based on didactic lectures. The clinical students would be largely affected since the priority of frontline healthcare workers had shifted to treating the rapidly incoming sick and vulnerable patients. This study aimed to evaluate students experience and their future perspective regarding online learning.

Overall, students have reported a general satisfaction with online learning, and they addressed the continues support they have received from during the transition to emergency online learning. They have reported the challenges they faced and how all troubleshot by the college administration within weeks of the transition. In fact majority feels they are better in term of adopting online learning compared to the first week of the transition which was reported earlier as well (Dhillon et al., 2020).

In our institute, several workshops have been conducted to rapidly prepare the educators and students for this shift. Technical support was readily available for both students and educators, although challenges were inevitable. In fact, Frehywot et al. evaluated online learning as part of a planned curricular change before COVID-19 (Frehywot et al., 2013). Despite the planning, a few barriers related to inadequate infrastructure, lack of face-to-face interaction, inadequate technical support, financial costs of maintaining the platform, and time commitment required from teachers were reported.

The challenges that have been reported by medical students in this study were mainly lack of proper interaction with the educators and colleagues and the feeling of isolation during the online asynchronous sessions. Knowing that interaction is a significant element in learning as it boosts learning outcomes, more engaging strategies need to be implemented in online learning through the use of interactive tools. Students did not report isolation as a challenge in synchronous sessions. In fact, the ability to interact with peers and educators was the top-reported benefit in synchronous sessions. They listed psychological issues, involvement in decision-making, technical support and communication as main areas that need to be considered to improve the experience. The listed reasons for this perception are similar to those reported in other studies (Farooq et al., 2020; Rahiem, 2021; Regmi & Jones, 2020).

Digital inequality with unstable internet connection, lack of devices where some students share the same device with siblings and the costly internet packages were frequently reported during the emergency remote learning but this was not a challenge in the followed semester (Cecilio-Fernandes et al., 2020; Zhang et al., 2020). Home atmosphere with non-academic responsibilities was another reason reported to hinder students' engagement and interaction in online environment (Baltà-Salvador et al., 2021). A fear of losing an academic year and lack proper hands-on training in pre-clinical practical and clinical training in clinical setting was reported earlier among medical students (Cao et al., 2020; Hasan & Bao, 2020; Izaias et al., 2020) (Grubic et al., 2020; Lin, 2020).

Another dimension of challenges is faced in the clerkship training of undergraduate medical students who have moved away from bedside teaching, a vital element of their training. Substituting bedside teaching with interactive online resources was the only resort but it can't substitute the soft and heard skills students gain from direct involvement with patients (Koumpouras & Helfgott, 2020). This has further exacerbated the anxiety and stress level of medical students because of the fear of inability to gain skills needed for graduation and to be competent doctors. Medical universities used several platforms to ensure a sufficient clinical exposure such as simulators, online video library, educational conferences and online atlases and interactive online picture diagnosis quizzes (Chandler, 2007; Dedeilia et al., 2020; Doubleday et al., 2011; Murphy, 2020).

Studies on the effectiveness of online clinical skills learning showed paradoxical results. It is true that it does not substitute direct bedside teaching and direct patient interaction, but it has been rated as beneficial especially the video conferencing and video libraries (Dedeilia et al., 2020; Gormley et al., 2009) (Feriandi et al., 2020). In our study, students did not perceive online learning as a good modality for clinical skills learning. However, they did rate videos as the best among all online modalities for such a purpose which is consistent with findings from other studies (Clay, 2011; Hansen et al., 2011). Therefore, educators should be trained in the use of videos in order to enhance students learning and engagement in clinical skills for a possible blended learning. This preference could be utilized in the future where videos can be constructed and distributed to students before the clinical sessions. This would help to reduce the time needed for illustration and theory. Instead, more time would be available for practice and constructive feedback.

Despite all reported challenges, online learning has created new opportunities such as improving digital literacy and the digital training for stakeholders. The implementation of innovative learning strategies to improve the online learning experience that ensure learners engagement, interactions and proper assessment was very noticeable across different geographical regions (Bao, 2020; Kay & Pasarica, 2019; Pather et al., 2020; Sandhu & de Wolf, 2020) (Arandjelovic et al., 2021).

5 Conclusion

Despite all challenges faced during the online learning due to COVID-19, lessons learned are reshaping the medical education. It has encouraged self-learning and technical literacy for both educators and learners. Experts are envisioning that online teaching should remain active in post-COVID-19 medical curriculum as a hybrid learning where online learning strategies are impeded along with face-to-face learning. A systematic understanding of the challenges would help stakeholders and medical education planners to pay more attention to overcome the challenges and plan an effective integration of technology and learning even after the pandemic.

Significance

The findings from this study hold significant implications for the future of medical education. The challenges and preferences expressed by students during the shift to online learning, especially in the field of medicine, highlight the need for a well-balanced approach in educational delivery. Addressing the concerns raised, such as the lack of hands-on clinical experience and the preference for combined synchronous and asynchronous learning methods, emphasizes the necessity for a hybrid model that incorporates both traditional in-person training and effective online resources. This highlights the importance of implementing innovative strategies to enhance the online learning experience, particularly in clinical skill acquisition, through video-based resources and interactive tools. Understanding the significance of maintaining clinical exposure and direct patient interactions for medical students underscores the need for adaptive approaches that simulate real-world experiences in a virtual setting. These insights will guide the development of more comprehensive and robust curricula that integrate technology effectively, balancing the strengths of in-person instruction with the flexibility and accessibility offered by online learning. Moreover, the study emphasizes the importance of addressing digital inequality, providing adequate technical support and fostering an engaging and interactive online environment to ensure a more equitable and effective learning experience for medical students. As medical education continues to evolve, these findings will contribute to shaping a more adaptable, inclusive and effective educational system that prepares future healthcare professionals for the dynamic and diverse challenges they will encounter in their careers.

Funding The authors declare that no funds, grants or other support were received during the preparation of this manuscript.

Competing Interests The authors have no relevant financial or non-financial interests to disclose.

References

Arandjelovic, A., Arandjelovic, K., Dwyer, K., & Shaw, C. (2021). *COVID-19: Considerations for Medical Education during a Pandemic [Version 1]*, 1–13.

Baltà-Salvador, R., Olmedo-Torre, N., Peña, M., & Renta-Davids, A. I. (2021). Academic and emotional effects of online learning during the COVID-19 pandemic on engineering students. *Education and Information Technologies, 26*(6), 7407–7434. https://doi.org/10.1007/s10639-021-10593-1

Bao, W. (2020). COVID-19 and online teaching in higher education: A case study of Peking University. *Human Behavior and Emerging Technologies, 2*(2), 113–115. https://doi.org/10.1002/hbe2.191

Cao, W., Fang, Z., Hou, G., Han, M., Xu, X., Dong, J., & Zheng, J. (2020). The psychological impact of the COVID-19 epidemic on college students in China. *Psychiatry Research, 287*. https://doi.org/10.1016/j.psychres.2020.112934

Cecilio-Fernandes, D., Parisi, M. C. R., Santos, T. M., & Sandars, J. (2020). The COVID-19 pandemic and the challenge of using technology for medical education in low and middle income countries. *MedEdPublish*, *9*, 74. https://doi.org/10.15694/mep.2020.000074.1

Chandler, C. (2007). Effective use of educational technology in medical education. *AAMC Institute for Improving Medical Education, March*, 1–18. https://members.aamc.org/eweb/upload/Effective%20Use%20of%20Educational.pdf

Clay, C. A. (2011). Exploring the use of mobile technologies for the acquisition of clinical skills. *Nurse Education Today, 31*(6), 582–586. https://doi.org/10.1016/j.nedt.2010.10.011

Davies, L. (2011). Understanding education's role in fragility: synthesis of four situational analyses. *Synthesis*, 69.

Dedeilia, A., Sotiropoulos, M. G., Hanrahan, J. G., Janga, D., Dedeilias, P., & Sideris, M. (2020). Medical and surgical education challenges and innovations in the COVID-19 era: A systematic review. *In Vivo, 34*, 1603–1611. https://doi.org/10.21873/invivo.11950

Dhillon, J., Salimi, A., & ElHawary, H. (2020). Impact of COVID-19 on Canadian medical education: Pre-clerkship and clerkship students affected differently. *Journal of Medical Education and Curricular Development*, *7*(X), 238212052096524. https://doi.org/10.1177/2382120520965247

Doubleday, E. G., O'Loughlin, V. D., & Doubleday, A. F. (2011). The virtual anatomy laboratory: Usability testing to improve an online learning resource for anatomy education. *Anatomical Sciences Education, 4*(6), 318–326. https://doi.org/10.1002/ase.252

Farooq, F., Rathore, F. A., & Mansoor, S. N. (2020). Challenges of online medical education in Pakistan during COVID-19 pandemic. *Journal of the*

College of Physicians and Surgeons Pakistan, 30(1), S67–S69. https://doi.org/10.29271/jcpsp.2020.Suppl.S67

Feriandi, Y., Wasliman, I., Hanafiah, N., Budiman, B., Putra, A. R., Rachmadini, N., Putri, C. R., & Yusuf, K. (2020). Blended E-learning on clinical skills learning from the medical student's perspectives. *Journal of Physics: Conference Series, 1469*(1). https://doi.org/10.1088/1742-6596/1469/1/012055

Frehywot, S., Vovides, Y., Talib, Z., Mikhail, N., Ross, H., Wohltjen, H., Bedada, S., Korhumel, K., Koumare, A. K., & Scott, J. (2013). E-learning in medical education in resource constrained low- and middle-income countries. *Human Resources for Health, 11*(1), 4. https://doi.org/10.1186/1478-4491-11-4

Gormley, G., Collins, K., Boohan, M., Bickle, I., & Stevenson, M. (2009). Is there a place for e-learning in clinical skills? A survey of undergraduate medical students' experiences and attitudes. *Medical Teacher, 31*(1), e6–e12. https://doi.org/10.1080/01421590802334317

Grubic, N., Badovinac, S., & Johri, A. M. (2020). Student mental health in the midst of the COVID-19 pandemic: A call for further research and immediate solutions. *International Journal of Social Psychiatry, 66*(5), 517–518. https://doi.org/10.1177/0020764020925108

Hansen, M., Oosthuizen, G., Windsor, J., Doherty, I., Greig, S., McHardy, K., & McCann, L. (2011). Enhancement of medical interns' levels of clinical skills competence and self-confidence levels via video iPods: Pilot randomized controlled trial. *Journal of Medical Internet Research, 13*(1). https://doi.org/10.2196/jmir.1596

Hasan, N., & Bao, Y. (2020). Impact of "e-Learning crack-up" perception on psychological distress among college students during COVID-19 pandemic: A mediating role of "fear of academic year loss." *Children and Youth Services Review, 118*. https://doi.org/10.1016/j.childyouth.2020.105355

Izaias, C., Filho, S., Conte De Las, W., Rodrigues, V., Beauchamp De Castro, R., Aparecida Marçal, A., Pavelqueires, S., Takano, L., Luis De Oliveira, W., & Neto, S. (2020). Impact of COVID-19 pandemic on mental health of medical students: A cross-sectional study using GAD-7 And PHQ-9 questionnaires. *MedRxiv*, 2020.06.24.20138925. https://www.medrxiv.org/content/10.1101/2020.06.24.20138925v1

Kay, D., & Pasarica, M. (2019). Using technology to increase student (and faculty satisfaction with) engagement in medical education. *Advances in Physiology Education, 43*(3), 408–413. https://doi.org/10.1152/advan.00033.2019

Koumpouras, F., & Helfgott, S. (2020). Stand together and deliver: Challenges and opportunities for rheumatology education during the COVID-19 pandemic. *Arthritis and Rheumatology, 72*(7), 1064–1066. https://doi.org/10.1002/art.41278

Lin, M. P. (2020). Prevalence of internet addiction during the covid-19 outbreak and its risk factors among junior high school students in Taiwan. *International Journal of Environmental Research and Public Health, 17*(22), 1–12. https://doi.org/10.3390/ijerph17228547

Molodynski, A., Lewis, T., Kadhum, M., Farrell, S. M., Lemtiri Chelieh, M., Falcão De Almeida, T., Masri, R., Kar, A., Volpe, U., Moir, F., Torales, J., Castaldelli-Maia, J. M., Chau, S. W. H., Wilkes, C., & Bhugra, D. (2021). Cultural variations in wellbeing, burnout and substance use amongst medical students in twelve countries. *International Review of Psychiatry, 33*(1–2), 37–42. https://doi.org/10.1080/09540261.2020.1738064

Murphy, B. (2020). Medical school assessment during COVID-19: shelf exams go remote. *American Medical Association*, 2020–2022. https://www.ama-assn.org/residents-students/medical-school-life/medical-school-assessment-during-covid-19-shelf-exams-go

P, S. (2020). Closure of universities due to coronavirus disease 2019 (COVID-19): Impact on education and mental health of students and academic staff. *Cureus, 12*(4), e7541. https://pubmed.ncbi.nlm.nih.gov/32377489/

Pather, N., Blyth, P., Chapman, J. A., Dayal, M. R., Flack, N. A. M. S., Fogg, Q. A., Green, R. A., Hulme, A. K., Johnson, I. P., Meyer, A. J., Morley, J. W., Shortland, P. J., Štrkalj, G., Štrkalj, M., Valter, K., Webb, A. L., Woodley, S. J., & Lazarus, M. D. (2020). Forced disruption of anatomy education in Australia and New Zealand: An acute response to the Covid-19 pandemic. *Anatomical Sciences Education, 13*(3), 284–300. https://doi.org/10.1002/ase.1968

Rahiem, M. D. H. (2021). Indonesian University students' likes and dislikes about emergency remote learning during the COVID-19 pandemic. *Asian Journal of University Education, 17*(1), 1–18. https://doi.org/10.24191/ajue.v17i1.11525

Rajab, M. H., Gazal, A. M., & Alkattan, K. (2020). Challenges to online medical education during the COVID-19 pandemic. *Cureus*. https://doi.org/10.7759/cureus.8966

Regmi, K., & Jones, L. (2020). A systematic review of the factors—Enablers and barriers—Affecting e-learning in health sciences education. *BMC Medical Education, 20*(1). https://doi.org/10.1186/s12909-020-02007-6

Sandhu, P., & de Wolf, M. (2020). The impact of COVID-19 on the undergraduate medical curriculum. *Medical Education Online, 25*(1). https://doi.org/10.1080/10872981.2020.1764740

Shraim, K., & Khlaif, Z. (2010). An e-learning approach to secondary education in Palestine: Opportunities and challenges. *Information Technology for Development, 16*(3), 159–173. https://doi.org/10.1080/02681102.2010.501782

WHO. (2020). World Health Organization. Coronavirus disease 2019 (COVID-19). *Situation Report, 32*(February), 1–16. https://covid19.who.int/?gclid=CjwKCAiA_Kz-BRAJEiwAhJNY74BJHWPUTVpLi2lBpngW2Cosw7Rpt8BXLW5gd3HYIDc_Eyg2hf_9tBoCDk4QAvD_BwE

Yurttas, I., Aktar, I., Bardak, M., & Goeschl, S. (2020). *Institutional report for COVID-19 impact on medical education.*

Zhang, W., Wang, Y., Yang, L., & Wang, C. (2020). Suspending classes without stopping learning: China's education emergency management policy in the COVID-19 outbreak. *Journal of Risk and Financial Management, 13*(3), 55. https://doi.org/10.3390/jrfm13030055

CHAPTER 9

The Impact of COVID-19 on Visitor's Footfall at National Science Centre, New Delhi: An Educational Resource

N. Ramdas Iyer and Bharat Bhusan Srivastava

1 Introduction

In March 2020, nearly overnight, each unit of the National Council of Science Museums (NCSM) closed their doors to the public. NCSM in India forms the largest network of science centres and museums in the world under single administrative umbrella (Srivastava, 2010). As aware, the country was facing a challenging situation due to COVID-19 pandemic and as per the directions of the Government of India, the science centres were closed for public from March 17, 2020, to November 9, 2020 (UNICEF and UNISCO, 2021). During second wave, NCSM was closed from April 16, 2021, to June 16, 2021, and during third wave of pandemic, NCSM was closed from January 8, 2022, to February 15, 2022. The government has imposed expenditure control and restricted the expenditure and reduction of basic grants. This has resulted in a

N. R. Iyer · B. B. Srivastava (✉)
National Science Centre of India, New Delhi, India
e-mail: sribharat40@gmail.com

A. Mishrif (ed.), *Perspectives on Human Capital Development*,
https://doi.org/10.1007/978-981-97-5246-1_9

severe funds crunch and as a result, the National Science Centre, Delhi (NSCD) had to reduce the manpower deployed for security, housekeeping, gardening, etc. and impose severe cuts on maintenance as far as possible. Despite this grave situation, the NSCD kept its spirit of working from home till it returned to work. National Science Centre, Delhi worked relentlessly to reach out to visitors through online programmes; social media handles, etc. and extended services to the visitors visiting the NSCD after its reopening. But the footfalls to the NSCD were seriously affected and thereby resulted in the impact on revenue generation.

2 National Science Centre in Delhi: An Eductional Resource

The National Science Centre, Delhi (NSCD) is a unit of the National Council of Science Museums (NCSM), which is an autonomous body under the Ministry of Culture of the Government of India (Srivastava, 2010). It is a pioneering institute engaged in the popularization of science among the people of the northern part of India in general and among the students in particular. The National Science Centre, Delhi (NSCD) is popularly known as Science Museum in Delhi. It was inaugurated on the 9th of January 1992 by the then Prime Minister of India. Since opening, the NSCD has rendered yeoman service to the cause of science popularization. There are permanent thematic galleries and other facilities/special shows for the visitors (NCERT, 2018; Mintz, 2005). The gallery on 'Water-The Elixir of Life' is aimed at creating awareness about this scarce and related issue. The exhibits give an account of the water available on the planet Earth, and even in living beings. One can check the water content in his/her organs in the body. Various characteristics of water such as turbidity, acidity, reaction with other chemicals, etc. have been elaborated. Any Indian individual can also calculate his/her water use in daily life in comparison with a national average use of an Indian. The gallery also gives an account of how much effort it takes to bring a drop of water from the raw source to the tap of Delhiites (Dierking & Falk, 2001). Hence the gallery especially tries to sensitize people about the misuse of water particularly in Delhi. Permanent gallery on 'Our Science & Technology Heritage' depicts a long history of 4500 years of Indian Science & Technology (Ministry of Education, Government of India, 2021). The past has always been inspiring the future in India. Our long and rich heritage in science and technology defines our strides as we march proudly towards the dream of becoming a strong, self-reliant, and developed nation. This gallery depicts now, in course of time, side by side with art and literature, grew up on Indian soil, a very rich scientific and technological culture (Emily, 2021).

A gallery on 'Human Biology' aims to portray the human body in all its aspects: anatomical, physiological, biochemical, structural, functional, and systemic. The gallery aims to address on immunity, diseases, and healthy living. It also makes the visitors aware of the new concepts in biology like Genetic Engineering and Biotechnology. 'Pre-historic Life' gallery is a recreation of a world that none of us have seen as it existed millions of years ago and many of its life forms have become extinct by now. Selected species of life forms of different ages such as Trilobites, Giant Scorpions, early birds, gigantic dinosaurs, and other living creatures up to Neanderthal man have been presented in the gallery with artificially created matching ambiance and special light and sound effects (Borun et al., 1996). Since most of the species displayed are electro-pneumatically animated, it adds a new dimension to the gallery.

A large cluster of interactive hands-on exhibits related with school curriculum are on display in 'Fun Science' gallery. The emphasis is to supplement the text bookish approach to learning with inquiry-based learning. Inquiry is a multifaceted activity that guides learners to inquire or generate meaningful questions that lead to the relevant answers (Anderson et al., 2003; Falk, 2001; Falk et al., 2004). In inquiry learning, learners are shown how knowledge is generated and transmitted and how they can acquire the knowledge and skills necessary to become life-long learners. This gallery tries to achieve these goals of learning through participatory and interactive exhibits. The 'Hall of Nuclear Power' gallery showcases myriad applications of nuclear energy and radiation in the service of mankind. The gallery has a fascinating audio-visual and interactive feast in store for the visitors depicting the various aspects of nuclear energy and applications of radiation for the betterment of human life and the environment. The story of evolution of communication technology from cave painting to internet in India is told in 'Information Revolution' gallery. While moving through time, one experiences the relation between technology and culture through history in this rare show. The gallery showcases the earliest as well as the latest forms of communication and their impact on society. A digital exhibition 'Uniting India: The Role of Sardar Vallabhbhai Patel' showcases the integration of India, and the contribution of Sardar Vallabhbhai Patel.

Participation is the key to learning. NSCD has about 500 exhibits many of which are of a participatory nature. In addition, NSCD conducts daily and regular shows like SDLs, 3D shows, Holo show, and Science on Sphere show & Fantasy Ride. These are all ticketed shows with limited seating capacity. Interactive hands-on session/workshops for students and teachers on nominal fee basis remain a regular activity. Renting out facilities like auditoriums and conference rooms to outside similar minded organization for organizing some educational programmes is also being done. The National Science Centre is an educational resource for school children & teachers and for the public in general (Chandasiri, 2020). The National Science Centre, Delhi remains open every day in a year except for two holidays due to festivals. The loss in revenue due to COVID-19 pandemic was indeed significant.

About ten years ago, NSCD used to receive more student visitors than public but in recent years, number of public visiting NSCD has gradually increased, and it has been more than student visitors. One of the reasons might be the 'word of mouth' publicity by the student community. NSCD provides discounted tickets to students and teachers for visiting and availing the facilities of NSCD. These students perhaps inform their parents, relatives, and friends. They also get enthused and visit NSCD in family groups, with relatives and friends.

Social media like YouTube, Facebook, Twitter and Instagram are performing a pivotal role in presenting NSCD as a vibrating hub of science communication. Using the science centres as science education resources for students, teachers as well as for public has been proven a beneficial strategy for inculcating scientific awareness among them. Both exhibits and activities (indoor and outdoor) are being utilized as powerful educational resources.

2.1 Supplementing Science Education

As per the New Education Policy 2020 (NEP 2020) in India, quality higher education must aim to develop good, thoughtful, well-rounded, and creative individuals(Chandasiri, 2020). It must enable an individual to study one or more specialized areas of interest at a deep level and develop character, ethical and constitutional values, intellectual curiosity, scientific temper, creativity, spirit of service, and twenty-first-century capabilities across a range of disciplines including sciences, social sciences, arts, humanities, languages, as well as professional, technical, and vocational subjects. Science Centres perform a significant role in inculcating these specialized areas of interest among the youth. Science centres have been identified as an important resource in encouraging students to choose higher education in science and technology (Emily, 2021). This NEP 2020 envisages that the extant 10+2 structure in school education will be modified with a new pedagogical and curricular restructuring of 5+3+3+4 covering ages 3–18 as shown in the representative Fig. 1.

Earlier, children in the age group of 3–6 were not covered in the 10+2 structure as Class 1 begins at age 6. In the new 5+3+3+4 structure, a strong base of Early Childhood Care and Education (ECCE) from age 3 is also included, which is aimed at promoting better overall learning,

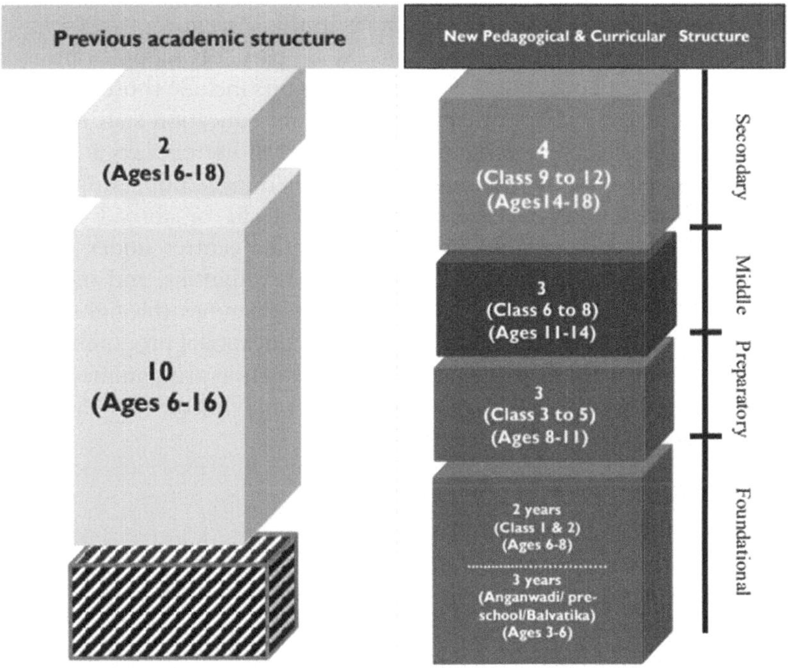

Fig. 1 School education to be modified with a new pedagogical and curricular restructuring of 5+3+3+4 covering ages 3–18 (*Source* National Education Policy 2020, Govt. of India publication)

development, and well-being. This New Education Policy aims to facilitate an inclusive, participatory, and holistic approach, which takes into consideration field experiences, empirical research, stakeholder feedback, as well as lessons learned from best practices (Ministry of HRD, Government of India, 2020). The current 10+2 system would be replaced by a new 5+3+3+4 curricular structure corresponding to ages 3–8, 8–11, 11–14, and 14–18 years respectively. It will bring the uncovered age group of 3–6 years under school curriculum, which has been recognized globally as the crucial stage for development of mental faculties of a child. It will also have 12 years of schooling with three years of Anganwadi/pre-schooling. Teaching up to at least Grade 5 in mother tongue/regional language is an excellent option which would remain available with schools. No language will be imposed on any student. Science centres have been striving to cope with changing scenarios and made efforts in this direction.

A science excursion to museums is a part of school outreach programmes for many schools. School group visits include those where an educational programme is provided by museum education staff or those where the schoolteachers make their own plans to use displays and other materials available at the museum (Falk & Dierking, 2000; Mukhopadhyay, 2005). All most all science centres in India or abroad work in two prong strategy—exhibits and activities. The centres under NCSM have permanent thematic galleries, temporary exhibitions, and travelling exhibition and organize many educational programmes throughout the year. NSCD organizes strategic and stratified educational programmes for children of different age groups. Teachers' orientation programmes for in-service and pre-service are being organized throughout the year (Ministry of HRD, Government of India, 2020).

2.2 *Objectives*

(a) To examine the effects of lockdown caused by the COVID-19 pandemic on student visitor's footfall at National Science Centre, New Delhi.
(b) To find its impact on educational activities for school children in particular as well as for public in general.
(c) To explore opportunities and challenges which the science teachers were experiencing during the COVID-19 pandemic in the lockdown period due to closure of NSCD.

(d) To find, develop and implement the tools, resources, and support system to supplement science education in schools.
(e) To explore the effectiveness of the ways and means for overall learning experience by teachers.

3 Methodology

The focus of this research was our investigation into how science teachers faced problems in their classroom teaching due to non-utilization of NSCD as an educational resource during lockdown. Another important exploration was to extend the possible support to science teachers pertaining to their online teaching. The research work critically analyzed the overall learning experience and to what extent the issues of the teachers were addressed. This was done by administering a specially designed questionnaire on teachers. Making a questionnaire is important as the expected outcome gives us direction for improvement in the existing infrastructure/facilities. Questionnaires give museums the unique opportunity to learn about experience of support extended by us, interests in future programmes, and take in valuable information directly from the target group whom we aim to serve. Providing a questionnaire ensures gaining insight into reliable data about the strengths and weaknesses of our programmes. We prepared the questionnaire after a brainstorming session with the education staff of NSCD as they are the front-end interface between visiting people and us. The questionnaire prepared by us was sent over mail to schools and teachers. The same was given on-site in person. After administering the questionnaire, the received information was collected and compiled. We analyzed and interpreted the results in pictorial format.

Another important focus of this research was to quantify the student visitor loss to NSCD due to closure of NSCD and schools in pandemic. A comparative study of the footfall statistics during reopening of NSCD in the intervening period with previous years was also done. NSCD has computerized ticketing system which works in offline mode. The records for study purposes were made available to the researchers from the preserved data in the server. Using visitors' data sheets available with NSCD record, an analysis was done with respect to footfall which also affected revenue generation. Based on data sheet available with NSCD for the period of consideration under research, impact on visitors' footfall was clearly visible.

3.1 *Operational Definitions*

This report refers to specific terminology, data collection, and analysis methods; these terms and processes are explained below:

(a) **Resource Centre**

A place available for you on offer to cater existing facilities/ services to you.

(b) **Science Centre—An Educational Resource**

Science centre can be regarded as active learning place/centre/ institution having rich educational resource available for the use to help students and teachers achieve something, especially in their work or study according to their requirement. The science teachers can evaluate the performance of students after making use of the facilities of the science centres. Tangible or intangible learning and its impact among teachers/students would indicate the meaningful educational resourcefulness of science centres. National Science Centre—An Educational Resource is called as 'NSCD' in this report.

(c) **Daily/Weekly/Monthly Visitor Attendance**

This is quantified data or maintenance of record of number of visitors/footfall to a museum/science centre for doing audience research or studying the entire group of visitors on daily/weekly/ monthly basis.

(d) **Financial Year**

In India, this 1-year period starts from 1 April and ends on 31 March. A financial year is a period of twelve months, used by government, business, and other organizations in order to calculate their budgets, profits, and losses. Here, we use it to calculate annual footfalls. For instance, if your financial year is from April 1, 2020, to March 31, 2021, then it is known as FY 2020–21.

(e) **Facilities/Shows and Sessions/Workshops**

National Science Centre conducts daily and regular shows like SDLs, 3D shows, Holo Shows, and Fantasy Ride. These are all ticketed shows with limited seating capacity. Interactive hands-on session/workshops for students and teachers on nominal fee basis remain a regular activity.

(f) **Blended Learning**

It is a hybrid form of teaching and holistic learning that involves both classroom and online learning, both structured and free choice learning.

3.2 *Sample*

The sample for the research was purposive. National Science Centre was visited by many students, teachers, and general public every day during pre-pandemic period. The annual footfall to NSCD was 609435, 561911, 561107, 73609, and 210508 in the last few financial years i.e. 2017–2018, 2018–2019, 2019–2020, 2020–2021, and 2021–2022, respectively. The visitor footfall includes the data of general public and student groups with accompanying teachers to NSCD on site and does not include the outreach activities data.

Teachers truly shape the future of our children—and, therefore, the future of our nation. It is because of this noblest role that the teacher in India was the most respected member of society. Teaching is a system. It is not a loose mixture of individual features thrown together by the teacher. It works more like a machine, with the parts operating together and reinforcing one another, driving the vehicle forward. Concerns and issues pertaining to the environment should be emphasized in every subject and through a wide range of activities involving outdoor project work. The high respect for teachers and the high status of the teaching profession must be restored to inspire the best to enter the teaching profession. The motivation and empowerment of teachers are required to ensure the best possible future for our children and our nation.

NSCD has developed a symbiotic linkage with schools to achieve educational benefits mutually. So, selecting a sample from the teacher's group was not very difficult. A group of about 100 teachers from schools in Delhi and NCR were selected for this study. The time frame chosen for the survey was from April to August 2022. However, for studying the student visitors' footfall, data sheet from the preserved records was used.

3.3 Tools

(a) Questionnaire was developed by researchers for determining the problems towards utility of NSC as an educational resource for teaching science and the impact of 'Blended learning' approach.
(b) Daily/Weekly/Monthly Visitor Attendance of the period under consideration for research purposes. The annual visitors' statistics used in this report are from year 2017, 2018, 2019, 2020, 2021, and 2022.

4 Data Analysis

NSCD was closed from March 17, 2020, to November 9, 2020; from April 16, 2021, to June 16, 2021, and from January 8, 2022, to February 15, 2022, for public. The visitors' footfall including general public and students in comparison to footfall statistics in the last three consecutive years was taken for comparative study. Similarly, after reopening, the visitors' footfalls statistics from November 10, 2020, to April 15, 2021; June 17, 2021, to January 7, 2022, and February 16, 2022, to June 30, 2022, are being taken for this research and also the visitors' footfall statistics in the last three consecutive years of the same date and period are also being taken in account for comparative study.

However, NSCD remained open for public since its reopening on February 16, 2022, and for this pilot project and practical purposes, we culminated the teachers' survey on June 30, 2022, starting from April 1, 2022. The survey was administered on teachers at schools in Delhi and NCR. Some schools are privately managed and some are government-funded. More than 100 teachers participated in the survey. The questions in the questionnaire were designed to seek answers on the impact on educational activities for school children, challenges faced by teachers, utility of NSCD as an Educational Resource and general opinion on blended learning approach during lockdown and reopening of NSCD. Some of the questions like 'Was there anyone infected from COVID-19 among your near & dear during first, second & third wave of corona?', 'Were you comfortable in online teaching during COVID-19 pandemic?', 'Did you get any support in teaching from NSCD during lockdown period?', 'Any online demo on some teaching related topic received from NSCD & if it served the purpose?', 'Was your salary affected by these lockdown?', Do you feel 'work from home' is a good alternative for teaching?, 'Would you be interested to vote for hybrid form of teaching i.e. online & offline mode?' and 'Do you believe that the students will learn more in offline teaching?' were prominent.

The teachers marked the rating in a 1–5 scale that National Science Centre can be utilized as a good Educational Resource Centre in the same survey form. Some of the questions have been clubbed and responses have been shown in percentage form in the pie chart. The following are the pictorial representation of response given by teachers (Fig. 2).

As per this survey, 56% of teachers confirmed that their relatives encountered this infection. However, the number of infected relatives was decreasing in third wave during January–February 2022. Averaging the percentage of responses, 20% were not encountered with any infected people. 24% teachers did not like to respond; perhaps they did not like to remember the horrific scenario of the pandemic (Fig. 3).

50% of teachers responded that their salary was affected during lockdown. However, 40% replies in negative. It is worth mentioning here that in the survey the teachers were from government-funded schools and some are privately managed. Most of the privately managed schools' teachers' salary was affected. As schools remained closed during pandemic, the majority of private schools reported a decrease in revenue, leading to a reduction in teachers' salaries. There was a major reduction in the number of new admissions in the academic year. The schools' revenues were hit by the inability of parents to pay fees regularly. These were some of the reasons due to which the teachers' salary was affected.

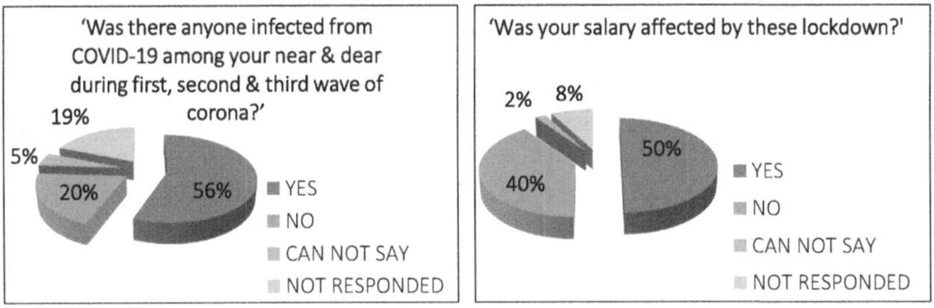

Fig. 2 The teachers' response on COVID-19 infection and their salary during lockdown (*Source* Survey Reports by National Science Centre, New Delhi)

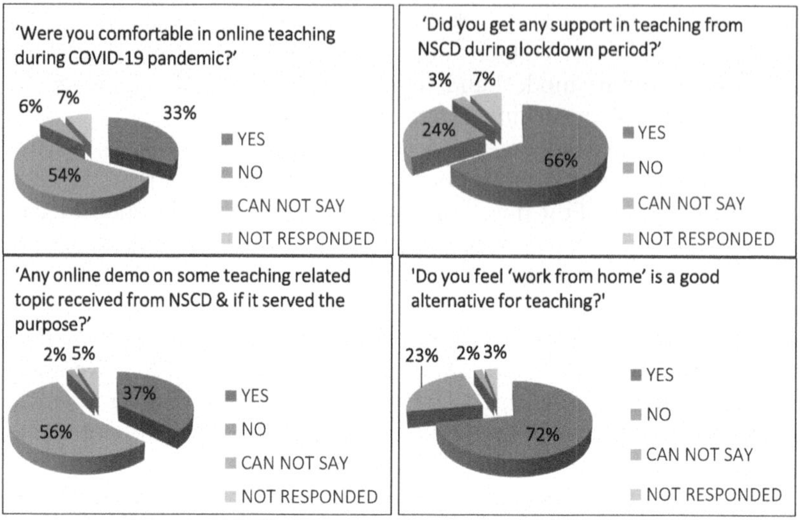

Fig. 3 The Teachers' response on online teaching during COVID-19 pandemic, getting online support during lockdown, getting online demo from NSCD & on 'Work from home' as good alternative for teaching (*Source* Survey Reports by National Science Centre, New Delhi)

54% teachers found online teaching not comfortable, and 66% teachers said that they received support from NSCD in teaching during lockdown. 37% teachers reported that online demonstration was really useful to supplement their online teaching. This is interesting to note that 72% teachers gave their consent that 'Work from home' is a good alternative for teaching. Indirectly, it supports that they support online teaching, or they might have groomed themselves to develop new skills in this digital era. 'Teaching from home', perhaps made them more convenient in teaching due to less formalities which otherwise they had to follow in normal school system. The COVID-19 pandemic flipped the world's classrooms on their heads. Teachers and students were catapulted into a virtual or hybrid environment overnight. Survival of the fittest meant those who had access to computer skills, could do well and contribute to teaching-learning process during pandemic. This is indeed a paradigm shift from pre-pandemic era (Fig. 4).

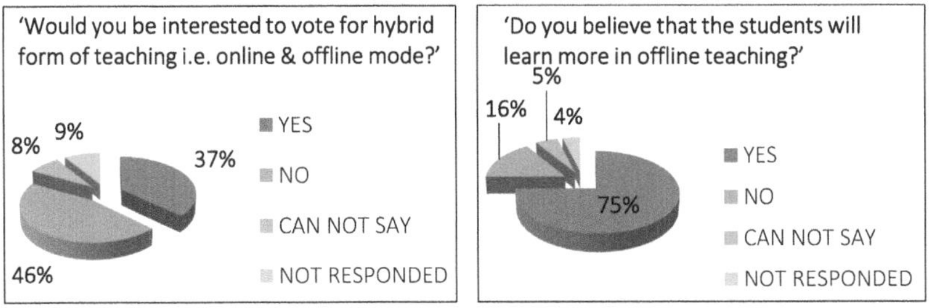

Fig. 4 The teachers' response on form of teaching mode and learning in offline mode (*Source* Survey Reports by National Science Centre, New Delhi)

Hybrid form of teaching or 'Blended learning' approach was supported by only 37% of teachers. 75% teachers opined that the students learn more in offline mode. The data revealed that it would take more time to adapt to the 'New Normal' scenario when the teachers will manage online and offline classes conveniently and comfortably.

56% of teachers felt very satisfied that NSCD catering services as a good educational resource centre and 37% expressed satisfaction. However, we need to make more efforts to shift the neutral opinion to satisfactory level. Organizing regular educational trips for students and teachers remains on one of the annual targets. We leave no stone unturned to provide an enriching experience while their visit to NSCD. Also, after talking to students and teachers, we realized that some school children take the educational tour as only fun trip i.e. having a day off from their normal school routine and some take it as learning trip. The school and museum's agenda often remains as learning outcome. Field trips are undertaken with a particular purpose. Some of the teachers view the field trip as a change of pace for students and a social experience. Some teachers expressing enrichment and social interaction instead focus the field trip in a cognitively oriented manner, by doing things such as providing and requiring students to use worksheets. A science centre's success should be measured by its impact on people, on the community where it exists, and on the economic status of its community. Its overall success should be anchored to its achievement in the development and/or promotion of science culture (Fig. 5).

The annual visitors' statistics for the financial years 2017–2018, 2018–2019, 2019–2020, 2020–2021, and 2021–2022 are shown in Fig. 6.

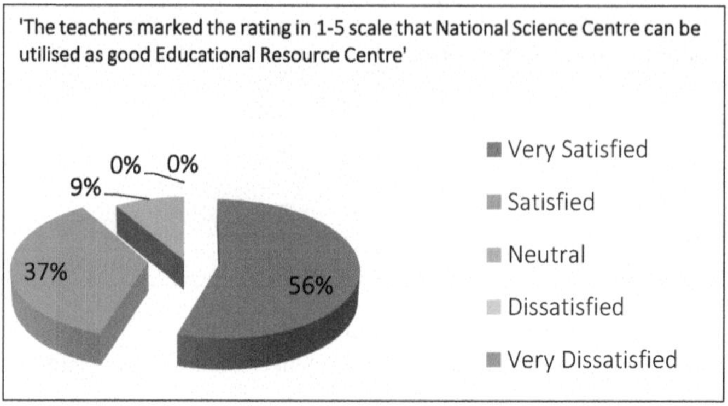

Fig. 5 The teachers' response on a rating scale (1-Very Dissatisfied to 5-Very Satisfied) about NSCD can be utilized as a good Educational Resource Centre (*Source* Survey Reports by National Science Centre, New Delhi)

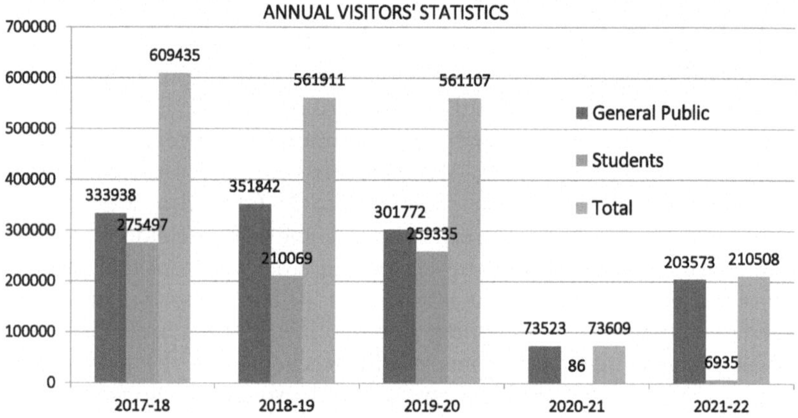

Fig. 6 Annual Visitors' footfall to NSCD in the past five years (*Source* Annual Reports of National Science Centre, New Delhi)

Through this comparative study of the visitor's footfall statistics, we have observed a great downfall in the number of visitors after this prolonged COVID-19 pandemic lockdown. In the financial year 2020–2021, there was a humungous 86.8% loss in the total number of visitors in comparison to the previous year i.e. 2019–2020 and 86.9% loss from

2018–2019. Similarly, with an 87.9% loss from 2017 to 2018, we have seen a 99.9% loss in the number of students for the year 2020–2021. This is such a huge number as the NSCD is an informal mode of studying various branches of science. If the pandemic did not happen, we could have easily converted this loss in the total number of general visitors and students to an exponential profit.

The following bar charts represent the footfalls including general public and students in comparison to footfall statistics in the last three consecutive years. It is worth mentioning here that NSCD was closed three times during COVID-19 pandemic i.e. from March 17, 2020, to November 9, 2020; from April 16, 2021, to June 16, 2021, and from January 8, 2022, to February 15, 2022, for public (Fig. 7).

During the first lockdown, when NSCD was closed, we could not get any visitors. Comparing the statistics for the last three consecutive years of the same time, we find 100% decrease (Fig. 8).

Also, if we compare the time period of closing the NSCD second time from April 16, 2021, to June 16, 2021, with last three years, we find 100% decrease (Fig. 9).

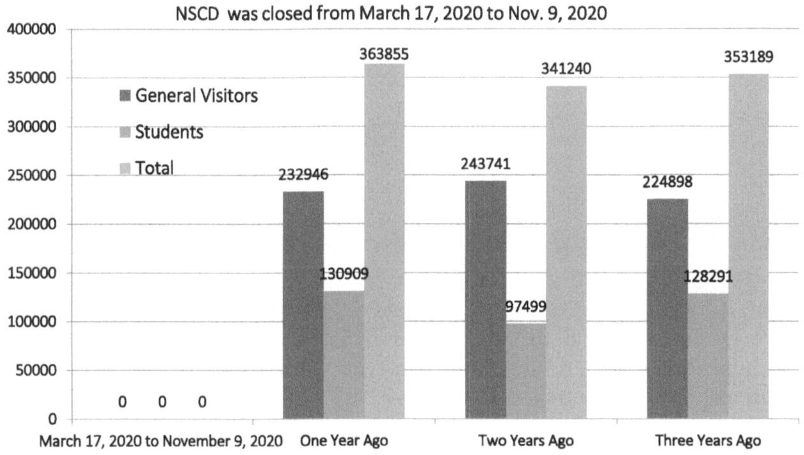

Fig. 7 Visitors' footfall to NSCD from March 17, 2020, to November 9, 2020, and during previous three consecutive years (*Source* Annual Reports of National Science Centre, New Delhi)

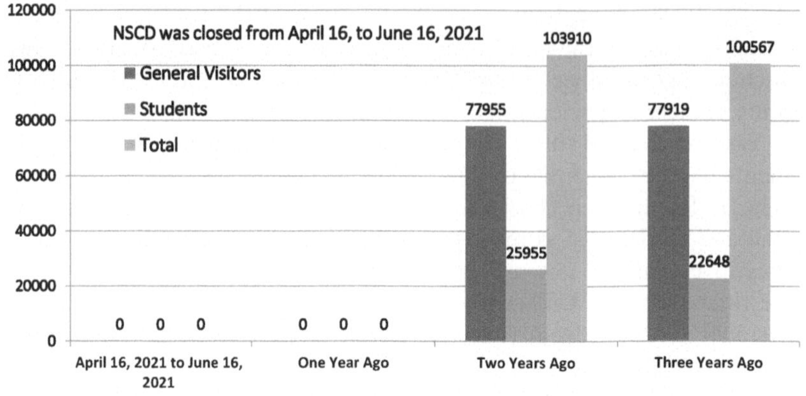

Fig. 8 Visitors' footfall to NSCD from April 16, to June 16, 2021, and during the previous three consecutive years (*Source* Annual Reports of National Science Centre, New Delhi)

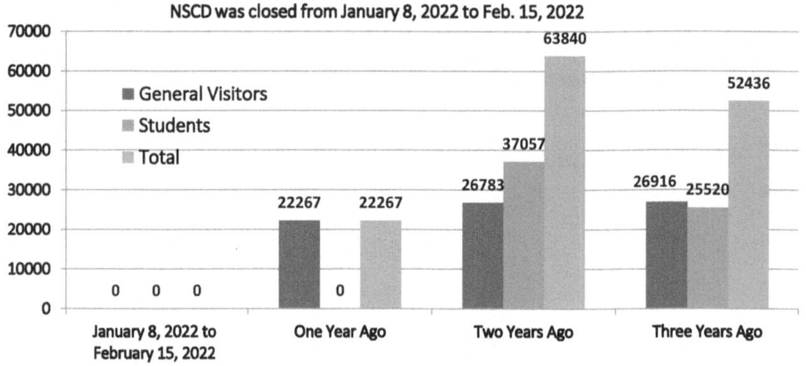

Fig. 9 Visitors' footfall to NSCD from January 8, 2022, to February 15, 2022, and during the previous three consecutive years (*Source* Annual Reports of National Science Centre, New Delhi)

Even when the NSCD was closed a third time, we found 100% decrease. The following bar charts represent the footfalls including general public and students during reopening of NSCD from November 10, 2020, to April 15, 2021; June 17, 2021, to January 7, 2022, and

February 16, 2022, to June 30, 2022, being taken for this research and also the visitors' footfalls statistics in the last three consecutive years of the same date and period is also being taken in account for comparative study (Figs. 10, 11, and 12).

On the other hand, the comparison of statistics in the past 3 years revealed that there was 67.9% loss in the total number of visitors when NSCD was reopened after first closing on November 10, 2020, and 35.1% loss after the second closing. Overall, the number of students visiting the NSCD saw a great downfall, as the schools were also closed at that time, whereas the general visitors were not tremendously affected just like the students.

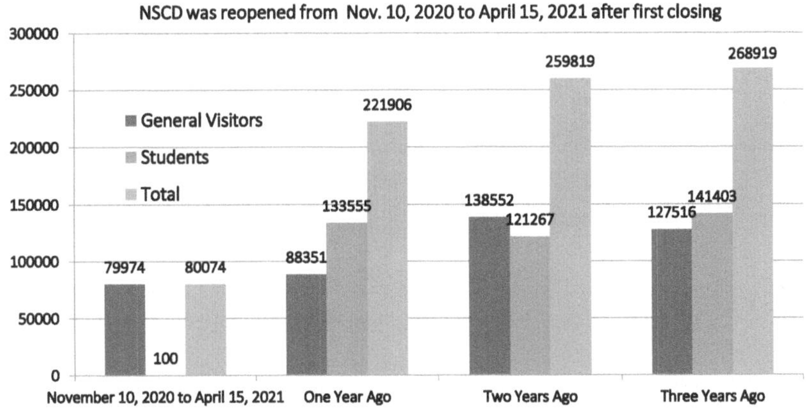

Fig. 10 Visitors' footfall to NSCD from November 10, 2020, to April 15, 2021, and during the previous three consecutive years (*Source* Annual Reports of National Science Centre, New Delhi)

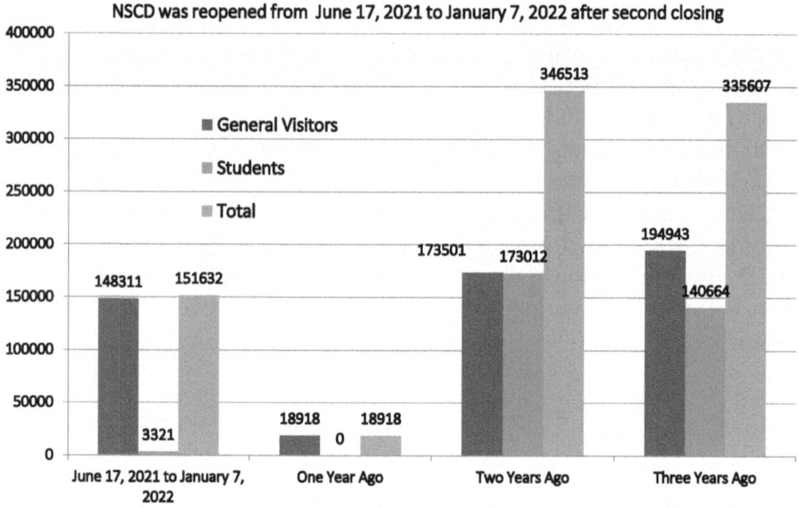

Fig. 11 Visitors' footfall to NSCD from June 17, 2021, to January 7, 2022, and during the previous three consecutive years (*Source* Annual Reports of National Science Centre, New Delhi)

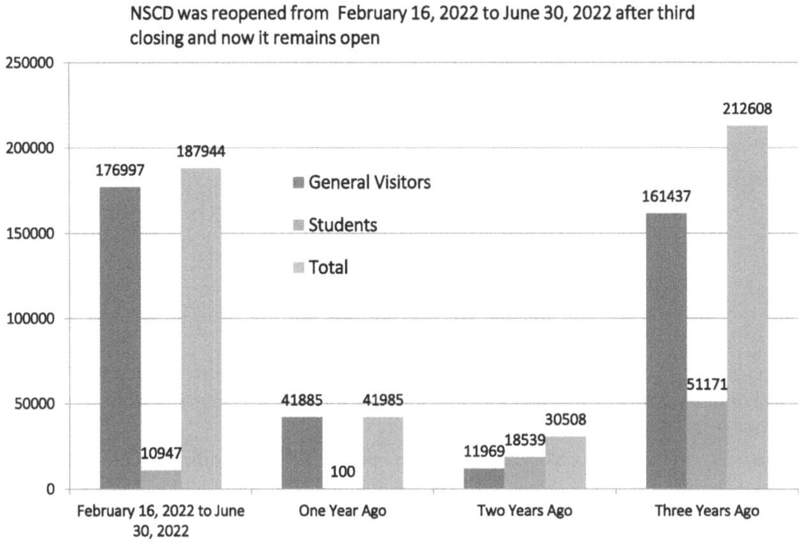

Fig. 12 Visitors' footfall to NSCD from February 16, 2022, to June 30, 2022, and during the previous three consecutive years (*Source* Annual Reports of National Science Centre, New Delhi)

5 Conclusion

Even though NSCD used interactive and pedagogy-led interpretation approaches, still we feel that due to this global outbreak of the COVID-19 pandemic, the benefits and importance of play-based learning could not be achieved as in pre-pandemic era. The reopening of NSCD after each closing cannot be equated to returning to pre-pandemic operations and facilities. One was supposed to follow COVID-19 protocols issued by the government for taking appropriate steps on maintaining standard hygiene-measures, such as masks, disinfectant, and social distancing, etc. In order to offer a low-risk interactive and playful museum experience for families, operations have to be adapted and changed dramatically. Most of the push button/touch button participatory exhibits involving 'hands-on' experience were modified by sensor-based touch-free switches. The efforts were made to extend 'hands-on' museum experiences to the visitors without affecting its learning outcome. Using our interactive prototype to explain some scientific principles to student community during lockdown, we tried to create free digital home schooling. 'Blended learning' approach may be now the 'New Normal' for teaching-learning process in the ensuing educational practices. As the teaching cannot be always 'Chalk & Talk', we can make children as well as adults aware of the practical science which is used frequently in our day-to-day lives through various interactive things. Curiosity leads to exploration; exploration makes us gain knowledge and the knowledge then enhances our mind.

References

Anderson, D., Lucas, K. B., & Ginns, I. S. (2003). Theoretical perspectives on learning in an informal setting. *Journal of Research in Science Teaching, 40*(2), 177–199.

Borun, M., Chambers, M., & Cleghorn, A. (1996). Families are learning in science museums. *Curator: The Museum Journal, 39*(2), 123–138.

Chandasiri, O. (2020). The COVID-19: Impact on education. *International Journal of Advanced Education and Research, 5*(3), 13–14. https://www.researchgate.net/publication/341960453

Dierking, L. D., & Falk, J. H. (2001). Learning from Science Centers: A Broader Perspective. *ASTC Dimensions.*

Emily, A. (2021). *How science museums reinvented themselves to survive the pandemic.* https://www.sciencenews.org/article/science-museums-online-exhibits-education-coronavirus-covid-pandemic

Falk, J. H. (2001). Free-choice science learning: Framing the discussion. In J. H. Falk (Ed.), *Free-choice science education. How we learn science outside of school.* Teacher College Press.

Falk, J. H., & Dierking, L. D. (2000). *Learning from museums: Visitor experiences and the making of meaning*. Altamira Press.

Falk, J. H., Scott, C., Dierking, L., Rennie, L., & Cohen Jones, M. (2004). Interactive and visitor learning. *Curator The Museum Journal, 47*(2), 171–198.

Ministry of Education, Govt. of India. (2021). *National Achievement Survey 2021.* https://nas.education.gov.in/home

Ministry of HRD, Govt. of India. (2020). *National Education Policy 2020.* https://www.education.gov.in/sites/upload_files/mhrd/files/NEP_Final_English_0.pdf

Mintz, A. (2005). *Science, Society and Science Centres.* https://www.researchgate.net/publication/7105459

Mukhopadhyay, I. K. (2005). *The Science Centre movement in India: A conspectus.* https://pubmed.ncbi.nlm.nih.gov/16676474/

NCERT, Govt. of India. (2018). *Handbook on understanding science through activities, games and toys*. NCERT.

Srivastava, B. B. (2010). *National Science Centre, Delhi—A critical study for its utilisation as educational resource*. NCSM, Kolkata.

United Nations Children's Fund (UNICEF) and (UNESCO). (2021). *India case study—Situation analysis on the effects of/and responses to COVID-19 on the education sector in Asia*.

CHAPTER 10

Digital Readiness and Higher Education Students' Socio-Emotional Perceptions: The Mediation of Perceived Stress in the Context of COVID-19

Fadi Abdelfattah, Abrar AL Alawi, Najla Yahya Al Mashaikhya, Ayman El-Saleh, and AbdulHakim Mohammed

1 Introduction

The novel viral propagation of the COVID-19 epidemic influenced all industries worldwide, including the education sector. The sudden emergence and spread of the COVID-19 pandemic have forced Higher Educational Institutions (HEIs) to shift the educational system from

F. Abdelfattah (✉)
Modern College of Business and Science, Muscat, Oman
e-mail: fadi.abdelfattah@mcbs.edu.om

A. AL Alawi
University of Nizwa, Nizwa, Oman

N. Y. Al Mashaikhya
Global College of Engineering and Technology, Muscat, Oman

A. Mishrif (ed.), *Perspectives on Human Capital Development*,
https://doi.org/10.1007/978-981-97-5246-1_10

conventional face-to-face to digital-based education in the direction of meeting the newly embarked social distancing policies (Abdulghani et al., 2020; Chen et al., 2020; Händel et al., 2020; Kulikowski et al., 2021). Hence, digital learning and developing digital teaching and learning tools in the twenty-first century enhanced remarkably to facilitate the learning process and leverage the perceived usefulness and ease of use.

Although the initiated platforms in the academic context provide digital learning that both instructors and students can be able to use, it is an arguable issue concerning the capability of utilized platforms in fulfilling the learning objectives (Azlan et al., 2020; Blayone et al., 2018; Portillo et al., 2020). Students of HEIs are expected to have adequate skills that enable them to deal with various software and hardware instruments that qualify them to interact actively with their colleagues and educators via the virtual digital learning system. However, students' acceptance and likeliness to cope with such circumstances are debated (Händel et al., 2020; Portillo et al., 2020). In this regard, Kee (2020) and Rodr et al. (2021) found that students' acceptance of digital learning is lacking due to the perceived lack of digital tools readiness in terms of technological, computational, communicational, and informational capability.

Meanwhile, many scholars illustrate that a low level of digital learning readiness causes a drawback in their acceptance of the digital learning system and raises perceived stress, which consequently impacts their socio-emotional perception (Blayone et al., 2018; Händel et al., 2020; Portillo et al., 2020; Rodr et al., 2021). Abdulah and Mohammed (2020) declared that students are more likely to improve negative socio-emotional perceptions when affected by a high level of experienced stress. In contrast with the conventional learning approach, the widespread spread of portable devices such as laptops and the generation of innovative technologies encouraged scholars to investigate its competency as a means of teaching. Compared to other countries, Oman confronts a short period to adopt e-learning methodologies (Al-Emran et al., 2020; Rashid

A. El-Saleh
College of Engineering (COE), A'Sharqiyah University, Ibra, Oman

A. Mohammed
College of Business Administration, A'Sharqiyah University, Ibra, Oman

Al-Senaidi & Gawande, 2013; Shorfuzzaman & Alhussein, 2016) as many physical and psychological factors affect the quality of the learning process. Hence, digital readiness is one of the most critical factors sought to affect student's perceived level of stress, illustrated by the stress caused by a lack quality of technological, computational, communicational, and informational readiness to effectively satisfy student's needs (Abdulghani et al., 2020; Chen et al., 2020; Portillo et al., 2020). This chapter examines the influence of digital readiness and perceived stress on students' socio-emotional perceptions among HEI students during the COVID-19 pandemic. Also, in the context of higher education students, this research will critically examine the mediate effect of perceived stress between digital readiness and students' socio-emotional perception under the conditions of the pandemic crisis. The results of this research are expected to provide valuable contributions for decision-makers and practitioners in HEIs, in which valuable insights will help regulate relevant digital learning authorities.

2 Literature Review and Constructs Development

2.1 Digital Readiness

Hong and Kim (2018) state that a student's digital readiness refers to "technology-related knowledge, skills, and attitudes and competencies for using digital technologies to meet educational aims and expectations in higher education". Nowadays, digital learning is one of the most popular technologies used globally by educational institutes such as schools, colleges, and universities (Bhaskar et al., 2020; Mailizar et al., 2020; Portillo et al., 2020). Technology integration as the complementary component of HEIs is vastly employed within the educational system. Across the world, technological materials concerning information and communication tools constitute an opportunity and advantage for HEIs (Bai, 2019; Rachmadtullah, 2020; Sarrab et al., 2018).

2.2 Socio-Emotional Perceptions

The management competencies of relationships, emotions, and feelings are the key to the socio-emotional perception of students (Moradi & Chemelnezhad, 2021; Rodr et al., 2021; Savage et al., 2020). However, socio-emotional perception is significantly affected by digital learning readiness for higher education students (Jamil, 2019). In the social and business context, the new digital technologies signify a dramatic change (Ciriello et al., 2018, 2020; Ziyadin et al., 2019). With the rapid advancement of technological infrastructure and the globalization of markets, organizations are increasingly confronting a complex and competitive environment (Foerster-Metz et al., 2018; Lee & Trimi, 2021). To overcome this challenge, organizations adapt to the organizational culture, employees, structure, and capabilities (Agrawal et al., 2019; Fischer et al., 2020).

2.3 Perceived Stress

Stress is a physiological or mental reaction to stimulate physical and/or psychological potential threats (Evans & Kelly, 2004). Stress is a psychological threat individuals perceive against a particular situation (Day & Livingstone, 2003). From another perspective, stress has positive benefits and harmful adverse effects. For instance, contextual behavior such as supportive assistance behavior and vocal behavior can also be affected by stress. Perceived stress results from a person's assessment of a stressor as threatening or non-threatening and the person's self-coping abilities (Liu et al., 2021). An individual personality trait can also affect how they appraise and respond to perceived stress under different conditions. For instance, the COVID-19 pandemic imposed exceptional learning, and the working environment impacts individuals perceived stress when dealing with various technological tools (Liu et al., 2022; Savage et al., 2020).

2.4 The Relationship Between Digital Readiness and Socio-Emotional Perceptions

Digital transformation aims to improve organizational entities by utilizing information technology, data, and new communication techniques to result in practical changes (Vial, 2021). Thus, HEIs must be prepared for the change that digital transformation brings, as it impacts a wide variety of areas and extends far beyond the mere adoption of information technology (Mirković et al., 2019; Osmundsen et al., 2018).

Azlan et al. (2020) and Moralista and Oducado (2020) argue that the complexity of digital educational platforms is the main influential factor affecting students' emotional perception of digital learning. Additionally, student training at HEIs was lacking at the stage of transformation from a conventional learning system to a blended technology-based learning system. Professional intervention in utilizing technological enhancement applications and inducing digital readiness will prominently qualify students with needed soft skills and raise their willingness and dedication to digital learning enforcement (Portillo et al., 2020). Hence, emotional intelligence was more predictive in facilitating the learner's self-control, reflecting an individual's online learning readiness levels (Flesia et al., 2020; Liu et al., 2022).

2.5 The Relationship Between Digital Readiness and Perceived Stress

Digital learning acceptance by higher education students is imperative to effectively and actively proceed with digital learning methodology. The digital learning role in HEIs is primarily driven by students' socio-emotional perceptions, such as anger, worries, and a sense of isolation toward using related-learning technological instruments (Kee, 2020; Portillo et al., 2020; Rodr et al., 2021). Moralista and Oducado (2020) declared that universities in developing countries had not theorized about the effect of students' perceived stress on students' emotional perception of digital learning. Besides, training on digital learning utilization, assessment tools, and knowledge sharing becomes necessary to reinforce the learning experience and mitigate the perceived and potential negative emotions (Jensen et al., 2017; Moralista & Oducado, 2020).

2.6 Perceived Stress and Socio-Emotional Perceptions

The rapid evolution in information and communication technologies increases the efficiency of teaching and learning approaches; teaching practices are no longer confined by the necessity of physical requirements such as classes, tables, and books. E-learning offers educators the flexibility of teaching anytime and anywhere. Thereby, priority was given to investigating educators' and students' readiness to acquire digital learning and the preparedness of related digital tools' influence on students' psychological health (Haider & Al-Salman, 2020; Razak & Din, 2020; Shorfuzzaman & Alhussein, 2016). Based on the Five-Factor Model, five broad personality traits include neuroticism (e.g., tendency to respond when things go wrong, worry, and experience anxiety), consciousness (e.g., being organized, hardworking, goal-oriented), extroversion (i.e., being sociable, assertive, cheerful, active), openness (e.g., being perceptive, creative, reflective, and appreciating fantasy, and aesthetics), and agreeableness (i.e., being kind, cooperative, altruistic, trustworthy, and generous) (Flesia et al., 2020). Meanwhile, stress hurts these behaviors, as illustrated by the fact that individuals are driven to acquire, protect, and retain resources like time, physical and emotional energy, and attention when stressed (Chung, 2018). Furthermore, stress hurts an individual's productivity, effectiveness, and job quality. Individuals who perceive a high stress level suffer from cognitive fatigue, which depletes an individual's energy while it is required for task accomplishment. On the other side, stress also creates adverse situations, such as information overload, which necessitates a substantial portion of one's attention and effort (Chung, 2018; Karaca et al., 2019; Russell et al., 2020).

2.7 *Perceived Stress as Mediation Construct Between Digital Readiness and Socio-Emotional Perceptions*

The shift from traditional learning to e-learning has created several issues for instructors and students from different disciplines (Giray, 2021; Hsu et al., 2019). With the rapid global switch to e-learning mode during the pandemic, many scholars argued that mental health consequences such as anxiety, depression, and perceived stress (Kabir et al., 2021; Müller et al., 2021). Various studies investigated the factors affecting perceived stress in different contexts. Saeed et al. confirmed that the most prominent factors influencing students' perceived stress were anxiety, hopelessness, restlessness, and depression. Optimism and self-efficacy were investigated as factors buffering perceived stress among human resources.

Researchers have found that students and the general public are less likely to experience high stress levels when they are more optimistic (Burger & Samuel, 2017; Denovan & Macaskill, 2017; Heinen et al., 2017). They found that adolescents' mental health status and self-efficacy correlated with higher self-efficacy (Arima et al., 2020; Piekarska, 2020; Rodriguez-Ayllon et al., 2019). Many scholars pay attention to investigating the perceived stress after COVID-19. They found that a pandemic increased the level of perceived stress remarkably. Therefore, different empirical studies have been conducted to examine and assess perceived stress and the associated factors and consequences (Achterberg et al., 2021; Babore et al., 2020; Brown et al., 2020; Torales et al., 2020; Whitehead, 2021). Awoke et al. (2021) reported that in the context of the

COVID-19 pandemic, undergraduate students' stress levels and coping techniques were lacking.

The present chapter posits the following hypotheses based on the aforementioned rationale.

- **H1**: Digital readiness significantly affects perceived stress by HEI students.
- **H2**: Digital readiness significantly affects socio-emotional perception by HEI students.
- **H3**: Perceived stress significantly affects socio-emotional perception by HEI students.
- **H4**: Perceived stress mediates the relationship between digital readiness and socio-emotional perception.

3 Study Framework

Based on a critical review of the literature, Fig. 1 shows the conceptual model has been developed that mainly proposes that student's socio-emotional perceptions are influenced by digital readiness and perceived stress.

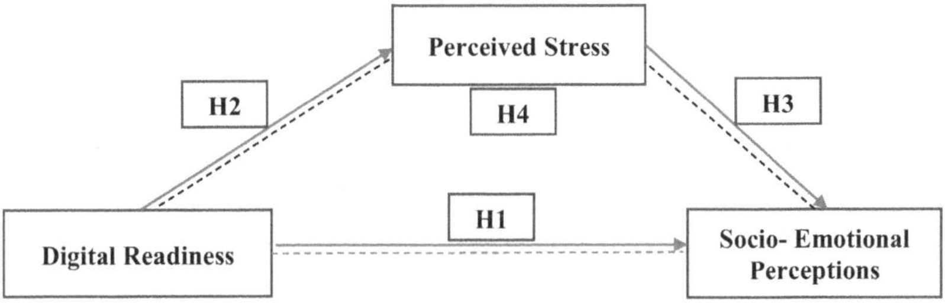

Fig. 1 Research framework (self developed)

4 Methodology

4.1 Material and Procedure

This cross-sectional study adhered to a positivist and quantitative research paradigm congruent with its delineated objectives. The research framework integrated primary and secondary data sources, with particular emphasis on the pivotal role of primary data in achieving the study's objectives. The primary data were garnered from students in higher educational institutions across diverse regions in Oman, encompassing various academic years and majors. The survey instrument encompassed inquiries related to digital readiness, perceived stress, and socio-emotional perception.

Given the absence of a comprehensive student listing, a non-probabilistic, purposive sampling strategy was employed, involving the distribution of a structured closed-ended questionnaire. The selection of non-probability purposive sampling was predicated on its adaptability to various non-probability sampling schemes, particularly in situations where a complete sampling frame for theoretical generalization is unavailable. While acknowledging the limitations on the generalizability inherent in purposive sampling, empirical evidence substantiates the reliability of data collected through such methodologies. In this context, students from higher educational institutions were specifically chosen as participants to assess hypotheses derived from the extant literature.

The data collection process involved the administration of a Google form survey distributed through social media platforms (e.g., Facebook and WhatsApp) and emails. The questionnaire, structured into three sections, sought participants' permission, addressed respondent profiles, and probed into the study variables of digital readiness, perceived stress, and socio-emotional perception. To accommodate the linguistic diversity among Omani respondents, the questionnaires were meticulously developed in both English and Arabic, adhering to recommended translation protocols. The questionnaire underwent pilot testing involving ten professors, resulting in minor adjustments to enhance clarity, validity, and reliability. All measures employed a five-point Likert response format (1 = strongly disagree; 5 = strongly agree).

A total of 300 voluntary responses were collected, ensuring confidentiality and exclusive use for research purposes. The acquired data underwent initial processing to eliminate bias or outliers, followed by a descriptive analysis in SPSS to present participant profiles in terms of

Table 1 Respondents' profile

Respondents characteristics		*Frequency*	*Percentage %*
Gender	Male	99	33.0
	Female	201	67.0
Education	Diploma	82	27.3
	Bachelor	201	67.0
	Master	4	1.3
	Other	13	4.3
Academic year	Year 1	66	22.0
	Year 2	74	24.7
	Year 3	40	13.3
	Year 4	34	11.3
	More than year 4	86	28.7

Source Author's own work and Author's calculations

frequency and percentage. Upon completion of data cleaning, Structural Equation Modeling by Partial Least Squares (SEM-PLS) was employed to scrutinize the proposed hypotheses. The data computation process utilized SPSS and SmartPLS3.2.8 software, with techniques such as the PLS Algorithm and Bootstrapping applied for rigorous analysis.

5 Data Analysis and Results

5.1 Students Characteristics

As shown in Table 1, the data were collected from three hundred students from higher educational institutions. Female students constitute the majority of the received responses. Most of the students are in the bachelor's degree level exceeds the fourth academic year.

5.2 Reliability and Validity Test

PLS-SEM measures the construct's internal consistency, convergent reliability, and discriminant validity. According to Hair et al. (2014), internal consistency is indicated from 0.7 or more Cronbach's Alpha scores, convergent reliability indicated from composite reliability valued at 0.7, and above, and validity of constructs demonstrated from the values of average variance extracted that equal or exceeded 0.5. The results in Table 2 confirm the excellent reliability and validity of the examined

Table 2 Reliability and validity

Study variables	*CA*	*CR*	*AVE*
Digital readiness	0.833	0.888	0.666
Perceived stress	0.864	0.917	0.787
Socio-emotional perception	0.888	0.918	0.694

Notes CA = Cronbach's Alpha, CR = Composite Reliability, AVE = Average Variance Extracted
Source Author's own work and Author's calculations

Table 3 Discriminant validity (Fornell-Larcker)

	Digital readiness	*Perceived stress*	*Socio-emotional perception*
Digital readiness	**0.816**		
Perceived stress	0.515	**0.887**	
Socio-emotional perception	0.518	0.825	**0.833**

Source Author's own work and Author's calculations

constructs. However, discriminant validity is evidenced from the square root of the average variance extracted when each variable correlated with the variable itself, given that the correlation of the variable to the same variable must record the highest value compared to the correlation of the variable with others. Table 3 demonstrates satisfactory discriminant validity. Figure 2 shows the good explanatory power of the dependent variables, including socio-emotional perception with R^2 equal to 0.629 and perceived stress with R^2 equal to 0.265.

5.3 *Hypotheses Testing*

This chapter investigates the factors predicting higher educational institutions' students' socio-emotional perceptions during the COVID-19 pandemic. Given the exceptional conditions imposed by the spread of COVID-19, this raises concerns about examining the impact of digital readiness and perceived stress on students' socio-emotional perception. The collected data was examined using structural equation modeling. Hence, a bootstrapping test was performed using a 5000 sub-sample. The results demonstrate that a significant direct relationship exists between

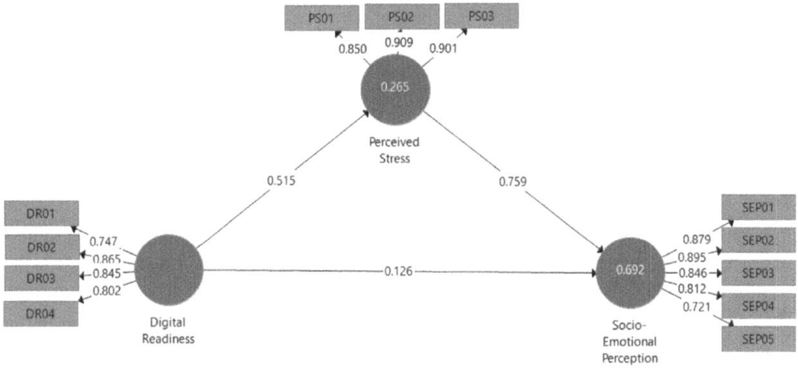

Fig. 2 PLS Algorithm (*Source* Author's own work)

digital readiness and perceived stress (β = 0.515, *t*-value = 12.027, *P* = 0.000), digital readiness and socio-emotional perception (β = 0.126, *t*-value = 2.659, *P* = 0.008), perceived stress and socio-emotional perception (β = 0.759, *t*-value = 20.128, *P* = 0.000). On the other side, the mediate influence of perceived stress was investigated. The findings confirm that a significant positive mediate impact by perceived stress between digital readiness and socio-emotional perception (β = 0.391, *t*-value = 9.909, *P* = 0.000). These findings confirm the results reached by previous studies that confirm students' feelings and emotions are driven by the educational system readiness and students' skills and knowledge that qualifies them to deal with such technologies (Aristovnik et al., 2020; Flores et al., 2021; Händel et al., 2020; Rodr et al., 2021) (Tables 4 and 5).

6 Discussion and Conclusions

In the preceding chapters, we have explored the intricate relationship between digital learning, socio-emotional perception, and the overall well-being of higher education students, particularly within the context of the COVID-19 pandemic in Oman. As we conclude this inquiry, several key insights emerge, offering both theoretical and practical implications for educational policymakers, institutions, and practitioners.

Our investigation has identified critical factors that significantly influence the socio-emotional perception of Omani higher education

Table 4 Direct effect test

Hypothesis	*Hypotheses direction*	*Original sample*	*Sample mean (M)*	*Standard deviation*	T *values*	P *values*
H1	Digital readiness -> Perceived stress	0.515	0.518	0.043	12.027	0.000
H2	Digital readiness -> Socio-emotional perception	0.126	0.126	0.048	2.659	0.008
H3	Perceived stress -> Socio-emotional perception	0.759	0.761	0.038	20.128	0.000

Source Author's own work and Author's calculations

Table 5 Indirect effect test

Hypothesis	*Hypotheses direction*	*Original sample*	*Sample mean (M)*	*Standard deviation*	T *values*	P *values*
H4	Digital readiness -> Perceived stress -> Socio-emotional perception	0.391	0.394	0.039	9.909	0.000

Source Author's own work and Author's calculations

students during their exposure to digital learning. These factors encompass not only technological readiness but also the psychological and emotional challenges induced by the abrupt shift in educational modalities. Recognizing that students' perceptions, emotions, and stress levels are profoundly affected by the sudden transition to digital learning, it becomes imperative to develop targeted interventions. Strategies aimed at mitigating obstacles encountered during technology utilization should be formulated, fostering an environment conducive to positive socio-emotional experiences. A key avenue for improvement lies in elevating the digital facilities' readiness to a level that aligns with the evolving needs of Omani students. By determining and implementing practical and user-friendly modifications, the stressors associated with technology use can be significantly reduced, promoting a more seamless integration of digital tools into the educational landscape.

The integration of interactive communication tools within the digital learning system emerges as a potent solution to alleviate students' feelings of alienation and loneliness. Creating a virtual space that fosters collaboration, engagement, and social interaction can contribute to a more positive mental health status among students. The effective management and efficiency of education in Oman hinge on the adaptive evolution of the digital learning system. Tailoring this system to better suit the unique needs and challenges faced by Omani students will not only enhance the overall educational experience but also empower students to overcome obstacles and thrive in the digital learning environment.

In conclusion, our exploration into the nexus of digital learning, socio-emotional perception, and student well-being underscores the importance of adaptability and targeted interventions. By proactively addressing the challenges unearthed in this study, educational stakeholders can contribute to a more resilient and student-centric learning ecosystem in Oman.

6.1 Practical Implications

This chapter's contribution to the knowledge of digital readiness in education has practical implications for various stakeholders. Educating researchers, managers, academic staff, and practitioners about the pivotal role of a student's socio-emotional perceptions in enhancing and delivering digital readiness can significantly improve the overall learning experience. Additionally, by expanding the existing knowledge of digital enthusiasm in an educational context, this research offers a valuable contribution, particularly in the Omani setting, which has been relatively underexplored in previous studies that predominantly focus on developed countries.

The practical implications extend to policymakers and practitioners, providing them with crucial insights and theoretical knowledge. This information is instrumental for the seamless implementation of a digital learning system, ultimately mitigating the negative psychological impact on students. In essence, the findings from this chapter offer practical guidance for enhancing digital readiness and enthusiasm, ensuring a more effective and positive learning environment in the context of Omani education.

7 Limitations and Future Research Suggestions

While this research contributes significantly, we must acknowledge its limitations. The chapter explores the link between digital readiness, perceived stress, and students' socio-emotional perspectives in education. However, the lack of comprehensive quantitative data limits generalization. This study sets the stage for additional empirical research, urging investigations into the connections among research constructs. The methodology offers potential replication in diverse domains, testing the conceptual model's generalizability.

Future research opportunities lie in examining the impact of self-image on students' socio-emotional perception and digital learning acceptance. Despite valuable insights, the dynamic nature of technology and education calls for ongoing research. Subsequent studies could explore emerging technologies and pedagogical approaches, especially in unforeseen disruptions, ensuring continued adaptability in this evolving educational landscape.

Acknowledgements The research leading to these results has received funding from the Ministry of Higher Education, Research and Innovation (MoHERI) of the Sultanate of Oman under the Block Funding Program with agreement no. MoHERI/BFP/ASU/01/2021.

References

Abdulah, D. M., & Mohammed, A. A. (2020). The consequences of the COVID-19 pandemic on perceived stress in clinical practice: Experience of doctors in Iraqi Kurdistan. *Romanian Journal of Internal Medicine, 58*(4), 219–227. https://doi.org/10.2478/rjim-2020-0020

Abdulghani, H. M., et al. (2020). Association of COVID-19 pandemic with undergraduate medical students' perceived stress and coping [response to letter]. *Psychology Research and Behavior Management, 13*, 1101–1102. https://doi.org/10.2147/PRBM.S292018

Achterberg, M., et al. (2021). Perceived stress as a mediator for longitudinal effects of the COVID-19 lockdown on wellbeing of parents and children. *Scientific Reports, 11*(1), 1–14.

Agrawal, P., Narain, R., & Ullah, I. (2019). Analysis of barriers in implementation of digital transformation of supply chain using interpretive structural modelling approach. *Journal of Modelling in Management, 15*(1), 297–317.

Al-Emran, M., et al. (2020). Examining the roles of students' beliefs and security concerns for using smartwatches in higher education. *Journal of Enterprise Information Management*. https://doi.org/10.1108/JEIM-02-2020-0052

Arima, M., et al. (2020). Factors associated with the mental health status of medical students during the COVID-19 pandemic: A cross-sectional study in Japan. *British Medical Journal Open, 10*(12), e043728.

Aristovnik, A., et al. (2020). Impacts of the COVID-19 pandemic on life of higher education students: A global perspective. *Sustainability (Switzerland), 12*(20), 1–34. https://doi.org/10.3390/su12208438

Awoke, M., et al. (2021). Perceived stress and coping strategies among undergraduate health science students of jimma university amid the COVID-19 outbreak: Online cross-sectional survey. *Frontiers in Psychology*, 12.

Azlan, C. A., et al. (2020, July). Teaching and learning postgraduate medical physics using Internet-based e-learning during the COVID-19 pandemic—A case study from Malaysia. *Physica Medica, 80*, 10–16. https://doi.org/10.1016/j.ejmp.2020.10.002

Babore, A., et al. (2020). Psychological effects of the COVID-2019 pandemic: Perceived stress and coping strategies among healthcare professionals. *Psychiatry Research, 293*, 113366.

Bai, H. (2019). Pedagogical practices of mobile learning in K-12 and higher education settings. *Association for Educational Communications & Technology*.

Bhaskar, P., Tiwari, C. K., & Joshi, A. (2020). Blockchain in education management: Present and future applications. *Interactive Technology and Smart Education*. https://doi.org/10.1108/ITSE-07-2020-0102

Blayone, T. J. B., et al. (2018). Profiling the digital readiness of higher education students for transformative online learning in the post-soviet nations of Georgia and Ukraine. *International Journal of Educational Technology in Higher Education, 15*(1). https://doi.org/10.1186/s41239-018-0119-9

Brown, S. M., et al. (2020). Stress and parenting during the global COVID-19 pandemic. *Child Abuse & Neglect, 110*, 104699.

Burger, K., & Samuel, R. (2017). The role of perceived stress and self-efficacy in young people's life satisfaction: A longitudinal study. *Journal of Youth and Adolescence, 46*(1), 78–90.

Chen, T., et al. (2020). The impact of the COVID-19 pandemic on user experience with online education platforms in China. *Sustainability (Switzerland), 12*(18). https://doi.org/10.3390/SU12187329

Chung, Y. W. (2018). Workplace ostracism and workplace behaviors: A moderated mediation model of perceived stress and psychological empowerment. *Anxiety, Stress, & Coping, 31*(3), 304–317. https://doi.org/10.1080/10615806.2018.1424835

Ciriello, R. F., Richter, A., & Schwabe, G. (2018). Digital innovation. *Business & Information Systems Engineering, 60*(6), 563–569.

Correani, A., et al. (2020). Implementing a digital strategy: Learning from the experience of three digital transformation projects. *California Management Review, 62*(4), 37–56.

Day, A. L., & Livingstone, H. A. (2003). Gender differences in perceptions of stressors and utilization of social support among university students. *Canadian Journal of Behavioural Science/Revue Canadienne des sciences du comportement, 35*(2), 73.

Denovan, A., & Macaskill, A. (2017). Stress and subjective well-being among first-year UK undergraduate students. *Journal of Happiness Studies, 18*(2), 505–525.

Evans, W., & Kelly, B. (2004). Pre-registration diploma student nurse stress and coping measures. *Nurse Education Today, 24*(6), 473–482.

Fischer, M., et al. (2020). Strategy archetypes for digital transformation: Defining meta objectives using business process management. *Information & Management, 57*(5), 103262.

Flesia, L., et al. (2020). Predicting perceived stress related to the COVID-19 outbreak through stable psychological traits and machine learning models. *Journal of Clinical Medicine, 9*(10), 3350. https://doi.org/10.3390/jcm9103350

Flores, M. A., et al. (2021). Portuguese higher education students' adaptation to online teaching and learning in times of the COVID-19 pandemic: Personal and contextual factors. *Higher Education*, 1389–1408. https://doi.org/10.1007/s10734-021-00748-x

Foerster-Metz, U. S., et al. (2018). Digital transformation and its implications on organizational behavior. *Journal of EU Research in Business, 2018*(S3), 1–14.

Giray, G. (2021). An assessment of student satisfaction with e-learning: An empirical study with computer and software engineering undergraduate students in Turkey under pandemic conditions. *Education and Information Technologies, 26*(6), 6651–6673.

Haider, A. S., & Al-Salman, S. (2020). Dataset of Jordanian university students' psychological health impacted by using e-learning tools during COVID-19. *Data in Brief, 32*, 106104. https://doi.org/10.1016/j.dib.2020.106104

Hair, J. F., et al. (2014). Partial least squares structural equation modeling (PLS-SEM): An emerging tool in business research. *European Business Review, 26*(2), 106–121. https://doi.org/10.1108/EBR-10-2013-0128

Händel, M., et al. (2020). Digital readiness and its effects on higher education students' socio-emotional perceptions in the context of the COVID-19 pandemic. *Journal of Research on Technology in Education*, 1–13. https://doi.org/10.1080/15391523.2020.1846147

Heinen, I., Bullinger, M., & Kocalevent, R.-D. (2017). Perceived stress in first-year medical students-associations with personal resources and emotional distress. *BMC Medical Education, 17*(1), 1–14.

Hong, A. J., & Kim, H. J. (2018). College students' Digital Readiness for Academic Engagement (DRAE) scale: Scale development and validation. *Asia-Pacific Education Researcher, 27*(4), 303–312. https://doi.org/10.1007/s40299-018-0387-0

Hsu, H.-C. K., Wang, C. V., & Levesque-Bristol, C. (2019). Reexamining the impact of self-determination theory on learning outcomes in the online learning environment. *Education and Information Technologies, 24*(3), 2159–2174.

Jamil, S. (2019). Preparedness of university students for the challenges of globalisation. *The Online Journal of Distance Education and e-Learning* (32007).

Jensen, B., Jensen, P., & Rasmussen, A. W. (2017, September). Does professional development of preschool teachers improve children's socio-emotional outcomes? *Labour Economics, 45*, 26–39. https://doi.org/10.1016/j.labeco.2016.11.004

Kabir, H., Hasan, M. K., & Mitra, D. K. (2021). E-learning readiness and perceived stress among the university students of Bangladesh during COVID-19: A countrywide cross-sectional study. *Annals of Medicine, 53*(1), 2305–2314.

Karaca, A., et al. (2019). The effect of cognitive behavioral group therapy on infertility stress, general health, and negative cognitions: A randomized controlled trial. *Journal of Rational-Emotive & Cognitive-Behavior Therapy, 37*(4), 375–394.

Kee, C. E. (2020). The impact of COVID-19: Graduate students' emotional and psychological experiences. *Journal of Human Behavior in the Social Environment*, 1–13. https://doi.org/10.1080/10911359.2020.1855285

Kulikowski, K., Przytuła, S., & Sułkowski, Ł. (2021, January). E-learning? Never again! On unintended consequences of COVID-19 forced e-learning on academic teacher motivational job characteristics. *Higher Education Quarterly, 76*(1), 174–189. https://doi.org/10.1111/hequ.12314

Lee, S. M., & Trimi, S. (2021). Convergence innovation in the digital age and in the COVID-19 pandemic crisis. *Journal of Business Research, 123*, 14–22.

Liu, S., et al. (2021). Personality and perceived stress during COVID-19 pandemic: Testing the mediating role of perceived threat and efficacy. *Personality and Individual Differences, 168*, 110351. https://doi.org/10.1016/j.paid.2020.110351

Liu, Y., Zhao, L., & Su, Y.-S. (2022). The impact of teacher competence in online teaching on perceived online learning outcomes during the COVID-19 outbreak: A moderated-mediation model of teacher resilience and age. *International Journal of Environmental Research and Public Health, 19*(10). https://doi.org/10.3390/ijerph19106282

Mailizar, M., et al. (2020). Secondary school mathematics teachers' views on e-learning implementation barriers during the COVID-19 pandemic: The case of Indonesia. *Eurasia Journal of Mathematics, Science and Technology Education, 16*(7). https://doi.org/10.29333/EJMSTE/8240

Mirković, V., et al. (2019). Key characteristics of organizational structure that supports digital transformation. In *International Scientific Conference Strategic Management and Decision Support Systems in Strategic Management.*

Moradi, A., & Chemelnezhad, M. (2021). Predicting emotional-social competence based on academic engagement, self-efficacy and perception of school climate in high school students. *Iranian Evolutionary and Educational Psychology Journal, 3*(4), 574–582.

Moralista, R. B., & Oducado, R. M. F. (2020). Faculty perception toward online education in a state college in the Philippines during the coronavirus disease 19 (COVID-19) pandemic. *Universal Journal of Educational Research, 8*(10), 4736–4742. https://doi.org/10.13189/ujer.2020.081044

Müller, A. M., et al. (2021). COVID-19 emergency e-learning and beyond experiences and perspectives of university educators. *Education Sciences, 11*(1), 19.

Osmundsen, K., Iden, J., & Bygstad, B. (2018). Digital transformation: Drivers, success factors, and implications. *MCIS*, 37.

Piekarska, J. (2020). Determinants of perceived stress in adolescence: The role of personality traits, emotional abilities, trait emotional intelligence, self-efficacy, and self-esteem. *Advances in Cognitive Psychology, 16*(4), 309.

Portillo, J., et al. (2020). Self-perception of the digital competence of educators during the COVID-19 pandemic: A cross-analysis of different educational stages. *Sustainability (Switzerland), 12*(23), 1–13. https://doi.org/10.3390/su122310128

Rachmadtullah, R. (2020). Use of blended learning with Moodle: Study effectiveness in elementary school teacher education students during the COVID-19 pandemic. *International Journal of Advanced Science and Technology, 29*(7), 3272–3277. https://www.scopus.com/inward/record.uri?partnerID=HzOxMe3b&scp=85085640272&origin=inward

Rashid Al-Senaidi, S., & Gawande, V. (2013). Factors affecting adoption of ICT among Omani faculty members in Sultanate of Oman. *International Journal of Computing Academic Research, 2*(5), 200–213. http://www.meacse.org/ijcar

Razak, N. S. A. A., & Din, R. (2020). Video usage among secondary school students during the COVID-19 pandemic. *Universal Journal of Educational Research, 8*(11A), 43–48. https://doi.org/10.13189/ujer.2020.082106

Rodriguez-Ayllon, M., et al. (2019). Role of physical activity and sedentary behavior in the mental health of preschoolers, children, and adolescents: A systematic review and meta-analysis. *Sports Medicine, 49*(9), 1383–1410.

Rodr, J., Mar, A., & Cord, E. (2021). The influence of digital tools and social networks on the digital competence of university students during COVID-19 pandemic. *International Journal of Environmental Research and Public Health.*

Russell, L. H., et al. (2020). The closed response style and posttraumatic stress: Examining the interaction between experiential avoidance and cognitive fusion among women experiencing sexual trauma. *Psychological Trauma: Theory, Research, Practice, and Policy, 12*(6), 627.

Sarrab, M., et al. (2018). Toward Educational Requirements Model for Mobile Learning Development and Adoption in Higher Education. *TechTrends, 62*(4), 635–646.

Savage, M. J., et al. (2020, June). Mental health and movement behavior during the COVID-19 pandemic in UK university students: Prospective cohort study. *Mental Health and Physical Activity, 19*, 100357. https://doi.org/10.1016/j.mhpa.2020.100357

Shorfuzzaman, M., & Alhussein, M. (2016). Modeling learners' readiness to adopt mobile learning: A perspective from a GCC higher education institution. *Mobile Information Systems*. https://doi.org/10.1155/2016/6982824

Torales, J., et al. (2020). Self-perceived stress during the quarantine of COVID-19 pandemic in Paraguay: An exploratory survey. *Frontiers in Psychiatry, 11*, 1155.

Vial, G. (2021). Understanding digital transformation: A review and a research agenda. In A. Hinterhuber, T. Vescovi, & F. Checchinato (Eds.), *Managing digital transformation: Understanding the strategic process* (pp. 13–66). Routledge.

Whitehead, B. R. (2021). COVID-19 as a stressor: Pandemic expectations, perceived stress, and negative affect in older adults. *The Journals of Gerontology: Series B, 76*(2), e59–e64.

Ziyadin, S., Suieubayeva, S., & Utegenova, A. (2019). Digital transformation in business. In *International Scientific Conference "Digital Transformation of the Economy: Challenges, Trends, New Opportunities"* (pp. 408–415). Springer.

CHAPTER 11

The Level of Early Awareness of the Pandemic Effects Among Arab Students in Turkey: A Qualitative Study

Iyad Abusahloub

1 Introduction

The World Health Organization (WHO) officially designated COVID-19 as a disease on February 11, 2020. This highly contagious respiratory illness was first documented in December 2019, with China being the initial epicenter. Subsequently, the WHO declared it a pandemic in March 2020. Common symptoms associated with COVID-19 include coughing, sore throat, difficulty in breathing, and fever (Singh & Singh, 2020).

Undoubtedly, the COVID-19 pandemic has left a profound mark on both the global economy and society. The extensive and far-reaching changes brought about by the pandemic have affected various facets of human existence. Yet, predicting the precise nature and extent of these transformations has proven to be a formidable challenge, especially during the initial months of the pandemic. The scarcity of information at that

I. Abusahloub (✉)
UIK: Université Ibn Khaldoun, Tunis, Tunisia
e-mail: iyadabusahloub@gmail.com; iyad.abusahloub@uik.ens.tn

A. Mishrif (ed.), *Perspectives on Human Capital Development*,
https://doi.org/10.1007/978-981-97-5246-1_11

time, coupled with the practical difficulties in conducting field research due to quarantine measures and restrictions on individual movement, made it a particularly daunting endeavor. Furthermore, the variability in economic, healthcare, and other capacities among different countries added to the complexity of the situation.

This article addresses the question of how COVID-19 has impacted the economy and society by examining the early awareness of its effects among Arab students in Turkey. The research adopts an inductive approach and employs qualitative methods, specifically manual coding using the Grounded Theory approach, involving a three-step coding process (open, axial, and selective). Semi-structured interviews (SSIs) with a descriptive/interpretive typology were conducted. The selective codes (or themes) derived from this research may serve as variables influenced by the COVID-19 pandemic, which can be employed in future deductive studies utilizing quantitative methods to assess the nature and strength of the pandemic's impact on these variables.

2 Theoretical Framework

Scholars' assessments of the COVID-19 pandemic's repercussions on humanity extend beyond common expectations. McCallion (2020) contends that even as humanity perseveres beyond this pandemic, its enduring impact will be profound. This global health crisis has laid bare the duality of human nature, revealing both altruism and selfishness, a pattern recurrent in history. Historical records demonstrate that pandemics not only shook the foundations of the Roman Empire but also precipitated a spiritual crisis from which Rome never fully recovered. In light of these historical precedents, McCallion raises two critical questions regarding the destiny of the world's largest nation, the United States of America: "Will Pax Americana face a similar fate? Will we meet this challenge and emerge strengthened?"

In every crisis, there are silver linings. Kumar et al. (2021) contend that the COVID-19 pandemic has engendered sweeping global transformations, affecting multiple spheres of life, notably business, agriculture, entertainment, tourism, and service industries. Intriguingly, despite these disruptions, there has been a notable reduction in environmental pollutants, manifesting in lower levels of air, soil, and water contamination.

2.1 The COVID-19 Pandemic and Society

The COVID-19 pandemic has had a far-reaching impact, with its effects being particularly pronounced among the most vulnerable segments of the population. Lockdowns and social distancing measures have created a significant social divide, impeding interpersonal relationships among friends and family. A notable consequence of reduced economic activity during the pandemic has been the revelation that life can be sustained with more restrained consumption.

Within the family sphere, there have been some positive outcomes, with fathers, in particular, drawing closer to their children and families. This shift is noteworthy as some fathers had comparatively limited engagement with their children before the pandemic (Verma & Prakash, 2020).

The containment measures necessitated by the COVID-19 outbreak have presented challenges to personal and community interactions. These restrictions, encompassing social distancing and isolation, have had a profound impact on social relationships, resulting in heightened feelings of loneliness, anxiety, depression, mental health disorders, and associated health risks, impacting both individuals and society at large (Singh & Singh, 2020).

Additionally, the pandemic has given rise to heightened fears and insecurities, primarily driven by concerns over potential job loss and income reduction. Government-imposed closures have, regrettably, contributed to an increase in incidents of domestic violence and child abuse, underscoring the far-reaching social consequences of this crisis (Debata et al., 2020).

2.2 The COVID-19 Pandemic and Environment

As outlined by Kumar et al. (2021), although COVID-19 has brought about adverse effects on globalization and society, it has, paradoxically, created an environment conducive to improvements in environmental health. This observation aligns with the findings of Verma and Prakash (2020), who note that in the initial months of 2020, the repercussions of the pandemic have led to substantial environmental recovery. This recovery holds the potential for a positive impact on global climate change. Furthermore, Debata et al. (2020) highlight that, in spite of the economic deceleration, the lockdown measures imposed in response to the pandemic have proven advantageous for the environment. This has been achieved through a reduction in pollution levels and a decreased discharge of effluents from factories into water bodies.

2.3 *The COVID-19 Pandemic and Economy*

COVID-19 is evidently instigating enduring transformations in global politics, particularly in sectors such as health, security, trade, employment, agriculture, industrial production, and scientific policies. This pandemic has inflicted severe negative consequences on various stakeholders, including employees, customers, supply chains, and financial markets, with the ominous specter of a global economic recession looming. The timing and scale of this downturn remain highly uncertain due to the ongoing nature of the pandemic (Açikgöz & Günay, 2020).

As emphasized by Raut (2020), COVID-19 presents a formidable dual challenge, impacting both health and the economy. The profound and adverse repercussions of this pandemic are set to exacerbate economic woes in numerous countries globally, necessitating immediate and future decisive measures.

The world's economies are seemingly teetering on the brink of recession, as asserted by Sułkowski (2020). This prospect has the potential to culminate in a worldwide economic downturn. The crisis has spurred contemplation of shifting government attitudes toward healthcare functions, the role of states, and the functions of international financial institutions. Simultaneously, there is a discernible surge in the utilization of virtual communication tools.

Lone and Ahmad (2020) underscore the detrimental impact of the pandemic on the most developed nations globally while serving as a major threat to low- and middle-income countries. The continent of Africa, home to a highly susceptible population regarding infectious diseases, is expected to bear a substantial burden from the protracted COVID-19 outbreak.

According to Verma and Prakash (2020), the pandemic has precipitated dire consequences for employment and income, resulting in a reduction in full-time jobs and factory closures. Salaries have become uncertain, causing further economic distress.

Kumar et al. (2021) draw attention to the scarcity of accurate data concerning the COVID-19 outbreak in some regions, a situation stemming from concerns related to the accompanying economic crisis.

2.4 The COVID-19 Pandemic and the Business Models

The COVID-19 pandemic has emerged as a transformative and pivotal event that has profoundly altered our way of life. Notably, businesses and their underlying models have experienced a substantial digital overhaul, prompting companies to adapt their daily operations. A predominant shift toward remote work has become the standard, with nearly all remote workers now relying on digital technologies as an integral part of their work (Stalmachova et al., 2021).

This pandemic has presented a diverse array of challenges to businesses, and their responses to this disruptive force have had a pronounced impact on their resilience and prospects for navigating this crisis successfully. Industries that primarily offer services have been particularly hard-hit. Consequently, companies are revisiting and adapting their business models to suit this evolving landscape (Gregurec et al., 2021).

The COVID-19 crisis has compelled organizations to explore digital alternatives and devise strategies for delivering their goods and services with minimal physical interaction, prioritizing safety. These alternative approaches have opened up avenues for innovation, enabling companies to reconfigure existing products, develop alternative digital offerings, and reimagine the channels and mechanisms for delivering their products and services. In this context, businesses are actively seeking positions and strategic partnerships within the emerging ecosystem (Seetharaman, 2020).

2.5 The COVID-19 Pandemic and Public Health

Emerging evidence from multiple countries underscores the persistence of socio-economic inequalities that have found resonance in the context of the COVID-19 pandemic. Much like in previous times, these disparities have resurfaced as a consequence of COVID-19, which both interacts with and exacerbates existing inequalities related to chronic diseases and the determinants of health. The pandemic has laid bare the deep-seated social, economic, and political disparities that preexisted it. Even prior to the outbreak, the UK and the United States had already witnessed a decline in life expectancy among the most disadvantaged segments of the population, and health inequalities had been on the rise in some European countries over the past decade. The future portends the likelihood of a global economic downturn in the post-COVID-19 era, which could further exacerbate health inequities, especially if health-damaging austerity policies are re-implemented (Bambra et al., 2020).

McCallion (2020) characterizes the pandemic as a public health crisis with profound moral implications, the ultimate outcome of which remains uncertain. While COVID-19 has been dubbed the "Great Equalizer" due to its potential to affect people regardless of their socio-economic status, it is only partially true. The wealthy have a statistically better chance of survival as they possess the financial means to practice strict social distancing in spacious homes, the resources to stay at home without facing financial hardship, and access to well-equipped hospitals. Dr. David Blumenthal, Chair of the Commonwealth Fund, highlights the enormous economic impact and fear of the virus, emphasizing the unprecedented challenge it presents to the healthcare system.

The COVID-19 pandemic has subjected the global healthcare systems to a rigorous test, exposing vulnerabilities and revealing fundamental flaws. Blumenthal et al. (2020) argue that the crisis has unveiled and exacerbated underlying issues in the US healthcare system, shedding light on the need for comprehensive reforms. This situation, they contend, provides an opportunity to address not only the challenges posed by future pandemics but also the fundamental healthcare needs of Americans. The pandemic underscores the importance of not letting a crisis go to waste, as Winston Churchill once aptly stated.

Moreover, the pandemic holds the potential to usher in profound changes in healthcare dynamics, leading to substantial investments in disease prevention infrastructure and accelerating the digital transformation of healthcare delivery. Furthermore, collaboration among various stakeholders has given rise to opportunities for the development of vaccines and treatments. Companies such as Johnson & Johnson, Vir Biotechnology, Novavax, and NanoViricides have announced collaborative efforts to develop a viral vaccine. Clinical trials for COVID-19 vaccines have been underway, with promising results (Nicola et al., 2020). This collective effort has culminated in the rapid development and distribution of vaccines across the globe in less than a year.

2.6 The COVID-19 Pandemic and Mental Health

The advent of the COVID-19 pandemic, triggered by the SARS-CoV-2 virus, presents humanity with an unprecedented stressor. This crisis has given rise to severe acute respiratory distress and, significantly, a widespread decline in physical fitness and mental resilience, the full ramifications of which remain challenging to gauge (Heitzman, 2020). As noted by Xiong et al. (2020), the pandemic has ushered in an unparalleled threat to mental health, affecting individuals in high, middle, and low-income countries alike. Beyond efforts to mitigate viral transmission, it is imperative to accord priority to the prevention of mental disorders, including major depressive disorder, post-traumatic stress disorder (PTSD), and suicide.

Tee et al. (2020) conducted a study during the early stages of the COVID-19 pandemic in the Philippines, revealing alarming statistics. Approximately one-fourth of the respondents reported experiencing moderate-to-severe anxiety, while one-seventh reported moderate-to-severe stress levels. A similar proportion, one-sixth, reported experiencing moderate-to-severe depression due to the profound psychological impact of the pandemic's outbreak in the Philippines. These findings underscore the profound and far-reaching mental health consequences of the ongoing pandemic.

2.7 *The COVID-19 Pandemic and Cybercriminals*

The COVID-19 pandemic has instigated comprehensive lifestyle changes that span various aspects of daily life. These alterations have given rise to novel lifestyle patterns necessitating adaptation. Notably, numerous institutions have transitioned to official online operations, students have shifted to e-learning platforms, and online shopping has experienced a notable upsurge. These circumstances have created a fertile ground for the proliferation of cybercriminal activities. Cybercriminals have seized upon these conditions, exploiting the heightened pressures experienced by individuals and organizations, thereby augmenting the success of their attacks (Khweiled et al., 2021).

A paper authored by Pranggono and Arabo (2021) investigates the cybersecurity challenges that have arisen in the context of the COVID-19 pandemic. The paper contends that during the pandemic, cybercriminals and Advanced Persistent Threat (APT) groups have leveraged the opportunity to target vulnerable individuals and systems. It underscores a direct association between the pandemic and the escalating frequency of cyberattacks directed at susceptible sectors. Furthermore, the paper highlights that the proliferation of anxiety and fear induced by the pandemic has contributed to an increase in the effectiveness of these cyberattacks.

2.8 The COVID-19 Pandemic and Education

The pandemic has laid bare the inadequacies of the current higher education system, highlighting the urgent need for enhanced training of educators in digital technology to better align with the rapidly evolving educational landscape. In the post-pandemic scenario, the utilization of eLearning and virtual education is poised to become an integral component of higher education. Higher education institutions and universities must formulate post-pandemic education and research strategies to ensure the attainment of desired student learning outcomes and the maintenance of educational quality standards (Rashid & Yadav, 2020).

As indicated by Pokhrel and Chhetri (2021), the COVID-19 pandemic has triggered the most extensive disruption in global education systems in recorded history, impacting approximately 1.6 billion learners across over 200 countries. School closures, institutional shutdowns, and the cessation of in-person learning have affected over 94% of the world's student population, bringing about profound alterations in various aspects of our lives. Social distancing measures and restrictions on movement have significantly disrupted traditional educational practices. The reopening of schools post-relaxation of restrictions presents another challenge, with the implementation of new standard operating procedures. This necessitates innovation and the adoption of alternative educational systems and assessment strategies.

The COVID-19 pandemic has afforded an opportunity to usher in digital learning, as discussed by Verma and Prakash (2020). It has had a global impact on educational systems, with the disruption in education and learning potentially yielding medium and long-term consequences for educational quality. Kumar et al. (2021) note that online learning mechanisms have been employed to compensate for theoretical concepts, although practical learning has suffered a considerable setback due to the pandemic.

2.9 The COVID-19 Pandemic and the Economic Sectors

The COVID-19 outbreak is having a profound and far-reaching impact on the aviation industry, causing a significant downturn in global aviation and tourism business. The International Air Transport Association (IATA) reports a substantial reduction in the global revenue of the airline industry, estimated at around USD 113 billion. Furthermore, the shipping and air freight sector has not been spared from the effects of COVID-19. The air freight business has experienced a sharp decline due to the widespread cancelation of passenger flights worldwide, creating disruptions in supply chains (Rahman et al., 2020).

Among the hardest-hit sectors, the hospitality and travel industry faces unprecedented challenges, especially affecting hourly workers. For instance, Marriott International, with approximately 174,000 employees, is considering placing tens of thousands of workers on furlough. Hilton Worldwide has proactively borrowed $1.75 billion under a revolving loan, signaling the need for financial flexibility amid global market uncertainties. The European hotel market, in particular, has witnessed significant declines due to the international distortions caused by the COVID-19 crisis. The tourism sector is one of the hardest-hit areas, affecting both travel supply and demand, with millions of jobs at risk according to The World Travel and Tourism Council (Nicola et al., 2020).

The COVID-19 pandemic is reshaping food supply chains, giving rise to the growth of the online grocery delivery sector and altering consumer preferences toward "local" food supply chains. Canadian food supply chains are facing several ramifications, with a critical emphasis on enhancing supply chain resilience (Hobbs, 2020).

In the realm of health markets, including the pharmaceutical sector, the COVID-19 pandemic is causing a major crisis. Recognizing these effects is crucial for informing policymakers as they plan strategies to address the associated challenges (Ayati et al., 2020).

The magnitude of the COVID-19 pandemic has had a profound impact on health systems and the pharmaceutical industry worldwide. Health services have been disrupted on a global scale, prompting the adoption of practices such as remote patient communication to ensure the safety of healthcare teams. The virus has emerged as a sudden threat with multifaceted implications, affecting not only healthcare but also the pharmaceutical industry. This crisis has yielded valuable lessons that extend beyond virus risk reduction, offering insights into the disruptions within the economic system (Almurisi et al., 2020).

2.10 *The COVID-19 Pandemic and Turkey*

In a study conducted by Bostan et al. (2020), the impact of the COVID-19 pandemic on society was assessed across three dimensions: pandemic sensitivity, pandemic protection, and social trust. The research findings revealed that individuals exhibited heightened sensitivity to the pandemic, exerted maximum efforts to protect themselves, and displayed an above-average level of social trust, although it slightly lagged behind in comparison to the other dimensions. Consequently, this chapter concludes that COVID-19 has exerted a significant impact on the Turkish population.

The COVID-19 pandemic has posed a substantial risk to students' mental health, as research indicates an increase in perceived stress and mental health issues during this crisis. An investigation involving 358 undergraduate students from 14 universities in Turkey utilized a hierarchical linear regression model to identify predictors of perceived stress, after accounting for gender and factors such as negative emotions, anxiety, and reduced physical activity. The findings underscore the substantial risk to students' mental well-being during the pandemic (Aslan et al., 2020).

In accordance with Adibelli et al. (2021), emotional violence levels are higher for women and their partners who are not employed during the pandemic. The researchers have concluded that emotional violence tends to be more pronounced during the pandemic, with non-participation in income-generating employment contributing to this phenomenon.

3 Method

This chapter employs an inductive approach, differing from the deductive method, which typically starts with an anticipated pattern that is tested against observations. Induction, on the other hand, commences with observations and seeks to discern patterns within them, as explained by Babbie (2010).

The research at hand adopts a qualitative methodology. As outlined by Williams and Moser (2019), qualitative research offers the opportunity to trace the origins of a phenomenon, explore potential reasons for its occurrence, elucidate the significance of the phenomenon to those involved, and ascertain whether it contributes to the development of a theoretical framework or conceptual understanding associated with the phenomenon. In contrast to quantitative research, which primarily aims to quantify and statistically analyze the frequency of a phenomenon and then generalize the findings, qualitative research delves deeply into the phenomenon to uncover its meaning, both during and after its occurrence. The qualitative approach supports the process of constructing meaning from the collected data, thereby making valuable contributions to the existing literature and enriching our comprehension of the world.

With the evolution of qualitative research and the maturation of data collection and organization methodologies, specific strategies and structures for managing data have emerged as standard practices. An integral component of data organization in qualitative research is coding. Coding encompasses a series of procedures that facilitate the organization, categorization, and thematic arrangement of collected data, providing a structured framework for the construction of meaning (Williams & Moser, 2019).

In this chapter, manual coding strategies aligned with qualitative research are applied, employing the Grounded Theory method's three-step coding process, which includes open, axial, and selective coding (Williams & Moser, 2019).

3.1 Technique

In this chapter, a Semi-Structured Interview (SSI) approach was employed. Analytically, SSI involves comparing participants' responses item by item. Since all participants are asked the same set of questions in the same order, the data collected are comparable and can be transformed into numerical form for quantitative analysis. Each piece of data is systematically analyzed, focusing on individual items, as explained by (McIntosh and Morse, 2015).

According to Merton and Kendall (1946), Morse and Field (1995), and Richards and Morse (2007), SSI is designed to elicit subjective responses from individuals regarding specific situations or phenomena they have encountered. It employs a relatively detailed interview guide and is typically used when there is sufficient objective knowledge about an experience or phenomenon, but subjective insights are lacking. The interview questions are structured to elicit responses from each participant, and they have the freedom to respond to these open-ended questions as they see fit, with the researcher probing for further insights. This combination of structure and flexibility characterizes the semi-structured nature of the method and sets it apart from other interview approaches, making it highly relevant to the research topic while remaining responsive to the participants (McIntosh & Morse, 2015).

In this chapter, a descriptive/interpretive classification of SSIs was used. This classification seeks to understand the empirical world from the perspective of the participants within their contextual dimensions. It recognizes the limited framework from the outset and values the importance of subjective knowledge in expanding it. The participants' perspectives may either confirm and expand the existing framework or challenge it, leading to the emergence of new categories, themes, and hypotheses for understanding the experience (McIntosh & Morse, 2015).

In this chapter, SSI was employed for qualitative research to generate categories and themes that will contribute to theory development and construct meaning. Subsequently, these categories and themes will be used to create a quantitative questionnaire to measure the impact of the COVID-19 pandemic on the selective codes (themes) analyzed through the three-step coding process. These themes represent the variables affected by the phenomenon under investigation, the COVID-19 pandemic.

3.2 Sampling

It is imperative that purposive sampling be employed in Social Science Inquiry (SSI) research. Purposive sampling plays a crucial role in SSI research, as it aims to optimize the validity of findings, making them applicable to a broader range of contexts. Various strategies are employed for purposive sampling, including convenient sampling (where eligibility criteria are publicized, and the initial volunteers who meet these criteria constitute the sample), snowball sampling (where individuals with insider knowledge of eligible participants facilitate their inclusion in the research project), homogeneous sampling (involving selection of participants with strong similarities), and variable sampling (in which participants represent the entire spectrum of the domain) (McIntosh & Morse, 2015). This chapter utilized the convenient sample strategy, conducting a total of 55 SSIs among Arab students in Turkey.

It is imperative that the principle guiding sampling for SSI research ensures that the collected data is sufficient. A minimum of 30 participants is recommended for initial recruitment to guarantee the adequacy of data collection. Adequacy of data in SSI research is assessed in both qualitative terms, considering the depth of collected data, and quantitative terms, focusing on the quantity of data. Given that SSI data is collected through interviews with participants answering the same set of questions, data analysis is conducted on an item-by-item basis. This approach lends itself to non-parametric statistical analysis, which necessitates a minimum sample size of 30 for meaningful results. In addition to qualitative and quantitative analysis, data derived from SSIs may be integrated into a mixed-method design, such as a QUAL-Quan sequential mixed-method design, wherein qualitative data is transformed for quantitative analysis. In this scenario, the QUAL sample size should be a minimum of 30 to ensure the adequacy of quantitative analysis (McIntosh & Morse, 2015). Therefore, this chapter conducted 55 SSIs, with 15 being conducted face-to-face, 20 via telephone, and 20 electronically using Google Meet.

3.3 Data Analysis

The initial step involves the extraction of codes from the data. The researcher's approach is to scrutinize responses item by item, commencing with a comprehensive examination of all participants' answers to a specific question. Subsequently, the researcher employs established coding techniques, which entail the identification and highlighting of significant words or phrases, alongside annotating noteworthy aspects within each response in the margin (McIntosh & Morse, 2015). Consequently, this chapter adhered to manual coding techniques typically associated with qualitative research, utilizing the Grounded Theory methodology. As proposed by Williams and Moser (2019), this methodology encompasses a three-step coding process, encompassing open coding, axial coding, and selective coding.

4 Findings

Through the questions that were asked to the students, their open answers revolved around phrases, words, or short phrases that were constantly repeated. The researcher picked up and then analyzed these words or short phrases using the Grounded Theory method that uses the three-step coding process (manual coding strategy) open, axial, and selective as shown in the following figures:

Referring to Fig. 1, the statements (reducing emissions, reducing industrial pollution, reducing pollution from transportation) formed the open codes that were picked up from the students' mouths during the interviews. These open codes formed a single axial code, which is (global climate improvement), which in turn constitutes a single selective code, which is (global climate). Accordingly, the theory can be developed, i.e., the following theoretical hypothesis is developed: "*There is a relationship between the pandemic and the global climate*".

Referring to Fig. 2, the statements (remote university, remote exams, distance training, distance certificates, remote work tasks, online services, and online individual projects) formed the open codes that were picked up from the students' mouths during the interviews. These open codes formed two axial codes, which are (distance education expansion, and remote work expansion), which in turn constitute a single selective code, which is (online activities). Accordingly, the theory can be developed, i.e., the following theoretical hypothesis is developed: "*There is a relationship between the pandemic and the online activities*".

Referring to Fig. 3, the statements (learn a new language, reading books, more time for hobbies, sports at home, dieting, reducing stress, closer to family) formed the open codes that were picked up from the students' mouths during the interviews. These open codes formed two axial codes, which are (exploiting free time, and healthy lifestyle), which in turn constitute a single selective code, which is (personal life). Accordingly, the theory can be developed, i.e., the following theoretical hypothesis is developed: "*There is a relationship between the pandemic and the personal life*".

Referring to Fig. 4, the statements (countries preoccupied with the pandemic, more cooperation between countries, and postponing disputes) formed the open codes that were picked up from the students' mouths during the interviews. These open codes formed a single axial code, which is (reduce the intensity of conflicts), which in turn constitutes

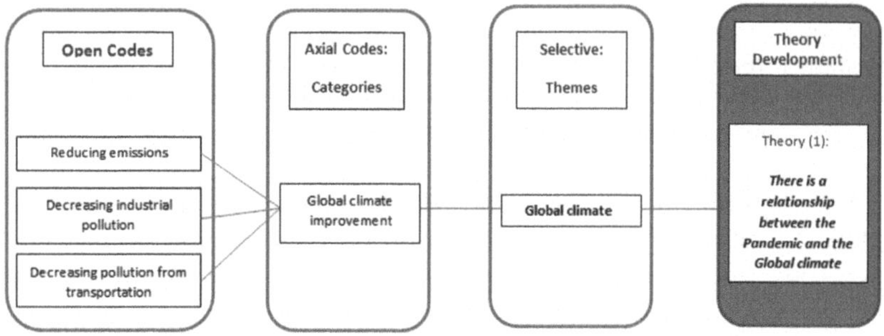

Fig. 1 The three-step coding process of (Global Climate) as a theme. *Source* Author's calculations

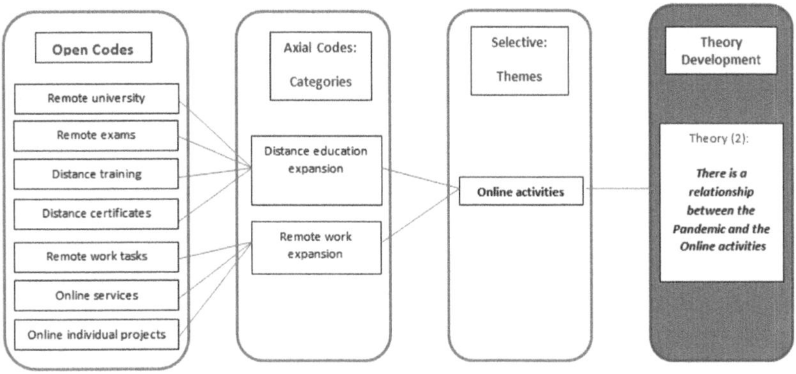

Fig. 2 The three-step coding process of (Online Activities) as a theme. *Source* Author's calculations

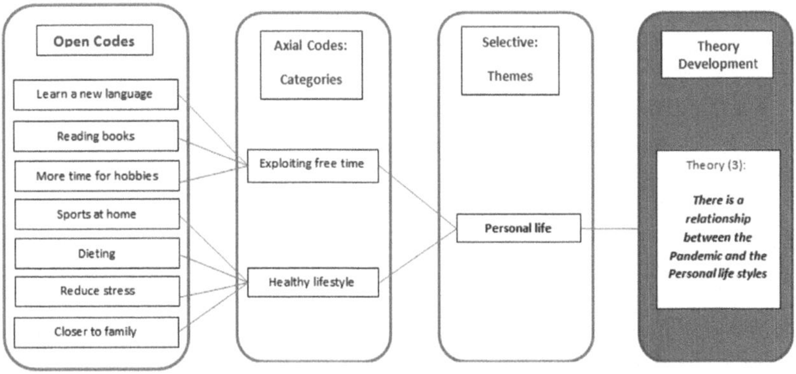

Fig. 3 The three-step coding process of (Personal Life) as a theme. *Source* Author's calculations

a single selective code, which is (world peace). Accordingly, the theory can be developed, i.e., the following theoretical hypothesis is developed: "*There is a relationship between the pandemic and the world peace*".

Referring to Fig. 5, the statements (restricting movement between cities, international travel restriction, compulsory medical examination, tourist activities disrupted, and quarantine) formed the open codes that were picked up from the students' mouths during the interviews. These

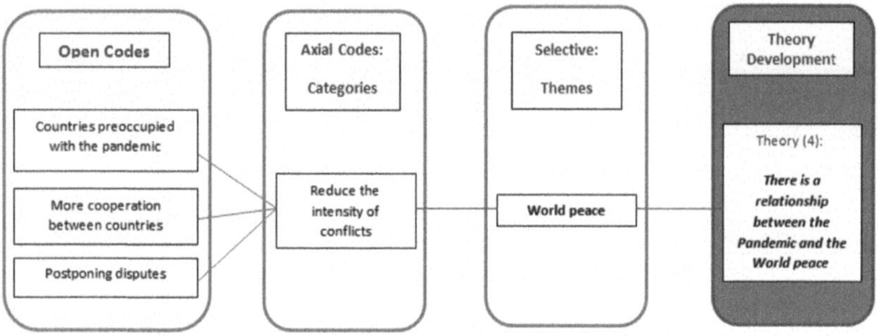

Fig. 4 The three-step coding process of (World Peace) as a theme. *Source* Author's calculations

open codes formed a single axial code, which is (restricting tourism and travel), which in turn constitutes a single selective code, which is (tourism and travel). Accordingly, the theory can be developed, i.e., the following theoretical hypothesis is developed: "*There is a relationship between the pandemic and the tourism and travel*".

Referring to Fig. 6, the statements (global economic recession, slow down trade, monopoly of important goods, production decline, preoccupation with pandemic, storage of raw materials, deficit in non-exporting countries, and slowing growth in developing countries) formed the open codes that were picked up from the students' mouths during the interviews. These open codes form three axial codes, which are (global economic downturn, supply chain disruption, and decline in the economies of developing countries), which in turn constitute a single selective code, which is (global economy). Accordingly, the theory can be developed, i.e., the following theoretical hypothesis is developed: "*There is a relationship between the pandemic and the global economy*".

Referring to Fig. 7, the statements (social distancing, problems arise in families, and restricting social activities) formed the open codes that were picked up from the students' mouths during the interviews. These open codes formed a single axial code, which is (problems in social and family relations), which in turn constitutes a single selective code, which is (family and society). Accordingly, the theory can be developed, i.e., the following theoretical hypothesis is developed: "*There is a relationship between the pandemic and the family and society*".

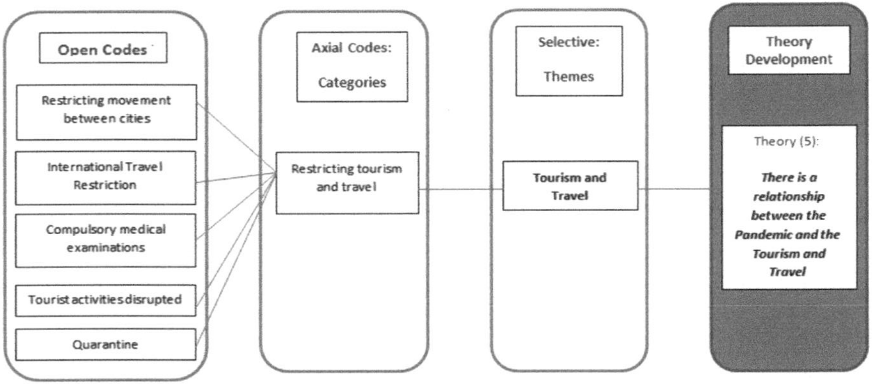

Fig. 5 The three-step coding process of (Tourism and Travel) as a theme. *Source* Author's calculations

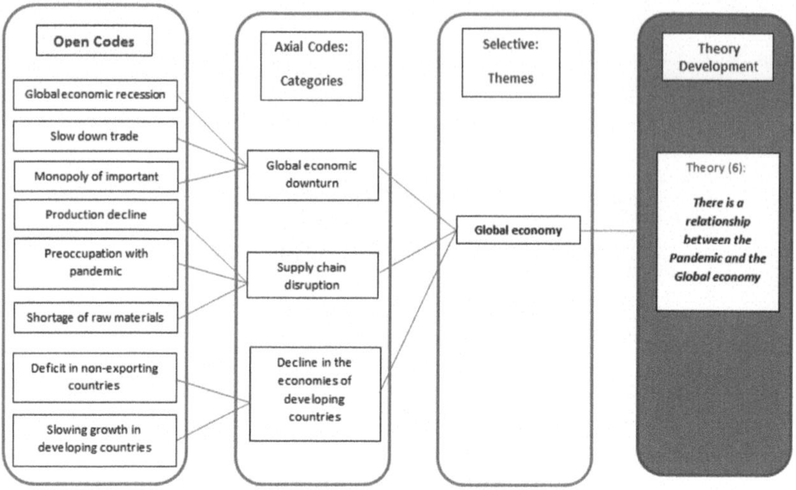

Fig. 6 The three-step coding process of (Global Economy) as a theme. *Source* Author's calculations

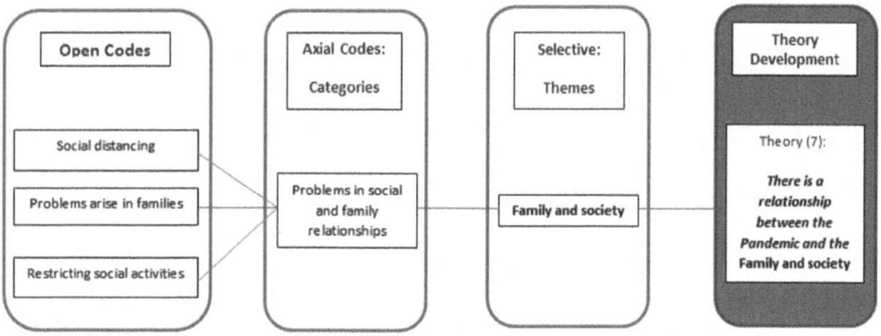

Fig. 7 The three-step coding process of (Family and Society) as a theme. *Source* Author's calculations

Referring to Fig. 8, the statements (fear of pandemic infection, fear of losing loved ones, stress, and anxiety, sitting for days at home, depression, and overly nervous) formed the open codes that were picked up from the students' mouths during the interviews. These open codes formed a single axial code, which is (mental health problems), which in turn constitutes a single selective code, which is (mental health). Accordingly, the theory

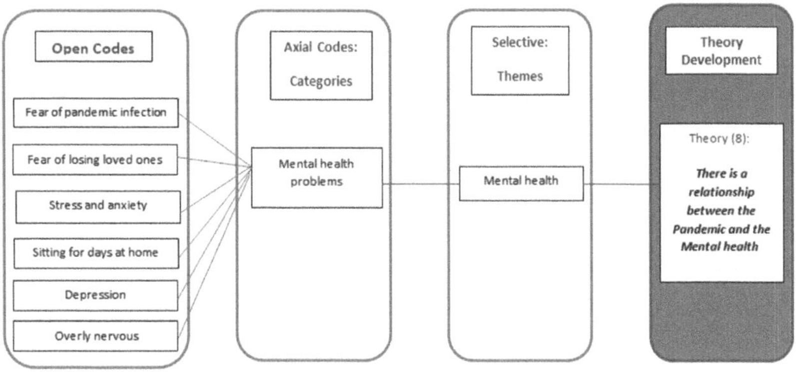

Fig. 8 The three-step coding process of (Mental Health) as a theme. *Source* Author's calculations

can be developed, i.e., the following theoretical hypothesis is developed: "*There is a relationship between the pandemic and the mental health*".

Referring to Fig. 9, it is clear that the statements (new delivery companies, demand for delivery, demand for mask, urgent need for oxygen, demand for vitamins and immune boosters, demand for goods, storage of some goods, rely on apps, communication-education-work via apps, competing to develop a vaccine, and compete to get vaccine) formed the open codes that were picked up from the students' mouths during the interviews. These open codes formed five axial codes, which are (delivery sector growth, growth of the medical consumable sector, retail sector growth, IT sector growth, and vaccine sector growth), which in turn they constitute a single selective code, which is (*specific economic sectors*). Accordingly, the theory can be developed, i.e., the following theoretical hypothesis is developed: "*There is a relationship between the pandemic and the specific economic sectors*".

Referring to Fig. 10, the statements (create virtual tourism, more virtual social networking, and more e-commerce) formed the open codes that were picked up from the students' mouths during the interviews. These open codes formed a single axial code, which is (create or grow new business models), which in turn constitutes a single selective code, which is (business models). Accordingly, the theory can be developed, i.e., the following theoretical hypothesis is developed: "*There is a relationship between the pandemic and the business models*".

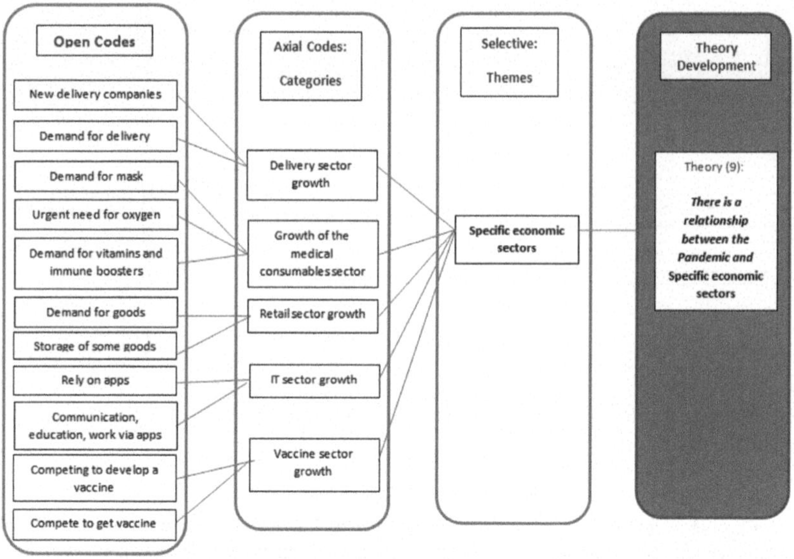

Fig. 9 The three-step coding process of (Specific Economic Sectors) as a theme. *Source* Author's calculations

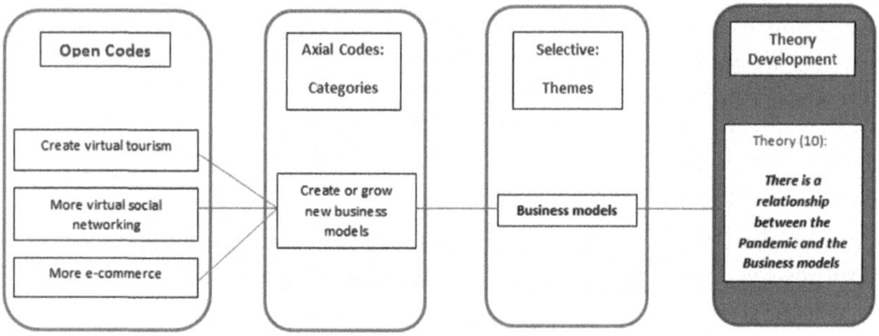

Fig. 10 The three-step coding process of (Business Models) as a theme. *Source* Author's calculations

Referring to Fig. 11, the statements (decrease in revenue, salaries shortfall, reducing the number of employees, travel restrictions limit opportunities, postponing admission to a university or a job, and postponing potential projects) formed the open codes that were picked up from the students' mouths during the interviews. These open codes formed two axial codes, which are (loss of current jobs, and loss of educational or job opportunities), which in turn constitute a single selective code, which is (professional and educational positions). Accordingly, the theory can be developed, i.e., the following theoretical hypothesis is developed: "*There is a relationship between the pandemic and the professional and educational positions*".

Referring to Fig. 12, the statements (transmission of disease, pandemic spread, vulnerable groups, and infection complication and death) formed the open codes that were picked up from the students' mouths during the interviews. These open codes formed a single axial code, which is (threats to public health), which in turn constitutes a single selective code, which is (public health). Accordingly, the theory can be developed, i.e., the following theoretical hypothesis is developed: "*There is a relationship between the pandemic and the public health*".

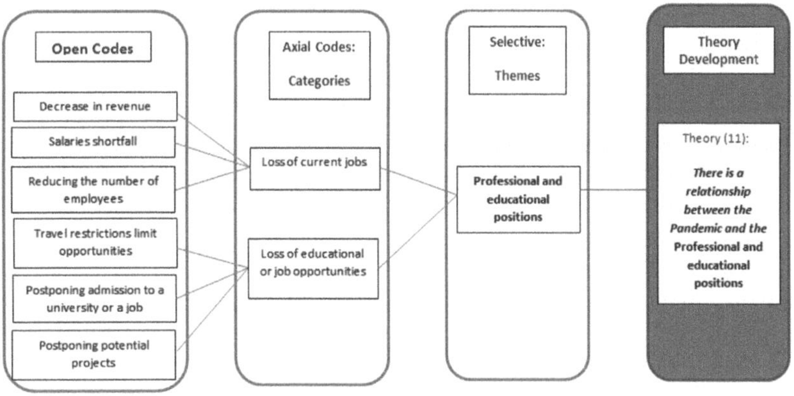

Fig. 11 The three-step coding process of (Professional and Educational positions) as a theme. *Source* Author's calculations

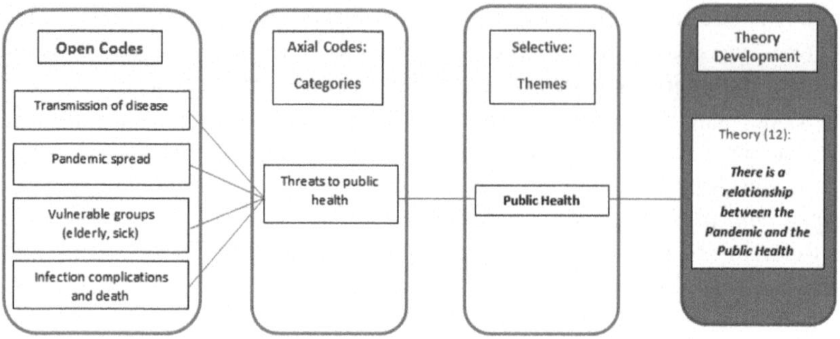

Fig. 12 The three-step coding process of (Public Health) as a theme. *Source* Author's calculations

5 Conclusion

Since the Grounded Theory Method helps in delving into phenomena and constructing meaning to develop theories and based on the 12 themes that this chapter codified as selective codes, this qualitative study has developed 12 theories that could be investigated in future quantitative studies to measure the nature and strength of the relationships among the pandemic and the 12 variables (themes) which are constituting the variables that are directly affected by the COVID-19 pandemic phenomenon according to this chapter findings.

Utilizing the Grounded Theory method for data analysis, this study unveiled intricate interrelationships between the COVID-19 pandemic and a wide array of life domains. These domains encompass global climate, online activities, personal lifestyles, world peace, tourism, the global economy, family and society dynamics, mental health, specific economic sectors, business models, professional and educational roles, as well as public health.

Hence, this chapter recommends researchers consider these 12 themes to construct a comprehensive quantitative questionnaire in order to measure quantitatively to what extent the COVID-19 pandemic affects these 12 variables so that the socio-economic impacts of the COVID-19 pandemic be investigated.

6 Practical Implications

The Development of Theoretical Frameworks: The qualitative analysis conducted in this chapter using the Grounded Theory method has led to the development of 12 theories that pertain to the impact of the COVID-19 pandemic on various aspects of life and society. These theories provide a valuable foundation for future research.

Identification of Key Variables: The chapter has identified 12 themes or variables that are directly affected by the COVID-19 pandemic. These variables encompass a wide range of areas, including global climate, online activities, personal lifestyles, world peace, tourism, global economy, family and society, mental health, specific economic sectors, business models, professional and educational positions, and public health.

Foundation for Quantitative Research: The 12 themes derived from this qualitative study serve as a basis for constructing a comprehensive quantitative questionnaire. This questionnaire can be used in future quantitative research to measure the nature and strength of the relationships between the pandemic and these 12 variables.

Socio-Economic Impact Analysis: The recommended quantitative questionnaire can help researchers assess the socio-economic impacts of the COVID-19 pandemic more comprehensively. By quantifying the effects on these 12 variables, a deeper understanding of the pandemic's consequences can be achieved.

Future Research Directions: The 12 theories developed in this qualitative study offer potential research directions for future studies. Researchers can investigate these theories quantitatively to gain a clearer understanding of how the pandemic has influenced various aspects of life, from economic sectors to mental health.

In summary, the research chapter provides a valuable foundation for future investigations that can quantitatively measure the impact of the COVID-19 pandemic on multiple aspects of society and the economy. The development of theoretical frameworks and the identification of key variables offer opportunities for more in-depth and structured research into the pandemic's effects.

References

Açikgöz, Ö., & Günay, A. (2020). The early impact of the COVID-19 pandemic on the global and Turkish economy. *Turkish Journal of Medical Sciences, 50*(9), 520–526.

Adibelli, D., Sümen, A., & Teskereci, G. (2021). Domestic violence against women during the COVID-19 pandemic: Turkey sample. *Health Care for Women International, 42*(3), 335–350.

Almurisi, S. H., Al Khalidi, D., AL-Japairai, K. A., Mahmood, S., Chilakamarry, C. R., Kadiyala, C. B. N., & Mohananaidu, K. (2020). Impact of COVID 19 pandemic crisis on the health system and pharmaceutical industry. *Letters in Applied NanoBioScience, 10*(2), 2298–2308.

Aslan, I., Ochnik, D., & Çınar, O. (2020). Exploring perceived stress among students in Turkey during the COVID-19 pandemic. *International Journal of Environmental Research and Public Health, 17*(23), 8961.

Ayati, N., Saiyarsarai, P., & Nikfar, S. (2020). Short and long term impacts of COVID-19 on the pharmaceutical sector. *DARU Journal of Pharmaceutical Sciences, 28*(2), 799–805.

Babbie, E. (2010). *The practice of social research.* Cengage Learning.

Bambra, C., Riordan, R., Ford, J., & Matthews, F. (2020). The COVID-19 pandemic and health inequalities. *Journal of Epidemiology and Community Health, 74*(11), 964–968.

Blumenthal, D., Fowler, E. J., Abrams, M., & Collins, S. R. (2020).COVID-19—Implications for the health care system. *New England Journal of Medicine, 383*(15), 1483–1488.

Bostan, S., Erdem, R., Öztürk, Y. E., Kılıç, T., & Yılmaz, A. (2020). The effect of COVID-19 pandemic on the Turkish society. *Electronic Journal of General Medicine, 17*(6), em237.

De Búrca, S., Fletcher, R., & Brown, L. (2004). *International marketing: An SME perspective.* Pearson Education.

Debata, B., Patnaik, P., & Mishra, A. (2020). COVID-19 pandemic! It's impact on people, economy, and environment. *Journal of Public Affairs, 20*(4), e2372.

Gregurec, I., Tomičić Furjan, M., & Tomičić-Pupek, K. (2021). The impact of COVID-19 on sustainable business models in SMEs. *Sustainability, 13*(3), 1098.

Heitzman, J. (2020). Impact of COVID-19 pandemic on mental health. *Psychiatria Polska, 54*(2), 187–198.

Hobbs, J. E. (2020). Food supply chains during the COVID-19 pandemic. *Canadian Journal of Agricultural Economics/revue Canadienne D'agroeconomie, 68*(2), 171–176.

Khweiled, R., Jazzar, M., & Eleyan, D. (2021). Cybercrimes during COVID-19 pandemic. *International Journal of Information Engineering & Electronic Business, 15*(2), 1.

Kumar, V., Alshazly, H., Idris, S. A., & Bourouis, S. (2021). Evaluating the impact of COVID-19 on society, environment, economy, and education. *Sustainability, 13*(24), 13642.

Lone, S. A., & Ahmad, A. (2020). COVID-19 pandemic–an African perspective. *Emerging Microbes & Infections, 9*(1), 1300–1308.

McCallion, K. F. (2020). *COVID-19 The virus that changed America and the world*. Brayant Park Press.

McIntosh, M. J., & Morse, J. M. (2015). Situating and constructing diversity in semi- structured interviews. *Global Qualitative Nursing Research, 2*, 2333393615597674.

Nicola, M., Alsafi, Z., Sohrabi, C., Kerwan, A., Al-Jabir, A., Iosifidis, C., Agha, M., & Agha, R. (2020). The socio-economic implications of the coronavirus pandemic (COVID-19): A review. *International Journal of Surgery, 78*, 185–193.

Pokhrel, S., & Chhetri, R. (2021). A literature review on impact of COVID-19 pandemic on teaching and learning. *Higher Education for the Future, 8*(1), 133–141.

Pranggono, B., & Arabo, A. (2021). COVID-19 pandemic cybersecurity issues. *Internet Technology Letters, 4*(2), e247.

Rahman, N. A. A., Rahim, S. A., Ahmad, M. F., & Hafizuddin-Syah, B. A. M. (2020). Exploring COVID-19 pandemic: Its impact to global aviation industry and the key strategy. *International Journal of Advanced Science and Technology, 29*(6), 1829–1836.

Rashid, S., & Yadav, S. S. (2020). Impact of COVID-19 pandemic on higher education and research. *Indian Journal of Human Development, 14*(2), 340–343.

Raut, D. N. (2020). Effects of COVID-19 on employment of India. *IRE Journals, 3*(11), 33–36.

Seetharaman, P. (2020). Business models shifts: Impact of COVID-19. *International Journal of Information Management, 54*, 102173.

Singh, J., & Singh, J. (2020). COVID-19 and its impact on society. *Electronic Research Journal of Social Sciences and Humanities, 2*(1), 5.

Stalmachova, K., Chinoracky, R., & Strenitzerova, M. (2021). Changes in business models caused by digital transformation and the COVID-19 pandemic and possibilities of their measurement—Case study. *Sustainability, 14*(1), 127.

Sułkowski, Ł. (2020). COVID-19 pandemic; recession, virtual revolution leading to de- globalization? *Journal of Intercultural Management, 12*(1), 1–11.

Tee, M. L., Tee, C. A., Anlacan, J. P., Aligam, K. J. G., Reyes, P. W. C., Kuruchittham, V., & Ho, R. C. (2020). Psychological impact of COVID-19 pandemic in the Philippines. *Journal of Affective Disorders, 277*, 379–391.

Verma, A. K., & Prakash, S. (2020). Impact of COVID-19 on environment and society. *Journal of Global Biosciences, 9*(5), 7352–7363.

Williams, M., & Moser, T. (2019). The art of coding and thematic exploration in qualitative research. *International Management Review, 15*(1), 45–55.

Xiong, J., Lipsitz, O., Nasri, F., Lui, L. M., Gill, H., Phan, L., Chen-Li, D., Lacobucci, M., Ho, R., Majeed, A., & McIntyre, R. S. (2020). Impact of COVID-19 pandemic on mental health in the general population: A systematic review. *Journal of Affective Disorders, 277*, 55–64.

CHAPTER 12

Toward a Teaching Model of the Entrepreneurship Course in Oman Using the Design Thinking Approach: The Inspiring COVID-19 Experience for Better Online Teaching

Ramzi Sallem, Hisham Ghunaimi, and Jawaher Al Balushi

1 Introduction

Investing in entrepreneurship education is no longer optional for universities. Henceforth, there is no need for scholars to ask whether entrepreneurs are born or are made. Though it is not so clear to

R. Sallem (✉) · H. Ghunaimi
A'Sharqiyah University, Ibra, Oman
e-mail: ramzi.sallem@asu.edu.om

H. Ghunaimi
e-mail: hisham.alghunaimi@asu.edu.om

J. Al Balushi
University of Technology and Applied Sciences, Muscat, Oman
e-mail: Jawaher.niz@cas.edu.om

A. Mishrif (ed.), *Perspectives on Human Capital Development*,
https://doi.org/10.1007/978-981-97-5246-1_12

what extent such education enables graduates to become more effective entrepreneurs (C. Jones, 2006; Kirby, 2004; Packham et al., 2006; Richardson & Hynes, 2008), the investment in entrepreneurship education is fruitful and valuable (Pittaway & Hannon, 2008; Solomon et al., 2008; Sowmya et al., 2010).

The actual challenges for the community of entrepreneurship scholars are to focus more on what and how entrepreneurship or enterprise education "is", when implemented in practice (Pittaway & Cope, 2007). For that, there is wide consensus on the importance of experiential entrepreneurship education (Hegarty & Jones, 2008; B. Jones & Iredale, 2010; P. Jones et al., 2008; Kabongo & McCaskey, 2011; Mwasalwiba, 2010). It seems clear that entrepreneurship education offers an innovative new paradigm for business school education that answers some of these challenges (Binks et al., 2006; Klapper, 2004; Klapper & Tegtmeier, 2010).

The researches focusing on the entrepreneurship education program effectiveness and efficiency are numerous, the unanimity suggests the use of unconventional pedagogy when teaching such courses (e.g., Ballantine & Larres, 2007; Pio & Haigh, 2007), while highlighting ontologically the actors roles in such courses, in which the students are no more passive and the teachers become simple animators (Karwowski et al., 2007; Seikkula-Leino et al., 2010).

The pedagogical "tool box" in such courses is very rich and many guides and books are available for the community of entrepreneurship instructors and trainers, however the question of "how" managing these practices in service of a successful program remain very challenging (Huq & Gilbert, 2017). In that sense, recent researches are investigating on the importance of the entrepreneurship education programs based on design thinking in order to foster innovative human resources (Suzuki, 2016), the majority of them are offering conceptual frameworks (Mansoori & Lackéus, 2020), however few of them have given empirical evidences (e.g., Pratomo et al., 2021; Sarfati, 2019).

In that sense and in the era of pandemics, the community of instructors that are convinced by the effectiveness of the design thinking approach has new challenges related to the way of how operationalizing the tools of the design thinking approach in the online context. Furthermore, the course of entrepreneurship in many countries, like Oman, is a university requirement, and from now on, one it would be ensured online for many of the universities in all the world, the toolbox of the design thinking approach should be revisited with creative and adequate pedagogical tool.

Obviously, there is a real need to share the experiences among the community of researchers to enrich the design thinking "toolbox" with practical activities. The research is aiming to identify the main effective pedagogical tools to use in design thinking approach while teaching online. Entrepreneurship as a field of research is mainly based on four paradigms: Individual, Innovation, Opportunity Recognition and New value creation (Verstraete & Fayolle, 2005).

Thus, an assessment of ideas generation, innovation and opportunity recognition remains necessary to the development of the way of enhancing learning entrepreneurial behavior (Penaluna & Penaluna, 2009; Penaluna et al., 2010). The literature is very reach in term of the empirical investigation dealing with the effectiveness of some pedagogical methods on students' creativity (Dewett & Gruys, 2007; Yang & Cheng, 2010), however few of research has focused on their alertness skill enhancement (e.g., Pratomo et al., 2021).

2 Enhancing the Creative Alertness Through the Entrepreneurship Teaching

2.1 The Concept of Entrepreneurial Alertness

This concept of entrepreneurial alertness was born in 1973 with the economist Israel Kirzner, who argues that entrepreneurs are not just risk-takers or innovators; they are individuals who possess a unique ability to perceive market disequilibrium and profit opportunities that result from the gaps between the current market situation and a potential equilibrium state. The development of the alertness trait concept based on Israel Kirzner's theory has led to the evolution of frameworks that explore the role of alertness in entrepreneurship. Some of them emphasized the role of alertness in identifying and evaluating opportunities based on existing information while focusing on the cognitive aspects of how entrepreneurs perceive and evaluate opportunities (Kaish et al., 1991). This framework has been soon supported by many researchers while offering refinement to the alertness scale (Lowell, 1996; Tang et al., 2012). Nowadays, the entrepreneurial alertness trait is an important ingredient of entrepreneurial processes. Indeed, entrepreneurial alertness influences how entrepreneurs recognize and capitalize on opportunities (Tang, 2008) and navigate the dynamic and uncertain landscape of entrepreneurship. They are more likely to take swift action when they identify an opportunity. They understand that timing is crucial in entrepreneurship, and they are willing to move quickly to exploit opportunities before they become saturated or obsolete (Gaglio & Katz, 2001). It has also an impact on the decision involving the maintenance of competitive advantage in more mature organization (Roundy et al., 2018). The alertness affects the passion among entrepreneurs to make strategic change (Montiel-Campos, 2021) or to build strong social networks allowing them to identify opportunities (Ma et al., 2020) while improving their self-efficacy and intention toward the entrepreneurial act (Jiatong et al., 2021). Hence successful entrepreneurs have a high level of entrepreneurial alertness enabling them to identify and capitalize on potential opportunities in the market that others might overlook (Sharma, 2019).

2.2 *Alertness Trait and Opportunity Evaluation Process*

Entrepreneurial alertness significantly and directly predicted opportunity recognition (Li et al., 2015; Mpeera Ntayi et al., 2022) which subsequently influences the entrepreneurial action (Neneh, 2019). Indeed, Alert individuals are attuned to changes, trends and signals within the market (Zaheer & Zaheer, 1997). They can spot shifts in consumer preferences, emerging technologies, regulatory changes and other factors that create opportunities for new products, services or business models (Srivastava et al., 2021) through the recognition of inefficiencies or suboptimal processes within industries (Shane, 2000). The entrepreneurs with high level of alertness are synthetizing information from different sources and disciplines to uncover novel opportunities at the intersection of various fields as the patterns they then perceive in these events or trends suggest ideas for new products and services (Baron, 2006).

2.3 *Creative Alertness as an Important Trait for the Students*

In a recent literature, the alertness and creativity traits have been well discussed in the intentional models tested among higher education students in many universities in all over the world (e.g., Gozukara & Colakoglu, 2016; Hu et al., 2018). The majority of the research are exploring the teaching courses learning outcomes regarding these two important traits that seem to gain the attention of the instructors while designing their entrepreneurship courses (Dosunmu et al., 2020). This attention is since there is a strong relationship between creativity and alertness traits among entrepreneurs. Indeed, thinking creatively is necessary for the students to generate innovative ideas, while to be alerted could be the good wind for them to recognize opportunities (Saadat et al., 2022).

The teaching activities need to help students to identify the market needs, think to solve real problems to create unique products and to be aware about the market trends (Srivastava et al., 2021). Creative thinking is to picture new solutions to existing problems which is essential for proposing new value that may procure the competitive advantage to the novel ideas they are discussing while preparing their business plan (Zhao et al., 2021).

Consequently, "Creative alertness" describes the mental clarity, receptivity to fresh perspectives and open-mindedness that these traits foster. It entails remaining alert and cognizant of the environment, thoughts and feelings while simultaneously remaining open to new ideas and inspiration. Students may improve their ability to solve problems, stimulate creativity and take a more creative approach to obstacles by incorporating creative alertness into their daily life.

3 Enhancing Students' Self-efficacy and Opportunity Evaluation Competency

3.1 *The Self-efficacy as Students' Entrepreneurial Intention Predictor*

There is an exhaustive literature review focusing on entrepreneurial intentional models, which seem to be a planned behavior. There are a boom intentional models that are using either the theory of the planned behavior of the planned Behavior (Ajzen, 1990) or the theory of the self-efficacy (bandura albert, 1982) or a combination between these two theories (Krueger et al., 2000; Siu & Lo, 2013). Indeed, the self-efficacy theory of bandura albert (1982) is analogical to the perceived behavioral control intentional antecedent of Icek Ajzen. Researchers are predicting the entrepreneurial intention among students through many traits and or skills to explain attitude and perceived behavioral control toward the entrepreneurial act.

Enhancing creative skills among students can help them to conceptualize their entrepreneurial ideas more clearly (Shahab et al., 2019). Indeed, creative thinking is an important stimulator to self-efficacy, which is the conviction that one can succeed in given circumstance. They become more self-confident and intentional toward the entrepreneurial act (Ferreira-Neto et al., 2023). Their belief in their capability to start a new business through active research of novel and feasible opportunities is highly probable (Díaz-Portugal et al., 2022).

Furthermore, developing students' alertness—the capacity to be attentive, perceptive and receptive to possibilities and changes in the environment—is essential to raising their level of entrepreneurial intention and self-efficacy (Urban, 2020). By learning how to undertake challenges before they become more serious, students enhance their self-efficacy and become cognitively flexible to entrepreneurial alertness (Gill et al., 2021; Jiatong et al., 2021). They feel more capable, self-assured and equipped to pursue entrepreneurial endeavors successfully, which increases their entrepreneurial self-efficacy and intention.

In conclusion, teaching accustoming students to solve problems through class activities leads to enhance their creative alertness. They would be equipped with a toolkit that combines alert observational abilities with creative thinking to increase their capacity to detect novel ideas to be concretized on exploitable opportunities (Yasir et al., 2020). Their self-efficacy is raised by this increased confidence in their skills, giving them the courage to take on obstacles, seize chances and successfully to be more intentional toward the entrepreneurial act (Eladl & Polpol, 2020).

3.2 *Opportunity Evaluation Skill as Important Outcome of the Entrepreneurship Course*

Since 2009 the number of publications focusing on the opportunity evaluation process has increased exponentially (Wood & Mckelvie, 2015), as it is a crucial step toward the entrepreneurial action (Mitchell & Shepherd, 2010). Indeed, the opportunity evaluation in entrepreneurship is a complex process that involves cognitive and rule-based decision-making through the perception of risk (Dali & Harbi, 2016; Hean Tat Keh et al., 2002; Riquelme & Alqallaf, 2020), the financial and social attributes of an opportunity (Smith et al., 2010) and mainly by concretizing existing and novel ideas into feasible prototypes (Pretorius et al., 2023). Entrepreneurs use socially constructed rules to evaluate opportunities, and that individual differences in knowledge and worst-case scenario thinking influence opportunity evaluation (Wood & McKinley, 2010). They evaluate opportunities based on their existing knowledge resources but may also pursue the acquisition of new resources that are inconsistent with their existing knowledge (Haynie et al., 2009). Hence, the opportunity evaluation process is a structured approach used by individuals, entrepreneurs and organizations to assess the potential of a business idea, project or venture before committing significant resources to it. This process involves gathering relevant information (Autio et al., 2013), analyzing various aspects of the opportunity and making informed decisions about whether to pursue or abandon the opportunity (Haynie et al., 2009, 2010; D. Shepherd & Haynie, 2009). Opportunity evaluation is a distinct and a very complex phenomenon and there is a tough passage from the opportunity evaluation stage to the one of action, which needs more exploration to understand this enigma. Indeed, some entrepreneurs might struggle with or delay the execution of opportunities even after evaluating them positively due to many factors psychological, cognitive and contextual factors that affect this critical phase of entrepreneurship, such as entrepreneurs' perception of uncertainty, their temporal orientation and the socio-cognitive challenges they face (McMullen & Shepherd, 2006; D. A. Shepherd et al., 2007). Does it represent the solid bridge between the stage of ideation and the one of creation (Williams & Wood, 2015; Wood & Williams, 2014)?

It may be argued that integrating theory into the classroom gives teachers the resources they need to support students in improving their opportunity recognition abilities (White & Hertz, 2022). It is necessary to enable students to evaluate their opportunities as it is an important component of the overall opportunity recognition process. This involves a deep analysis regarding the challenges that face their opportunities when reflecting them to environmental changes and hazards (Bailey et al., 2021; Cohen et al., 2021; Yasir et al., 2020). Understanding how to assess some factors that can help them to increasing the likelihood of their project success like a real entrepreneur.

4 The Effectiveness of the Design Thinking Approach in Reaching the Entrepreneurship Courses Outcomes

4.1 *The Design Thinking Approach*

Despite the use of design thinking in the entrepreneurial courses in Standford University since 1948, the efficacy of impact of this approach on the entrepreneurial student's mindset remains a very fresh topic of research (Chou, 2018; Huq & Gilbert, 2017; Sarooghi et al., 2019). Thus, a conceived entrepreneurship course based on the design thinking approach has a big chance to enhance the creative alertness trait, the self-efficacy and the opportunity evaluation competency among the students. The system of the design thinking has tridimensional spaces: inspiration, ideation and implementation, while the process is articulated progressively and iteratively in five main steps: empathizing, defining, ideating, prototyping and testing (Von Kortzfleisch et al., 2013).

4.2 *The Impact of the Design Thinking Approach on the Student's Entrepreneurial Creative Alertness, Self-efficacy and Opportunity Evaluation Competency*

As many successful startups have been founded by heterogeneously competencies team members, sensitizing students to build a team regardless their friendship is one of the crucial steps of the design thinking approach (Chasanidou et al., 2014; Thi-Huyen et al., 2021). In fact, embracing design thinking is contingent on shifting focus from individual knowledge work to team-based collaboration (Mansoori & Lackéus, 2020). Activities that insulate critical thinking and creativity are the pillars of innovation and opportunity creation among students. The problem-based learning remains one of the essential tools in design thinking approach to help student to get creative opportunities (Garbuio et al., 2018; Tselepis & Lavelle, 2020). Learning by doing is the principle of any successful entrepreneurship course! Enrolling students in projects and inviting them to be based on their own experience is capital to let them, not only discovering their potential, but also to be more entrepreneurial as individuals. Creativity and alertness can be improved by a design thinking approach using experiential learning (Pratomo et al., 2021).

Students' resilience, confidence and positive outlook can all be fostered by integrating the design thinking method into the classroom, which raises their self-efficacy. Long-term impacts on their academic achievement, problem-solving ability and general personal and professional growth may result from this heightened self-belief (Liu et al., 2023). Furthermore, inviting students to prepare a prototype "fast, fail ad cheap" is one indispensable ingredient of the design thinking practices which is motivating them toward the entrepreneurial action. Indeed, prototyping and entrepreneurial activity are related, and the Prototype-It Challenge's pedagogical focus is on the importance of basic prototypes in opportunity identification and evaluation (Noyes, 2018) (Fig. 1).

Integrating design thinking into entrepreneurship courses may equip students with problem-solving skills and develops the confidence, creative alertness and opportunity evaluation competency needed to succeed as entrepreneurs. Design thinking provides a holistic approach that nurtures both the mindset and skill set essential for entrepreneurial action (Chaney et al., 2020; Mansoori & Lackéus, 2020; Pratomo et al., 2021; Sarooghi et al., 2019).

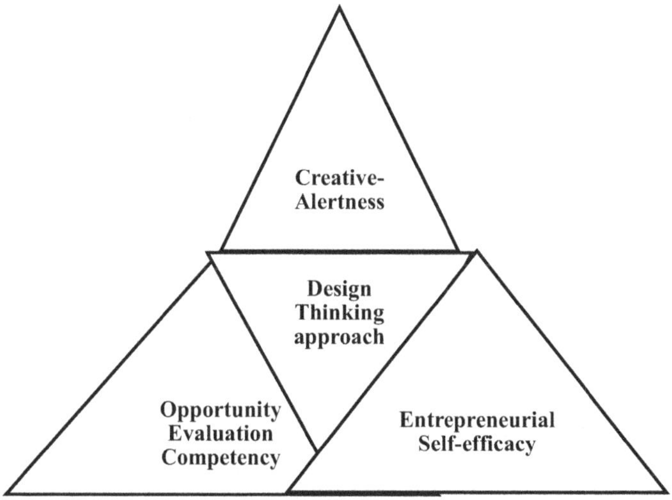

Fig. 1 Entrepreneurship teaching model using the design thinking approach

5 The Application of the Design Thinking Approach Through the Online Mode

To apply the design thinking approach thorough the online mode, the toolkit is rich in terms of teaching methods and templates used by the community of entrepreneurship instructors. These teaching practices are directly related to the design thinking teaching practices, such as the lean canvas, the empathy map, the Business Model Canvas, the value proposition canvas, the idea napkin. The application of these templates and methods is highly recommended on the online teaching as it helps the students not only to respond to the most pertinent entrepreneurial questions but also, they are easy and useful tools to organize students' project. Based on some previous entrepreneurship experiences, and inspired from the design thinking pedagogical toolbox, the following online teaching practices and templates have been used during the entrepreneurship courses given to Omani students in the period of the COVID-19 pandemic. The expected learning outcomes after 45 online hours of online teaching are to enhance the students "creative alertness, self-efficacy and opportunity evaluation competencies".

5.1 Team Building

Team building is the most crucial step in the online course as well as in any entrepreneurial process started by a shared a single idea by team members (Brennan & Dooley, 2005; Craft, 2001; Dewett & Gruys, 2007; Gryskiewicz et al., 1985; Sawyer, 2006; Yang & Cheng, 2010). To assist students to form their team, students were invited to know each other in an unconventional way. That's why a shared Google drive document containing a table was put in Moodle and given to the students to fill useful information concerning them: their passions, their strengths, their weaknesses. A WhatsApp group was created to facilitate the students networking. It is expected that the more the team is heterogeneous in terms of competencies the more the performance in terms of entrepreneurial outcomes is guaranteed. Each team should name one interlocutor who has a mission to deal with the teacher during the lecture to follow the advancement of the teamwork. Each team should also have a leader, who will have many tasks mainly:

- To ensure the good quality of the different deliverables as per the given templates.
- To arrange the schedule of the team meetings.
- To guarantee an equitable tasks distribution.
- To ensure that all the assignments are deposited with the respect of all the deadlines. To motivate the team members to be more creative and more hard working.

5.2 *Inspiration*

Inspiration is one of the crucial steps to invite teams to get creative ideas. Students are enrolled in a series of activities to constitute a bank of further interesting ideas. The inspiration process is continuous throughout the semester; each new discussed idea during the lectures is registered in the database of the class ideas. The main aim of the following activities is to arise in the lectures an interesting dialogue about the way to enrich the Omani Market with local product and services "Made in Oman".

Activity 1 (Observation as the First Resource of Inspiration): In this activity each student is called to imagine and look for a simple imported product and/or service that could be easily produced in Oman. They are invited then to write their ideas in the MS Team chat, the first time, and after a discussion within a group the class is voting the top 10 ideas of products that may be "made in Oman" for the first time. These ideas are registered in the class bank of ideas as the first inspirational activity output.

Activity 2 (Iteration): Critical Thinking as the Second Resource of Inspiration/Criticizing a List of Omani Products/Services

Now the students are invited to choose some product made in Oman and to think about the anomalies related to their functionality, packaging, components, then they are discussing within the class the way of how promoting these products and services. They also vote and register the top ten ideas as the second inspirational activity deliverable.

Activity 3 (Iteration): Problems as the Third Resource of Inspiration

To "fall in love with problems" is the golden rule of the inspiration stage for any nascent entrepreneurs. The students are called to think deeply about the problems and worries that are encountering them daily, they detect some of them and unconsciously they start to find some solutions. Rich discussions are triggered, and the top ten ideas are voted on and registered in table.

5.3 Team Performing (Iteration)

The teams are brainstorming about the main entrepreneurial traits of the entrepreneurs and what makes a successful entrepreneurial team. Some successful teams are presented as success stories (e.g., AIRBNB, IBM, TWITTER) and teams start to dispatch the role among them, they are applied to register on the table the name of the team leader and the interlocutor to deal with during the lecture while briefly explaining the reason of their choice. Each team is invited to choose from the class bank of ideas a problem to solve, while discussing their choice with the other students during the lectures. They must find an adequacy between their competencies and the problems they are assigned to solve.

5.4 Solutions vs Trends

The teams have brainstormed and have already developed some solutions to the problems they have chosen, in accordance with their members' logic, knowledge and competencies. To verify if their concepts are original and in the core of trends, two activities are given to them.

Activity 4 (Inspiration/Iteration): Exploration of Mega Trend Maps

The teams are called to explore the "Maga Trends and Technologies map",[1] they must improve their solutions while taking for granted the trends by trend lines and their intersections. They should confirm that the solutions are at the core of trends.

[1] https://toptrends.nowandnext.com/wp-content/uploads/2017/05/Mega-trends-LR.jpg.

Activity 5: Concretizing the Solutions by Products or Services

They are visiting some websites (e.g., trendhunter.com, ted.com...) and they are applied to find similar concepts while thinking about the development of their own concept. This activity is very important to them to position their concept and to start to think about the importance of the value proposition.

At the end of this stage teams are teams are conscious about the main trends, they are aware about the concept of innovation, and they will no more "reinvent the wheels!".

5.5 Empathizing and Developing Solutions (Iteration)

To be more aware of the importance of the unique value proposition, the teams are focusing more on the problems of their customers; they are motivated to know them more and to refine their couple problems/solutions. An important tool is given to them through the activity of empathy map.

Activity 6: Empathy Map

The teams are applied to fill the empathy map with a lot of attention. An example of an empathy map is discussed within the lecture and the students are projecting better their solutions into the real needs of their customer or user. They are also used to make a checklist of their early adopters and potential business-to-business (B2B) or business-to-consumer (B2C) customer segments. Henceforth, they are aware of the importance of the customer for the continuity of the startup.

5.6 Prototyping and Validating Ideas

To concretize their ideas teams are sensitized to the prototyping as an important activity to any new product launch. They are invited to conceive and design a first version of their high- or low-tech product or service. It is a challenging task due to the online teaching, however thanks to some new applications and platforms (e.g., uizard.io or wikicell.org,) students could make their first prototype design "fast, fail and cheap".

Activity 7: Prototype-It—"Fast, Fail and Cheap"

The students are applied to conceptualize their idea by designing their product and preparing an explicative support (video, image, process, web or application front page) to discuss within the lecture with the other students and to get a prior feed-back. They are noting the remarks, and they are profiting from the other user's experiences to improve their concept and to get prior users and customer feed-back.

Stage 7: Customer Testing (Iteration)

Each team must create a free page or group through a virtual social network (Facebook, Instagram, Twitter, LinkedIn.). The prior objective of this virtual space is to get the customers' and users' comments to improve their prototype and their potential products and /or services. They are in competition to see which team would have the biggest number of followers. This step is considered as a prior "proof of concept" that may motivate them to be more engaged toward the act of startup launch.

5.7 *Opportunity Validation and the "Proof of Concept"*

The teams are now conscious of the importance of the customer testing and the prototyping step. They would like to prove that their concept is a real opportunity. They are refining their unique value proposition and their high-level concept by referring mainly to the trends and the new technologies of information and communication. They should deliver the first version of their lean canvas.

Activity 8: The Lean Canvas

The teams should fill all the blocs of the lean canvas; this activity will help them to capitalize on all the previous activities and to start acting as nascent entrepreneurs' team. Meanwhile some other successful start-up's lean canvas is discussed during the lecture to help them to prepare a pertinent first lean canvas.

5.8 *Opportunity Evaluation*

As the students are from many disciplines (engineering, health, veterinary, management and other sciences), they are obsessed by the business plan preparation which seems to them the heaviest task of the entrepreneurship course. Two templates were prepared to vulgarize this deliverable. The parts of the business plan were deeply highlighted by video links and examples, the students could share with the teacher a Google drive document to ask for possible responses to any business plan element. Furthermore, another Excel template was given to them to develop the profitability analysis part.

Activity 9: The Business Model/Plan

The teams should develop their lean canvas and deliver the business plan templates. They are accompanied individually by the teacher to ensure this part in the right way. They are evaluating their opportunities, and they start to use the language of numbers.

6 Implication and Further Research

The pandemic situation has introduced the world to the new normal education system which is typically known as "Online Learning", the adaptability skills allow the students to prepare them for real-world situations and empower them to overcome the challenges. Also, entrepreneurship education empowers students to think critically about challenging situations and allows them to take strategic actions to answer some of the challenges that they encounter. The current chapter emphasizes the importance of entrepreneurship education programs based on design thinking to foster innovative human resources. The design thinking approach emphasizes a user-centric and collaborative approach thus teaching students to be collaborative even in an online setting. Entrepreneurial education serves as a significant tool that facilitates students to start their businesses. Also, the design thinking approach allows the students to analyze the real-world challenges in a business context and helps them to find innovative ways out. Entrepreneurship is multidisciplinary thus incorporating a design thinking approach equips the necessary skills and mindsets to the students that allow the students to be successful entrepreneurs in this competitive world. Thus, adopting the design thinking approach in entrepreneurship courses in Oman can have a significant on the online teaching experience. The approach allows the students to adapt to change, fosters collaboration, makes them familiar with advanced technology, and real-life challenges, and teaches them problem-solving skills. Thus, this can be said that by incorporating the design thinking approach Oman can introduce the future generation of entrepreneurs to a more innovative world.

7 Conclusion

In conclusion, constructing the entrepreneurial attention of students becomes one of the common attributes of graduates in all higher education institutions in Oman. Entrepreneurship course as a common requirement in all majors is a significant tool that facilitates the road for all students to have the potential and willingness to start their own business. However, building the content of this model needs to be updated, comprehensive and well-designed. This chapter clearly shows that during COVID-19 program needs much more development in terms of the content and teaching approach. Therefore, it aims to construct to test the efficacy and effectiveness of a conceived online entrepreneurship program using the "design thinking" approach. Through the stages of the "design thinking" approach that has been applied to teaching entrepreneurship courses online, the literature shows that there is a positive relationship between the approach applied to the self-efficacy, alertness and opportunity evaluation competency of the students.

References

Ajzen, I. (1990). The theory of planned behavior. *Organizational Behavior and Human Decision Process, 50*, 179–211.

Autio, E., Esmt, L. D., & Frederiksen, L. (2013). Information exposure, opportunity evaluation, and entrepreneurial action: An investigation of an online user community. *Academy of Management Journal, 56*(5), 1348–1371. https://doi.org/10.5465/amj.2010.0328

Bailey, J., Read, J., Linder, B., & Neeley, L. (2021). Interdisciplinary team-based learning: An integrated opportunity recognition and evaluation model for teaching business, engineering and design students. *Entrepreneurship Education and Pedagogy, 4*(2), 143–168. https://doi.org/10.1177/2515127420979190

Ballantine, J., & Larres, P. M. C. (2007). Cooperative learning: A pedagogy to improve students' generic skills? *Education and Training, 49*(2), 126–137. https://doi.org/10.1108/00400910710739487

bandura albert. (1982). Self-efficacy mechanism in human agency. *American Psychologist, 37*(2), 122–147.

Baron, R. A. (2006). Opportunity recognition as pattern recognition: How entrepreneurs "connect the dots" to identify new business opportunities executive overview. *Academy of Management Perspectives, 20*(1), 104–119.

Binks, M., Starkey, K., & Mahon, C. L. (2006). Entrepreneurship education and the business school. *Technology Analysis & Strategic Management, 18*(1), 1–18.

Brennan, A., & Dooley, L. (2005). Networked creativity: A structured management framework for stimulating innovation. *Technovation, 25*(12), 1388–1399. https://doi.org/10.1016/j.technovation.2004.08.001

Chaney, B. H., Christensen, T. W., Crawford, A., Ford, K., & Godwin, W. W. (2020). Best practices in honors pedagogy: Teaching innovation and best practices in honors pedagogy: Teaching innovation and community engagement through design thinking community engagement through design thinking. *University of Nebraska-Lincoln*, 71–92. https://digitalcommons.unl.edu/nchchip

Chasanidou, D., Gasparini, A. A., & Lee, E. (2014). *Design thinking methods and tools for innovation in multidisciplinary teams*. http://goo.gl/g

Chou, D. C. (2018). Applying design thinking method to social entrepreneurship project. *Computer Standards and Interfaces, 55*, 1339–1351. https://doi.org/10.1016/j.csi.2017.05.001

Cohen, D., Hsu, D. K., & Shinnar, R. S. (2021). Identifying innovative opportunities in the entrepreneurship classroom: A new approach and empirical test. *Small Business Economics, 57*(4), 1931–1955. https://doi.org/10.1007/s11187-020-00387-z

Craft, A. (2001). *An analysis of research and literature on creativity in education report prepared for the qualifications and curriculum authority.*

Dali, N., & Harbi, S. (2016). The effect of risk perception and cognitive biases on the evaluation of opportunity in family and non-family entrepreneurs: The case of Tunisian entrepreneurs. *Journal of Enterprising Culture, 24*(3), 281–312. https://doi.org/10.1142/s0218495816500114

Dewett, T., & Gruys, M. L. (2007). Advancing the case for creativity through graduate business education. *Thinking Skills and Creativity, 2*(2), 85–95. https://doi.org/10.1016/j.tsc.2007.04.001

Díaz-Portugal, C., Delgado-García, J. B., & Blanco-Mazagatos, V. (2022). The influence of the positive affective trait on the willingness to act entrepreneurially: The mediating effect of opportunity evaluation. *International Small*

Business Journal: Researching Entrepreneurship, 40(5), 592–617. https://doi.org/10.1177/02662426211047920

Dosunmu, M., Abolaji, B., Oludare Olatoye, A., Moronke Dosunmu, M., & Bukki, A. O. (2020). Prior knowledge, creativity and entrepreneurial alertness of undergraduate students in Ogun State-owned universities. *KIU Journal of Social Sciences, 6*(2), 24–251. https://www.researchgate.net/publication/359822739

Eladl, A. M., & Polpol, Y. S. (2020). The effect of self-regulated learning strategies on developing creative problem solving and academic self-efficacy among intellectually superior high school students. In *International Journal of Psycho-Educational Sciences, 9*(1). https://www.journals.lapub.co.uk/index.php/IJPES

Ferreira-Neto, M. N., de Carvalho Castro, J. L., de Sousa-Filho, J. M., & de Souza Lessa, B. (2023). The role of self-efficacy, entrepreneurial passion, and creativity in developing entrepreneurial intentions. *Frontiers in Psychology, 14*. https://doi.org/10.3389/fpsyg.2023.1134618

Gaglio, C. M., & Katz, J. A. (2001). The psychological basis of opportunity identification: Entrepreneurial alertness. *Small Business Economics, 16*(2), 95–111. https://doi.org/10.1023/A:1011132102464

Garbuio, M., Dong, A., Nidthida, L. I. N., Tschang, T., & Lovallo, D. (2018). Demystifying the genius of entrepreneurship: How design cognition can help create the next generation of entrepreneurs. In *Academy of management learning and education* (Vol. 17, pp. 41–61). George Washington University. https://doi.org/10.5465/amle.2016.0040

Gill, S. A., Bencheva, N., Karayel, S., & Usman, M. (2021). Does entrepreneurial self-efficacy moderate effects of cognitive flexibility and entrepreneurial alertness on entrepreneurial intentions? *Entrepreneurial Business and Economics Review, 9*(3), 25–41. https://doi.org/10.15678/EBER.2021.090302

Gozukara, I., & Colakoglu, N. (2016). Enhancing entrepreneurial intention and innovativeness of university students: The mediating role of entrepreneurial alertness. *International Business Research, 9*(2), 34. https://doi.org/10.5539/ibr.v9n2p34

Gryskiewicz, S. S., Holt, K. D., Faber, A. M., & Sensabaugh, S. (1985). From experience: Demystify creativity, enhance innovation. *Journal of Product Innovation Management, 2*(2), 101–106.

Haynie, J. M., Shepherd, D. A., & Mcmullen, J. S. (2009). An opportunity for me? The role of resources in opportunity evaluation decisions. *Journal of Management Studies, 46*(3), 337–361.

Haynie, J. M., Shepherd, D., Mosakowski, E., & Earley, P. C. (2010). A situated metacognitive model of the entrepreneurial mindset. *Journal of Business Venturing, 25*(2), 217–229. https://doi.org/10.1016/j.jbusvent.2008.10.001

Hean Tat Keh, Maw Der Foo, & Boon Chong Lim. (2002). Opportunity evaluation under risky conditions: The cognitive processes of entrepreneurs. *Entrepreneurship Theory and Practice, 27*(2), 125–148. https://doi.org/10.1111/1540-8520.00003

Hegarty, C., & Jones, C. (2008). Graduate entrepreneurship: More than child's play. *Education and Training, 50*(7), 626–637. https://doi.org/10.1108/00400910810909072

Hu, R., Wang, L., Zhang, W., & Bin, P. (2018). Creativity, proactive personality, and entrepreneurial intention: The role of entrepreneurial alertness. *Frontiers in Psychology, 9*(Jun). https://doi.org/10.3389/fpsyg.2018.00951

Huq, A., & Gilbert, D. (2017). All the world's a stage: Transforming entrepreneurship education through design thinking. *Education and Training, 59*(2), 155–170. https://doi.org/10.1108/ET-12-2015-0111

Jiatong, W., Murad, M., Li, C., Gill, S. A., & Ashraf, S. F. (2021, September). Linking cognitive flexibility to entrepreneurial alertness and entrepreneurial intention among medical students with the moderating role of entrepreneurial self-efficacy: A secondorder moderated mediation model. *PLoS One*, *16*(9). https://doi.org/10.1371/journal.pone.0256420

Jones, B., & Iredale, N. (2010). Enterprise education as pedagogy. *Education + Training, 52*(1), 7–19. https://doi.org/10.1108/00400911011017654

Jones, C. (2006). Enterprise education: Revisiting whitehead to satisfy Gibbs. In *Education And Training*, *48*(5), 356–367. https://doi.org/10.1108/00400910610677045

Jones, P., Jones, A., Packham, G., & Miller, C. (2008). Student attitudes towards enterprise education in Poland: A positive impact. *Education and Training, 50*(7), 597–614. https://doi.org/10.1108/00400910810909054

Kabongo, J. D., & McCaskey, P. H. (2011). An examination of entrepreneurship educator profiles in business programs in the United States. *Journal of Small Business and Enterprise Development, 18*(1), 27–42. https://doi.org/10.1108/14626001111106415

Kaish, S., Gilad, B., Kaish, S., & Gilad, B. (1991). Characteristics of opportunwies search of entrepreneurs versus executives: Sources, interests, general alertness. *Journal of Business Venturing, 6*, 45–61.

Karwowski, M., Gralewski, J., Lebuda, I., & Wiśniewska, E. (2007). Creative teaching of creativity teachers: Polish perspective. *Thinking Skills and Creativity, 2*(1), 57–61. https://doi.org/10.1016/j.tsc.2006.10.004

Kirby, D. A. (2004). Entrepreneurship education: Can business schools meet the challenge? *Education + Training, 46*, 510–519. https://doi.org/10.1108/00400910410569632

Klapper, R. (2004). Government goals and entrepreneurship education—An investigation at a Grande Ecole in France. *Education + Training, 46*(3), 127–137. https://doi.org/10.1108/00400910410531787

Klapper, R., & Tegtmeier, S. (2010). Innovating entrepreneurial pedagogy: Examples from France and Germany. *Journal of Small Business and Enterprise Development, 17*(4), 552–568. https://doi.org/10.1108/14626001011088723

Krueger, N. F., Reilly, M. D., & Carsrud, A. L. (2000). Competing models of entrepreneurial intentions. *Journal of Business Venturing, 15*(5–6), 411–432.

Li, Y., Wang, P., & Liang, Y. J. (2015). Influence of entrepreneurial experience, alertness, and prior knowledge on opportunity recognition. *Social Behavior and Personality, 43*(9), 1575–1584. https://doi.org/10.2224/sbp.2015.43.9.1575

Liu, X., Gu, J., & Xu, J. (2023). The impact of the design thinking model on pre-service teachers' creativity self-efficacy, inventive problem-solving skills, and technology-related motivation. *International Journal of Technology and Design Education.* https://doi.org/10.1007/s10798-023-09809-x

Lowell, W. B. (1996). Research on entrepreneurial alertness. *Journal of Small Business Management, 34*(4), 35–44.

Ma, C., Yang, J., Chen, L., You, X., Zhang, W., & Chen, Y. (2020). Entrepreneurs' social networks and opportunity identification: Entrepreneurial passion and entrepreneurial alertness as moderators. *Social Behavior and Personality, 48*(2). https://doi.org/10.2224/sbp.8659

Mansoori, Y., & Lackéus, M. (2020). Comparing effectuation to discovery-driven planning, prescriptive entrepreneurship, business planning, lean startup, and design thinking. *Small Business Economics, 54*(3), 791–818. https://doi.org/10.1007/s11187-019-00153-w

McMullen, J. S., & Shepherd, D. A. (2006). Entrepreneurial action and the role of uncertainty in the theory of the entrepreneur. *Academy of Management Review, 31*(1), 132–152. Academy of Management. https://doi.org/10.5465/AMR.2006.19379628

Mitchell, J. R., & Shepherd, D. A. (2010). To thine own self be true: Images of self, images of opportunity, and entrepreneurial action. *Journal of Business Venturing, 25*(1), 138–154. https://doi.org/10.1016/j.jbusvent.2008.08.001

Montiel-Campos, H. (2021). Moderating role of entrepreneurial alertness on the relationship between entrepreneurial passion and strategic change. *Journal of Organizational Change Management, 34*(5), 1107–1124. https://doi.org/10.1108/JOCM-12-2020-0386

Mpeera Ntayi, J., Pagano, A., Bo, C., Xue Zhou, I., Neumeyer, X., & Jiang, B. (2022). Impact of different types of entrepreneurial alertness on entrepreneurial opportunities identification. *Frontiers in Psychology, 13*(4), 1–19.

Mwasalwiba, E. S. (2010). Entrepreneurship education: A review of its objectives, teaching methods, and impact indicators. *Education and Training, 52*(1), 20–47. https://doi.org/10.1108/00400911011017663

Neneh, B. N. (2019). From entrepreneurial alertness to entrepreneurial behavior: The role of trait competitiveness and proactive personality. *Personality and Individual Differences, 138*, 273–279. https://doi.org/10.1016/j.paid.2018.10.020

Noyes, E. (2018). Teaching entrepreneurial action through prototyping: The prototype-it challenge. *Entrepreneurship Education and Pedagogy, 1*(1), 118–134. https://doi.org/10.1177/2515127417737289

Packham, G., Jones, P., Thomas, B., & Miller, C. (2006). Student and tutor perspectives of on-line moderation. *Education and Training, 48*(4), 241–251. https://doi.org/10.1108/00400910610671915

Penaluna, A., Coates, J., & Penaluna, K. (2010). Creativity-based assessment and neural understandings: A discussion and case study analysis. *Education and Training, 52*(8), 660–678. https://doi.org/10.1108/00400911011088971

Penaluna, A., & Penaluna, K. (2009). Assessing creativity: Drawing from the experience of the UK's creative design educators. *Education and Training, 51*(8), 718–732. https://doi.org/10.1108/00400910911005262

Pio, E., & Haigh, N. (2007). Towards a pedagogy of inspirational parables. *Education + Training, 49*(2), 77–90. https://doi.org/10.1108/00400910710739441

Pittaway, L., & Cope, J. (2007). Entrepreneurship education: A systematic review of the evidence. *International Small Business Journal, 25*(5), 479–510. https://doi.org/10.1177/0266242607080656

Pittaway, L., & Hannon, P. (2008). Institutional strategies for developing enterprise education: A review of some concepts and models. *Journal of Small Business and Enterprise Development, 15*(1), 202–226. https://doi.org/10.1108/14626000810850937

Pratomo, L. C., Siswandari, & Wardani, D. K. (2021). The effectiveness of design thinking in improving student creativity skills and entrepreneurial alertness. *International Journal of Instruction, 14*(4), 695–712. https://doi.org/10.29333/iji.2021.14440a

Pretorius, M., Le Roux, I., & Millard, S. (2023). Understanding opportunity evaluation prototypes in search of more entrepreneurs. *Southern African Business Review*. https://doi.org/10.25159/1998-8125/11588

Richardson, I., & Hynes, B. (2008). Entrepreneurship education: Towards an industry sector approach. *Education + Training, 50*(3), 188–198. https://doi.org/10.1108/00400910810873973

Riquelme, H. E., & Alqallaf, A. (2020). Anticipated emotions and their effects on risk and opportunity evaluations. *Journal of International Entrepreneurship, 18*(3), 312–335. https://doi.org/10.1007/s10843-019-00262-3

Roundy, P. T., Harrison, D. A., Khavul, S., Pérez-Nordtvedt, L., & McGee, J. E. (2018). Entrepreneurial alertness as a pathway to strategic decisions and organizational performance. *Strategic Organization, 16*(2), 192–226. https://doi.org/10.1177/1476127017693970

Saadat, S., Aliakbari, A., Alizadeh Majd, A., & Bell, R. (2022). The effect of entrepreneurship education on graduate students' entrepreneurial alertness and the mediating role of entrepreneurial mindset. *Education and Training, 64*(7), 892–909. https://doi.org/10.1108/ET-06-2021-0231

Sarfati, G. (2019). Entrepreneurship and the face of Janus of institutions: Stimulus policies for high-impact entrepreneurs in Brazil and Russia. *Teoria e Prática Em Administração, 9*(1), 15–28. https://doi.org/10.21714/2238-104x2019v9i1-40753

Sarooghi, H., Sunny, S., Hornsby, J., & Fernhaber, S. (2019). Design thinking and entrepreneurship education: Where are we, and what are the possibilities? *Journal of Small Business Management, 57*(S1), 78–93. https://doi.org/10.1111/jsbm.12541

Sawyer, R. K. (2006). Educating for innovation. *Thinking Skills and Creativity, 1*(1), 41–48. https://doi.org/10.1016/j.tsc.2005.08.001

Seikkula-Leino, J., Ruskovaara, E., Ikavalko, M., Mattila, J., & Rytkola, T. (2010). Promoting entrepreneurship education: The role of the teacher? *Education and Training, 52*(2), 117–127. https://doi.org/10.1108/00400911011027716

Shahab, Y., Chengang, Y., Arbizu, A. D., & Haider, M. J. (2019). Entrepreneurial self-efficacy and intention: Do entrepreneurial creativity and education matter? *International Journal of Entrepreneurial Behaviour and Research, 25*(2), 259–280. https://doi.org/10.1108/IJEBR-12-2017-0522

Shane, S. (2000). Prior knowledge and the discovery of entrepreneurial opportunities. *Organization Science, 11*(4), 448–469.

Sharma, L. (2019). A systematic review of the concept of entrepreneurial alertness. *Journal of Entrepreneurship in Emerging Economies, 11*(2), 217–233. https://doi.org/10.1108/JEEE-05-2018-0049

Shepherd, D., & Haynie, J. M. (2009). Birds of a feather don't always flock together: Identity management in entrepreneurship. *Journal of Business Venturing, 24*(4), 316–337. https://doi.org/10.1016/j.jbusvent.2007.10.005

Shepherd, D. A., McMullen, J. S., & Jennings, P. D. (2007). The formation of opportunity beliefs: Overcoming ignorance and reducing doubt. *Strategic Entrepreneurship Journal, 1*(1–2), 75–95. https://doi.org/10.1002/sej.3

Siu, W. S., & Lo, E. S. C. (2013). Cultural contingency in the cognitive model of entrepreneurial intention. *Entrepreneurship: Theory and Practice, 37*(2), 147–173. https://doi.org/10.1111/j.1540-6520.2011.00462.x

Smith, B. R., Kickul, J. R., & Wilson, F. (2010). Entrepreneurial opportunity evaluation: A discrete choice analysis of financial and social entrepreneurial opportunity attributes. *Values and opportunities in social entrepreneurship* (pp. 121–140). Palgrave Macmillan.

Solomon, G., Dickson, P. H., Solomon, G. T., & Weaver, K. M. (2008). Entrepreneurial selection and success: Does education matter? *Journal of Small Business and Enterprise Development, 15*(2), 239–258. https://doi.org/10.1108/14626000810871655

Sowmya, D. V., Majumdar, S., & Gallant, M. (2010). Relevance of education for potential entrepreneurs: An international investigation. *Journal of Small Business and Enterprise Development, 17*(4), 626–640. https://doi.org/10.1108/14626001011088769

Srivastava, S., Sahaym, A., & Allison, T. H. (2021). Alert and awake: Role of alertness and attention on rate of new product introductions. *Journal of Business Venturing, 36*(4). https://doi.org/10.1016/j.jbusvent.2020.106023

Suzuki, K. (2016). Entrepreneurship education based on design thinking and technology commercialization in Japanese Universities. *Proceedings—2016 5th IIAI International Congress on Advanced Applied Informatics, IIAI-AAI 2016*, 779–784. https://doi.org/10.1109/IIAI-AAI.2016.257

Tang, J. (2008). Environmental munificence for entrepreneurs: Entrepreneurial alertness and commitment. *International Journal of Entrepreneurial Behaviour & Research, 14*(3), 128–151. https://doi.org/10.1108/13552550810874664

Tang, J., Kacmar, K. M. M., & Busenitz, L. (2012). Entrepreneurial alertness in the pursuit of new opportunities. *Journal of Business Venturing, 27*(1), 77–94. https://doi.org/10.1016/j.jbusvent.2010.07.001

Thi-Huyen, N., Xuan-Lam, P., & Thanh Tu, N. T. (2021). The impact of design thinking on problem solving and teamwork mindset in a flipped classroom. *Eurasian Journal of Educational Research*, *96*, 30–50. https://doi.org/10.14689/ejer.2021.96.3

Tselepis, T. J., & Lavelle, C. A. (2020). Design thinking in entrepreneurship education: Understanding framing and placements of problems. *Acta Commercii, 20*(1). https://doi.org/10.4102/ac.v20i1.872

Urban, B. (2020). Entrepreneurial alertness, self-efficacy and social entrepreneurship intentions. *Journal of Small Business and Enterprise Development, 27*(3), 489–507. https://doi.org/10.1108/JSBED-08-2019-0285

Verstraete, T., & Fayolle, A. (2005). Paradigmes Et Entrepreneuriat. *Revue De L'entrepreneuriat, 4*(1), 33–52. https://doi.org/10.3917/entre.041.0033

Von Kortzfleisch, H. F. O., Zerwas, D., & Mokanis, I. (2013). Potentials of entrepreneurial design thinking® for entrepreneurship education. *Procedia—Social and Behavioral Sciences, 106*, 2080–2092. https://doi.org/10.1016/j.sbspro.2013.12.237

White, R. J., & Hertz, G. T. (2022). Teaching opportunity recognition: meeting the challenges of message, method and measurement. *The Journal of Entrepreneurship, 31*(2_suppl), S52–S78. https://doi.org/10.1177/09713557221107436

Williams, D. W., & Wood, M. S. (2015). Rule-based reasoning for understanding opportunity evaluation. *Academy of Management Perspectives, 29*(2), 218–236. https://doi.org/10.5465/amp.2013.0017

Wood, M. S., & Mckelvie, A. (2015). Opportunity evaluation as future focused cognition: Identifying conceptual themes and empirical trends. *International Journal of Management Reviews, 17*(2), 256–277. https://doi.org/10.1111/ijmr.12053

Wood, M. S., & McKinley, W. (2010). The production of entrepreneurial opportunity: A constructivist perspective. *Strategic Entrepreneurship Journal, 4*(1), 66–84. https://doi.org/10.1002/sej.83

Wood, M. S., & Williams, D. W. (2014). Opportunity evaluation as rule-based decision making. *Journal of Management Studies, 51*(4), 573–602. https://doi.org/10.1111/joms.12018

Yang, H. L., & Cheng, H. H. (2010). Creativity of student information system projects: From the perspective of network embeddedness. *Computers and Education, 54*(1), 209–221. https://doi.org/10.1016/j.compedu.2009.08.004

Yasir, N., Mahmood, N., Jutt, A. A., Babar, M., Irfan, M., Jamil, F., Shaukat, M. Z., Khan, H. M., & Liren, A. (2020). How can entrepreneurial self-efficacy, proactivity and creativity enhance sustainable recognition opportunity? The effect of entrepreneurial alertness is to mediate the formation of sustainable entrepreneurial intention. *Revista Argentina de Clínica Psicológica, XXIX*(5), 1004–1023. https://doi.org/10.24205/03276716.2020.1097

Zaheer, A., & Zaheer, S. (1997). Catching the wave: Alertness, responsiveness, and market influence in global electronic networks. *Management Science, 43*(11), 1493–1509. https://doi.org/10.1287/mnsc.43.11.1493

Zhao, W., Yang, T., Hughes, K. D., & Li, Y. (2021). Entrepreneurial alertness and business model innovation: The role of entrepreneurial learning and risk perception. *International Entrepreneurship and Management Journal, 17*(2), 839–864. https://doi.org/10.1007/s11365-020-00637-2

CHAPTER 13

Students' Perceptions of Emergency Remote Teaching During COVID-19: The Case of Sultan Qaboos University

Sabah Al Balushi and Mohammed Athar Khan

1 Introduction

In response to the COVID-19 pandemic, higher education institutions (HEIs) across the globe closed their doors to stop it from spreading (Ren et al., 2020), which disrupted higher education services (Ana et al., 2020; Obaid AI-Youbi et al., 2020). This closure forced HEIs to transition quickly to what is commonly known as Emergency Remote Teaching (ERT), i.e., 'a temporary shift of instructional delivery to an alternate delivery mode due to crisis circumstances' (Hodges et al., 2020, p. 6). They had to move to uncharted territories while grappling with e-learning. However, most of the HEIs quickly embraced the dynamics of online learning to deliver remote teaching (Burns et al., 2020; EUA, 2020; OECD, 2020; Rastogi & Priya, 2020), relying primarily on asynchronous learning (for example, video lectures) and at times, synchronous

S. Al Balushi (✉) · M. A. Khan
Sultan Qaboos University, Muscat, Oman
e-mail: sabah@squ.edu.om

A. Mishrif (ed.), *Perspectives on Human Capital Development*,
https://doi.org/10.1007/978-981-97-5246-1_13

learning (video conferencing) to enhance their students' learning experiences (Hashim et al., 2020; Salman et al., 2020). For virtual interactive sessions, teachers had to conduct lessons through applications, some of which they had not used or known about, such as Zoom, WebEx, Adobe Connect, Skype for Business, Big Blue Button (BBB), and Edu Meet, among others (Arora & Srinivasan, 2020; World Bank, 2020).

This unexpected situation led to a variety of problems for both teachers and their students (Longhurst et al., 2020; Obaid AI-Youbi et al., 2020;), which affected education adversely. Indeed, Rapanta et al. (2020) state that the shift to ERT shocked institutions, teachers, and students. Moreover, according to Shin and Hickey (2020), this unprecedented transition was massive and profoundly transformed the lives and learning experiences of higher education students the most. For instance, the pandemic resulted in students' isolation, which unsettled them (Araújo et al., 2020) and caused a lack of self-discipline (Bao, 2020). Even quantitatively, more than 1.6 billion students were affected, i.e., around 91% of all students worldwide (DeVaney et al., 2020). This makes it mandatory that research is consistently devoted to investigating the experiences, perspectives, and insights of the primary customers and most critical stakeholders of tertiary education, i.e., students (Bond et al., 2021; Quinn et al., 2009; Raaper et al., 2022). Several studies (Crick et al., 2020; Mohmmed et al., 2020; Osman, 2020; Shim & Lee, 2020; Toquero, 2020) have suggested exploring students' experiences of ERT. Although some studies have done so (Dong & Ishige, 2022; Guskaroska et al., 2022; Jeyaraj, 2023), there is still a dearth of literature on this aspect.

To fill this gap, the chapter investigates perceptions of ERT. It explores the issues faced by tertiary education students at Sultan Qaboos University (SQU) during COVID-19. The findings can be similar or different to other regional and worldwide contexts. They can thus inform policymaking in ways that can improve different higher education systems, particularly regarding online and distance learning plans.

2 ERT Versus Online Learning

ERT, as discussed earlier, is a temporary shift of instruction from face-to-face to online mode during a crisis or emergency. According to Hodges et al. (2020), ERT is not a robust educational system. However, it provides temporary access to instruction and instructional support that is quickly set up and remains in place as long as an emergency or crisis exists.

Recognizing the differences between ERT and online learning is crucial because the experiences students acquire will affect their attitude toward online learning, which can help policymakers handle such emergencies.

According to Bozkurt et al. (2020), online education is purely based on theoretical and practical knowledge of online learning. It includes well-thought-of activities that expose the students to various experiences by keeping them engaged, responsible, and flexible (Bozkurt & Sharma, 2020). ERT, on the other hand, is an alternative learning process. Mohmmed et al. (2020) report that ERT courses are developed within days without prior planning and design, and the course quality, learning management, and support environment might be compromised. Hodges et al. (2020) stress that ERT should not be mistaken for long-term solutions but accepted as a temporary solution to an immediate problem. Online courses take a long time to design and develop and are iterated, whereas ERT lacks these features. ERT instructors and institutions neither have the expertise nor the time to deliver proper online courses. Furthermore, online practitioners are well-versed in challenges such as effective asynchronous communication and online student–student interaction, whereas students, teachers, administrators, and family members are not aware of the huge obstacles in ERT courses (Dietrich, 2021; Fisher et al., 2020).

Hodges et al. (2020) do not consider remote learning experiences during crises as 'online courses' but categorize them as a subset of distance education called ERT. Similarly, Williamson et al. (2020) refer to remote learning experiences as Emergency Remote Education (ERE). According to Aristovnik et al. (2020), students' ERT experience differs from one place to another depending on educational access, continuity, and quality. Therefore, students' perceptions of learning experiences depend on how distance courses (online or ERT) are designed, developed, and delivered (Bozkurt & Sharma, 2020). In the given scenario, recognizing the differences between ERT and online courses can help us understand ERT challenges.

3 ERT Challenges for Students

As mentioned in the previous section, transitioning to the ERT mode of teaching and learning was challenging for teachers and students. However, since this chapter is concerned with students, the focus is on the challenges ERT presents to students.

3.1 Lack of Access to Technology

Di Pietro et al. (2020) report that the ERT mode of teaching and learning results in loss of learning. Some challenges emanate from their socioeconomic status, such as the availability and usage of the internet and technology and the support they get at home from their parents and other family members. Although technological equity (internet availability, utilization of educational opportunities) is essential, it still does not exist (Hippe et al., 2016). It gets amplified in crisis situations like the implementation of ERT (Rohs & Ganz, 2015). Di Pietro et al. (2020) report that students from remote areas may not show good academic progress because of the lack of access to broadband internet service and technology (computer, laptop, tablet, or smartphone). Moreover, home environments that do not support students will likely compromise the online teaching mode as they increase students' stress levels (Duraku & Hoxha, 2020) and reduce their self-directed learning (Taskeen, 2020). This situation can hurt students' ability to adapt to a new and unfamiliar situation.

3.2 Lack of Time Management Skills

Another challenge concerns time management in the ERT mode of teaching and learning (Di Pietro et al., 2020). Because students had to adapt fast and flexibly while transitioning to ERT, they were suddenly forced to manage their time and self-regulate their learning. Yates et al. (2020) observed that some students find it challenging to manage their time during online learning as they feel they have more freedom from being supervised, as is the case in face-to-face teaching, which can lead to reduced motivation and, consequently, a lack of learning (Wang et al., 2020).

3.3 Changed Means of Communication

During ERT, one of the most critical changes that students had to navigate was the sudden change in how they communicated with their teachers and peers, shifting from the realms of the classroom to the virtual world. Yates et al. (2020) report that students prefer face-to-face communication because of the support and feedback they get from teachers. On the other hand, communication through Google Meet, Microsoft Teams,

Zoom, etc., appears unnatural to students (Gonzalez et al., 2022). Moreover, students often turn off their cameras and microphones as they feel uncomfortable asking questions in front of the whole class, which hinders teacher interaction (Castelli & Sarvary, 2021). Even informal communication among peers in traditional classrooms can become challenging during the ERT mode of online classes (Yates et al., 2020).

3.4 Emotions and the Emotional State of Students

Research shows that both emotions and the emotional state of students' minds play an essential role in teaching and learning. The emotions could range from positive to negative along a continuum and can support or undermine learning. For example, positive emotions may include engagement, interest, curiosity, passion, creativity, etc., which can motivate students and facilitate learning. However, negative emotions like anxiety, stress, disengagement, etc., can impede learning (Osika et al., 2007). In the context of ERT, Bozkurt and Sharma (2020, p. 3) raise the issue of emotions and emotional state of mind in the following way:

> In a time of crisis, when people are under trauma, stress and psychological pressure, should we focus on teaching educational content or should we focus on teaching how to share, collaborate and support? We should remember when things go back to normal, people will not remember the educational content delivered, but they will remember how they felt, how we cared for them, and how we supported them.

3.5 The Stress Level of Students in ERT

The ad-hoc shift to ERT presented an entirely new situation for students for which they were not ready. Di Pietro et al. (2020) confirm that stress and adaptability to the new learning environment were among the challenges students faced. Such a sudden massive shift puts students under considerable psychological stress (Bozkurt & Sharma, 2020), contributing to the development of anxiety (Asanov et al., 2021) that can directly impact their mental well-being. During the lockdown, some students showed signs of fear, panic, despair, stress, anxiety, confusion, and passiveness (Duraku & Hoxha, 2020).

Several cross-sectional studies report higher student stress levels (Obermeier et al., 2022). This increased stress level could emanate from the change in the means of communication (Bozkurt et al., 2020), lesser contact with teachers and peers (Hopp et al., 2021), a higher level of loneliness, which affects well-being and motivation (Keyserling et al., 2021), and mental exhaustion, and higher cognitive load during video conferencing (Fauville et al., 2021).

Furthermore, the digital readiness of students determines students' perception of stress in ERT (Handel et al., 2020). Those students who lack digital readiness experience negative emotions and lower performance levels (Hadwin et al., 2022); male students appear to be better equipped with digital readiness (Senkbeil et al., 2021) compared to female students (Voltmer et al., 2021).

4 ERT and Policymaking in Higher Education

The United Nations (2020) reported that the pandemic has created the most extensive disruption of the education system in history, affecting 1.6 billion learners and 63 million teachers in more than 190 countries. Due to unprecedented challenges because of COVID-19, higher education institutions have been the most affected in the entire education system since they are the gateway to employment (Tilak & Kumar, 2022). They further state that a large proportion of students have found the experience of learning so frustrating that they risk losing interest in education. The question haunting the policymakers is: will adaptations made during ERT become part of higher education forever? Qamar (2021) acknowledges the importance and use of technology as an effective instrument to enhance the quality of education but warns that we should not deduce that future education will be all virtual.

In light of COVID-19 experiences, policy reformers in higher education should consider that 'failure to sustain effective tertiary systems can lead to perilous social upheavals, as youth fall outside the education system, unable to engage in active learning and uncertain about the future of their education and prospects' (World Bank, 2020, p. 1).

In addition, the shift to remote teaching during the pandemic forces the policymakers to raise the issue of the use of technology that 'may provide indications both on how Educational Technology scenarios may end up being reconfigured beyond this pandemic, and on how to deal with future educational emergencies' (Manca & Delfino, 2021, p. 1397). As a result, much research has focused on updating and reconstructing educational policies during the crisis, such as adapting and designing new instructional activities (Baran & Al Zoubi, 2020; Kier & Clark, 2020), formulating educational frameworks that serve ERT in the future Whittle et al., (2020), creating sustainable education that is equitable, accessible, and empowering (Veletsianos & Houlden, 2020) and promoting active learning and civic participation (Greenhow & Chapman, 2020).

5 Recent Changes in Higher Education Due to COVID-19

In response to the pandemic, many transformative measures have already been adopted in higher education, which are likely to have lasting implications on the way we approach and deliver education in the future, leading to the evolution of the higher education landscape even in underdeveloped parts of the world. Some recent developments include the following:

5.1 Transformation of Teachers' Digital Skills

To ensure that faculty and students are adequately prepared for the inevitable transformation to online education, a swift acquisition of digital teaching skills and the redesign of courses to fit the virtual landscape have been deemed necessary. So, educators have delved into pedagogical adaptations in the digital environment. Hira and Anderson (2021) outlined practical strategies for online teaching that included clear communication, well-structured course materials, and engaging digital content. These strategies aimed to replicate the interactive and dynamic nature of in-person instruction in the virtual realm. Furthermore, fostering student engagement has become a central concern for educators (Chu, 2022), calling for innovative approaches, including multimedia elements, discussion forums, and virtual office hours. These measures aim to maintain a sense of community among students and encourage active participation, ensuring that the quality of education remained strong despite the shift in the learning environment (Salta et al., 2022). In addition, bridging the digital divide and access issues, which came to the forefront as significant impediments (Graham & Sahlberg, 2020), has been a pivotal adjustment to ensure equitable education opportunities for all.

5.2 Technological Infrastructure and Support

Another significant shift that was triggered by the pandemic is how HEIs approach technology and infrastructure investments. A vital element of this transformation was the rapid adoption of Learning Management Systems (LMS) (Cavus et al., 2021), which are indispensable tools for managing online courses, facilitating content delivery, and tracking student progress. LMS platforms not only help streamline the educational process but also ensure that students and faculty have a centralized platform for accessing course materials and engaging in the virtual classroom. In addition to LMS adoption, ensuring technical support for students and faculty has been imperative (Toquero, 2020) to deal with the increased reliance on technology and address issues related to software, hardware, and connectivity. Thus, HEIs work diligently to provide robust technical support services for students and faculty (Al Amoush et al., 2020; Cavus et al., 2021).

5.3 Student Experience and Well-being

The COVID-19 pandemic has also brought a profound transformation to the student experience and well-being within the HE landscape. A vital component of this adjustment has focused on addressing the effects on student mental health caused by the sudden shift to online learning and the broader uncertainties of the pandemic (Meda et al., 2021). Therefore, innovative strategies such as virtual social events, online support groups, and peer mentoring programs have emerged as ways to combat the emotional toll of isolation and disconnectedness (Leal Filho et al., 2021), fostering a sense of community and belonging in the virtual realm. Cao et al. (2020) emphasize that universities must prioritize academic and emotional support to ensure students feel connected to their educational experience.

5.4 Changes in Institutional Governance

The need for effective leadership and decision-making in times of turbulence has led to significant transformations in institutional governance in HEIs (started during COVID-19). On the one hand, the pandemic placed an unprecedented level of responsibility on the shoulders of university leaders, demanding agility, adaptability, and crisis management skills

(Kells, 2021), as they had to make quick and often difficult decisions related to campus closures (Asio & Bayucca, 2021) and shift to online teaching. On the other hand, collaborative governance models emerged as a critical approach to decision-making (Özer, 2020) since the complex challenges presented by the pandemic required inclusive, collective efforts involving multiple stakeholders, including faculty, staff, and students. For example, in Metchik et al.'s (2021) collaborative approach, university leaders sought input from various corners of the institution and other institutions, ensuring a more comprehensive understanding of the issues at hand and fostering a sense of shared responsibility and ownership in decision-making. Mao (2020) asserts that this model enhanced transparency and engendered a sense of community in times of crisis. Indeed, COVID-19 provided administrators with an opportunity to rethink the educational system (Canese & Amarilla, 2020) giving more importance to faculty involvement in decision-making (Lepp et al., 2021). This has allowed for the development of policies and practices more attuned to the academic needs of students and the institutional mission.

Although research is available on policymaking in times of crisis, it is mostly from administrators, policymakers, teachers, and researchers' points of view. Yet, there is a dearth of research that attempts to adopt a bottom-up approach, i.e., involving students and their experiences in policymaking to deal with future emergencies in higher education.

6 Methodology

As the aim was to investigate students' experiences with online learning, particularly ERT, during COVID-19, the best way to collect the data in this unique situation was via an online student survey. Given the circumstances of forced distance learning, using a completely online data collection tool was inevitable. Online surveys have almost replaced conventional paper-and-pencil questionnaires years before the pandemic. In recent years, they have become one of educational research's most popular data collection instruments (Saleh & Bista, 2017).

Despite some problems with online data collection methods, for example, weak internet connectivity, online surveys are cost-effective and less time-consuming. Moreover, if given adequate time to answer, they can be reliable in achieving a high return response rate as they allow researchers to reach participants in different geographical locations (Lefever et al., 2007).

The online survey not only collected students' feedback but also reinforced the use of online learning modality (i.e., fit for purpose). Students' opinions were captured using structured close-ended items that yielded quantitative data. The researchers used Google Forms to design the survey questionnaire, which was emailed to all students enrolled in a foundation or credit-based course offered by the Center for Preparatory Studies (CPS) at Sultan Qaboos University. A total of 337 responses were received and analyzed. Both descriptive and inferential statistics were used to report the findings.

For descriptive statistics, charts and graphs with numbers and percentages were generated to summarize the data. For inferential statistics, chi-square (X^2) was performed to determine relationships and associations based on the nature of the variables available. More specifically, gender, type of device used, internet provider, service strength, location of internet service, and technical skills before ERT were examined to check whether there are dependencies with the target variable representing the students' satisfaction with online learning during ERT through the final survey statement '***Online learning was a good experience***'.

To improve the robustness of the chi-square test, two variables, namely 'strength of the internet' and 'technical skills before ERT', were reduced to three levels of agreement instead of the initial five-point Likert scale. In addition, the area/governorate variable was excluded because it included many levels that statistically affected the test conducted. Moreover, before running the test, the data was pre-processed and cleaned. As a result, the final sample size for inferential statistics was 254, sufficient to conduct the test.

7 Results

The respondents (n = 337) were almost evenly distributed in terms of gender, with the majority belonging to the 18–20 age group (Table 1). However, they were enrolled in different courses. Most of them were still doing the general foundation program (GFP) with three independent components or subjects: English, Math, and IT. It takes one to three semesters, depending on the starting level, provided that a student progresses without failing any course. However, another significant proportion of the respondents had finished the GFP and was taking a CELP, or credit English language program from the CPS, in addition to other undergraduate courses as per their college study plan. Table 1 provides a summary of the participant's background.

In terms of gender, it is clear from Table 2 that no relationship existed between this variable and the students' satisfaction with online learning during ERT ($X^2 = 0.254$; $p = 0.706$).

The participants conducted ERT from different governorates, mostly from Al Dakhiliya, followed by Muscat and North Al Batinah, South Al Batinah and Al Dhahirah (Fig. 1). The remaining regions/ governorates were not that well represented. This finding is similar to SQU statistics on the distribution of undergraduate students across the different Governorates of the Sultanate. For example, in the academic year 2019–2020 (Planning & Statistics Department, 2020, p. 10), Al Dakhiliyah came first with 21.3% and 23.2% of the total number of students admitted and registered. North Al Batinah Governorate was second, with 15% admitted and 16.9% registered students. In third place was South Al Batinah with 12.8% and 14.7%, followed by Muscat with 12.7% and 13.3%. The other regions of Oman shared the rest.

Table 1 Participants' background

Variable		*Number*	*Percentage*
Gender	Male	169	51.1%
	Female	168	49.9%
Age group	18–20	306	90.8%
	19–22	29	8.6%
Main courses students were enrolled in	FPEL0603[a]	70	20.8%
	CELP Humanities[b] (Existed the FP and are in colleges)	53	15.7%
	FPMT[c]	50	14.8%
	CELP Sciences (Exited FP & are in colleges)	47	13.9%
	FPCS[d]	42	12.5%
	FPEL0560	45	13.4%
Total	337		

[a]FPEL = Foundation Program, English Language
[b]CELP = Credit English Language Program
[c]FPMT = Foundation Program, Math
[d]FPCS = Foundation Program, Computer Science
Source Authors' calculations

Table 2 Gender and satisfaction of students with online learning

Chi-Square Tests					
	Value	*Df*	*Asymp. Sig. (2-sided)*	*Exact Sig. (2-sided)*	*Exact Sig. (1-sided)*
Pearson Chi-Square	**0.254**[a]	**1**	**0.614**		
Continuity Correction[b]	0.143	1	0.706		
Likelihood Ratio	0.254	1	0.614		
Fisher's Exact Test				0.706	0.353
Linear-by-Linear Association	0.253	1	0.615		
No of Valid Cases	254				

[a]0 cells (0.0%) have an expected count of less than 5. The minimum expected count is 58.00
[b]Computed only for a 2 × 2 table
Source Authors' calculations

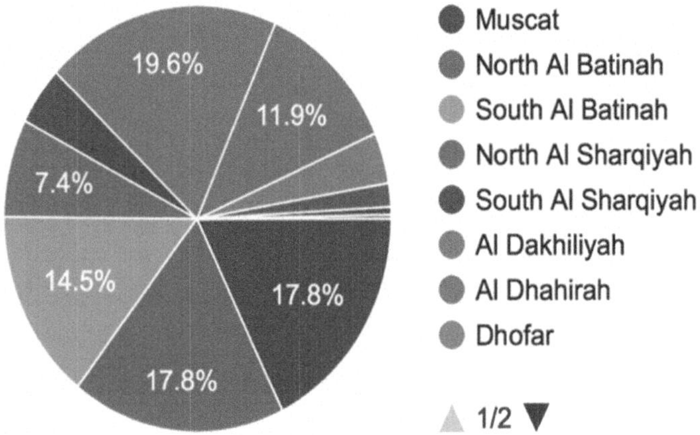

Fig. 1 Geographical locations of students in Oman during ERT (*Source* Authors' calculations)

Different factors determine readiness for online learning (e.g., McVay, 2001; Smith et al., 2003). One essential element is technological readiness, i.e., whether students can access the Internet quickly and when needed, which is conditioned by the possession or availability of a suitable device to conduct online learning. First, concerning the latter factor (Fig. 2), most respondents reported using smartphones during ERT while a large percentage also had personal laptops or desktop computers. A tablet is not a very popular device among SQU students compared to smartphones or computers. A sizable proportion of the students also indicated that they shared a laptop or desktop computer (most probably with family members). Very few students said that they borrowed a more suitable device for online learning. It must be noted that, based on the numbers, students used more than one device, for example, a smartphone and a computer.

The device (personal or shared laptop or desktop/smartphone) affected satisfaction with online learning during ERT ($X^2 = 14.91$; $p = 0.001$), as seen in Table 3 and Fig. 3.

As to having an accessible Wi-Fi or internet connection, the most popular networks used were, as expected, the government-owned

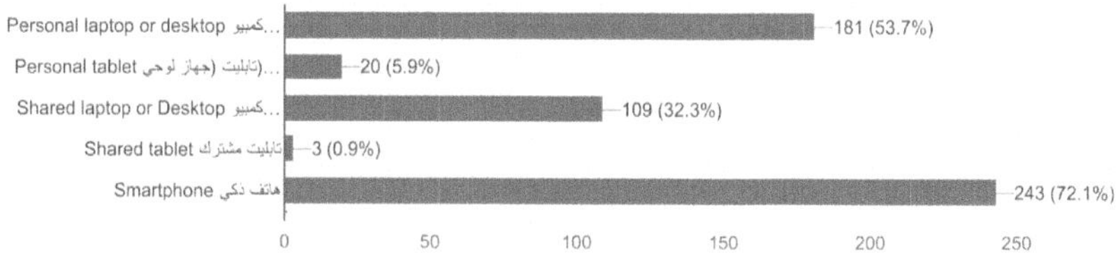

Fig. 2 Types of devices students used during ERT (*Source* Authors' calculations)

Table 3 Device used and satisfaction of students with online learning

Chi-Square Tests			
	Value	*Df*	*Asymp. Sig. (2-sided)*
Pearson Chi-Square	**14.914**[a]	2	**0.001**
Likelihood Ratio	15.196	2	0.001
Linear-by-Linear Association	10.519	1	0.001
No of Valid Cases	254		

[a]0 cells (0.0%) have an expected count of less than 5. The minimum expected count is 18.72
Source Authors' calculations

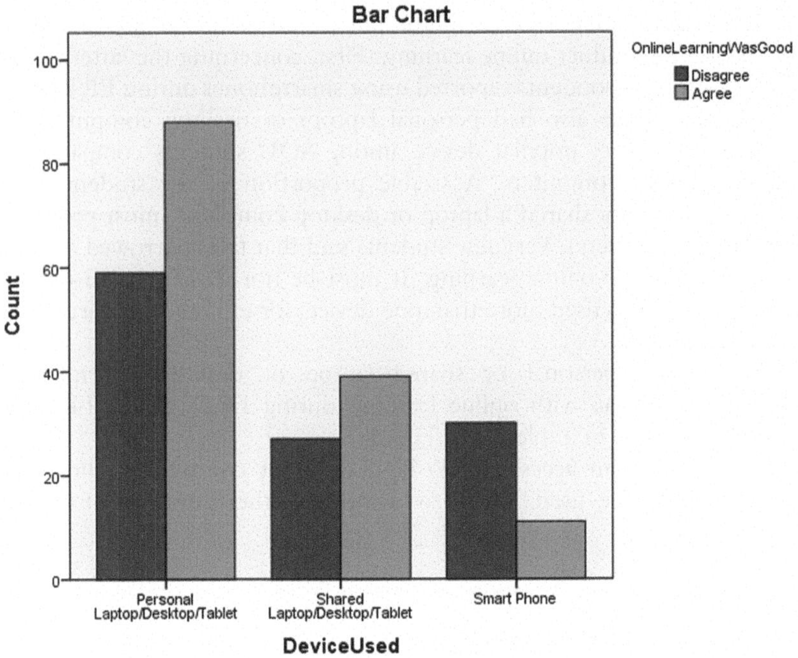

Fig. 3 Device used and satisfaction of students with online learning (*Source* Authors' calculations)

Omantel, followed by Ooredoo. Awaser was also used by 8.3% of them. Figure 4 illustrates the home environment of internet companies as reported by the respondents.

Table 4 shows that the internet provider companies (Omantel/Oreedo/Awaser) did not influence satisfaction with online learning during ERT ($X^2 = 4.48$; $p = 0.213$). This may indicate that the services provided by the different companies are more or less the same.

Relevant to this but even more important, 34.1%, 32%, and 21.1% of the respondents rated their internet service (Fig. 5) as average, poor, or good, respectively. Only 3.3% enjoyed excellent service.

Indeed, there was a clear correlation between students' satisfaction with online learning during ERT and internet strength ($X^2 = 33.319$; $p = 0.000$), as presented in Table 5 below.

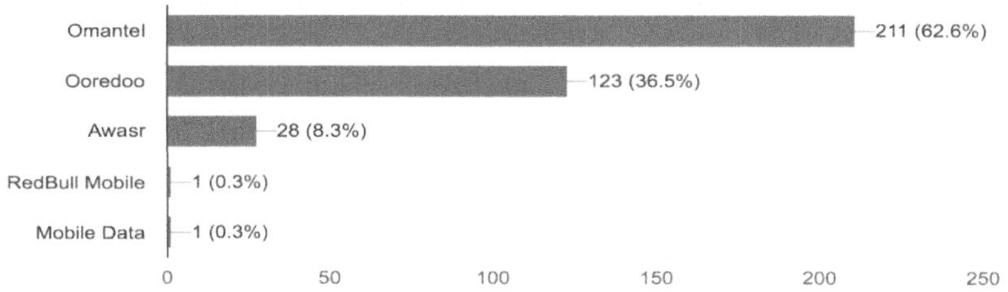

Fig. 4 Type of internet service at students' homes (*Source* Authors' calculations)

Table 4 Internet provider and satisfaction of students with online learning

Chi-Square Tests			
	Value	*Df*	*Asymp. Sig. (2-sided)*
Pearson Chi-Square	**4.488**[a]	3	**0.213**
Likelihood Ratio	4.678	3	0.197
Linear-by-Linear Association	2.321	1	0.128
No of Valid Cases	254		

[a]0 cells (0.0%) have an expected count of less than 5. The minimum expected count is 10.05
Source Authors' calculations

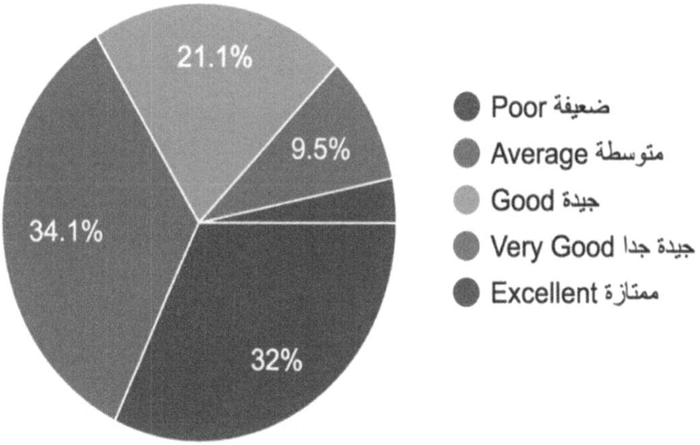

Fig. 5 Quality of students' internet service during ERT (*Source* Authors' calculations)

Table 5 Internet service strength and satisfaction with online learning

Chi-Square Tests			
	Value	*Df*	*Asymp. Sig. (2-sided)*
Pearson Chi-Square	**33.319**[a]	2	**0.000**
Likelihood Ratio	34.105	2	0.000
Linear-by-Linear Association	29.214	1	0.000
No of Valid Cases	254		

[a]0 cells (0.0%) have an expected count of less than 5. The minimum expected count is 15.98
Source Authors' calculations

Moreover, most reported that they had Wi-Fi at home while a little less than 50% also used their mobile phone data to learn online. Unfortunately, about 10% used other people's Wi-Fi, and a similar percentage had to leave their homes or villages to find more robust and more stable connectivity (Fig. 6).

A correlation was observed (as shown in Table 6 and Fig. 7) depending on where or/and how the students got a good internet service (home Wi-Fi/ mobile data/ other locations from where they lived, or a mix (unstable). When the students changed their locations or networks to find better connectivity, their satisfaction with ERT decreased ($X^2 = 22.072$; $p = 0.000$).

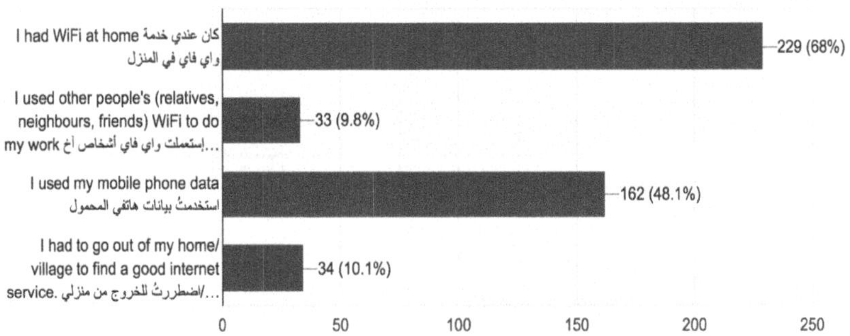

Fig. 6 Location of internet service (*Source* Authors' calculations)

Table 6 Where and how students got their internet and satisfaction with ERT

Chi-Square Tests

	Value	*Df*	*Asymp. Sig. (2-sided)*
Pearson Chi-Square	22.072[a]	3	0.000
Likelihood Ratio	22.442	3	0.000
Linear-by-Linear Association	3.769	1	0.052
No of Valid Cases	254		

[a]0 cells (0.0%) have an expected count of less than 5. The minimum expected count is 16.44
Source Authors' calculations.

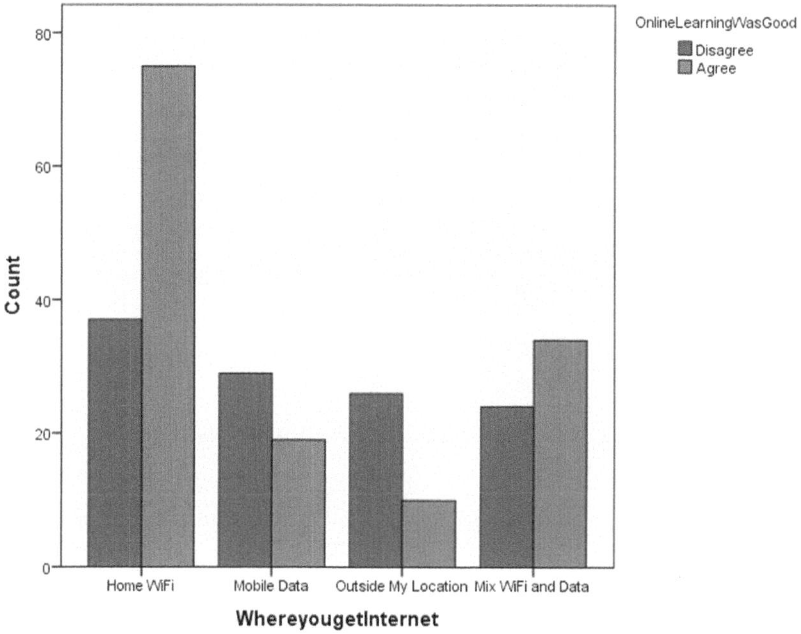

Fig. 7 Where students got their internet and satisfaction with online learning (*Source* Authors' calculations)

The students also rated their technical/IT skills before engaging with ERT, and the results in Fig. 8 indicate that they believed that they had adequate knowledge and capabilities.

Interestingly, according to data from Table 7 and Fig. 9 below, students' previous knowledge of IT was not a significant factor affecting their satisfaction with online learning ($X^2 = 4.362$; $p = 0.113$).

Moving on to the virtual learning environment, the students mentioned the applications (apps) they used to conduct their online learning, i.e., attending classes, communicating, and submitting assignments (See Fig. 10 for a comparison of the three aspects). The choice of apps was usually determined for the students by the course instructors.

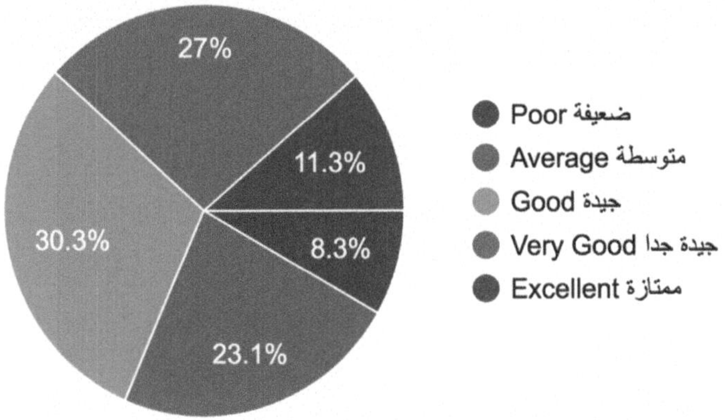

Fig. 8 Students' IT skills prior to ERT (*Source* Authors' calculations)

Table 7 Previous technical knowledge and satisfaction with online learning

Chi-Squared Tests			
	Value	*Df*	*Asymp. Sig. (2-sided)*
Pearson Chi-Square	**4.362**[a]	2	**0.113**
Likelihood Ratio	4.399	2	0.111
Linear-by-Linear Association	1.120	1	0.290
No of Valid Cases	254		

[a]0 cells (0.0%) have an expected count of less than 5. The minimum expected count is 8.68
Source Authors' calculations

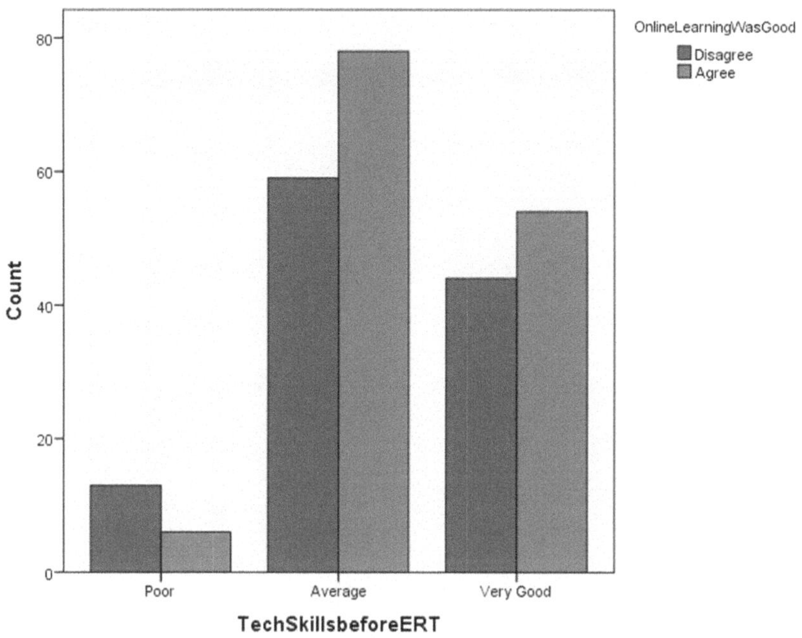

Fig. 9 Technical skills before ERT and satisfaction with online learning (*Source* Authors' calculations)

However, due to the condition of their internet, some students may have opted or been forced to use a different but more accessible tool.

Using a five-point Likert scale, the final two questions zoomed in on the following three issues:

a. Students' readiness for the sudden shift to online learning;
b. Their courses and teachers during ERT;
c. The overall perception of online learning during ERT.

Some highlights from the main findings are reported below (sample size 337). 'Neutral' and N/A responses were disregarded but not excluded.

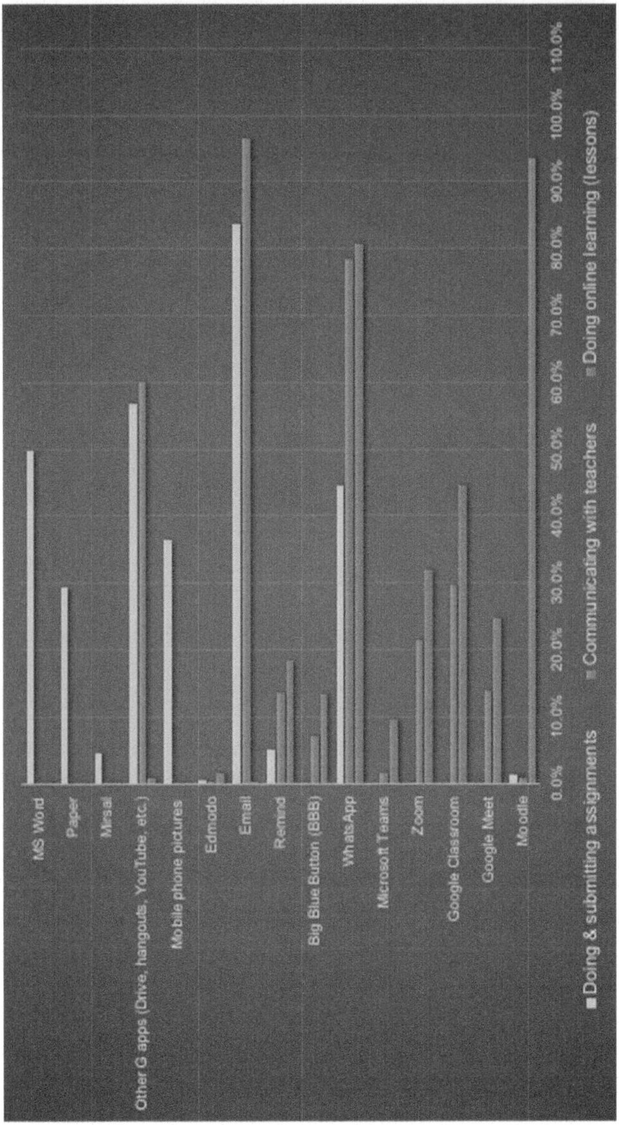

Fig. 10 Apps students used for online learning during ERT (*Source* Authors' calculations)

First, regarding their technical and personal readiness, some of the most salient results showed that:

- Around 72% encountered problems with their internet service during ERT.
- About 61% were technically ready for online learning; however, about one-third had issues using the course tools.
- Half of the students felt they needed training for online learning.
- About 40.4% were not happy about joining online classes.

Second, in respect of courses, the results indicate that:

- 66% had problems understanding materials during online lessons.
- Although around 47.5% of the students had difficulties completing their assignments and homework, submission was an easy task for about 46%.
- Approximately 60% found it challenging to work independently.
- A majority of students (67%) said that they did their homework independently; yet, about 51% and 32% confessed that they got help either from the internet or their family and friends, respectively.
- Course workload was not considered good by 40%.

Students also expressed their satisfaction with their teachers during ERT.

- Approximately 53% of students said that their teachers helped them with problems.
- In terms of communication with teachers, 47.2% said that it was easy; however, the interaction was deemed effective only for 35.6%.
- Around 40% of the students did not abide by communication rules and attempted to connect with their teachers outside of working hours (8 am–4 pm).
- Only 37% had teachers who motivated them to learn.

Finally, their overall perceptions of ERT indicate that:

- Online learning improved the technical skills of about 52% of the participants.
- More than half of them (51.3%) did not believe that online learning was more effective than face-to-face classes.
- Approximately 41% were not happy about the online learning experience.
- Around 38.9% noted that online learning harmed their personal life.
- Online learning was a good experience for 40.9%.

8 Discussion

The purpose of this chapter was to understand how students, as end-receivers, perceived Emergency Remote Teaching (ERT) by understanding their experiences when they transitioned from on-campus classes to online learning during COVID-19. This abrupt shift did not allow for much preparation for HEIs to deliver appropriate online instruction. The students were too unprepared to receive this kind of learning, and they were impacted the most. Unfortunately, they are not heard enough. Therefore, the researchers realized the need for and importance of adopting a bottom-up approach to gather students' feedback to help practitioners, administrators, and policymakers to critically assess the ERT experience and identify opportunities for improvement. This section will discuss the main findings under six categories.

8.1 Readiness of Students

The student's readiness can be looked at from two angles, namely technological and technical. The former refers to the availability of suitable devices and network accessibility and quality. The results indicate that this significantly affected students' online learning experience. For example, ensuring that all students had access to suitable laptops or desktops (equity) would have facilitated their learning. More importantly, the quality of the internet at home may lead to a lack or loss of learning, as Di Pietro et al. (2020) reported. On the other hand, technical skills involve awareness and knowledge of applications, tools, and platforms the HEIs adopt to offer online courses. The findings show that although students possessed adequate technical skills for online learning, some students had problems handling the different tools for online lessons and doing assignments which might lead to stress (Handel et al., 2020) and lower performance levels (Hadwin et al., 2022).

8.2 Communication and Interaction With Teachers

There was an overnight change in how students communicated with their teachers and peers in ERT. Communication became completely virtual, for which neither teachers nor students were ready in an absolute sense. It is well-established that virtual communication appears unnatural to students (Gonzalez et al., 2022). However, this chapter also reveals that teachers used a variety of platforms to communicate with students. Sometimes, these platforms also varied from one course to another, which compromised the effectiveness of communication and interaction (Yates et al., 2020) even more. In addition, teachers used various platforms to deliver instruction (Burns et al., 2020; OECD, 2020). This could have also caused distraction and confusion among the students trying to keep pace with all the changes.

8.3 Course Materials

The results show that most students were unhappy with the course material, which is in line with what research has to say about the lack of preparation in planning, designing, and development of ERT course materials (Hodges et al., 2020; Mohmmed, et al., 2020). Further, these course contents were delivered by teachers who have been teaching students in the mortar and concrete walls of the classroom and probably did not have much experience delivering online instruction (Hodges et al., 2020; Rapanta et al., 2020). This would have led the students to report feeling overwhelmed during online learning because of issues related to the content, course workload, or lack of motivation by teachers.

8.4 Online Learning and Gender Ability

An interesting finding is that both male and female respondents demonstrated equal ability and willingness to deal with online learning. This contrasts sharply with available literature that shows that male students are better equipped with digital readiness (Senkbell et al., 2021) compared to female students (Voltmer et al., 2021). This could be attributed to different contexts and the policies adopted by governments to impart equal opportunities for education to both genders in the Sultanate.

8.5 *Students' Well-being and Emotions During ERT*

The well-being of students is another critical aspect of the findings since many respondents said that they felt confused as they began the online learning journey. Feelings of frustration were also reported, especially around the middle of the semester. In addition, many students described being stressed, afraid, and worried throughout ERT. The sudden shift to online learning coupled with a lack of information and insufficient digital and psychological readiness presented a new and different environment for students. This was expected to cause a flux of negative emotions. Indeed, a significant increase in tension and worry compared to a decrease in happiness was reported by Obermeier et al. (2022) among students during ERT. Added to that is the general fact that in crises, people are already under trauma because of the pandemic and its consequences on personal and social life (Bozkurt & Sharma, 2020).

8.6 *Overall ERT Experience*

The results show that students had mixed experiences. Many of them felt that online learning was ineffective compared to face-to-face teaching. This resonates with what Hodges et al. (2020) warn us of ERT being a temporary solution to an immediate problem. Some students were also unhappy about online learning experiences, which matches with Aristovnik et al.'s (2020) assertion that students' ERT experiences vary from place to place depending on educational access, continuity, and quality. Some students faced specific issues such as not being able to complete their assignments and finding it challenging to work independently. As a result, they had to take help from friends and family. In addition, students' isolation during the pandemic could have unsettled them (Araújo et al., 2020) and caused a lack of self-discipline (Bao, 2020) and lower confidence in the later stages of ERT.

9 Limitations

The objective of this chapter was to gain a thorough understanding of ERT from the students' perspectives, as there is limited research on this particular aspect in Oman. Most ERT studies in this context focus on teachers, curriculum, and administration issues. This bottom-up approach has certain limitations. To begin with, it is a small-scale research confined to one higher education institution in the Sultanate of Oman, and thus, generalizations must be made with care. Moreover, the findings are derived from a single instrument, namely an online questionnaire survey. Conducting sample follow-up interviews could have enriched the data.

10 Conclusion and Implications

Emergency remote teaching or ERT has received much attention due to the COVID-19 pandemic. However, students' perceptions and experiences of this phenomenon have not been researched enough, especially in higher education. To this end, the chapter gains importance in contributing to this under-researched area. Students, as we know, constitute the most critical segment of tertiary education since they are its most vital stakeholders. Moreover, their experiences can help educators and policymakers critically assess any learning process, particularly in emergencies, to improve future experiences. That is, to help develop good policies should there be any other such crisis.

The findings provide insights for heads of institutions, administrators, researchers, and policymakers to make decisions that can help avoid the potential pitfalls of ERT and related practices. They also help online and blended learning practitioners in their choice of approach to technology for teaching and learning, as well as in devising policies to integrate online with on-site classes to complement learning.

The fact that the results show no significant correlation between students' gender and prior technical skills and their satisfaction with ERT suggests that both genders are ready to undertake online learning. However, they may need some training for the specific or specialized educational tools decided by each HEI in their given context. This finding invites HEIs to rethink their approach to education and eventually integrate some aspects of remote teaching/e-learning into their standard teaching, i.e., adopting a hybrid approach is inevitable.

Nevertheless, the main factor affecting student satisfaction with ERT is related to technological infrastructure, i.e., availability of network services, quality of internet, and type of device. This has enormous implications for the Ministry of HE and Research and Innovation in the Sultanate of Oman and internet service providers (ISPs) to revisit their policies and enter into agreements to upgrade their services to meet the requirements of the twenty-first century. In addition, it is recommended that HEIs create a live database of students' technological and technical readiness to help implement their strategic plans.

Acknowledgements The authors would like to thank Dr. Mohammed Hadra, IT senior instructor at the Center for Preparatory Studies, Sultan Qaboos University, Oman, for his valuable assistance in conducting an inferential statistical analysis of the data.

References

Al Amoush, A. B., & Sandhu, K. (2020). Digital transformation of learning management systems at universities: Case analysis for student perspectives. In K. Sandhu (Ed.), *Digital transformation and innovative services for business and learning* (pp. 41–61). IGI Global.

Al-Youbi, A. O., Al-Hayani, A., Bardesi, H. J., Basheri, M., Lytras, M. D., & Aljohani, N. R. (2020). The King Abdulaziz University (KAU) pandemic framework: A methodological approach to leverage social media for the sustainable management of higher education in crisis. *Sustainability, 12*(11), 4367.

Ana, A., Minghat, A. D., Purnawarman, P., Saripudin, S., Muktiarni, M., Dwiyanti, V., & Mustakim, S. S. (2020). Students' perceptions of the twists and turns of E-learning in the midst of the COVID-19 outbreak. *Romanian Journal for Multidimensional Education/Revista Romaneasca pentru Educatie Multidimensionala, 12*, 15–26.

Araújo, F., de Lima, L., Cidade, P., Nobre, C. B., & Neto, M. (2020). Impact of Sars-Cov-2 and Its reverberation in global higher education and mental health. *Psychiatry Research, 288*, 112977. https://doi.org/10.1016/j.psychres.2020.112977

Aristovnik, A., Keržič, D., Ravšelj, D., Tomaževič, N., & Umek, L. (2020). Impacts of the COVID-19 pandemic on life of higher education students: A global perspective. *Sustainability, 12*(20), 8438.

Arora A. K., & Srinivasan R. (2020). Impact of pandemic COVID-19 on the teaching-learning process: A study of higher education teachers. *Prabandhan*

Indian Journal of Management, 13(4). https://doi.org/10.17010/pijom/2020/v13i4/151825

Asanov, I., Flores, F., McKenzie, D., Mensmann, M., & Schulte, M. (2021). Remote-learning, time-use, and mental health of Ecuadorian high-school students during the COVID-19 quarantine. *World Development, 138*, 105225. https://doi.org/10.1016/j.worlddev.2020.105225

Asio, J. M. R., & Bayucca, S. (2021). Spearheading education during the COVID-19 rife: Administrators' level of digital competence and schools' readiness on distance learning. *Journal of Pedagogical Sociology and Psychology, 3*(1), 19–26. https://doi.org/10.33902/JPSP.2021364728

Bao, W. (2020). COVID-19 and online teaching in higher education: A case study of Peking University. *Human Behavior and Emerging Technologies, 2*, 113–115. https://onlinelibrary.wiley.com/doi/pdf/10.1002/hbe2.191

Baran, E., & AlZoubi, D. (2020). Human-centered design as a frame for transition to remote teaching during the COVID-19 pandemic. *Journal of Technology and Teacher Education, 28*(2), 365–372.

Bond, M., Bedenlier, S., Marín, V. I., & Händel, M. (2021). Emergency remote teaching in higher education: Mapping the first global online semester. *International Journal of Educational Technology in Higher Education, 18*(1), 1–24.

Bozkurt, A., & Sharma, R. C. (2020). Emergency remote teaching in a time of global crisis due to CoronaVirus pandemic. *Asian Journal of Distance Education, 15*(1), i–vi.

Bozkurt, A., Jung, I., Xiao, J., Vladimirschi, V., Schuwer, R., Egorov, G., Lambert, S. R., Al-Freih, M., Pete, J., Olcott, D., Rodes, V., Aranciaga, I., Bali, M., Alvarez, A. V., Roberts, J., Pazurek, A., Raffaghelli, J. E., Panagiotou, N., ... & Paskevicius, M. (2020). A global outlook to the interruption of education due to COVID-19 pandemic: Navigating in a time of uncertainty and crisis. *Asian Journal of Distance Education, 15*(1), 1–126.

Burns, A., Danyluk, P., Kapoyannis, T., & Kendrick, A. (2020). Leading the pandemic practicum: One teacher education response to the COVID-19 crisis. *International Journal of E-Learning & Distance Education, 35*(2), 1–25.

Canese, V., & Amarilla, J. (2020). Educational administrators facing COVID-19 measures in Paraguay. *Journal of Educational Technology Development and Exchange* (JETDE), *13*(1), 4. https://aquila.usm.edu/jetde/vol13/iss1/4/

Cao, W., Fang, Z., Hou, G., Han, M., Xu, X., Dong, J., & Zheng, J. (2020). The psychological impact of the COVID-19 epidemic on college students in China. *Psychiatry Research, 287*, 112934. https://doi.org/10.1016/j.psychres.2020.112934

Castelli, F. R., & Sarvary, M. A. (2021). Why students do not turn on their video cameras during online classes and an equitable and inclusive plan to encourage them to do so. *Ecology and Evolution, 11*(8), 3565–3576.

Cavus, N., Mohammed, Y. B., & Yakubu, M. N. (2021). Determinants of learning management systems during COVID-19 pandemic for sustainable education. *Sustainability, 13*(9), 5189. MDPI AG. https://www.mdpi.com/2071-1050/13/9/5189

Chu, T. L., & (A.). (2022). Applying positive psychology to foster student engagement and classroom community amid the COVID-19 pandemic and beyond. *Scholarship of Teaching and Learning in Psychology, 8*(2), 154–163. https://doi.org/10.1037/stl0000238

Crick, T., Knight, C., Watermeyer, R., & Goodall, J. (2020, September). The impact of COVID-19 and "Emergency Remote Teaching" on the UK computer science education community. In *United Kingdom & Ireland Computing Education Research conference* (pp. 31–37).

Devaney, S., Miola, J., Cave, E., Purshouse, C., & Heywood, R. (2020). Healthcare professional standards in pandemic conditions: The duty to obtain consent to treatment. *Journal of Bioethical Inquiry, 17*(4), 789–792. https://doi.org/10.1007/s11673-020-10048-1

Di Pietro, G., Biagi, F., Costa, P., Karpiński, Z., & Mazza, J. (2020). *The likely impact of COVID-19 on education: Reflections based on the existing literature and recent international datasets* (Vol. 30275). Publications Office of the European Union.

Dietrich, J., Greiner, F., Weber-Liel, D., Berweger, B., Kämpfe, N., & Kracke, B. (2021). Does an individualized learning design improve university student online learning? A randomized field experiment. *Computers in Human Behavior, 122*, 106819.

Dong, Y., & Ishige, A. (2022). Studying abroad from home: An exploration of international graduate students' perceptions and experiences of emergency remote teaching. *Education Sciences, 12*(2). https://doi.org/10.3390/educsci12020098

Duraku, Z. H., & Hoxha, L. (Preprint) The impact of COVID-19 on education and on the well-being of teachers, parents, and students: Challenges related to remote (online) learning and opportunities for advancing the quality of education. https://www.researchgate.net/publication/341297812

Duraku, Z. H., & Hoxha, N. (2020). The impact of COVID-19, school closure, and social isolation on gifted students' wellbeing and attitudes toward remote (online) learning. In Z. H. Duraku (Ed.), *Impact of the COVID-19 Pandemic on Education and Wellbeing* (pp. 130–169).

EUA. (2020). *COVID-19 and Universities*. European University Association, Brussels, Belgium. www.eua.eu/issues/27:covid-19-and-universities-in-europe.html

Fauville, G., Queiroz, A. C., Hambrick, L., Brown, B. A., & Bailenson, J. N. (2021). Participatory research on using virtual reality to teach ocean acidification: A study in the marine education community. *Environmental Education Research, 27*(2), 254–278.

Filho, W. L., Wall, T., Rayman-Bacchus, L., Mifsud, M., Pritchard, D. J., Lovren, V. O., Farinha, C., Petrovic, D., & Balogun, A. (2021). Impacts of COVID-19 and social isolation on academic staff and students at universities: A cross-sectional study. *BMC Public Health, 21*(1213). https://doi.org/10.1186/s12889-021-11040-z

Fisher, D., Frey, N., & Hattie, J. (2020). *The distance learning playbook, grades K-12: Teaching for engagement and impact in any setting*. Sage Publications.

González-Calvo, G., Barba-Martín, R. A., Bores-García, D., & Hortigüela-Alcalá, D. (2022). The (virtual) teaching of physical education in times of pandemic. *European Physical Education Review, 28*(1), 205–224.

Graham, A., & Sahlberg, P. (2020, March 26). Schools are moving online, but not all children. *The Conversation*. https://theconversation.com/schools-are-moving-online-but-not-all-children-start-out-digitally-equal-134650

Greenhow, C., & Chapman, A. (2020). Social distancing meet social media: Digital tools for connecting students, teachers, and citizens in an emergency. *Information and Learning Sciences, 121*(5/6), 341–352. https://doi.org/10.1108/ILS-04-2020-0134

Guskaroska, A., Dux Speltz, E., Zawadzki, Z., & Kurt, Ş. (2022). Students' perceptions of emergency remote teaching in a writing course during COVID-19. *Frontiers in Education, 7*. 965659. https://doi.org/10.3389/feduc.2022.965659

Hadwin, A. F., Sukhawathanakul, P., Rostampour, R., & Bahena-Olivares, L. M. (2022). Do self-regulated learning practices and intervention mitigate the impact of academic challenges and COVID-19 distress on academic performance during online learning? *Frontiers in Psychology, 13.*

Händel, M., Stephan, M., Gläser-Zikuda, M., Kopp, B., Bedenlier, S., & Ziegler, A. (2020). Digital readiness and its effects on higher education students' socio-emotional perceptions in the context of the COVID-19 pandemic. *Journal of Research on Technology in Education*, 1–13.

Hashim, S., Masek, A., Abdullah, N., Aini, N., Paimin, A., & Muda, W. (2020). Students' intention to share information via social media: A case study of COVID-19 pandemic. *Indonesian Journal of Science and Technology, 5*(2), 236–245. https://doi.org/10.17509/ijost.v5i2.24586

Hippe, R., Araújo, L., & Dinis da Costa, P. (2016). Equity in education in Europe. Publications Office of the European Union; EUR 28285 EN, https://doi.org/10.2791/255948

Hira, A., & Anderson, E. (2021). Motivating online learning through project-based learning during the 2020 COVID-19 pandemic. *IAFOR Journal of Education, 9*(2), 93–110.

Hodges, C., Moore, S., Lockee, B., Trust, T., & Bond, A. (2020). The difference between emergency remote teaching and online learning. *Educause Review*. https://er.educause.edu/articles/2020/3/thedifference-between-emergencyremote-teaching-and-online-learning

Hopp, M. D. S., Handel, M., Bedenlier, S., Glaeser-Zikuda, M., Kammerl, R., Kopp, B., & Ziegler, A. (2021). The structure of social networks and its link to higher education students' socio-emotional loneliness during COVID-19. *Frontiers in Psychology*, 12. https://doi.org/10.3389/fpsyg.2021.733867

Jeyaraj, J. J. (2023). Drawing on students' lived experiences in emergency remote teaching (ERT): Reflections from a critical pedagogy inspired writing class. *Asia Pacific Journal of Education, 43*(2), 450–462. https://doi.org/10.1080/02188791.2021.1941756

Kells, L. M. (2021). *Educational administrators' decision-making experiences during COVID-19 pandemic: A phenomenological study*. Available from ProQuest Dissertations & Theses Global. https://www.proquest.com/dissertations-theses/educational-administrators-decision-making/docview/2545627167/se-2

Keyserling, K., Janetos, E., & Sprague, C. (2021). Teaching telehealth during a pandemic and beyond: An intern's survival guide for virtual medicine. *Journal of General Internal Medicine, 36*(10), 3219–3223.

Kier, M., & Clark, K. (2020). The rapid response of William & Mary's School of Education to support preservice teachers and equitably provide mentoring to elementary learners in a culture of an international pandemic. *Journal of Technology and Teacher Education, 28*(2), 321–327. Society for Information Technology & Teacher Education. https://www.learntechlib.org/primary/p/216153/

Lefever, S., Dal, M., & Matthíasdóttir, Á. (2007). Online data collection in academic research: Advantages and limitations. *British Journal of Educational Technology, 38*(4), 574–582. https://doi.org/10.1111/j.1467-8535.2006.00638.x

Lepp, L., Aaviku, T., Leijen, Ä., Pedaste, M., & Saks, K. (2021). Teaching during COVID-19: The decisions made in teaching. *Education Sciences, 11*(2), 47. https://doi.org/10.3390/educsci11020047

Longhurst, G. J., Stone, D. M., Dulohery, K., Scully, D., Campbell, T., & Smith, C. F. (2020). Strength, weakness, opportunity, threat (SWOT) analysis of the adaptations to anatomical education in the United Kingdom and Republic of Ireland in response to the COVID-19 pandemic. *Anatomical Sciences Education, 13*(3), 301–311.

Manca, S., & Delfino, M. (2021). Adapting educational practices in emergency remote education: Continuity and change from a student perspective. *British Journal of Educational Technology, 52*(4).

Mao, Y. (2020). Combating COVID-19 through collaborative governance: Lessons from East Asia. *Chinese Public Administration Review, 11*(2), 132–141. https://doi.org/10.22140/cpar.v11i2.255

McVay, M. (2001). *How to be a successful distance learning student: Learning on the internet*. Prentice Hall.

Meda, N., Pardini, S., Slongo, I., Bodini, L., Zordan, M. A., Rigobello, P., Visioli, F., & Novara, C. (2021). Students' mental health problems before, during, and after the COVID-19 lockdown in Italy. *Journal of Psychiatric Research, 134*, 69–77. https://doi.org/10.1016/j.jpsychires.2020.12.045

Metchik, A., Boyd, S., Kons, Z., Vilchez, V., Villano, A. M., Lazar, J. F., Anand, R. J., Jackson, P., & Stern, J. (2021). How we do it: Implementing a virtual, multi-institutional collaborative education model for the COVID-19 pandemic and beyond. *Journal of Surgical Education, 78*(4), 1041–1045. https://doi.org/10.1016/j.jsurg.2020.12.012

Mohmmed, A. O., Khidhir, B. A., Nazeer, A., & Vijayan, V. J. (2020). Emergency remote teaching during coronavirus pandemic: The current trend and future directive at Middle East College Oman. *Innovative Infrastructure Solutions, 5*, 1–11. https://doi.org/10.1007/s41062-020-00326-7

Obermeier, R., Gläser-Zikuda, M., Bedenlier, S., Kammerl, R., Kopp, B., Ziegler, A., & Händel, M. (2022). Stress development during emergency remote teaching in higher education. *Learning and Individual Differences, 98*, 102178.

OECD. (2020). *Learning remotely when schools close: How well are students and schools prepared? Insights from PISA*.https://www.oecd.org/coronavirus/policy-responses/learning-remotely-when-schools-close-how-well-are-students-and-schools-prepared-insights-from-pisa-3bfda1f7/

Osika, W., Friberg, P., & Wahrborg, P. (2007). A new short self-rating questionnaire to assess stress in children. *International Journal of Behavioral Medicine, 14*(2), 108–117.

Osman, M. E. (2020). Global impact of COVID-19 on education systems: The emergency remote teaching at Sultan Qaboos University. *Journal of Education for Teaching, 46*(4), 463–471.

Özer, M. (2020). Educational policy actions by the Ministry of National Education during COVID-19. *Kastamonu Education Journal, 28*(3), 1124–1129. https://doi.org/10.24106/kefdergi.722280

Planning & Statistics Department. (2020). *Annual statistics Book 2019–2020*. Sultan Qaboos University, Oman. https://www.squ.edu.om/Portals/0/DNNGalleryPro/uploads/2020/9/3/AnnualStatisticsBOOK_2019-2020_compressed.pdf

Qamar, F. (2021). Technological transformation in higher education: Myths and realities. *The Rise*. https://therise.co.in/6888/technological-transformation-in-higher-education/

Quinn, N., Wilson, A., MacIntyre, G., & Tinklin, T. (2009). 'People look at you differently': Students' experience of mental health support within higher education. *British Journal of Guidance & Counselling*, *37*(4), 405–418. https://doi.org/10.1080/03069880903161385

Raaper, R., Brown, C., & Llewellyn, A. (2022). Student support as social network: Exploring non-traditional student experiences of academic and well-being support during the COVID-19 pandemic. *Educational Review, 74*(3), 402–421.

Rapanta, C., Botturi, L., Goodyear, P., Guàrdia, L., & Koole, M. (2020). Online university teaching during and after the COVID-19 crisis: Refocusing teacher presence and learning activity. *Postdigital Science and Education, 2*(3), 923–945.

Rastogi, R., & Priya, A. (2020). Recent trends in Indian higher education system. *International Journal of Advanced Science and Technology, 29*(8), 2216–2222.

Ren, J., Li, X., Chen, S., Chen, S., & Nie, Y. (2020). The influence of factors such as parenting stress and social support on the state anxiety in parents of special needs children during the COVID-19 epidemic. *Frontiers in Psychology, 11*, 565393. https://doi.org/10.3389/fpsyg.2020.565393

Rohs, M., & Ganz, M. (2015). MOOCs and the claim of education for all: A disillusion by empirical Dana. *International Review of Research in Open and Distributed Learning, 16*(6). https://doi.org/10.19173/irrodl.v16i6.2033

Saleh, A., & Bista, K. (2017). Examining factors impacting online survey response rates in educational research: Perceptions of graduate students. *Journal of MultiDisciplinary Evaluation, 13* (2), 63–74.

Salman, M., Mustafa, Z. U., Asif, N., Zaidi, H. A., Hussain, K., Shehzadi, N., Khan, T. M., & Saleem, Z. (2020). Knowledge, attitude and preventive practices related to COVID-19: A cross-sectional study in two Pakistani university populations. *Drugs & Therapy Perspectives*, *36*(7), 319–325. https://doi.org/10.1007/s40267-020-00737-7

Salta, K., Paschalidou, K., Tsetseri, M., & Koulougliotis, D. (2022). Shift from a traditional to a distance learning environment during the COVID-19 pandemic: University students' engagement and interactions. *Science & Education, 31*(1), 93–122.

Senkbeil, J. C., Griffin, D. J., Sherman-Morris, K., Saari, J., & Brothers, K. (2021). Improving tornado warning communication for deaf and hard of hearing audiences. *Journal of Operational Meteorology*, *9*(2), 18–35. https://doi.org/10.15191/nwajom.2021.0902

Shim, T. E., & Lee, S. Y. (2020). College students' experience of emergency remote teaching due to COVID-19. *Children and Youth Services Review, 119*, 105578.

Shin, M., & Hickey, K. (2020). Needs a little TLC: Examining college students' emergency remote teaching and learning experiences during COVID-19. *Journal of Further and Higher Education, 45*(7), 973–986.https://doi.org/10.1080/0309877X.2020.1847261

Smith, P. J., Murphy, K. L., & Mahoney, S. E. (2003). Towards identifying factors underlying readiness for online learning: An exploratory study. *Distance Education, 24*(1), 57–67. https://doi.org/10.1080/01587910303043

Taskeen, A. (2020). The privilege of #pivotonline: A South African perspective. *Open Development and Education*. https://opendeved.net/2020/04/22/the-privilege-of-pivotonline/

Tilak, J. B., & Kumar, A. G. (2022). Policy changes in global higher education: What lessons do we learn from the COVID-19 Pandemic? *Higher Education Policy*, 1–19.

Toquero, C. M. (2020). Emergency remote teaching amid COVID-19: The turning point. *Asian Journal of Distance Education, 15*(1), 185–188.

United Nations. (2020). Policy brief: Education during COVID-19 and beyond. https://unsdg.un.org/sites/default/files/2020-08/sg_policy_brief_covid-19_and_education_august_2020.pdf

Veletsianos, G., & Houlden, S. (2020). Radical flexibility and relationality as responses to education in times of crisis. *Postdigital Science and Education, 2*(3), 849–862.

Voltmer, K., Hormann, O., Pietsch, M., Maehler, C., & Von Salisch, M. (2021). Teaching the teachers about language support strategies: Effects on young children's language development. *Frontiers in Psychology, 12*, 660750. https://doi.org/10.3389/fpsyg.2021.660750

Wang, G., Zhang, Y, Zhao J., Zhang, J., & Jiang, F. (2020). Mitigate the effects of home confinement on children during the COVID-19 outbreak. *Lancet, 395* (10228). https://doi.org/10.1016/S0140-6736(20)30547-X

Whittle, C., Tiwari, S., Yan, S., & Williams, J. (2020). Emergency remote teaching environment: A conceptual framework for responsive online teaching in crises. *Information and Learning Sciences., 121*(5/6), 311–319. https://doi.org/10.1108/ILS-04-2020-0099

Williamson, B., Eynon, R., & Potter, J. (2020). Pandemic politics, pedagogies and practices: Digital technologies and distance education during the coronavirus emergency. *Learning, Media and Technology, 45*(2), 107–114.

World Bank. (2020). The COVID-19 crisis response: Supporting tertiary education for continuity, adaptation, and innovation. *World bank Group Education*, Washington, DC, http://pubdocs.worldbank.org/en/621991586463915490/WB-Tertiary-Ed-and-Covid-19-Crisis-for-public-use-April-9.pdf

Yates, A., Starkey, L., Egerton, B., & Flueggen, F. (2020). High school students' experience of online learning during COVID-19: The influence of technology and pedagogy. *Technology, Pedagogy and Education*. https://doi.org/10.1080/1475939X.2020.1854337

CHAPTER 14

Learning Loss in Lockdown: Impact of COVID-19 on Schooling in India

Sameer Ahmad Khan and Furqan Qamar

1 Introduction

The history of coronavirus goes back to the mid-1960s when D.A. Tyrrell and M.L. Bynoe, whilst studying cultivation of virus, found a new kind of virus associated with the common cold. It was not until the late 70s that the group of viruses affecting humans and animals was classified as "the coronavirus", because of its crown-like appearance. The studies conducted resulted in findings that indicated coronavirus to be responsible for a lot of respiratory infections, however, the pathogenicity was considered to be low (Tyrrell & Bynoe, 1966). Five decades later, a novel virus from the same group has wreaked havoc across the globe. COVID-19 was first reported from Wuhan, Hubei province of China in December 2019. The origins of the Sars-cov-2 are still a topic of debate in the

S. A. Khan (✉) · F. Qamar
Department of Management Studies, Jamia Millia Islamia, New Delhi, India
e-mail: sameer2009148@st.jmi.ac.in

F. Qamar
e-mail: fqamar@jmi.ac.in

A. Mishrif (ed.), *Perspectives on Human Capital Development*,
https://doi.org/10.1007/978-981-97-5246-1_14

academic community but, a majority of academicians believe it to have "jumped" from a Pangolin to a human after direct contact.

The pandemic not only claimed human lives in an unprecedented manner but crippled the economy in a way that affected every sector of the country. Education has been no exception. The Indian education system boasts of being one of the largest education systems in the world catering to the needs of more than 250 million students, from pre-primary to higher secondary levels. To prevent the outbreak, India announced its first nationwide lockdown on the 24th of March 2022. As a part of this exercise, schools and educational institutions were to remain shut for the period, which was later extended multiple times. The government had instructed the schools, both public and private, to continue the delivery of classes in online mode until further notification. The initial phase was characterized by confusion and uncertainty, but by the end of May 2020, the majority of schools had implemented some form of remote education. However, attempts to reopen schools resulted in a significant increase in COVID-19 cases, leading to the subsequent closure of schools once again.

Days turned into weeks and weeks turned into months, India ended up recording the second longest pandemic-induced school closure, at 82 weeks, missing the first spot by just one week to Uganda. In a country like India which relies heavily on the traditional methods of teaching, where digital and remote education is still catching up, the closure of schools had a serious impact on schooling and the state of education in the country.

The closure of schools had far-reaching consequences, especially for marginalized communities, socially disadvantaged groups, and rural populations. These groups faced greater challenges due to the significant digital divide and limited access to technology. The absence of proper guidance from both parents and teachers further exacerbated the educational setbacks faced by students during this period.

This chapter aims to quantitatively measure the impact of the COVID-19 pandemic on the Indian school education system and assess the extent of the damage caused. By analysing various key indicators, such as enrolment rates, dropout rates, learning loss, and the overall quality of education, researchers seek to provide insights into the magnitude of the challenges faced by the education system and the potential long-term implications for students' academic progress and future opportunities.

Through this chapter, policymakers, educators, and stakeholders can gain a comprehensive understanding of the repercussions of the pandemic on the education sector. This knowledge can inform the development of targeted interventions, revised policies, and budgetary allocations to address the specific needs and challenges arising from the disrupted schooling experience

2 Literature Review

The schools of 180 countries were forced into closure because of the outbreak (Azevedo et al., 2020). It was expected that the closure would prevail for at least two semesters urging countries to adopt Emergency Remote Education. Despite the promptness and the efforts, the concerns about learning losses persisted.

According to The Glossary of Education Reform, learning loss refers to any specific or general loss of knowledge and skills or reversals in academic progress, most commonly due to extended gaps or discontinuities in a student's education. Whilst learning loss during the pandemic is a unique situation, and the literature on the subject is limited, there is existing research on the loss of learning and its impact on students in various contexts. For example:

A. Learning During Normal School Days vs. Holiday Breaks: Researchers have compared student learning during regular school days to learning during holiday breaks, such as summer or winter vacations. This can provide insights into the potential learning loss experienced during prolonged school closures. The results consistently indicate that students experience approximately a one-month learning loss during summer breaks, with an even greater loss observed in socially and economically disadvantaged communities (Alexander et al., 2004; Cooper et al., 1996; Slade et al., 2017).
B. Learning Loss During Natural Calamity: Academic studies have examined the impact of natural disasters or weather-related school closures on student learning. These studies can offer insights into the effects of sudden disruptions to the education system on student performance. (Andrabi et al., 2021) used the case of Pakistan where they assessed the impact of school closure due to an earthquake in 2005 which forced students out of school for about 14 weeks. They reported that learning losses were as high as 1.5 years of learning

in the most affected regions. These results are in line with the (Sacerdote, 2012) who found that scores of students affected by Hurricane Katrina and Rita fell sharply.

C. Learning Loss due to Absenteeism: Research on student absenteeism, including extended periods of absence from school, can provide insights into the potential consequences of prolonged disruptions to education. These studies may help understand the impact of extended school closures on student learning outcomes. (Santibañez & Guarino, 2021) observed decline in learning outcome, specifically in numeric abilities as the rate of absenteeism grew in students.

It wouldn't be far-fetched to say that school closures during the COVID-19 pandemic encompass elements of all three types of learning losses. The only point of difference between the two situations was the introduction of Emergency Remote Education. As reported by (Oxfam, 2020), 75% of the government schools reported WhatsApp as their preferred medium for Emergency Remote Education. The situation in the private sector was found to be similar where WhatsApp emerged as the most used medium of education. Albeit WhatsApp emerged as the most dominant medium, it serves as a platform for disseminating information rather than conducting classes. (Muñoz-Najar et al., 2021) highlighted that the countries in the high-income group could rely on internet-based solutions, whilst the countries in the lower-income group had to use a multi-modal approach for the delivery of the lessons. Furthermore, (Pokhrel & Chhetri, 2021) found that the pedagogy used for online education was the same as in-person education and, hence, not very effective.

Pedagogical deficiencies, prolonged closure, inadequate online learning platforms, and loss of livelihood amongst the people are some of the causes that contribute to the learning losses. It is also of uttermost importance to the researchers and the policymakers to reflect on where these losses are most and what should be our way forward. Hence, quantification of the learning loss, both in terms of subject skill and loss of learning opportunity, becomes a key factor in devising policies and remedial framework.

An advantage that developed countries had in this regard was standardized scores. Standardized scores allowed countries to identify problem stratum and employ remedial practices accordingly. For an instance, (Maldonado & De Witte, 2022) used grade 6 standardized scores of past six batches and compared them to the scores of class of 2020 to identify the problem areas. 0.19 standard deviation in Math and 0.29 deviation in Dutch was found amongst the students with learning losses more pronounced in the students from disadvantaged group. Another study in England by (Rose et al., 2021) used national score results of 2017 with post-pandemic score to conclude that 3 months of absence from school affected both reading and mathematical abilities of the students, again, learning losses more pronounced in students belonging to disadvantaged group.

The point identification of the learning deficiencies was possible because of standardized testing. Whilst the majority of studies addressing the quantification of learning losses focus on Western countries, where pre-COVID and post-COVID test results were compared using standardized testing, regrettably, there is a scarcity of empirical evidence from less fortunate and underdeveloped nations, including India. Fortunately, a study conducted (Singh et al., 2022) provides a glimpse of the grim situation by using panel data of 19,000 students from remote village of Tamil Nadu. (Singh et al., 2022) found out 0.34 SD in language and 0.80 SD in numeric abilities. And just like their counterparts from the west, the learning deficiencies were found to be more in socially and economically deprived students.

In the absence of standardized testing, the only option left for policymakers is to assess learning losses in terms of missed opportunities for learning. This leaves a wide room for doubt regarding learning losses in terms of skills, the effect of which is most likely pronounced in the socially-economically backward groups.

Government schools play a crucial role in providing education to marginalized communities and addressing social inequalities. Nevertheless, government schools frequently encounter substantial obstacles such as insufficient infrastructure, a shortage of qualified teachers, and limited available resources. The pandemic has further exacerbated these issues, widening the educational disparities faced by students in these schools. Serious concerns have been raised by experts regarding the future of 32.2 million students, a number that may potentially double in the post-pandemic period, particularly with students from marginalized communities being disproportionately impacted (KMPG & CII, 2021).

The loss of opportunity for students stems from the prolonged disruptions in the education system. School closures and the shift to remote learning have affected students differently based on their socio-economic backgrounds, access to technology, and parental support. Many students, particularly those from marginalized communities or rural areas, have faced barriers to accessing online education and have been disproportionately affected.

3 Research Methods

The primary objective of the chapter is to develop a comprehensive and detailed analysis of the learning loss caused by the pandemic-linked closure of the schools, with a special focus on the children belonging to the socially and economically backward community that relies on the government for schooling. We approach the issue in its entirety by taking key indicators like Total enrolment, Gross Enrolment Ratio (GER), Net Enrolment Ratio (NER), and flow rates like Dropout rates, promotion rate, and repetition rate into consideration to quantify the loss in learning opportunity amongst the students belong to socially backward and economically deprived communities.

The analysis was conducted using secondary data from various government reports namely Unified District Information System for Education (UDISE+), School Education in India—Flash statistics, and Education Statistics—At a Glance (ESG) annual report. Apart from the aforementioned, various studies from independent bodies, like ASER (Annual Survey of Education Report—rural) and Oxfam were also utilized to incorporate any aspects omitted by the government reports.

The chapter uses a counter-factual approach using the time series analysis to analyse the data from UDISE+, Flash statistics, and ESG, to statistically create a hypothetical state of absence of the pandemic and compare it to the actual state. To maintain data consistency, only official government reports have been used, where the period between 2015 and 2020 is referred to as the "pre-pandemic" period, and from 2020 to 2021 is referred to as the "pandemic" period. The modeling of the hypothetical state was done using a one-dimensional time series model with exponential triple smoothening model on MS-Excel. Exponential Triple Smoothing is a forecasting technique that employs three orders of smoothing. This choice was made with the intention of allowing the method to capture any existing seasonality, should it be present.

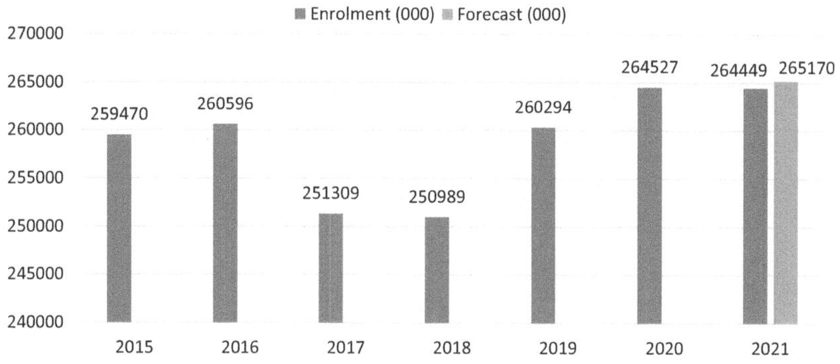

Fig. 1 Total enrolment of students (000) (*Source* [1] Data from 2015–2018: As reported by school education in India—flash statistics 2017–2018; [2] Data from 2019–2021: As reported by UDISE+)

4 Results

4.1 Total Enrolment of Students

Total enrolment of students refers to the number of children, regardless of their age, enrolled at any stage, that is primary, secondary, or higher secondary in an academic year. It reflects the total number of new enrolments at all levels in an academic year (Fig. 1).

From 2015 to 2016, there was a marginal increase in enrolment, with the number of students rising from 259,470 (000) to 260,596 (000). However, in 2017, a decline in enrolment was observed, dropping to 251,309 (000). The trend continued in 2018, with enrolment remaining relatively stable at 250,989 (000). By 2019, there was a recovery and the positive momentum sustained till 2020. The total enrolment of students in the year 2021 was 264,449 (000), recording a minor decline of 643 (000) pupils when compared to the preceding year. Despite the total enrolment exceeding 264,449 (000) across pre-primary to higher secondary levels, India falls short of the projected value of 265,170 (000) by 721 (000) students.

4.2 Gross Enrolment Ratio

The gross enrolment ratio refers to the total number of students admitted to any level of education during an academic year to the population of

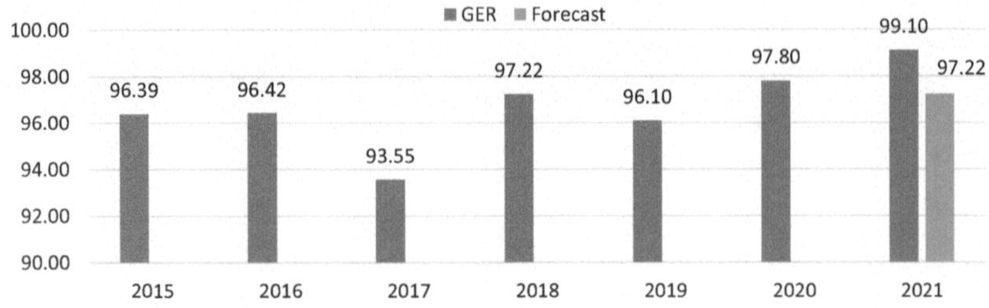

Fig. 2 Gross enrolment ratio (GER) elementary level (1–8) (*Source* [1] Data from 2015–2018: As reported by school education in India—flash statistics 2017–2018; [2] Data from 2019–2021: As reported by UDISE+)

the age group that corresponds to a specific level. The gross enrolment ratio is usually spread on a spectrum of 0 to 100, but sometimes, it can exceed the ceiling. The aforementioned situation happens because of late entrants, early entrants, and grade repetition. In an ideal condition, the higher the GER, the more desirable the condition is.

4.2.1 *Elementary Level (1–8)*

Gross enrolment ratio for the elementary level is calculated as: Number of students enrolled in grade 1–8 ÷ Projected population between the ages of 6 and 13 * 100 (Fig. 2).

Overall, data shows some fluctuation in the GER. The GER slightly increased in the year 2016 by 0.03% and then dropping to 93.55% in the year 2017. The trend reversed and an upward trend can be seen as GER increases to 97.22%, 96.10%, 97.80%, and 99.10%, respectively in the following years. In 2021, the actual GER was 99.10%, surpassing the forecasted value of 97.22% by 1.88%, indicating a positive outcome for enrolment in the elementary level of education.

4.2.2 *Secondary Level (9–10)*

Gross elementary ratio for secondary level is calculated as: Number of students enrolled in grades 9–10 ÷ Projected population between the ages of 14 and 16 * 100 (Fig. 3).

The data shows fluctuation in the GER over the years, with a mix of positive growth, stability, and decline. Initially, it increases for the year 2016 by 2.39% and plateaus for the next. It falls sharply next year by 2.88%. It recovers in the following year gradually before settling at

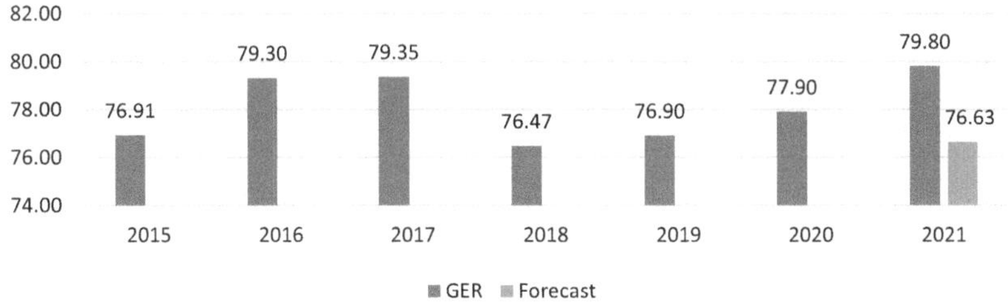

Fig. 3 Gross enrolment ratio (GER) secondary level (9–10) (*Source* [1] Data from 2015–2018: As reported by school education in India—flash statistics 2017–2018; [2] Data from 2019–2021: As reported by UDISE+)

79.80% in 2021, recording the steepest incline of 1.9%. The actual GER for 2021 surpassed the forecasted value by 3.17%, indicating a more positive enrolment outcome.

4.2.3 *Higher Secondary Level (11–12)*

Gross elementary ratio for higher secondary level is calculated as: Number of students enrolled in grades 11–12 ÷ Projected population between the ages of 16 and 18 *100 (Fig. 4).

Data reveals fluctuations in the GER, where it initially increases by 3.49% in the year 2016, before slipping to 55.40 in the year 2017. A further sharp decline can be seen for the year 2018 where it dropped to 48.13. The trend reverses thereon, registering a growth of 1.37%, 1.30%, and 2.40% in the following years. It surpasses the projected value by 5.5%.

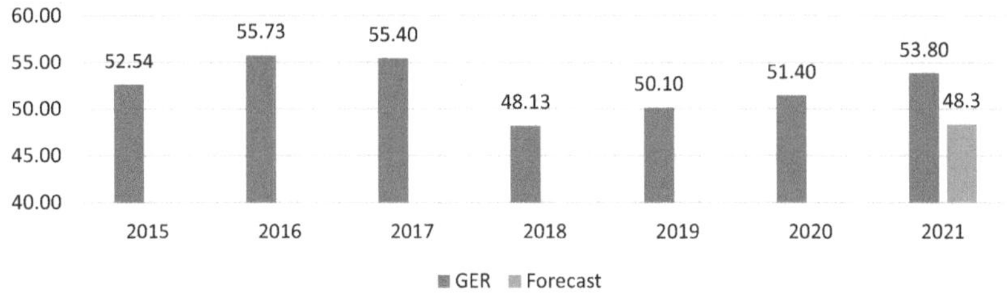

Fig. 4 Gross enrolment ratio (GER) higher secondary level (11–12) (*Source* [1] Data from 2015–2018: As reported by school education in India—flash statistics 2017–2018; [2] Data from 2019–2021: As reported by UDISE+)

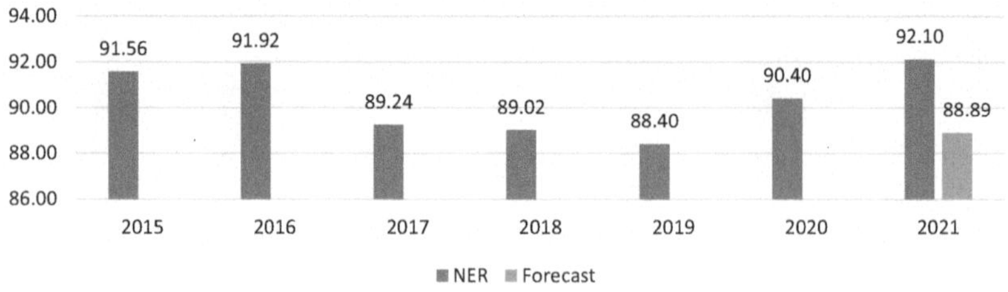

Fig. 5 Net enrolment ratio (NER) elementary level (1–8) (*Source* [1] Data from 2015–2018: As reported by school education in India—flash statistics 2017–2018; [2] Data from 2019–2021: As reported by UDISE+)

4.3 Net Enrolment Ratio

The net enrolment ratio refers to the number of students enrolled at a specific level of education, expressed as a percentage of the projected population of that age group. Since the net enrolment ratio matches the enrolment to the age group, it factors out the overage, underage, and repeat students. Hence, it can never be zero.

4.3.1 Elementary Level (1–8)

Net elementary ratio is calculated as: Number of students studying at the elementary level of ages 6–13 ÷ Population between the ages of 6 and 13 * 100 (Fig. 5).

The NER increased slightly in 2016 by 0.36% before dipping to 89.24% in the year 2017. It further falls to 89.02% in 2018 and to 88.40% in 2019. The trend reverses henceforth showing substantial increase over the next two years. The first surge is registered for the year 2020 where NER increases by 2.00% and 1.7% for the year 2021. It surpasses the projected value by 3.21%.

4.3.2 Secondary Level (9–10)

Net enrolment ratio (secondary) is calculated by: Number of students studying at the secondary level of ages 14–16 ÷ Projected population between the ages of 14 and 16 (Fig. 6).

The data shows a positive growth between 2015 and 2017, where it increased from 48.04 to 51.77%, an increase of 3.73%. However, it declines to 50.23% in 2018 and further to 48.60% in the year 2019. By 2020, there was a recovery, and the NER increased to 50.20%. A further

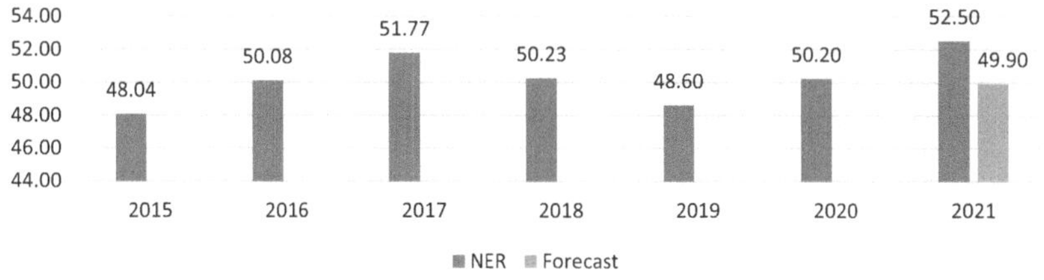

Fig. 6 Net enrolment ratio (NER) secondary level (9–10) (*Source* [1] Data from 2015–2018: As reported by school education in India—flash statistics 2017–2018; [2] Data from 2019–2021: As reported by UDISE+)

increase of 2.3% was recorded in the year 2021, taking the final NER to 52.50%, 2.7% more than the projected forecast of 49.90%.

4.3.3 Higher Secondary Level (11–12)

The net enrolment ratio for the higher secondary level is calculated by: Number of students studying at higher secondary of ages 16–18 ÷ Projected population between the ages of 16 and 18 *100 (Fig. 7).

The data follows a downward trend followed by subsequent recovery. It starts off by decreasing slightly in the year 2016 by 0.37, followed by a further decrease of 1.1% in 2017, and final decrease of 3.18% in 2018. The trend reverses thereon, increasing by 3.03% in 2019, 1.5% in 2020, and 2.40% in 2021. It surpasses the forecasted value of 2021 by 3.64%.

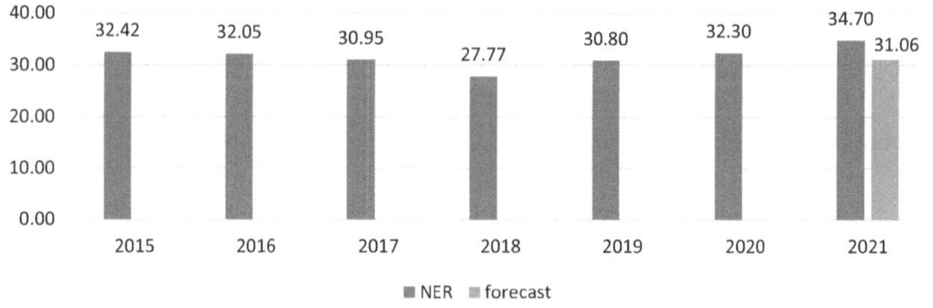

Fig. 7 Net enrolment ratio (NER) higher secondary level (11–12) (*Source* [1] Data from 2015–2018: As reported by school education in India—flash statistics 2017–2018; [2] Data from 2019–2021: As reported by UDISE+)

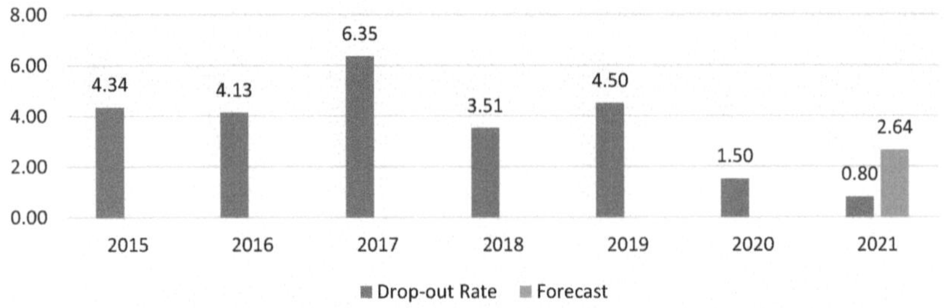

Fig. 8 Dropout rate (DR) primary level (1–5) (*Source* [1] Data from 2015–2018: As reported by school education in India—flash statistics 2017–2018; [2] Data from 2019–2021: As reported by UDISE+)

4.4 *Flow Rate*

Flow rates are referred to as the category of rates that explain the flow of students in and out of the school system. Each of flow rate is a non-negative, and dropout rate + promotion rate + repetition rate = 100

4.4.1 Dropout Rate

The proportion of people enrolled in the same age group and grade in a given academic year who are no longer enrolled in the following year. It is one of the key indicators to monitor and analyse the flow of students in an educational cycle. Dropout rate is calculated by: Promotion rate—repetition rate. Any educational system aims to reduce the dropout rate to a bare minimum—in ideal conditions to 0%. Two consecutive years' data is analysed to compute the dropout rate. By comparing rates across levels, problem levels can be identified that require more policy consideration.

Primary Level

The data shows periods of increase in dropout rates, particularly in 2017, followed by periods of improvements and lower dropout rates in subsequent years. The dropout rate decreased slightly to 4.13% in 2016, before surging to 6.35 in 2017. It quickly recovers and dropout rate falls to 3.51% for the year 2018. It increases by 1.49% for the succeeding year and then drops to 1.50% in 2020 and further to 0.80% in 2021. The forecasted dropout rate was 2.1%, 1.3% more than the actual dropout rate (Fig. 8).

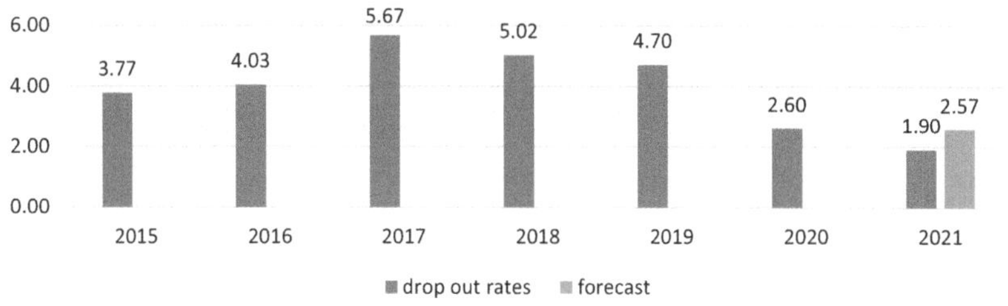

Fig. 9 Dropout rate (DR) upper primary level (6–8) (*Source* [1] Data from 2015–2018: As reported by school education in India—flash statistics 2017–2018; [2] Data from 2019–2021: As reported by UDISE+)

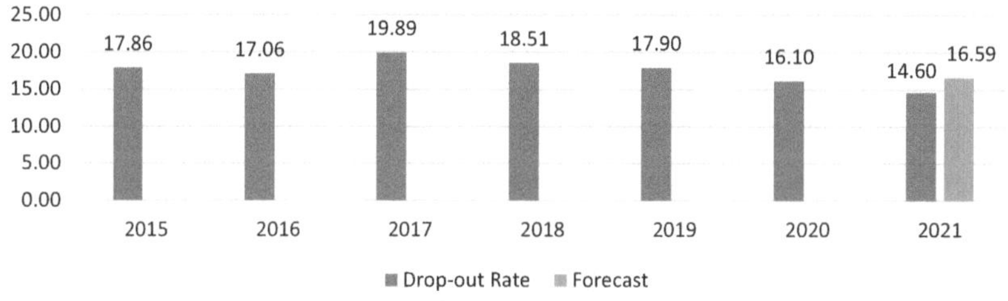

Fig. 10 Dropout rate (DR) secondary level (9–10) (*Source* [1] Data from 2015–2018: As reported by school education in India—flash statistics 2017–2018; [2] Data from 2019–2021: As reported by UDISE+)

Upper Primary Level (6–8)

The dropout rate exhibited an upward trend, experiencing a 0.26% increase in 2016. Subsequently, a significant surge of 1.64% was observed in 2017. However, in the following year (pre-pandemic), there was a decrease of 0.65% and 0.32% consecutively. During the pandemic period, the dropout rate further declined to 2.60% and 1.90%, which is 0.67% lower than the projected value of 2.57% (Fig. 9 and 10).

Secondary Level (9–10)

The dropout rate for secondary level began with a decrease of 0.80% in 2016, followed by a substantial surge to 19.89% in 2017. Subsequently, a downward trend is evident in the graph, leading to a final rate of 14.60% during the pandemic year. This value is 1.99% lower than the projected forecast of 16.59%

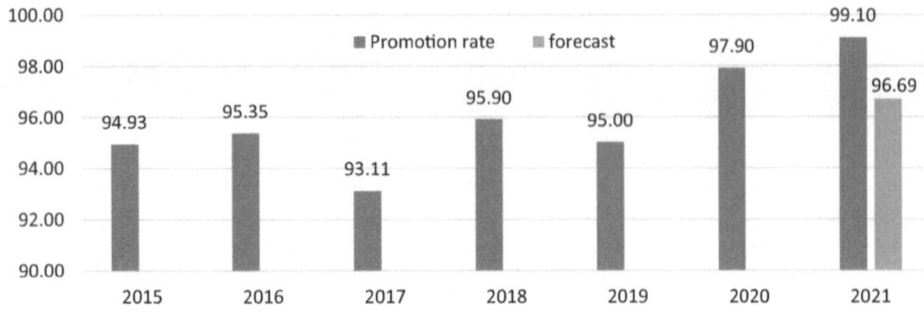

Fig. 11 Promotion rate (PR) primary level (1–5) (*Source* [1] Data from 2015–2018: As reported by school education in India—flash statistics 2017–2018; [2] Data from 2019–2021: As reported by UDISE+)

4.4.2 Promotion Rate

The proportion of people enrolled in the same age group and grade in a given academic year who study in the next grade in the following academic year. It measures the performance of an educational institution in promoting a student from one grade to another in an educational cycle. The goal is to have a high promotion rate. Ideally, the rate should reach 100%. Promotion rates are calculated by analysing data from two academic years; hence consistency should be maintained whilst reporting the data. Data across levels can be analysed to identify levels with low promotion rates so that remedial steps could be taken.

Primary Level (1–5)

The data shows periods of decline in the promotion rate, particularly in 2017, followed by periods of improvement and higher promotion rates in subsequent years. The promotion rate increases from 94.93% in 2015 to 95.35% in 2016. It dips down to 93.11% in the year 2017. The trend reverses in 2018 and promotion rate increases by 2.79%. It remains mostly stable for the next year registering a slight decrease of 0.90%, followed by an upward trend for the remaining two years. In 2021, promotion rate clocked at 99.10%, 2.41% more than the projected value of 96.69% (Fig. 11 and 12).

Upper Primary Level (6–8)

The promotion rate at the upper primary level experienced a slight decline, slipping from 95.74% in 2015 to 95.61% in 2016. Additionally, in

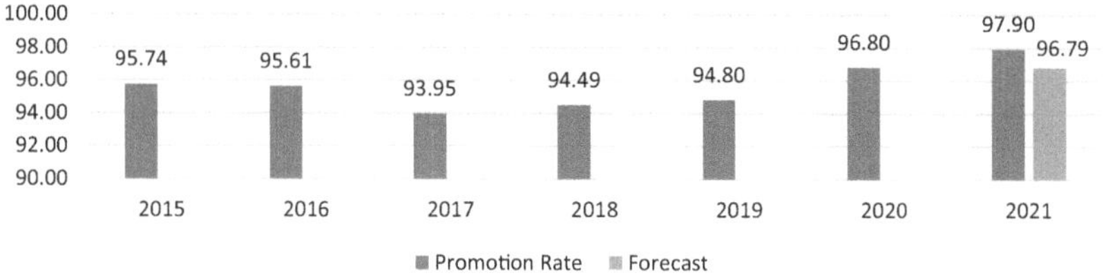

Fig. 12 Promotion rate (PR) upper primary level (6–8) (*Source* [1] Data from 2015–2018: As reported by school education in India—flash statistics 2017–2018; [2] Data from 2019–2021: As reported by UDISE+)

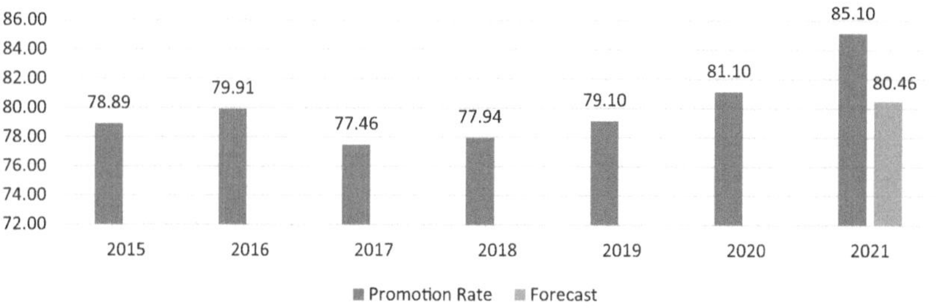

Fig. 13 Promotion rate (PR) secondary level (9–10) (*Source* [1] Data from 2015–2018: As reported by school education in India—flash statistics 2017–2018; [2] Data from 2019–2021: As reported by UDISE+)

2017, there was a further decrease of 1.66%. However, an upward trend is visible thereafter, culminating in a rate of 97.90% in 2021. This value surpasses the projected forecast by 1.11%.

Secondary Level (9–10)

The data shows slight increment in the promotion rate in 2016 of 1.02%. It declines to 77.46% in the year 2017, and then follows an upward trend in the subsequent years. The positive momentum continues taking the promotion rate for the pandemic year 2021 to 85.1%, registering an increase of 4% over the preceding year 2020. It was also more than the forecasted value by 4.6% (Fig. 13).

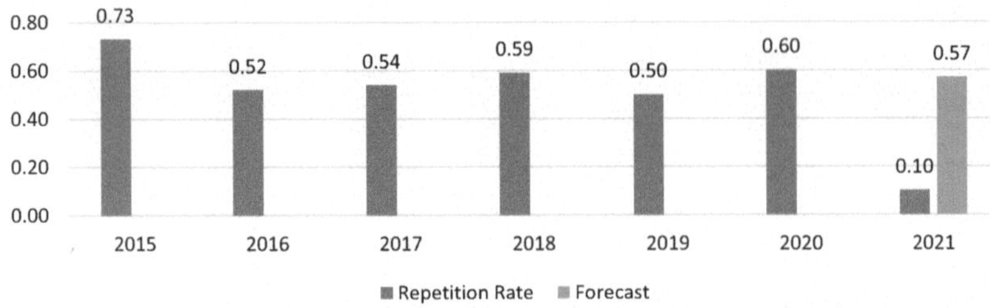

Fig. 14 Repetition rate (RR) primary level (1–5) (*Source* [1] Data from 2015–2018: As reported by school education in India—flash statistics 2017–2018; [2] Data from 2019–2021: As reported by UDISE+)

4.4.3 Repetition Rate

The proportion of people enrolled in the same age group and grade in a given academic year who study in the same grade in the following academic year. The repetition rate in an ideal world should be 0%. Like other flow rates, it is derived by analysing the data of two consecutive academic sessions, and data across different levels of education can be compared to find out problem areas that require special attention.

Primary Level (1–5)

The data shows a mix of both upward and downward trend in the beginning before falling steeply in the final year. It decreases slightly by 0.21% in the year 2016. It shows stable growth over the next two years, 0.2% and 0.5%. By 2020, there was a slight increase in the repetition rate to 0.60%, indicating a small rise in the number of students repeating the grade. The forecasted number suggested that it would remain unchanged at 0.57% for the year 2021 as it was in 2020. However, a further decline of 0.5% was reported for the year 2021, bringing it down to 0.1% (Fig. 14 and 15).

Upper Primary Level (6–8)

The repetition rate decreased in 2016 to 0.36%, suggesting a decline in the number of students repeating the grade. The repetition rate at the upper primary level demonstrates a consistent upward trend from there on until 2020. It slightly increases in 2017 by 0.1%. It further creeps to 0.49% in 2018 and 0.50%. It finally increases to 0.70% in 2020. However,

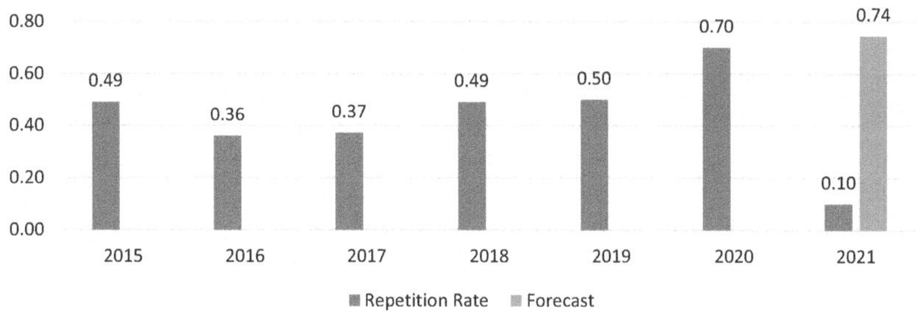

Fig. 15 Repetition rate (RR) upper primary level (6–8) (*Source* [1] Data from 2015–2018: As reported by school education in India—flash statistics 2017–2018; [2] Data from 2019–2021: As reported by UDISE+)

Fig. 16 Repetition rate (RR) secondary level (9–10) (*Source* [1] Data from 2015–2018: As reported by school education in India—flash statistics 2017–2018; [2] Data from 2019–2021: As reported by UDISE+)

in 2021, it dropped to 0.10%, which is 0.64% lower than the projected value.

Secondary Level (9–10)

The repetition rate dropped from 3.25% in 2015 to 3.03% in 2016, and further to 2.65% in 2017. It jumped to 3.54% in 2019. A downward trend from thereon can be witnessed. It declines to 3.00% in 2019 and to 2.80% in 2020. The repetition rate for the year 2021 was 0.3%, 2.5% less than the preceding year, and 2.8% less than the projected number of 3.1% (Fig. 16).

5 Discussion

The analysis of key indicators reveals an intriguing pattern, with India surpassing the forecasted numbers in all areas except for the total enrolment of students. Despite outperforming expectations and exhibiting a growth trend in most indicators, it would be inaccurate to conclude that the Indian education system remained unaffected by the pandemic.

Examining the overall trend across the key indicators, we observe a consistent performance in the initial years of 2015 and 2016, followed by a significant decline in 2017. Whilst there was a partial recovery in 2018, it was not enough to fully regain the previous levels. However, from 2019 onwards, there was a steady and gradual improvement in the indicators, continuing into 2020 and 2021.

To shed light on this trend, it is essential to consider the impact of a significant event in India's recent history: the demonetization of 500 and 1000 Rs notes announced on 8th November 2016. This move rendered the specified currency notes invalid as legal tender overnight, with citizens given a window to deposit them in their bank accounts. The demonetization aimed to tackle issues like black money, terror financing, and bringing cash hoarded outside the formal economy back into circulation. However, the process had repercussions.

The economic cost of demonetization was substantial, resulting in a 1.5% decline in GDP. Numerous small and medium enterprises (SMEs) were forced to shut down, leaving millions of daily wage earners without a means of earning. A report by the State of Working India (Foundation, 2019) revealed that between 2016 and 2018, five million people lost their jobs. It is well-established that the loss of livelihood and increased poverty have a direct impact on education, leading to a decline in educational indicators.

Therefore, the downward trend observed in the data can be attributed, at least in part, to the consequences of demonetization. The subsequent recovery and gradual improvement in the key indicators reflect the resilience and efforts of the education system to overcome the challenges posed by the pandemic and other economic disruptions.

Considering the severe impact of demonetization on India, which resulted in a significant decline in performance across various indicators in 2017, one might wonder how the country managed to make a remarkable recovery and achieve substantial progress in the following years. To understand this, it is important to consider the change in the reporting agency that happened in 2018–2019.

The UDISE (Unified District Information System for Education) was the primary agency responsible for data collection in the education sector. However, it was replaced by UDISE+ (Unified District Information System for Education Plus), which submitted its first report for the academic session 2018–2019. U-DISE+ claims to have "rectified" errors in the reporting methodology and offers significant advantages over its predecessor.

The introduction of UDISE+ and its refined data collection methodologies could explain the sudden surge in the upward trend of the indicators. The improved accuracy and reliability of data collection might have provided a more comprehensive and realistic picture of the education system's performance. It is possible that the previous system, U-DISE, may have underestimated certain indicators or had limitations in capturing the complete data, which could have affected the reported trends.

The transition to UDISE+ presents a two-sided situation. On the positive side, it implies that the data collected now is potentially more reliable and precise. However, on the flip side, the change in reporting agency and methodology raises concerns that the data might be underreported due to the alterations made. There is a strong possibility that school dropout rates in India during the COVID-19 pandemic were underreported. Like many countries, India's education systems have been greatly disrupted by the pandemic. The transition to online learning, school closures, and various socio-economic challenges faced by families have created conditions where some dropout cases may have been overlooked or not properly documented. Additionally, limited access to technology and connectivity issues could have hindered the accurate tracking and reporting of dropout rates. However, it is important to acknowledge that without specific data or studies on underreporting, it is speculative to make definitive conclusions about the extent of underreporting in India's school dropout rates during the pandemic.

An additional factor that could contribute to misleading data is the potential change in data collection and computation methods. This change in methodology has the potential to impact the accuracy and reliability of the reported information. It is possible that alterations in how data is collected and processed during the COVID-19 pandemic may introduce discrepancies or inconsistencies, leading to a distorted representation of school dropout rates. Therefore, it is crucial to consider the influence of changes in data collection and computation methodologies when interpreting the reported figures.

Dr. Arun C. Mehta questions the reliability of the dropout rates data presented by UDISE+. He argues that the methodology used for calculating flow rates, which include dropout, transition, and retention, has changed. Previously, these rates were calculated based on common schools between two reporting periods. However, the current approach considers all schools, leading to potential discrepancies and undermining the accuracy of the data. Mehta's argument suggests that the change in methodology has impacted the reliability of the reported dropout rates. He further suggests that UDISE+ should either resort to the previous methodology or state the benefit of using all schools instead of common schools.

Dr. Arun C. Mehta also raises concerns regarding the use of a digital platform for reporting data. Whilst digital platforms offer advantages, the lack of basic infrastructure in schools becomes a significant hurdle. Many schools do not possess the necessary resources to go digital. Amongst the 1.5 million schools covered under UDISE+, only 32.66% have access to computers, and a mere 18.73% have an internet connection. The situation is even more challenging in government schools, where 75.94% of schools lack internet connectivity. As a result, school staff members have had to rely on cybercafes or the office of the BRC coordinator, which also face network-related issues. These limitations have implications for the accuracy and efficiency of data reporting.

Amongst the various key indicators, total enrolment is the only one that aligns closely with the predicted values in the forecast. Despite an increase in overall enrolment numbers during the pandemic year, it falls short of the forecasted value. This can be attributed to various factors such as delayed admissions, economic hardships leading to loss of livelihood, and the unfortunate loss of guardians in some cases. However, it is important to note that enrolment does not necessarily guarantee attendance, which has been a pre-existing issue even before the pandemic. There could be cases where children are enrolled in schools but do not attend classes regularly, and the shift to online learning has further exacerbated this issue.

Whilst the government data presents a positive outlook, it is crucial to explore beyond official statistics to fully grasp the gravity of the situation. Independent organizations like PRATHAM Foundation's ASER (Annual Survey of Education—Rural) report and Oxfam India's report

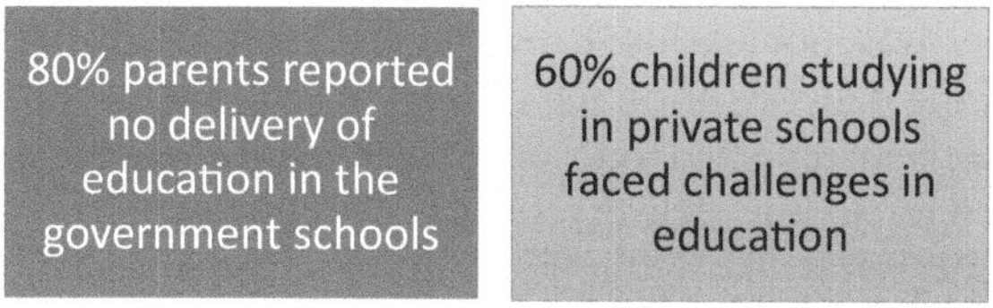

Fig. 17 *Source* As per Oxfam India's study: status report—government and private school during COVID-19

on the status of government and private schools during the COVID-19 pandemic provide a different perspective. These studies shed light on the challenges and disparities faced by students and schools, highlighting the need to consider alternative sources of information for a comprehensive understanding of the education landscape during these unprecedented times.

5.1 *Delivery of Education*

The government had notified all the schools, both public and private, to continue with the classes in online mode through different mediums. But the same could not be translated into actions. According to (Oxfam, 2020) report, 80% of parents report non-delivery of education in government schools. The same study reported close to 60% of children in private schools suffered interruption in the delivery of education. What could be inferred from the data is: (1) Lack of awareness regarding online education, or (2) Lack of accessibility. All the evidence points out the latter (Fig. 17).

5.2 *Lack of accessibility*

There are some prerequisites for digital/online education to take place, such as device, internet connection, and digital literacy to navigate your way through the software. (Oxfam, 2020) reports that 8 out of 10 parents reported one or a combination of reasons that caused hindrance in the education of their children. The majority of the people cited network issues as the main cause of hindrance, followed by data packs being too expensive. What comes next is a more fundamental issue of not owning a mobile phone, digital illiteracy, and no internet connection. The problem of accessibility was not exclusive to the students, teachers had to face challenges in the delivery of online classes as well (Fig. 18 and 19).

87% of teachers reported one or a combination of the reasons that caused challenges in the delivery of classes digitally. The situation was grimmer in the states like Uttar Pradesh and Chhattisgarh, where 80% and 67%, respectively, didn't have the appropriate device for the delivery of lectures (Fig. 20).

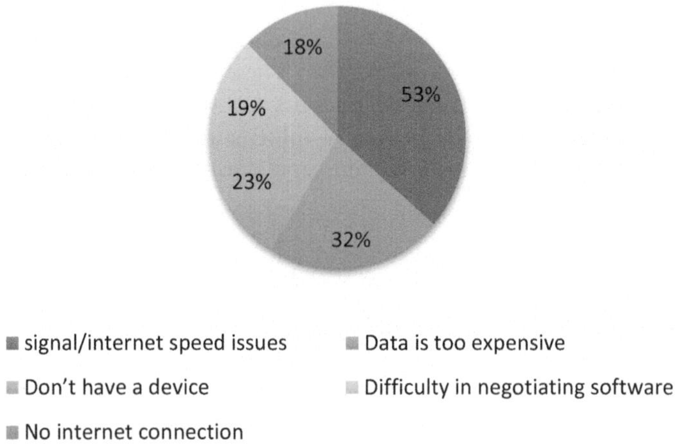

Fig. 18 Issues regarding accessibility (*Source* As per Oxfam India's study: status report—government and private school during COVID-19)

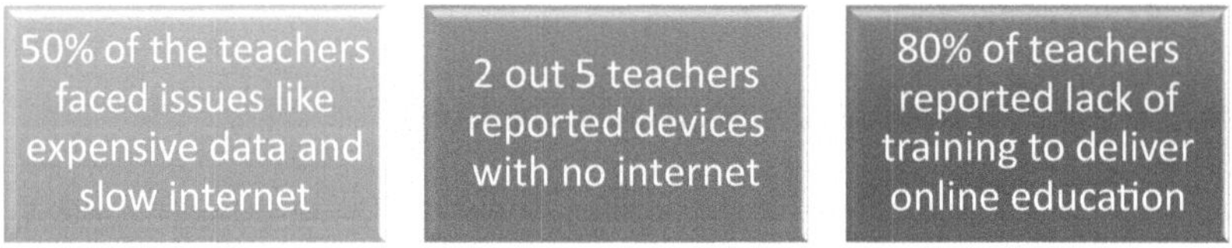

Fig. 19 *Source* As per Oxfam India's study: status report—government and private school during COVID-19

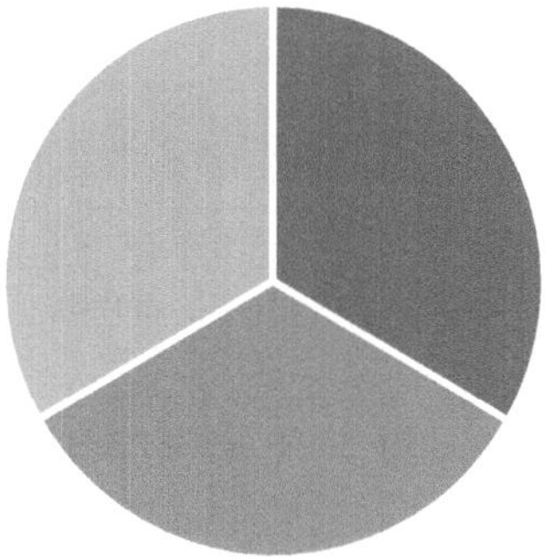

Fig. 20 Basis for digital divide

5.3 Digital Divide

The digital divide can be looked upon from three fronts. They are as follows:

(1) Economic Divide - As per the (ASER, 2021), smartphone ownership in India has almost doubled in India since 2018. It has increased substantially from 61.8 to 67.6%. But, even then only 27% of students report it to be available at all times, and 26.1% report it to be not available.
(2) Usability or Digital Literacy Divide: The usability divide is even worse than the economic divide. It presents a situation where even if the devices are provided to the people, they wouldn't be able to use them. In urban areas, digital literacy is reported to be 61%, whilst in rural areas, it is 25% only (Mothkoor & Mumtaz, n.d.)
(3) Empowerment or Gender Usage Divide: Another aspect of the digital divide is gender-based. Participation inequality is the trickiest of all. Even if devices and digital training are imparted, a gender wouldn't utilize those opportunities. The gender usage divide is significant in India. As of 2021, only 33.3% of internet users in India are women, whereas 57.1% of internet users are male (Statista, n.d.). Adopting completely digital methods of teaching

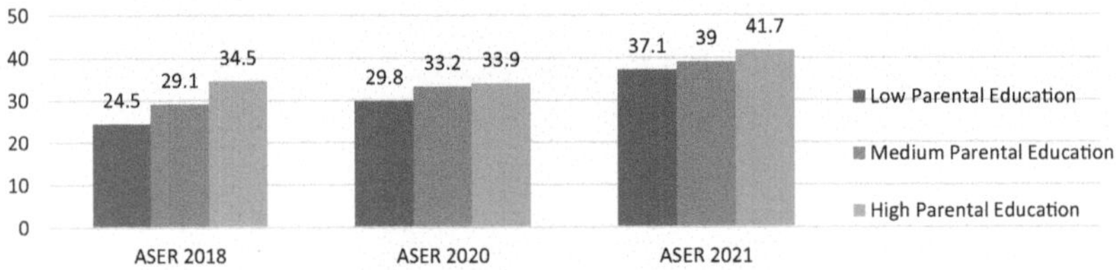

Fig. 21 Enrolment in private tuition by parent's education (*Source* As per Annual Status of Education Report 2021 by PRATHAM)

could result in substantial population of female students lagging behind.

5.4 *Enrolment in Private Tuitions*

According to the (ASER, 2021), the overall percentage of the students taking tuition is 39.2%, an increase of 6.7% over the previous year. The increase has been observed at all levels of education. However, what is interesting is the fact that most increase in the number of students taking private tuition happened in the children with parents of low education. With the delivery of education reduced to "dissemination of information" and no parental support at home, a large number of students had to rely on private tuitions to keep up pace with the curriculum (Fig. 21).

5.5 *Mid-Day Meal*

Although the Supreme Court of India directed that mid-day meals should be provided to those enrolled at the elementary stage of education, it could not be translated into action completely (Fig. 22).

(Oxfam, 2020) study reports that 35% of students did not receive their mid-day meal in any form. It is one of the major incentives that brings poor children to school, to get one proper meal of the day (Paul and Mondal, 2012). By failing to deliver a fair share of the meal, close to 1/3rd of the children falls into the risk category of being malnourished.

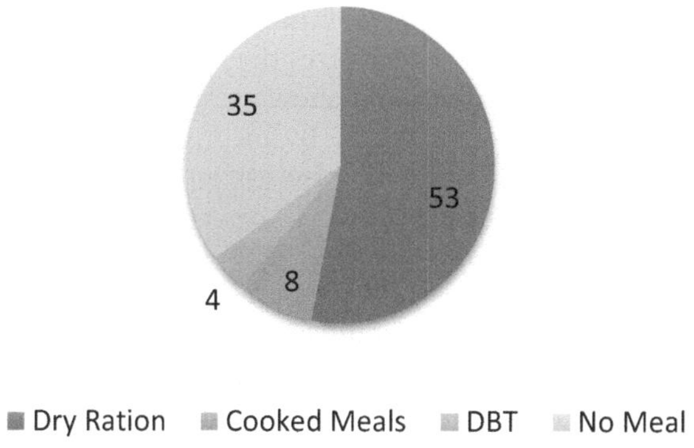

Fig. 22 Status of mid-day meal program (*Source* As per Oxfam India's study: status report—government and private school during COVID-19)

5.6 Loss of Livelihood and Shift to Government Schools

According to (ASER, 2021), there is a big jump in the total enrolment of the government schools, and a sharp decline in the total enrolment in the private schools. Enrolment in the private schools had dropped from 32.5% in 2018 to 24.4% in 2021. And, enrolment in the government schools had gone up by 5.3% at 70.3%. (Tribune, 2021) primarily cites the financial distress on parent because of loss of livelihood as the main reason. Closure of small unrecognized private school and reverse migration are also reasons for the surge in the number of enrolments in the private schools.

6 Suggestions to the Policy Makers

The COVID-19 wasn't the first, and certainly won't be the last crisis to affect humans. But, the experience of what worked and what did not can help us improve our crisis response. As a result of this chapter, following suggestions are made:

A. **Recognize the Losses:** The very first step towards solving a problem is to recognize its existence. Whilst achieving 100% accuracy may be an unrealistic expectation, striving towards it can be a worthwhile mission. Alternatively, adopting the principle of prudence, commonly used in business, can serve as a practical approach. This principle emphasizes the importance of not overestimating the positive aspects and allowing sufficient room for potential challenges or shortcomings. By incorporating these measures, a more reliable and comprehensive assessment of the educational landscape can be attained.

B. **Introduce Standardized Testing:** The government data captures only one side of the story that is of learning losses in terms of opportunity. It fails to capture anything related to learning losses in terms of skills. Standardized testing needs to be introduced so that diagnostic testing can be implemented to identify the problem areas. Western countries could identify and rectify the problem because of the availability of standardized scores. Hence, the introduction of standardized testing on a national level is the need of the hour.

C. **Introduce Bridge Courses:** (Foundation, 2019) conducted a study in 2021 which found that 92% of children had lost at least one language ability, like reading, speaking, or writing. The same study also found that 82% of children were having difficulty in doing mathematical operations. Similar findings were reported by (ASER, 2021) where the reading ability percentage amongst students was found to be 24.2%, a sharp decline of 17.6% from 2018. To address these learning losses, the introduction of bridge courses is crucial so that students can be brought up to speed with their present curriculum. One of the bridge courses that was launched in the rural areas of Tamil Nadu was "Illam Thedi Kalvi" (The Education at Doorstep). The course proved to be a massive success and contributed about 24% to the redressal of learning losses. The program included more than 200,000 volunteers who were not necessarily educators but were at least high school graduates. The sheer magnitude of this initiative made it one of the most significant education initiatives around the globe. Similar programs are needed at all levels of education throughout the country.

D. **Revised Budgetary Allocations:** Finally, revised budgetary allocations should be done. Budgetary allocations play a critical role in tackling learning loss by providing the necessary financial resources to implement remedial measures and adequately compensate teachers. By allocating funds specifically for addressing learning gaps, educational institutions can invest in resources, programs, and interventions that effectively support students in their academic recovery.

7 Conclusion

In conclusion, the pandemic exposed vulnerabilities within our education system and inflicted damage whose true magnitude is difficult to fully comprehend. The state of education is so grim that remedial measures are essential at all levels. By implementing the suggestions provided, we can fortify our education system from the calamities of tomorrow. At last, there is a lot of work to be done, and without collective effort, it will be the students to bear the brunt.

References:

Alexander, K. L., Entwisle, D. R., & Olson, L. S. (2004). Schools, achievement, and inequality: A seasonal perspective. *Summer Learning: Research, Policies, and Programs, 23*(2), 25–51. https://doi.org/10.4324/9781410610362

Andrabi, T., Daniels, B., & Das, J. (2021). Human Capital Accumulation and Disasters: Evidence from the Pakistan Earthquake of 2005. *Journal of Human Resources*, May, 0520-10887R1. https://doi.org/10.3368/jhr.59.2.0520-10887r1

ASER. (2021, January). Annual Status of Education Report 2021.

Azevedo, J. P., Hasan, A., Goldemberg, D., Aroob, S., & Koen Geven, I. (2020, June). *Simulating the Potential Impacts of COVID-19 School Closures on Schooling and Learning Outcomes* (Policy Research Working Paper No. 9284).

Cooper, H., Nye, B., Charlton, K., Lindsay, J., & Greathouse, S. (1996). The effects of summer vacation on achievement test scores: A narrative and meta-analytic review. *Review of Educational Research, 66*(3), 227–268. https://doi.org/10.3102/00346543066003227

Foundation, A. P. (2019). *State of working India*. http://www.unicef.org/sowc2011/

KMPG, & CII. (2021). *The impact of COVID-19 on school education and road to recovery* (pp. 1–31).

Maldonado, J. E., & De Witte, K. (2022). The effect of school closures on standardised student test outcomes. *British Educational Research Journal, 48*(1), 49–94. https://doi.org/10.1002/berj.3754

Mothkoor, V., & Mumtaz, Fa. (n.d.). Ideas for India.

Muñoz-Najar, A., Gilberto, A., Hasan, A., Cobo, C., Azevedo, J. P., & Akmal, M. (2021). Remote learning during COVID-19: Lessons from today principles for tomorrow. *Report, 1*(1), 62.

Oxfam. (2020). *Status Report-Government and private schools during COVID-19 Findings of rapid surveys* (p. 34).

Paul, P. K., & Mondal, N. K. (2012). Impact of mid-day meal programme on academic performance of students: Evidence from few upper primary schools of Burdwan district in West Bengal. *International Journal of Research in Social Sciences, 2*(3), 391–406.

Pokhrel, S., & Chhetri, R. (2021). A literature review on impact of COVID-19 pandemic on teaching and learning. *Higher Education for the Future, 8*(1), 133–141. https://doi.org/10.1177/2347631120983481

Rose, S., Badr, K., Fletcher, L., Paxman, T., Lord, P., Rutt, S., Styles, B., & Twist, L. (2021, December). *Impact of school closures and subsequent support strategies on attainment and socio-emotional wellbeing in Key Stage 1.* Education Endowment Foundation. https://www.nfer.ac.uk/media/4119/schools_responses_to_covid_19_the_challenges_facing_schools_and_p

Sacerdote, B. (2012). When the saints go marching out: Long-term outcomes for student evacuees from hurricanes Katrina and Rita. *American Economic Journal: Applied Economics, 4*(1), 109–135. https://doi.org/10.1257/app.4.1.109

Santibañez, L., & Guarino, C. M. (2021). The effects of absenteeism on academic and social-emotional outcomes: Lessons for COVID-19. *Educational Researcher, 50*(6), 392–400. https://doi.org/10.3102/0013189X21994488

Singh, A., Romero, M., & Muralidharan, K. (2022). COVID-19 learning loss and recovery: Panel data evidence from India. *National Bureau of Economic Research*, 1–23.

Slade, T. S., Piper, B., Kaunda, Z., King, S., & Ibrahim, H. (2017). Is 'summer' reading loss universal? Using ongoing literacy assessment in Malawi to estimate the loss from grade-transition breaks. *Research in Comparative and International Education, 12*(4), 461–485. https://doi.org/10.1177/1745499917740657

Statista. (n.d.). Internet usage rate among women and men in urban and rural India between 2019 and 2021.

Tribune. (2021). *Students shifting from private to govt schools, finds Annual Status of Education Report*. https://www.tribuneindia.com/news/nation/students-shifting-from-private-to-govt-schools-finds-annual-status-of-education-report-339358

Tyrrell, D. A., & Bynoe, M. L. (1966). Cultivation of viruses from a high proportion of patients with colds. *Lancet, 1*(7428), 76–77. https://doi.org/10.1016/s0140-6736(66)92364-6

CHAPTER 15

The Prospect of Human Capital Development in Post-pandemic

Ashraf Mishrif

1 Introduction

The devastating impact of the COVID-19 pandemic on education and health considerably affected human capital development worldwide. The policy measures taken to protect the public from the spread of the virus, including lockdown and closure of commercial centers, businesses, schools and colleges affected the lifestyle and behavior of individuals in terms of spending, consumption and social interaction with one another, even within the same family. The closure of businesses and factories resulted in the layoff of many employees and loss of income to millions of people, many of them were unable to meet their basic needs and some were pushed into extreme poverty. In health, the belonged duration of the pandemic over three or four years (2019–2022) paralyzed health-care systems across the world. This is apparent in the reduction in the types and quality of service provisions, postponement, and cancelation of most non-COVID-19 medical procedures and surgeries, and reduced

A. Mishrif (✉)
Humanities Research Centre, Sultan Qaboos University, Muscat, Oman
e-mail: ashraf.mishrif@gmail.com

A. Mishrif (ed.), *Perspectives on Human Capital Development*,
https://doi.org/10.1007/978-981-97-5246-1_15

number of medical staff, who suffered from the high risk of infection, died, or forced to leave the profession. The psychological impact of the crisis on medical staff, healthcare workers, and the public cannot also be ignored. Millions of people were unable to cope with the consequences of the pandemic and suffered from stress, anxiety, and depression, putting further strains on the medical and healthcare professions.

Meanwhile, the COVID-19 pandemic disrupted the education system, with considerable effects on students, teachers, instructors, and other service providers. The most notable impact was on students and teachers, who were not able to attend classes due to the lockdown and social distance, service delivery, and connectivity. Students suffered from these disruptive effects and complained about their loss of learning. By the end of the first year of the pandemic, there was an apparent loss of knowledge acquisition, particularly in developing countries, low-income countries, and the least developed countries, where parents and students were unable to cover the cost of internet connectivity and equipment for online education. It is worth noting here that educational institutions succeeded in introducing alternative modes of delivery, shifting to online education, and adopting new teaching methods and assessments to enable students to acquire the necessary knowledge and skills for their employability.

Indeed, the causes and consequences of the pandemic have been thoroughly examined in this book. Consequently, this chapter aims to focus solely on underlining and summarizing the key strategies for recovery in health and education and elaborating on the prospect of human capital development in the post-pandemic era. It explains how academic and health institutions are innovative in designing and implementing effective methods and tools to overcome the negative consequences of the pandemic. It also evaluates the effectiveness of policy implementation, identifies the types of new methods, techniques and innovative technologies created and introduced during the pandemic, and the expected effect of these policies and technologies in the development of human capital in the foreseeable future.

2 Public Health Strategy in Post-pandemic

COVID-19 was a public health crisis that required rapid and comprehensive response by the entire healthcare system to contain the disease. The response to this public health crisis began in 2019, with the establishment of political bodies and health committees to lead on the initiation and implementations of various policy measures to control the disease (Al Ghafri et al., 2021). Public institutions were actively providing guidelines, initiatives, and monitoring the implementation of containment strategies that aimed at protecting the medical staff, healthcare workers, and the public from the spread of the virus. In fact, there were multisectoral strategies and several public policy approaches, supported by public–private partnerships, to ensure the continuous supply of main goods and services and minimize the disruption in the domestic markets. For example, the logistics and supply chain strategies were effective in providing the supply of medical goods and equipment that were essential in fighting the pandemic, while guaranteeing the food security by continuously supplying food and nutrition materials and supplements. The application and use of information and communication technology (ICT) were also critical in connecting people and helping to restore confidence in the education system (Al Khalili et al., 2021).

The pandemic crisis illustrated the importance of collaboration between the public and private sectors during national and global health crises. The contribution of the private sector hospitals to the public health crisis exemplified in various forms, including admitting COVID-19 patients, conducting PCR tests, and giving COVID-19 vaccinations, all of these services eased pressure on public hospital and government-run health institutions and helped in sustaining and strengthening the healthcare system. Indeed, the collective efforts made by all sectors and social forces facilitated the implementation of the public health policies that helped in reducing the disruptions of the pandemic and warranted the provision of essential health services in most developed countries (WHO, 2022). Meanwhile, implementing public health prevention programs and hospital-based interventions succeeded in combating the pandemic in developing countries. These policy interventions were instrumental in effectively combating the pandemic and restoring essential health services (Hussain & Arif, 2021).

Several factors allowed for the success of the health strategy. Chief among these factors is the preparedness of the public health institutions to mitigate the impact of the pandemic on the health system and respond effectively to public health threats. Empirical evidence shows that, while dealing with the severe COVID-19 cases, the healthcare system was capable of absorbing and accessing non-COVID patients to have safe healthcare, especially for vulnerable people, disabled patients, emergency cases, and chronic diseases. This does not, however, ignore that fact that some countries experienced a decrease in admissions for cardiovascular diseases during the pandemic, including Italy (Filippo et al., 2020), Switzerland (Rachamin et al., 2021), the USA (Bhatt et al., 2020), and Japan (Morishita et al., 2022). This reduction in admissions for chronic diseases stopped after building a huge number of field hospitals for admitted COVID-19 cases.

The second success factor is the resilience of the healthcare system. The degree of flexibility exhibited in the healthcare system globally helped in minimizing the negative consequences of the pandemic disruptions. The use of technology facilitated access to the health services, with telemedicine being rapidly used in the initial peak of the pandemic in many developed countries; for example, this was effectively applied for Dutch patients with chronic diseases in the primary healthcare (Auener et al., 2020).

The third factor is the successful management of the public health crisis. Successful management was not only limited to close monitoring of patients and early treatment, but also in the early recognition of severity factors that effectively helped in monitoring hospitalized COVID-19 patients and reducing fatality cases and medical expenditure. Despite the decline in outpatient visits, hospitalizations, surgical, and radiological procedures in the initial two months (March and April 2020) of the pandemic due to restrictions applied to the public such as lockdown and quarantine, our findings reveal that all kinds of health services adapted to the pandemic by May 2020.

The fourth factor is the effectiveness of rigorous healthcare policies implemented to curb the pandemic. The success of the COVID-19-related policies highlights the importance of the speed of introducing the lockdown and social distance as an early response mechanism to contain the virus, the strength of the government mandates, and the lengthy implementation of the policy measures. It also underscores the trust and confidence of the public in the soundness of the policies and the quality of the healthcare service provisions in the fight against infectious disease. The success of the recovery strategy also underlines the importance of effective communication strategies to convey the need of compliance to the population and to address the concerns of different demographic and social groups, particularly the elderly, patients with chronic diseases, and those having doubts about the nature and threat of the virus. The government's rapid response to the pandemic strengthened the healthcare system by providing adequate medical resources, increasing healthcare accessibility, and enhancing the capacity of critical care.

The fifth success factor in the recovery strategy is global leadership and collective actions taken by the major industrial nations in terms of levels of investment in research and development (R&D) in creating an effective vaccine. The success of the investment strategy is evident in the levels of investment made in R&D in the fields of medicine and pharmaceutical industries. Most countries provided financial support to enable researchers and medical scholars to investigate ways to control COVID-19 and end the pandemic. They also invested in innovative methods and new technologies to apply them in the medical field such as telemedicine and other software programs that enabled medical doctors and specialists to operate remotely on patients elsewhere. They also devoted tens of billions of dollars to develop vaccines.

Undoubtedly, the vaccination policy is the most important development in the fight against the pandemic. Despite the precautionary measures introduced by governments such as curfews, masks, quarantining, and institutional closures that proved limited in controlling the virus, it was the vaccine that stopped the spread of the virus, reduced its transmission, and lowered the rates of morbidity and mortality over the world (Moghadas et al., 2021). As a result, countries were forced to accelerate previously scheduled vaccine doses to prevent the spread of the infection and thereby minimize the repercussions (NHS England and NHS Improvement, 2021). This policy underlines the importance of investing and developing the immunization process to keep the nation protected from infectious diseases (Hinston et al., 2021).

In the case of the Sultanate of Oman that is extensively examined in this book, the vaccination policy was a great success in the fight against COVID-19 for several reasons. First, Oman prioritized those groups of persons who needed the vaccine due to early supply constraints and high demand. Healthcare providers, frontline staff, and persons with co-morbid disorders such chronic lung or renal ailments and obesity were initially targeted when the vaccination deployment began in December 2020 (Al Wahaibi et al., 2021). Second, an effective strategy was established to cover 70% of the total population, with a deployment plan for delivering the vaccine in two phases, according to priority group, with 30% starting in late 2020, then 40% from July to October 2021. This process was accomplished by purchasing vaccines directly from vaccine producers at substantially higher prices than those obtained through

COVAX and by partnering with the corporate sector to create mega vaccination facilities in several governorates. Third, the government introduced new legislations and enforcement mechanisms, making vaccination mandatory for the ages 12 years old and above. Figure 1 shows that the number of vaccine doses were given in Oman reached more than 7 million (including the first, second and third doses), while elaborating the vaccination coverage that reached 135.8 per 100 people by the end of May 2022.

In fact, the healthcare strategy for post-pandemic recovery was a success in Oman. After some neighboring countries such as Saudi Arabia and the United Arab Emirates loosening their own COVID restrictions, Oman's Supreme Committee for monitoring COVID-19 lifted all COVID-19 restrictions at the end of May 2022. It is the higher vaccination coverage among people that encouraged the government to lift all restrictions, including musk mandate and PCR tests that are no longer required of international entrants, either before departure or upon arrival (Bodell, 2022).

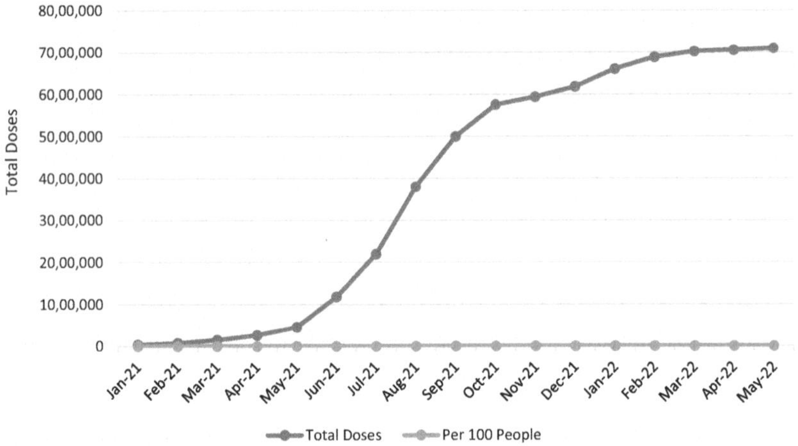

Fig. 1 Number of total doses given and vaccination coverage in Oman (Jan 2021–May 2022) (*Source* World Health Organization (WHO), 2022)

3 Education Strategy in Post-pandemic

The spread of COVID-19 disrupted the entire education system globally, resulting in the closure of schools and colleges, loss of learning, shift to online education without training and support services, and huge drops out of schools due to lack of connectivity and cost of internet and equipment in many developing countries. The financial and technological capacity of these countries to increase their investment in education is limited, which considerably affects human and social development in the post-pandemic era. Despite all these challenges, the lessons learned from the pandemic are reshaping the education system. The pandemic encouraged self-learning and technical literacy for both educators and learners. Education experts are envisioning that online teaching should remain active in post-COVID-19 medical curriculum as a hybrid learning, where online learning strategies are impeded along with face-to-face learning.

After almost four years of the outbreak of COVID-19, the education system showed resilience and adaptability to the changing circumstances. These characteristics, together with developing a systematic understanding of the challenges faced education in the past few years, helped policymakers and stakeholders to create and develop innovative means to integrate technology and creative learning after the pandemic. The first and foremost factor that contributed to the success of education strategy is effective utilization of technology, which played a significant role in the continuation of learning and teaching during the pandemic, as well as allowing for the potential use of blended education in the post-pandemic era. It is also technology that facilitated the shift to online education in a very short time.

The second factor is that online platforms and visual systems offered a low-risk interactive environment and facilitated the interaction between students and their educators to minimize the loss of learning. Even in applied sciences, most of the push button/touch button participatory exhibits involving hands-on experience were modified by sensor-based touch free switches. The advancement of technology enhanced the learning process and extended hands-on laboratory experiences to the students without affecting learning outcomes. It also allowed for the creation of free digital home schooling, where teachers use their interactive and prototypes to explain scientific principles to the student community during lockdown. In the post-pandemic, technological advancement in education makes it easy to continue with blended learning approaches as the new normal in the subsequent educational practices.

The third success factor is the ability of the education system to develop targeted intervention strategies to mitigate the socio-economic and socio-emotional ramifications of the pandemic on students. There was a considerable financial and technical support provided by the schools and universities to enable both instructors and students to easily access the online materials, lectures, chatrooms, and online assessment methods, all of them addressed the digital inequality, particularly after providing students with electronic devices and internet access to facilitate their learning at home during the pandemic. Moreover, digital readiness played a critical role in reducing the socio-emotional effects of the pandemic on students across the entire education system. This emotional effect was noticeable after the sudden transition to digital learning; hence, policy intervention based on technology utilization created and fostered an environment conducive to positive socio-emotional experiences. This type of intervention also helped in alleviating students' feelings of alienation and loneliness. This objective was attained by implementing practical and user-friendly application, elevating the digital facilities' readiness to a level that matches the evolving needs of students, and promoting a more seamless integration of digital tools into the educational landscape.

The fourth factor that featured in this publication is the emerging importance of entrepreneurship education programs based on design thinking to foster innovative human resources. The acceptance of online learning as the new normal education system facilitated the so-called 'adaptability skills' that allow the students to empower and prepare themselves for real-world situations. Entrepreneurship education empowers students to think critically about challenging situations and allows them to take strategic actions to answer some of the challenges that they encounter in real life. The advantage of the design thinking approach lies in its user-centric and collaborative approach that encourages students to be collaborative whether they are in an online setting or real-time situation. This approach does not only allow students to analyze real-world challenges and find solutions, but it also serves as a significant tool that enables students to start their businesses and be successful entrepreneurs in this increasingly competitive marketplace.

The fifth factor that contributed to the success of the education strategy after the pandemic is the rise of the concept 'emergency remote teaching,' which was designed in the education context and borrowed by the government and corporate sectors to allow students, workers, and employees to conduct their academic and professional activities remotely. This concept broadened the scope and pace of both education and work practices, offering employees a great deal of freedom in the way they conduct their activities and allowing employers to reduce the cost of operations, effectively assess the work patterns and practices, prepare alternative strategies for emergencies, and develop good policies and governance systems should there be any similar crisis in the future. In the education settings, the development of the emergency remote teaching method helped senior management and policy makers to underline and eliminate any pitfalls in the method and its related practices, while enabling online and blended learning practitioners in their choice of technology for teaching and learning and integrating online with on-site classes to complement learning.

Indeed, the pandemic experience provides sufficient training, knowledge, and practice for specialized educational tools that will enable students and practitioners to effectively engage in distance learning or adopt hybrid approach in the future. However, I must stress here that the greatest challenge facing the education system is the insufficient investment in the technological infrastructure, including the availability of network services in remote areas, quality of internet, and types of devices that enable students to connect to the system. Internet service providers and educational institutions must upgrade their services to meet the requirements of the twenty-first century.

4 Repercussions and Policy Recommendations for Human Capital Development

The impact of the pandemic was multidimensional, with direct and indirect effects on people's life at the social, economic, political, and ecological levels. It impacted on the operational capacity and functions of the government and public institutions, while disrupting the local and global value chains, causing significant shortages in the availability of base goods, commodities, and services. The pandemic repercussions caused significant damage to the global economy, with millions of people losing their jobs, main sources of income, and access to basic services such as education and health. The repercussions also caused huge concerns of global health security and the capacity of one country or organization to deal with the pandemic. In fact, the pandemic exposed the weakness of the healthcare system to deal with health emergencies in developed and developing countries alike. The experience shows that the healthcare system was unprepared for the pandemic, together with lack of access to effective public health services, made the pandemic worse and belonged it over a period of three years. So, there is an urgent need to propagate and adopt the concept of global health security, with effective measures and mechanisms to protect people from pandemics, natural disasters, and other public health threats and their subsequent health, social and psychological consequences.

Global health security requires global leadership to gear all countries toward greater awareness, cooperation, and collaboration in the fight against public health threats. It also requires the development of effective ways and measures to provide worldwide protection against the threats of infectious diseases, backed by revised and more powerful international health regulations. We appreciate the efforts of the World Health Organization in the fights against infectious diseases, but the experience of the organization in dealing with COVID-19 is marked by lack of effective mechanisms to curb the virus and slow motion in terms of preparedness. As global insecurity increases due to a growing tendency toward engagement in biological and chemical warfare and emergence of new types of infectious diseases, this chapter suggests a few policy measures to be considered by governments and national and international organizations.

In terms of education, the pandemic experience holds significant implications for the future of education. This experience underlines the difficulties and challenges faced by students and educators when shifting to online learning, especially in the fields of medicine, nursing, engineering, and other applied sciences. It also highlights the urgent need for a well-balanced approach in educational delivery. A blended approach can address the concerns expressed by medical, nursing, and laboratory-based science students of the lack of hands-on clinical experience and supports their preference for combined synchronous and asynchronous learning methods. In fact, the introduction of a hybrid model that incorporates both traditional in-person training and effective online resources is imperative for the continuation of education in post-pandemic. However, the success of this model depends on the capacity of the country to invest heavily in the development of information technology and implementation innovative strategies to enhance the online learning experience, particularly in technical skill acquisition, through video-based resources and interactive tools.

The pandemic experience also underlines the need for new curricula that combine theoretical understanding and practical exposure to real-time practices. This is imperative for capacity building and technical skills acquisition, whereby science-oriented students and practitioners appreciate the exposure and direct interaction that simulate real-world experiences in a virtual setting. These insights when designing new courses can guide the development of more comprehensive and robust curricula that integrate technology effectively, balancing the strengths of in-person instruction with the flexibility and accessibility offered by online learning. Curriculum development should also consider adjusting and changing learning outcomes and assessment methods to reflect on the quality of education.

As the education system continues to evolve, we expect that all aspects of education development must exhibit a higher degree of accessibility, adaptability, flexibility, inclusiveness, employability, and practicality. Policymakers and senior educators must find ways to address social exclusion, gender inequality, digital inequality, and the mismatch between education outcomes and labor market needs. As the labor market is expected to experience a significant transformation in the type of jobs and skills, it is impressive that the education system should consider ways to bridge the gap between higher education, labor market, and Industry 4.0 technologies. We expect both graduates and employees to be knowledgeable, skillful, and well-trained in data analytics, machine learning, internet of things, artificial intelligence, digital marketing, digital finance, cloud computing, and cybersecurity (Mishrif et al., 2023).

Bridging the gap between the education system and Industry 4.0 requires reforming both the education system and the labor market. In terms of education reforms, several procedures could be taken including updating curriculum according to the capabilities and skills required in the labor market, adding more technical courses relating to Industry 4.0, offering training courses to students through specific companies that are highly connected to Industry 4.0. Academic institutions and companies should also consider developing their own and joint initiatives for training and professional, as well as adapting to the changes driven by Industry 4.0 and labor market needs. Meanwhile, students, educators, and senior management of academic institutions must realize that future labor market needs will depend on four categories of skills: workforce readiness, soft skills, technical skills, and entrepreneurship. As for the latter category, entrepreneurial skills must be integrated within all branches of sciences because they include innovations, initiatives, resilience, resourcefulness, optimism, risk taking, business acumen, courage, and curiosity (Mishrif et al., 2023).

Basic on the data analysis and discussions presented in this book, this chapter summarizes some of the key policy recommendations for human capital development:

First, the revision of existing health polices and development of new public health policies to serve as a guiding principle in protecting the health of communities.

Second, it is imperative that health authorities must focus on preparing vaccines and treatments for the most common virus and infectious diseases that could cause such pandemics.

Third, WHO must equip itself with a rapid task force, proper planning, preparation, training, and coordination with countries, while galvanize itself from the selfish politics of accusations and claims exhibited by the USA and China on who is responsible for the spread of COVID-19.

Fourth, global leadership and international collaboration must focus on data sharing, which is pivotal for a coordinated global response to pandemics. This requires coordinated actions among governments and public authorities to share knowledge, experiences, and best practices to collectively combat infectious diseases.

Fifth, global leadership must find means of overcoming the disparities, inequalities, and discrimination in the way vaccines were distributed among countries. It must bring together people of all ages, genders, races, cultures, ethnicities, and regions in an equitable manner, regardless of where they live, for the protection of humanity.

Sixth, the pandemic recovery and achieving health security can best be attained by political will and effective economic policies that set up long-term fiscal goals. Deep fiscal-monetary coordination is required to scale down the macroeconomic risks and uncertainties, including cutting the interest rates as interest payments divert resources away from development finance. Collective actions and coordination at the global level is also fundamental to addressing the economic impact of the pandemic such as food insecurities, undernourishment, economic inequalities, and lack of opportunities in education, employment, and health.

Seventh, the key to the pandemic recovery is the commitment by governments to heavily invest and develop the digital infrastructure, as digital readiness in education has practical implications for various stakeholders. In fact, educating researchers, academic staff, managers, and practitioners about the pivotal role of digital readiness can significantly improve students' overall learning experience.

Eighth, the pandemic experience illustrates the important role of information and communication technology in shifting education from classrooms to online learning. Thus, it is recommended that governments must continuity invest and upgrade this sector that has become essential for the prospect of human capital development. I must also draw attention here to the importance of this sector in upgrading skills and facilitating the development and acquisition of Industry 4.0 technologies.

Ninth, the education system should be adaptable, flexible, innovative, and capable of withstanding any similar crises or pandemics in the future. Education institutions should develop blended approaches that combine traditional learning with online learning, hence investing in developing both digital infrastructure and digital readiness to overcome any digital inequality.

Tenth, entrepreneurship should be considered core courses across the entire education system to enable students to develop entrepreneurial knowledge and skills and determine their own career in the future.

Eleventh, human security must shape the global research agenda in a multidisciplinary fashion with more investments in R&D across all disciplines. The objective of global human security cannot be attained without the integration and collaboration of medical science, social science, natural sciences, technology, ecology, law, economics, and politics.

5 Conclusion

This chapter described the ways in which COVID-19 affected human capital development, with particular focus on health and education. It analyzed both the health and education strategies for post-pandemic recovery. Although the pandemic impacted directly on human capital development by putting the lives of medical staff and healthcare workers at risk, the chapter concludes that the policy intervention by the states were effective in minimizing the health threats and restoring the supply of healthcare services, with the vaccination policy putting an end to the pandemic by May 2022. Meanwhile, the pandemic disruption to the education system was gradually eliminated by the successful utilization of digital technology and shifting to online learning. Despite some shortfalls such as digital inequality in some developing countries, persistent policy intervention and technical support helped in restoring the process of learning during the pandemic. Moreover, this chapter also identified and explained the factors that influenced and contributed to the success of both the health and education strategies. It ends by providing some new insights and policy recommendations that could be useful for human capital development.

References

Al Ghafri, T., Al Ajmi, F., Al Balushi, L., Mohan Kurup, P., Al Ghamari, A., Al Balushi, Z., Al Fahdi, F., Al Lawati, H., Al Hashmi, S., Al Manji, A., & Al, S. A. (2021). Responses to the pandemic COVID-19 in primary health care in Oman: Muscat experience. *Oman Medical Journal, 36*(1), e216. https://doi.org/10.5001/omj.2020.70

Al Khalili, S., Al Maani, A., Al Wahaibi, A., Al Yaquobi, F., Al-Jardani, A., Al Harthi, K., Alqayoudhi, A., Al Manji, A., Al Rawahi, B., & Al-Abri, S. (2021). Challenges and opportunities for public health service in Oman from the COVID-19 pandemic: Learning lessons for a better future. *Frontiers in Public Health, 9*, 770946. https://doi.org/10.3389/fpubh.2021.770946

Al Wahaibi, A., Al Rawahi, B., Patel, P. K., Al Khalili, S., Al Maani, A., & Al-Abri, S. (2021). COVID-19 disease severity and mortality determinants: A large population-based analysis in Oman. *Travel Medicine and Infectious Disease, 39*, 101923.

Auener, S., Kroon, D., Wackers, E., Dulmen, S. V., & Jeurissen, P. (2020). COVID-19: A window of opportunity for positive healthcare reforms. *International Journal of Health Policy Management, 9*(10), 419–422. https://doi.org/10.34172/ijhpm.2020.66

Bhatt, A. S., Moscone, A., McElrath, E. E., et al. (2020). Fewer hospitalizations for acute cardiovascular conditions during the COVID- 19 pandemic. *Journal of the American College of Cardiology, 76*, 280–288. https://doi.org/10.1016/j.jacc.2020.05.038

Bodell, L. (2022, June 1). Oman drops all COVID-19 travel restrictions. *Simple Flying*. Retrieved June 14, 2022, from https://simpleflying.com/oman-drops-all-COVID-19-travel-restrictions/

Filippo, O., D'Ascenzo, F., Angelini, F., et al. (2020). Reduced rate of hospital admissions for ACS during Covid- 19 outbreak in northern Italy. *New England Journal of Medicine, 383*, 88–89. https://doi.org/10.1056/NEJMc2009166

Hinson, R. E., Hein, W., Tettey, L. N., Nartey, B. A., Harant, A., Struck, N. S., & Fobil, J. N. (2021). Critical prerequisites for COVID-19 vaccine acceleration: A developing economy perspective. *Journal of Public Affairs, 21*(4), e2723.

Hussain, R., & Arif, S. (2021). Universal health coverage and COVID-19: Recent developments and implications. *Journal of Pharmaceutical Policy and Practice, 14*, 23. https://doi.org/10.1186/s40545-021-00306-x

Mishrif, A. et al. (2023). Bridging the gap between Gulf higher education and labour market in Industry 4.0. In Ashraf Mishrif et al (Eds.), *Nationalization of Gulf labour markets: Higher education, skills development in Industry 4.0* (pp. 293–332). Palgrave Macmillan.

Moghadas, S. M., Vilches, T. N., Zhang, K., Wells, C. R., Shoukat, A., Singer, B. H., Meyer, A. L., Neuzil, K. M., Langley, J. M., Fitzpatrick, C. M., & Galvani, A. P. (2021). The impact of vaccination on coronavirus disease 2019 (COVID-19) outbreaks in the United States. *Clinical Infectious Diseases, 73*(12), 2257–2264.

Morishita, T., Takada, D., Shin, J.-H., et al. (2022). Trends, treatment approaches, and in- hospital mortality for acute coronary syndrome in Japan during the coronavirus disease 2019 pandemic. *Journal of Atherosclerosis and Thrombosis., 29*(5), 597–607. https://doi.org/10.5551/jat.62746

NHS England and NHS Improvement. (2021). Published letter regarding "Acceleration of second doses for all cohorts." https://www.england.nhs.uk/coronavirus/wp-content/uploads/sites/52/2021/07/C1342-second-dose-interval-letter-6-july-21.pdf (accessed June 12, 2022).

Rachamin, Y., Senn, O., Streit, S., Dubois, J., Deml, M. J., & Jungo, K. T. (2021). Impact of the COVID-19 pandemic on the intensity of health services use in general practice: A retrospective cohort study. *International Journal of Public Health, 66*, 635508. https://doi.org/10.3389/ijph.2021.635508

World Health Organization. (2022). *World health statistics report*. Monitoring health for the Sustainable Development Goals.

Index

A. Mishrif (ed.), *Perspectives on Human Capital Development*,
https://doi.org/10.1007/978-981-97-5246-1

The manufacturer's authorised representative in the EU is Springer Nature Customer Service Centre GmbH, Europaplatz 3, 69115 Heidelberg, Germany. If you have any concerns regarding our products, please contact ProductSafety@springernature.com

Printed and bound by CPI Group (UK) Ltd, Croydon, CR0 4YY
01/10/2026
02225854-0014